Planning
for educational mass media

Alan Hancock

Longman
London and New York

Longman Group Limited London

*Associated companies, branches and representatives
throughout the world*

*Published in the United States of America
by Longman Inc., New York*

First published 1977

Library of Congress Cataloging in Publication Data

Hancock, Alan, fl. 1965–
   Planning for educational mass media.

   Bibliography: p.
   Includes index.
   1. Audio-visual education.   2. Mass media.
I. Title.
LB1043.H327   371.33   76–22496
ISBN 0 582 41055 X

Set in IBM Journal 10 on 11pt
and printed in Great Britain by
Richard Clay (The Chaucer Press) Ltd,
Bungay, Suffolk

Preface

This book, like its predecessor, *Planning for ETV* (Longman, 1971) is essentially practical; it is designed as a handbook for those engaged in, or contemplating, media projects at local, regional or national levels — educational planners and technologists, curriculum specialists, producers and practitioners, teachers and tutors, in both schools and colleges and in the wider adult community.

Originally, the book was envisaged as an updating of the earlier volume. But on settling down to write, it became clear to me that, even after an interval of less than 5 years, the field has changed radically and a new approach is required. It is much less possible today to speak of a single medium such as educational television: the promise of multi-media working has become, in the intervening years, far more of a reality. Indeed, many of the developments previewed in Part 5 of the earlier book have become, if not commonplace, at least familiar and recognised, and must now be considered within the main fabric of the educational argument, not as a predictive annexe. Moreover, educational media are finally escaping from the confines of the school, and adult and non-formal education, community education and development are featuring more largely in comprehensive media systems.

The scope of the present handbook has therefore been widened, to review progress both in and out of school, and to consider the integrated planning of a triad of educational mass media — television, radio, and audio-visual support services. The emphasis is still however, on *mass* media (there are plenty of handbooks available on the planning of individual, classroom-based forms), though much of the argument concerns access to, participation in, and the individualisation of, mass channels.

The text has deliberately been written in a summary style. It is a presentation of current thoughts, trends, experimental forms and formats in the organisation, planning and utilisation of mass media in education; as such it is heavily indebted to other writers and researchers (and the debt is warmly acknowledged). It should also be noted that problems of adapting general media production to educational ends are treated in a separate volume (*Producing for Educational Mass Media*, published by Unesco and Longman in association).

The book is divided into four parts. Part 1 is discursive: it summarises past and present thinking about educational mass media and their functions. Part 2 deals with the planning process *per se* and with media selection, Part 3 with programme and materials development, and Part 4 with media use and evaluation. The Appendix is a description of characteristic media installations, and is followed by a Select bibliography and an Index.

Alan Hancock

v

Acknowledgements

We are grateful to the following for permission to reproduce copyright material:

The British Council for an extract from an article entitled 'Planning for the Development for Educational Media in Thailand' by Nicholas Bennett in *Educational Broadcasting International*, December 1974, Vol. 7, No. 4; The Authors for an abridged extract from *The Media Selection Process* by Peter Combes and John Tiffin; Canadian Radio-television and Telecommunications Commission for an extract from an article entitled 'A Survey of Activities' by Linda Mitchell; Harcourt Brace Jovanovich Inc. for a chart 'Curriculum' from *Curriculum Development: Theory and Practice* by Hilda Taba © 1962 by Harcourt Brace Jovanovich Inc. and reproduced with their permission; Harper and Row Publishers Inc. for a figure and table from *Instructional Technology: Its Nature and Use* by Walter A. Wittich and Charles F. Schuller © Harper and Row, 1973; Information Centre on Instructional Technology and respective authors for tables from, *Big Media—Little Media* by Dr Wilbur Schramm, published by the Institute for Communication Research at Stanford University, as one of the AID Studies in Educational Technology, distributed by the Information Centre on Instructional Technology and funded by the Technical Assistance Bureau of the United States Agency for International Development, *Educational Reform and Instructional Television in El Salvador: Costs, Benefits and Pay-Offs* by Prof. Richard E. Speagle, published and distributed by the Information Centre on Instructional Technology and funded by the Technical Assistance Bureau of the United States Agency for International Development, *The Effectiveness of Alternative Instructional Media: A Survey* by Dean Jamison, Patrick Suppes and Stuart Wells, published by the Institute for Communication Research at Stanford University and distributed by the Information Centre on Instructional Technology as one of the AID studies in Educational Technology financed by the Technical Assistance Bureau of the United States Agency for International Development; Rand Corporation for figures by Rudy Bretz; AV Communications Review for a chart by William H. Allen, published in *AV Communications Review*; Educational Testing Service for a figure by Ball and Bogatz; International Council for Adult Education for an extract from the report 'Development Campaigns in Rural Tanzania'; International Extension College for an extract from *Multi-media Approaches to Rural Education* by Tony Dodds, IEC Broadsheets on Distance Learning, No. 1,

1972. Reproduced by permission; Ontario Institute for Studies in Education for an extract from a report entitled 'Challenge for Change' by Laura Sky in *Community use of Media for Lifelong Education* by the Ontario Institute for Studies in Education; Unesco for extracts from the Unesco Reports on *Preinvestment Study of Educational Mass Media in Thailand*, 1974, *Media Accessibility and Use in an Open University Study Centre* by Marilyn Cooperman, *Studying Instructional Television: What Should Be Evaluated?* by E. McAnany, R. C. Hornik and J. K. Mayo. All published by permission of Unesco.

Whilst every effort has been made to trace the owners of copyright, in a few cases this has proved impossible and we take this opportunity to offer our apologies to any authors whose rights may have been unwittingly infringed.

Author's acknowledgements

I would like to express my appreciation to those who have offered their assistance freely during the compilation of this handbook. I mention in particular David Barlow, Tony Bates, Nicholas Bennett, Frances Berrigan, Norman Davey, Peter Dye, George Klein, Florence Marriott, Jack Moore, Lian Fook Shin, Bernard Webster, Hugh Williams, Stanley Wilson, but there are many others whom I do not have space to name.

I am also grateful for help received from the British Council, from the Ministry of Education, Thailand (and especially the Director General and staff of the Department of Educational Techniques), to fellow members of the Preinvestment Study Team of Educational Mass Media in Thailand, and to colleagues in the Division of Development of Communication Systems, Unesco.

Special thanks are due to the media services of the University of Glasgow, the Universiti Sains Malaysia, Penang, the Singapore Educational Media Service, the Malaysian Educational Media Service, the Hong Kong Educational Television Service, the City of Plymouth Educational Television Service, TELED Halifax, and the Open University.

Finally, three studies have been of especial value in preparing this book. The first is Bernard Webster's *Technology and Access to Communications Media*, written for the Unesco series *Reports and Papers on Mass Communication*. The second is the *Pre-Investment Study of Educational Mass Media in Thailand*, which was above all a team creation. The third is Wilbur Schramm's invaluable study, *Big Media—Little Media*, available only in draft at the time of writing, but promised for publication in 1977.

Contents

Part 4   Media utilisation, evaluation and research

The role of education: mass media

The role of educational mass media

Chapter 1

The evolution of media systems

What are the functions of educational mass media?

The question is fundamental, but still difficult. The difficulty in answering it stems, not so much from its complexity, as from placing a dateline on the response. In most educational fields, fashions change, opportunities are extended, patterns of use differ, new emphases emerge. This is the reason why some of the answers proposed in 1970 (when this handbook's predecessor, *Planning for Educational Television*, was written) are either no longer valid or have assumed a lower priority. But in the case of educational media, change is not merely the result of fashion, or of new technological opportunities — the whole relationship between educational philosophy and method, and between media, has been redefined. Media are now treated (far more generally than a few years ago) within an overall systems framework, and their success or relevance is seen as proportional to their integration with a number of related processes. It is new habits of thinking about education in general which have had the most marked effect upon media planning.

A framework for media

So while most handbooks begin with a list of contents, this book begins with a matrix. It is reproduced in Fig. 1.1 and is the basis of the descriptions and analyses which follow in Part 1.

The model is one of growth: tracing the evolution of media theory and practice from a traditional base (such as persisted up to the 1950s), through a transitional phase which is still largely with us, to a future, some of which is clear, some obscure, and for much of which a number of options are still available. The process of transition is described according to a number of basic parameters, affecting media planning, development and use.

The purpose of the matrix

Why begin in this way?

Primarily, to relate what is said in the following pages to a particular

	Traditional	Transitional	Innovatory
Educational Structures	Centralised or decentralised	Relaxation of structures	Interactive system
Media Organisation	Broadcasting or education control	Diversification	Interactive system
Educational Method	Teacher and syllabus based	Curriculum renewal	Dynamic curriculum
Media Technology	Broadcast transmission	Recording techniques	New technologies
Media Function	Enrichment or direct teaching	Curriculum support	Instructional system
Media Evaluation	*Ad hoc* reporting	Summative evaluation	Formative and process research and evaluation

Fig. 1.1 Development of educational media systems.

time-scale and theoretical base. Different truths have been held to be self-evident in educational media at various points of time, and it is important to know of which era we are speaking. In the main, we are now in the transitional phase – at least where general practice is concerned. But many of the processes of media cannot be understood without reference to the past which shaped them, and in some areas the forms of innovation have gone further than in others. With a framework of this kind, we can at least see where we are placed.

The limitations of the matrix

However, we must be careful not to make too many claims for what is essentially a means of description, not a tool of analysis. There is, for example, no necessary temporal or causal relationship between processes listed as 'transitional' or 'innovatory'. This is not to say that such relationships do not exist – indeed they must, but tracing them is a larger and broader academic matter, not part of a practical handbook. It is difficult to say, for example, with any precision whether technology has created some of the modern forms of educational media, or whether changes in educational thinking have forced technology to adopt a particular route. The important thing for the planner and practitioner to remember is that there is a definite relationship between the two, however it was derived.

The framework must therefore be read with caution. If it is taken simply as a means of displaying and clarifying a multi-faceted process, in such a way that the facets can be logically distinguished, it will serve its purpose.

The theme of change

The matrix is mostly concerned with change. It maps a departure from the traditional, through fluid transitional forms which mirror a challenge but not necessarily a solution, to a more precise future. It is not a process which has any definite beginning or end — from where we stand the past is always traditional, the business of grappling with current problems always innovatory. But in this transition, one trend is dominant, and that is the move towards greater coordination, precision and the planned use of resources.

In the development of modern media management, there is a growing concern with *systems*. A good deal will be said in this book about systems approaches, but simply defined a system is 'a collection of related components (things or people), working together for more or less well defined purposes'. It is easy to see its relevance to educational innovation, where there is equally a growing sense of interrelationship between methods and materials, and the precise establishment of objectives.

Systems approaches

The term 'system' is one of those portfolio words which occurs in such diverse phrases as 'postal system', 'educational system', 'parliamentary system', often implying little more than a degree of organic unity and coordinated planning. A more precise use of the term stemmed from early work on electronic amplifiers, when the notion of 'feedback' was first introduced. (In an amplifier, a small portion of the output is fed back into the input, where it is automatically re-amplified.) Later, it was recognised that there are common elements to all systems, and it was this recognition which led to the development of applied systems approaches, as a general tool of management and planning. Not surprisingly, the same electronically-based terms have been retained as descriptors ('feedback', 'input', 'output' and the like).

The function of systems planning is to ensure efficiency and stability; it is an attempt to take account of all those variables which may lead, if uncontrolled, to confused or wasteful performance. These include such factors as uncertainty over the true objectives of a system, duplication of processes, the use of inappropriate 'components' (methods, techniques, materials), friction, broken links, a lack of feedback, extraneous interference or 'noise'. It is easy to see that, even though the vocabulary is technical, the factors under scrutiny are human as well as machine-based. Indeed, in media systems it is the interaction between human beings and machine processes which is critical and which has to be built into the systems design.

Systems design is a technique which simply had to be invented, to cope with the proliferating demands of modern technology, in particular complex production processes. Without such planning controls, it would be impossible to plan, say, for the manufacture of a satellite, or the production of a supersonic aircraft. The process has naturally been assisted by a growing sophistication in computer-based monitoring devices, but put simply, the main elements involved are:

1. Consideration of the total working environment of a product.
2. A definition of production objectives.
3. Specifying (and where necessary inventing or improving) methods and materials for meeting production objectives.
4. Planning a system (broken down into operational stages) to meet these objectives.
5. Actual production, beginning with prototypes which are tested and the results fed back into the production process.

Educational technology

This sequence can easily be transferred to the situation of educational media or materials. Indeed, the phrase 'educational technology' has been coined principally to express the notion of men, machines and materials working together to improve the relevance of both teaching and learning processes.

The term 'educational technologist' is often used rather ambiguously, because it describes an approach, an attitude of mind and a perspective, rather than a formal programme of study. (The field is new enough for its representatives to come to the discipline by many different routes — from curriculum, from management, from media, from educational planning or systems analysis — rather than through academic programmes.) This approach is characterised by a concern with 'instructional systems'.

Instructional systems

In an 'instructional system', different channels of communication are blended together to achieve specific educational objectives. In this way, mass media become part of an overall educational strategy, and the same media may be part of a number of different systems, as television, for example, may be a component in a curriculum renewal scheme, a language teaching method, a literacy programme or an in-service teacher training programme.

The systems approach is founded upon two main assumptions. First, it is held that each educational medium has particular strengths and qualities, which will be of use in introducing, illustrating or reinforcing specific aspects of the total educational message. (Apart from the curriculum renewal examples already quoted, we may instance the combination of television and radio with correspondence courses, seminars, programmed texts, etc., as is being operated by the Open University in the UK; or a combination of programmed texts, language drill tapes, radio, etc., for language studies.)

Second, it is argued that education (like commerce or technology) is susceptible to breakdown and analysis in terms of objectives, tasks and paths: a process of inputs, models and outputs. This particular assumption has, predictably, raised many eyebrows. How can education, with its many intangibles, be compared to the mechanical process of an assembly line? Yet the assumption is worth taking further, if only because the techniques of network analysis were developed initially to make full use of techno-logical advances; they were intended to identify specific functions required to achieve various goals, and to divide these functions appropriately between men and machines. Our objectives in education, if we are seriously concerned to make the best use of the new media, are more than approximately parallel. We have already seen that a major problem is one of coordination — how to fit the various channels of communication together in a way which makes them genuinely interdependent. Or, to put it another way, our problem is how to reinterpret the philosophy of instruction — to regard it as a unified process of communication in which various channels, including the teacher, are combined to present a total message or to meet specific objectives, working in association (as opposed to the traditional approach in which the teacher is a solitary communica-tions agent, reinforced by supplementary, and subordinate, presentation aids). In the traditional manner, any component may be replaced, if neces-sary, by the teacher; with proper integration each component has its own unique function.

Some diagrammatic illustration may help at this point. Figure 1.2 shows the broad evolution of the systems approach: the way in which conventional instruction, mass instructional technology and individualised instructional technology (or 'programmed learning') may combine to produce a new coherence, through which the strengths of one channel may be used to counteract the weaknesses of another.

Figure 1.3 illustrates this relationship in a more detailed form. Here, the association and interaction between different channels is shown on a modular principle, with the feedback processes between them sketched in by connecting lines.

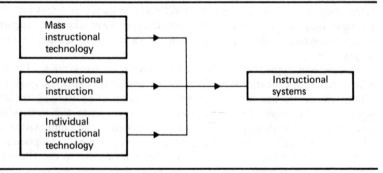

Fig. 1.2   Evolution of the systems approach.

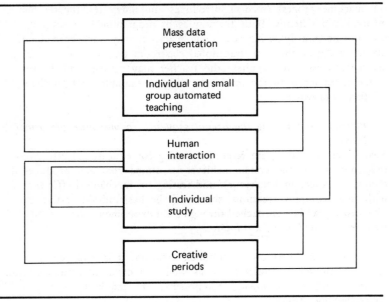

Fig. 1.3   Interaction between channels in the systems approach.

Even in this simplified sketch, it is clear that systems design can be an exacting business. But the main stages involved in the design can still be isolated for an instructional as opposed to an industrial system.

(i) The specification of achievement or performance goals
The word 'goal' is important; we are not trying to indicate general educational 'aims', but a specific target — a particular concept or group of concepts, a motor skill, an information sequence, which is to be mastered or completed.

(ii) The translation of these goals into sub-systems of general and specific functions
We have to state precisely how we can achieve the goal, breaking down the process into stages, as a linked sequence, in much the same way that we design a laboratory experiment or a computer program.

(iii) The specification of the means of executing these functions, and the isolation of components within the system
Different stages will be achieved by different means, and these means will interact within the sequence, as smaller or sub-systems.

(iv) The isolation of personal from machine functions
This is the crux of the problem. What should be left to the teacher, and what can best be performed by the machine? Traditionally, for example,

the machine process (media) introduces and illustrates, the teacher reinforces and extends. With techniques of programmed instruction, this may not necessarily be the case; a whole activity may sometimes be undertaken by the machine. In traditional classroom teaching, of course, the reverse process often applies: the teacher may present and illustrate a concept, leaving it to the textbook, with its examples and problems, to reinforce and extend.

(v) Planning and testing the overall sequence to maximise performance levels

Two kinds of testing are required: testing for educational effectiveness (whether or not the system achieves its stated goal and produces the required changes in behaviour), and testing for mechanical efficiency (as with most complex creations, there may be basic administrative snags). This testing can be approached through pilot experiments in the field, or it may be simulated, using a computer.

A system is, therefore, a complex creation. It is made up of many administrative and tutorial links, as well as a nexus of communication channels. All the following components are required to ensure its controlled operation:

1. Educational planning machinery and administration.
2. Teaching (the instructional system itself).
3. Production for multiplying media.
4. Transmission and distribution channels.
5. Administrative links.
6. Tutorial guidance and leadership.
7. Observable responses and active learning.
8. Feedback channels and continuous evaluation.
9. Refurbishing and maintenance machinery.

A statement of belief

This is probably the time at which to insert a personal opinion, which is addressed to the 'anti-planner' (a common phenomenon among creative producers). It is a principle of this book that planning for educational media can reduce wastage and improve efficiency, without in any way sacrificing the human qualities of education.

Many educators and producers react against educational technology because it is based on the same thought processes as are applied to creating the model of industrial technology. The emotive reaction, however carefully disguised, usually incorporates some reference to education being concerned with people rather than a factory production-line for inanimate objects: this is followed by a plea for 'effectiveness' to be given precedence over 'efficiency'.

The criteria argued for effectiveness, in addition to 'achievement of agreed objectives', usually include satisfaction with the learning process and the personal growth, development or enhancement of individuals or groups.

None of these criteria preclude the idea that more consideration should be given to efficiency, since anything which is efficient should by definition also be effective. However, the converse is not automatically true. For this reason, this book is dedicated to the premise that planning is not always a good thing, but the absence of planning is usually disastrous.

Planning through objectives

With this declaration of interest, we can come down more concretely to the business of planning. In many ways, media planning can be described as the art of being specific. When we speak (as the educational technologist usually speaks) of planning through objectives, the inference is that whatever is undertaken is directed to some precise end: it is planning to cater for a particular situation, environment or problem, which works towards equally precise outcomes.

Again, there is a terminology to be mastered (as with the systems approach), and again it is a language which is based upon straight-forward concepts. The overall framework is one of moving from a diagnosis, the analysis of a problem, to the consideration of alternative strategies for dealing with the problem, and thence to an operational plan. In this process, the environment is first of all considered, the *frame of reference* in which the problem occurs and the *target population* which is involved. From this analysis, *needs* are derived (deficiencies or gaps in the learner's experience or range of skills), and subsequently, after a further process of analysis and classification, *goals* are set — generalised descriptions of outcomes, indications of how learners are expected to respond to particular stimuli or sets of instructions. These general prescriptions are further refined into *objectives* — careful statements of intent, which describe how the more general goal can be achieved. Thus, the goal of an educational programme might be to develop patterns and habits of original thinking, but this is too vague and grand a notion to be of much use to the producer or teacher in formulating an instructional programme. His concern is far more specific; he deals more with the capacity, for example, of a student to read and research a subject on his own account, to write fluently and originally on a chosen topic, to master a set of skills or techniques. The value of setting objectives is that, being specific and referring to precise learning outcomes, they carry within them the seed of how they are to be achieved — and so to the practical producer they throw up ideas of how (with the use of media tools) they may be approached. In other words, they lead to a *strategy* for media use.

In a condensed form, this kind of discussion sounds arid and academic (though it will seem less so to the student who wishes to go more deeply into the literature of systems analysis). Certainly, it is not infallible. It will be as good, not merely as the system which is finally designed, but also as the people who operate it. But it still has a better chance of success than random development.

A simple model for planning educational media

As a concrete example, Fig. 1.4 illustrates the main stages in evolving a national media system. The process begins with the establishment of

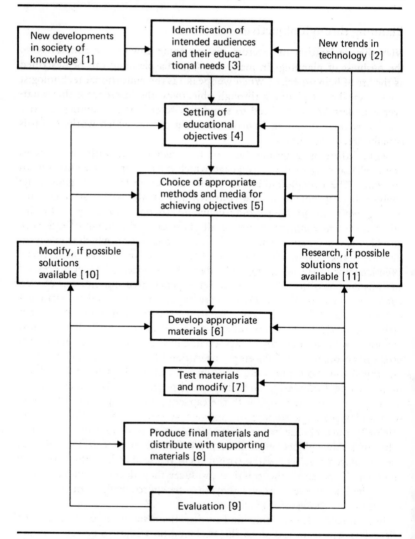

Fig. 1.4   The planning and development process.

educational priorities, and with the setting of educational objectives (steps [1]–[4]). Every country has its own goals, given concrete expression in a development plan, usually written to cover a specific period of time (commonly 5 years). From this development plan, and from an analysis of the social and educational condition of the country, goals and objectives are derived. In a country where there is a high rate of illiteracy, for example, a main goal may be to improve literacy standards. At the same time, the need to modernise, or to diversify job opportunities, may be felt; this could lead to a programme of functional literacy, where the teaching of basic skills of reading and writing is associated with teaching vocational skills. In other words, the farmer is not simply taught to read and write; those texts and aids which he uses are related to his job, and contain information and vocabulary which are useful to him in his work.

Though each society is likely to have only a limited number of overall goals — to modernise, to democratise, to improve living standards and so on — when these goals are reduced to objectives, and sub-objectives, the picture becomes very complex indeed.

Some objectives are quantifiable (literacy, for example, can be measured, at least in gross terms), but others are of a more abstract kind. 'To develop habits of self respect and self reliance' is a difficult concept to pinpoint, and to plan for, in a meaningful way; it will have to be broken down into much more specific elements, amounting to a programme of action by which such a change in psychological behaviour can be induced.

However, the basic purpose of formulating objectives remains the same. It is to isolate priorities, important features of a social or educational process, in such a way that they can be related precisely to means, and if possible, in such a way that success in achieving them can also be measured. This means that the framing of objectives is itself a skilled task, which should involve a number of specialists who are used to such work. It is, above all, a process of refinement. Broad goals are translated into objectives for particular audiences and social groups. These in turn are translated into sub-objectives and related to subject areas and levels. The more detail the better — if only because detail implies that a good deal of rigorous thinking and questioning has taken place.

Selection of media

The next stage of Fig. 1.4 relates objectives to media (step [5]): matching the benefits of particular media forms against their limitations and constraints, in the context of a particular subject area, function or audience. Much more will be said later in this book about the use of media in special situations; it should be stressed, however, that in a coherent media system we are not only talking about individual media, but about mixed, or *multi-media*. We can balance the strengths of one medium against the weaknesses of another; so, the non-visual drawbacks of radio can be offset by a range of printed support materials, or the expensiveness of television can be minimised, by using it only to introduce and describe key concepts (in say science or language teaching), while relying upon radio to provide follow-up discussion or practice drills.

In this exercise, we are dependent both upon experience and upon research. Experience provides the intuitive judgements upon which media producers base their decisions; research tells how far these intuitions can be substantiated. Both are necessary, and it will be a recurrent theme of this book that a mixture of disciplines, of minds and talents, pooled to face a common problem, is a prerequisite to media success.

Development and testing

Next comes the development and testing (*or piloting*) of materials (steps [6]–[7]). It is obviously in the best interests of both producers and audiences if materials are made first in prototype form, and pre-tested with typical audiences before they are finalised for transmission or produced in bulk. At this stage, a full investment has not yet been made in transmission or replication, and mistakes can be corrected, or materials revised. In other words, the development process has its own checks, to protect it against errors — exactly as, in electronic systems, prototypes are first built and tested, and fail-safe mechanisms introduced wherever possible.

Production, distribution and utilisation

Once pre-testing is complete, the best known parts of the system can proceed: the production and distribution of finished materials, taking full account of whatever has been discovered (step [8]). The impetus so far has been one of *pre*-planning, to make sure that what is produced is as relevant to its audiences' needs as can be contrived. But the system does not end here; it has its own built-in monitoring arrangements.

The context of use is extremely important. Media are not produced in a vacuum, and the physical, social and psychological environment of their users is necessarily part of systems design. More than this, their use is often subject to special controls (such as when TV is used in a classroom, or radio is heard in a group setting, with the active participation of a monitor). So, the strategy of media development tests its materials in advance, produces them for a known audience, and offers them up in a recognised, sometimes specially created setting.

Evaluation

The system, if it is to remain efficient, must also have arrangements for assessment and adequate feedback incorporated in its design (steps [9]–[11]). In practice it will be found that any existing system (mechanical, institutional or human) has considerable inertia — a quality which helps to protect it from violent disturbances, but also one which tends to inhibit new developments. It is therefore very important for those who wish to bring about changes in an existing system to be able to identify the true nature of inertia in the environment where they are working. Evaluation can employ many tools — statistical, subjective, or a combination of both. But its main purpose is to induce dialogue between producer and user, and to allow for rapid modification in the system design, immediately weaknesses are discovered.

Completing the cycle

Once evaluation is seen in this way, the model is dynamic rather than static. It allows for continual re-thinking of objectives, continuous monitoring of results, regular re-working of both new and old materials. Only in this way can it keep pace with changing circumstances.

Practical implications

The process just described is, of course, an *idealised* process and one which is by no means invariably followed. While the general aims of education are seldom in dispute, it is still comparatively rarely that specific *objectives* have been set for an educational process. Equally, systematic evaluation is rare. Various national and international agencies carry out 'state-of-the-art' surveys from time to time, but the process is often haphazard and at best the results percolate slowly through to those who can most usefully profit from them. The design and development of new methods and materials in education lag far behind most industrial technologies. When one compares the percentage of total expenditure devoted to research and development in education with that put to the same purpose in the electronics industry, it is obvious that the latter will have a development rate many times faster.

However, in this description, we have the nucleus of media planning as carried out within an instructional system. It has, deliberately, been put simply; those in search of more exact technical definitions can refer to the Bibliography, p. 363. It is a model which is followed in the body of this handbook (in Part 2), where it is fleshed out with the practicalities of media organisation.

It is certainly not a model which can be taken for granted (and probably never will be). Whatever the range of one's thinking, there will always be obstacles to logicality — the invested authority of tradition, misunderstandings, individual preferences and prejudices, cultural variations. And often the imperfections (if they are truly imperfections) have to be accounted for, at the operational planning stage, with quite as much care as goes into the overall planning formula. Systems design is a pragmatic, not a theoretical art.

Media functions

It is for this reason that Part 1 opened with a matrix of change, to which we can now return. It has already been noted that the matrix has two vectors — of innovation (along the horizontal axis), and of function (displayed vertically). The vector of innovation is expressed, crudely, as a continuum, from original and traditional encounters with media to newer forms. Functions are more carefully subdivided, to include the major components of *planning* (method, structure, function and technological invention), *development* (programme generation, organisational forms, production formats and distribution) and *use* (including evaluation). If we were dealing with an environment where planning always took place within a disciplined framework of objectives, there would be no problem. But innovation is a dynamic force, which feeds upon change, and which can only grow out of experiment and investigation. There would be no innovation, no systems approaches, if the need for these had not been demonstrated empirically, through trial and error. And, of course, the final column of Fig. 1.1 is not finite; the innovatory solutions will, in time, cease to be innovatory as they also cease to be ideal.

It is important therefore in this first section to review, with practical examples, the historical processes which have led to our current thinking about media use — and which are still, in practice, very much with us in the educational world. It is this background, more than anything, which will allow us to base our planning upon realistic premises. In doing so, we will treat each media function in turn, and trace its progress towards modernity.

Chapter 2

Educational structures

We start with an environment within which change must occur. There are few, if any, societies which are so undeveloped that some existing framework does not affect growth. So we should begin by looking at two organisational traditions — the structures of education, and those of media. These will have their effect upon new forms, even if only negatively.

Historically, educational systems have been organised in various ways, reflecting degrees of centralisation. At one extreme, we find a completely centralised version — where the Ministry of Education is part of the principal administrative machinery, and where local units derive their authority from the centre. In the industrial West, traditionally France has been representative of this category (though the system's viability is now being questioned). At the other extreme is the situation of the USA, where education derives its authority from the local community, and where, in broad terms, State and Federal authority stem finally from these local units. In between comes the model of the United Kingdom, with a shifting balance of national and local control.

So, in the centralised system, under the direction of a Ministry or Department of Education, curricula and frequently schemes of work and textbooks are devised nationally. The opposite tradition is far more diffuse, giving schools considerable autonomy in devising their programmes, syllabi, and teaching methods, albeit under the general supervision of an Inspectorate.

Both systems have their pros and cons. The centralised version is convenient in administrative and economic terms, but can inhibit the personal development and motivation of teachers, who will prefer to gear materials and teaching programmes to the level of their own pupils. The decentralised form, on the other hand, can make it difficult to introduce major innovative programmes, and to have them accepted by large numbers of participating schools.

In recent times, far more countries have tended to query the autocratic model and to experiment with greater delegation of powers to the community, or to the individual school. But in the developing world, such a trend can produce new problems, because in most cases planning and control over economic affairs, and the overall development process, are highly centralised, so that it is natural for this centralisation to be reflected in other spheres. When this works against traditional practice, it can create formidable tensions. In India, for example, the management of the economic plan is completely centralised, but education is given, constitutionally, to the States, who often refuse to recognise the authority of the All-India government in educational planning and development. Compromises, in practice, are hard to find, and all too often the pretence is maintained that federal authority exists, when in practice it may be minimal.

This kind of constitutional debate may seem far removed from media, but its practical effects are considerable. Mass media depend for their efficiency on a concensus among their users that they are working in support of common problems and philosophies. It is only in centralised systems that materials can be produced which are of direct curricular relevance throughout the system. This has been an historic issue, for example, in the United Kingdom, where for many years only 'enrichment' materials could be contemplated by the educational television organisations (except in new curricular areas, such as in the Nuffield programmes). In a decentralised system, the accent is more upon locally produced materials, and cable television systems, local broadcasting and micro-media (such as closed-circuit television) assume a heightened significance.

The problem is compounded by innovation. The newer forms of community media work from the ground upwards, and while in the sophisticated countries of the West there is room for investment and experiment within forms, in the developing world such mixed investments are not easy (especially when the overriding problem of economic development must be approached at a central level). The problem, in fact, again mirrors the perennial difficulty of mass media — a possible blurring of individuality, to ensure the advantages of mass distribution. The major investment required of a national mass media system demands full utilisation if it is to be economically viable; yet full utilisation tends to infer uniform styles, directed from the centre. Compromises are possible (they are discussed later in this handbook), but they can only stem from a frank recognition of the realities of planning and control.

It should be added that, although the problem has been presented in a global context, it also exists at the micro level. Within a single campus, say in a university, there is a basic choice to be made between a centralised system, probably using a wired distribution network, and a complex of smaller units, or some kind of mobile strike force. Planning has therefore to include a realistic appraisal of the attitudes, and willingness to compromise, of all users.

Chapter 3

Media organisation

A parallel situation exists with communications media, where there is a classic debate as to who should control educational broadcasting — educators or broadcasters? It is simple enough to advance theoretical arguments for and against both positions. When in the hands of professional broadcasters, there will be an inherently strong production capability, a full use of media techniques, creative and sophisticated programming. Timing and transmission arrangements are likely to be excellent, and access to broadcast networks easier, since the producing agency has a vested interest in distribution. On the other hand, sharpness in educational perspective, relevance in programming and the involvement of teachers in programme planning may be lacking. There may be less attention paid to the niceties of utilisation, less willingness to experiment on educational rather than production grounds, less acknowledgement that what is good for general broadcast may not be so as part of an instructional system, and almost certainly less concern for evaluation, unless it is concerned with audience levels.

Control by educators is likely to be the mirror image of the above: with a proper concern for educational matters, and less concern (largely because of lesser experience) with media potential. On balance (and speaking personally), control by educators is probably preferable. It is easier, in practice, to convert a teacher into a good broadcaster, than to instil into a broadcaster the sensitivities and experience of the teacher. There are, around the world, a growing number of production units in the hands of education departments and ministries which provide ready-made programmes for transmission over regular broadcasting channels. The growth of closed-circuit systems, of cable and community media, and the greater availability of production tools to the amateur (in less costly, non-professional versions) has provided a wider familiarity with production techniques.

Yet this theoretical debate is rarely worthwhile, since the planner's first concern is to come to grips with existing patterns of media use and control. What is needed most of all is to exploit present resources to the full, and to bring about, not opposition, but a lively interface between broadcasters and educators — within the limits of their retaining structures.

Characteristic broadcasting structures range from the purely State-controlled organisation, through intermediate systems in which public corporations operate with a constitutional requirement of 'responsibility' but with considerable autonomy, to much more varied systems, where commercial organisations are allowed to act independently, in mutual competition.

The first model creates a State monopoly, within a Ministerial framework or alternatively as a State bureau; the Eastern European countries, including the Soviet Union, are characteristic examples. The second model usually features a public corporation, over which Government control can theoretically be exercised through a veto sanction, but which in practice is often given substantial freedom (witness the BBC). An alternative to this form is one in which the State is actually a major stockholder, but with a good deal of executive responsibility vested in private minority stockholders; Italy, Sweden and Switzerland are illustrations. With the third model, in a commercial environment as in the USA, broadcasting is mostly a private concern. Additionally, there also exist in the world a number of non-profit-making corporations, using broadcasting to foster a special set of goals – often political or religious. 'Radio Free Europe', and some of the Catholic radio stations, fall into this category.

This is not to deny that, at all levels, controls exist. In technical matters, especially frequency allocation and regulation, broadcasting systems are subject to both national and international regulation (such as through the Federal Communications Commission (FCC), in the USA, or through the mechanisms of the International Telecommunications Union, which acts as a forum for international telecommunications debate and agreement). But the control may, at times, be little more than nominal and may also be subject to political circumstances; the position of the FCC, for example, has veered radically over the past few decades.

In the main, the determining factor is cultural, deriving from the climate in which broadcasting was first introduced – whether one of public responsibility, as in Britain, or one of free enterprise, as in the United States. As in other spheres, the countries of the developing world have tended to follow the cultural indicators of their sponsors. There are many systems modelled upon the BBC in the countries of Africa and Asia; until recently, the Philippines, Thailand, the countries of Latin America, were analogues of North America. But there are significant differences when it comes to control. There are relatively few countries in the developing world which have felt confident enough to create broadcasting corporations with anything like autonomy: the persuasive power of broadcasting in the interest of 'national development' has been too great to resist. At the time of its last political upheaval, the Philippines – traditionally a network of commercial stations – withdrew much of its support of free enterprise, because of the overt dangers of anti-Government use. It is most common in the developing world to find broadcasting organisations which are extensions of, or adjuncts to, Government bodies – in Asia, in Africa, in the Arab States, if not in Latin America.

The organisation of educational broadcasting follows the same pattern, since it arises from the same traditions. In those countries where there has been a strong State ownership or public service history there was also — at a relatively early stage of development — an incentive to create educational programmes. So school programmes have a comparatively long history in Great Britain, France, Australia, Canada, Japan, Singapore, Malaysia, Nigeria, India. In the main, at the national level at least, this tradition has been continued, with a strong element of centralisation in educational media planning, even though (as in Malaysia and Singapore) control may have been shifted from the Information to the Education authorities, or some new model may have been evolved, based upon partnership (as in the United Kingdom, where the Open University was set up in partnership with the BBC).

Other models under discussion, such as the proposal by one faction for an educational broadcasting corporation in Britain, to operate a new fourth channel, are equally founded upon a concept of public interest and government commitment.

In a more commercially oriented culture, the incentive towards educational broadcasting was not so strong, because the profit motive was lacking. It was therefore left to the educator to create instructional media systems, often working hand in glove with the smaller, public service community stations, as happened in the USA.

It must be emphasised that the understanding of educational broadcasting in the USA is very different from that in Europe. The commercial predominance meant that the range of programming throughout the networks was much narrower, with cultural programmes relatively few. So the term 'educational television' in the USA reflects all kinds of public broadcasting, not simply instructional programmes (known in North America as ITV), and including feature and drama programmes which might, in other situations, be expected to figure in general broadcasting schedules.

A landmark in the development of public broadcasting in the USA came with the Carnegie Commission's report, 'Public Television: A Programme for Action', which formed the basis of the Public Broadcasting Act of 1967. This act established the Corporation for Public Broadcasting (CPB), which was to provide a greater coherence for the national network of independent stations, and centralise financial awards. In 1970, the Corporation joined with a group of elected television representatives to create the Public Broadcasting Service (PBS), which is an organised federation of educational television stations. (For radio, there is also in existence National Public Radio (NPR), though NPR actually produces radio programmes, while PBS does not: it obtains programmes from its member organisations and from other agencies which are partially funded through CPB.)

The problems of public broadcasting did not end here. Long-range financing remained a major issue, and in 1973, a special task force of the CPB produced a plan calling for a matching grant formula from Federal funds, in the hope that this would resolve the uneasy opposition between the need for Federal support and the fear of Federal interference. A bill was submitted to Congress in 1974, proposing 1 dollar of Federal finance for every 2½ dollars raised elsewhere. The relationship between CPB and PBS was still ambivalent, and the two bodies produced a seven-point agreement in 1973, defining their roles more precisely. The problem of interconnection (a 'coast to coast' public broadcasting facility) is still unresolved, and solutions proposed include a public broadcasting satellite consortium.

The outcome is an attempt to come to grips, collectively and democratically, with a free enterprise situation. The result is a network of interconnected institutions, including several national programme libraries, many independent stations who can both sell and acquire programmes from each other, regional and State associations concerned with programme acquisition, professional societies for working producers, and federal organisations which help to channel production funds, programme information, and which offer corporate representation during negotiations with Government. Such a system is as good as the individuals who operate it, and as the degree of unanimity among its members.

Such changes indicate, most of all, a new responsiveness to existing conditions. If educational mass media were being developed from the grass roots upwards (as they were in American Samoa), there might be an ideal model; but generally, they are the result of compromise. It is the success of this compromise, in meeting both the objectives of media and entrenched interests and existing skills, which causes us most concern. The erosion of rigid patterns shows that this is being, gradually, achieved.

Chapter 4

Educational method

With the supporting structures recognised, we can turn to those changes in educational philosophy which have, more than anything, affected the character of educational mass media. These changes have been both gradual and cumulative; they reflect a synthesis of many disciplines, including the psychologist, the sociologist and the linguist as well as the educational theorist, which has brought together a body of empirical research on how, in what circumstances, for what reasons and with what kinds of assistance children and adults learn.

Although these changes are reflected in all quarters, from educational administration to classroom layout and design, it is the area of *curriculum* that has produced the greatest emphasis on learning systems, with media seen increasingly as agents in a total process rather than as independent additions to a teaching programme. The traditional environment of teacher and classroom, working to an agreed but generalised and content-oriented syllabus, now has a wider perspective. The teacher is not detached from the educational system which recruits and trains him; the classroom is not divorced from the external world.

The first, transitional development was the emergence of a curriculum which was more modern in content − which was up to date in ideas, took account of the external world, acknowledged new discoveries and processes. This was reinforced by new methods of teaching, particularly those which emphasised learning through discovery with the teacher encouraging pupils to find their own direction. At the same time, team teaching techniques, group activities, and new open plan styles of planning school buildings and organising classrooms, made it possible for students to work more at their own pace, basing their learning on personal enthusiasms, and tracing the interconnections between disciplines rather than the rigid outlines of a specialism. In the end this crystallised as a new sense of curriculum − a dynamic process, where methods and objectives are inseparable from content.

It is important, in this process, to differentiate again between two versions of curriculum construction. In some centralised educational systems (for example, in Eastern Europe), the main preoccupation has been the creation of a common core curriculum, stressing unity and uniformity rather than variety. The same is true of many developing countries, where, for reasons of economy, the limited numbers and quality of the teaching force and political ideology, standardisation has been the norm. Even in the earlier curriculum experiments in the USA (e.g. in the Biological Sciences Curriculum Study, the Physical Sciences Curriculum Study or the Chemical Education Materials Project), although the individuality of the pupils involved, and the need for personal discovery, was emphasised, materials — including pupils' texts, films, and audio-visual materials — were often produced according to a pre-determined plan.

Later developments in Europe and North America are of a different order, working upon the imagination and professional drive of the teacher as the best mediator between a subject and its students, but recognising that he may be in need of guidance to realise his own potential.

The nature of curriculum change

Modern curriculum approaches, therefore, consider a whole range of learning and teaching experiences. Curriculum planning is seen as a continuous process; it follows the same cycle of determining objectives, of establishing content, of allocating and assigning methods and of evaluating results.

In practice, the process is not made up of simple, discrete functions. Objectives, for example, are not generic; they have to be framed in the light of the quality of the teacher, the resources available and the needs and situation of the learner. An objective is not to teach the principle of relativity, but to teach it to a particular audience, in a particular environment. Equally, content is more than subject matter — it must include the mental processes which are mastered by acquiring a particular function, as well as the body of knowledge which is digested.

In the broadest sense, we can consider the educational process as the result of combining and applying various kinds of resource or input. These will include matching aims and priorities, students, teachers, aids and technologies, management procedures, content, quality controls, finances and research indicators. The result is a workable system.

Clearly, in a system of this kind, a good deal of group or team work is required, with specialists pooling their resources to analyse and reconstitute the system components. Objectives can only be established by reference to a body of information about the level of development of pupils, their needs and interests, the social conditions and problems which they are likely to encounter, the nature of the subject matter and the types of learning which can arise from a study of the subject matter. Thus in establishing objectives the disciplines of the sociologist, the psychologist and the curriculum specialist are equally necessary.

The organisation of content, and the assignment of methods, materials and techniques, also requires a broad spread of disciplines if the result is to be realistic. Once objectives are clearly devised, and teaching units organised, they have to function in the average classroom, applied by the teaching force at the system's disposal, using the resources available. Evaluation is the same; it must be framed in such a way that its findings can be communicated to all the parties involved, in the classroom as well

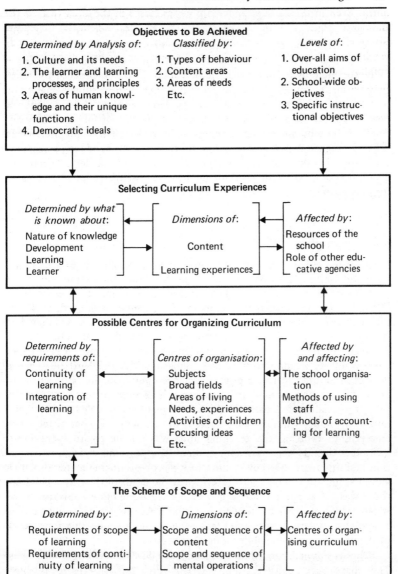

Objectives to Be Achieved

Determined by Analysis of:
1. Culture and its needs
2. The learner and learning processes, and principles
3. Areas of human knowledge and their unique functions
4. Democratic ideals

Classified by:
1. Types of behaviour
2. Content areas
3. Areas of needs
   Etc.

Levels of:
1. Over-all aims of education
2. School-wide objectives
3. Specific instructional objectives

Selecting Curriculum Experiences

Determined by what is known about:
Nature of knowledge
Development
Learning
Learner

Dimensions of:
Content
Learning experiences

Affected by:
Resources of the school
Role of other educative agencies

Possible Centres for Organizing Curriculum

Determined by requirements of:
Continuity of learning
Integration of learning

Centres of organisation:
Subjects
Broad fields
Areas of living
Needs, experiences
Activities of children
Focusing ideas
Etc.

Affected by and affecting:
The school organisation
Methods of using staff
Methods of accounting for learning

The Scheme of Scope and Sequence

Determined by:
Requirements of scope of learning
Requirements of continuity of learning

Dimensions of:
Scope and sequence of content
Scope and sequence of mental operations

Affected by:
Centres of organising curriculum

Fig. 4.1   A model for curriculum design.

as on the curriculum planning committee.

For this reason it is in *implementation* that most of the problems occur. It is not too difficult to evolve a model of what curriculum theory involves (one example devised by Hilda Taba is reproduced in Fig. 4.1). It is far more difficult to adjust this model to life-size situations.

The logical inference of all of this might well be that every curriculum must be different. Still, the more recent attempts to create common curricula (which in the developing world may be especially necessary, as guides to practice for teachers who are without the training or experience to create their own conceptual frameworks) do try to proceed by reference to ideas, concepts and behaviours, rather than to subject matter or content. In this way, they can offer guidance without insisting upon a dogmatic sequence of teaching, or a fixed progression of subjects. They lay emphasis on why something is being taught, rather than on precisely what is being taught. This is certainly helpful to the media producer, since he is able to use his skills to see how a particular instructional demand can best be approached, rather than taking an arbitrary list of topics as a scenario for illustration.

Some examples

Some characteristic examples of curriculum development can be taken from the United Kingdom: those of the Nuffield Foundation and, more recently, of the Schools Council. A shortfall in mathematicians and a sense of inadequacy in mathematics teaching programmes produced, in 1964, the first stages of the Nuffield Mathematics Project, which was aimed at the age level 5 to 13. Bridging primary and secondary education, it was designed to improve interest in the subject by attacking the spirit and content of its introductory phases. Subsequently, the Nuffield Science Project attempted to revise primary science courses in the same spirit. In both of these, the curriculum was devised by groups of teachers, parents, subject specialists and administrators, and materials were extensively pre-tested in pilot schools, coordinated by a national committee. The emphasis in evolving the teaching units was on the environment itself, beginning outside the classroom and stressing learning through participation and discovery. Moreover, the stress was on producing materials which would stimulate teachers into catering for the needs of their own children; there was no attempt (indeed it would have been quite contrary to the spirit of the project) to develop a set of materials which could be construed as a 'syllabus', with rigid lesson plans and a supporting framework of sequenced, commercially produced illustrations.

Schools Council curriculum projects have developed along similar lines. They have begun with feasibility trials, which put forward ideas about curriculum gaps and possibilities for discussion with teachers, employers, specialists and parents before systematic enquiry and prototyping are undertaken. Then the curriculum project itself has been entrusted to an overall director, who gathers around him a writing team. Materials are created in prototype and given field tests at all stages, with briefing and training provided for participating teachers. Afterwards, in a second phase before final materials are published, a second wave of pilot schools is involved, on the very reasonable premise that diffusion will be much improved if a substantial group of schools is concerned with extensive pre-testing.

The Schools Council has been in existence only for a decade and its work is still in a trial stage; evaluation (even the development of appropriate instruments for evaluation) is still incomplete. But it can be seen that once again the delicacy and detail of the systems approach is being used to allow, quite contrary to conventional opinion, for the greater involvement and freedom of individual students.

The case is somewhat different in the developing world. Many of the creations of the Schools Council stress the autonomy and professional competence of the classroom teacher, who needs drawing out, not force-feeding. The same is intrinsically true of teachers everywhere, but in more basic situations, the availability and level of training of teachers, their motivation, the conditions under which they work and the numbers with which they cope, often necessitate a much greater sense of direction, with the production of more concrete lesson plans, specific materials for pupils and teachers alike and a greater unity of scheduling (particularly when broadcasting is involved). In the process of curriculum reform, as in media development, we are in search of a transitional model, which allows for immediate assistance to meet temporary situations, but which also permits over the long term, greater teacher independence and control.

Chapter 5

Media technology

The remaining feature in mapping the environment in which media planning is conducted is that of technology itself. Technology is constantly changing and in general its theoretical capacity is far ahead of its reality, because any new technical development requires a weight of investment, of public or private market support. Except in such urgent cases as defence, or where international commercial cartels are involved, the lag between development and diffusion is protracted. In the case of the motion picture and television, for example, two decades intervened.

The influence which technological opportunity has upon educational media is therefore variable and it is likely to be most immediate in the industrialised countries, where investment possibilities and supporting infrastructures are already present. Yet in the lifetime of educational media there have been some transitions which can now be held to be general, even in the developing world. Until relatively recently, educational mass media were distributed by only one means: broadcast distribution. There was in consequence an innate rigidity in the use of media, because programmes had to be accepted at whatever time they were scheduled. Some refinements were possible (multiple repeats of programmes, consultation with users on appropriate schedules, statistical surveys of school timetables), but in principle the educational user had to accommodate to the medium rather than vice versa, and this inflexibility took its toll.

Taping

One developmental strand which has therefore been of major significance is that of *recording*. Once materials could be taped, they could be used at will by individual teachers and integrated, after preview, into a personal scheme of work. Although widespread in audio this process is still at a relatively early stage for video forms, though with the emergence of simpler, more practical video recorders, cassettes and discs, and the spread of low cost television equipment, the passive conditions of earlier mass media systems are rapidly being broken down.

The new technology

Once we move beyond taping, the position is very variable and vastly different as between the developed and the developing world. The new technologies are precise on the drawing board, reasonably clear in the laboratory or in prototype and less so in the schools. All that we can do at this point, therefore, is to review the main directions of current technology and see where some of the future trends lie. After all, while the planner has to keep a firm grasp of reality, he also has to look ahead, to ensure that whatever he is planning is compatible with the future, does not run contrary to present trends or make his recommended system obsolete in an uneconomic space of time. For this he has to be both knowledgeable and wary; the hardware salesmen can be extremely persuasive.

New possibilities exist at both macro and micro levels. At the macro level, where broadcasting was once confined to terrestrial transmission, we now have the availability of satellite distribution (for subsequent retransmission over ground networks), and the experimental existence of direct broadcasting by satellite to community receivers. At the micro level, a greater miniaturisation of equipment, with more reliable solid state technology, has meant that media can be used more extensively.

Micro technologies, which do not involve expensive transmission systems, are clearly easier for experiment; the portapak camera, the video-cassette, do not require a national grid. But curiously enough, the gap in potential between industrialised and developing countries is not so obvious at the macro level. In the developed West, there is already a major commitment to telecommunications to radio and television systems, and to advocate any change, in order to take advantage of a new technology, is difficult. In the developing countries, this degree of investment has not occurred and more speculation is often possible. Even more important in view of the urgency of communication and education needs in the developing world, macro technologies may represent the only solution which can affect radical change, and penetrate widely, in the measurable future. It was for this reason, for example, that India moved ahead to experiment with direct broadcasting satellite reception (in the SITE experiment), that Indonesia is committing itself to satellite communications as the one means of diffusing information across such a widely scattered country, and that Iran and the Philippines are following suit.

New trends

While the ability of technology to come up with the right answers depends ultimately on the right questions being asked, there are certain basic developments which have made the small revolution we have already experienced possible and which are important for the future.

The first of these is the transition from *valves* to *transistors*, and so to *integrated circuits*. The result is both greater miniaturisation and greater speed. The original valve amplifiers suffered from ageing, thus requiring adjustment and replacement, while the transistor is much more stable, needing little or nothing in the way of maintenance or operational skill.

The progression to circuit integration is producing a different impact again, particularly with computer technology. It is now possible, using photographic techniques, to put thousands of circuits on to a tiny chip of silicon which is itself barely visible to the naked eye. This method of 'large scale integration' has produced a new dimension in micro-technology.

Another critical development has been the move from *analogue* to *digital* techniques. A few years ago, all amplifiers accepted a voltage which was analogous to some such quality as the shape of a wave form, and this was amplified, at the output stage, to the same pattern. Digital techniques employ a pulse code system, which is much faster in dealing with the same volume of information, using a varying series of numbers rather than a varying physical quality. Although digital television cameras are still in the prototype stage, digital techniques are already used in television converters (translating American standard 525-line, 60 Hz signals into European 625-line 50 Hz signals), as well as in videotape recording and editing (to identify individual frames) or in systems which make it possible to 'hide' programme sound, after first converting it to digital form, in gaps in the television signal, so extending channel capacity.

A third development in the extension of channel capacity is by moving up the *frequency spectrum*. Mostly, radio frequencies are in the LW, MW and VHF bands, and television occupies VHF and UHF bands, with the SHF band (or microwaves) used in broadcasting for line-of sight connections, as between a production centre and transmitter. But the development of lasers, which are coherent light emitting sources, has opened up new possibilities. Light waves can be modulated and guided along optical fibre cables; a complete cable containing 50 conductors may be only 1 cm in diameter. Where the broadcasting spectrum is congested, this opens up a completely new vista.

The influence of technology is all-pervasive, but for the benefit of this argument it is convenient to consider three main areas — of *production*, of *distribution* and of *retrieval and interaction.* In this way, the main components of the educational media system (or indeed of any communication system) are covered.

Production

The main benefit which technology can offer to producers is in the increased flexibility, portability and reduced cost which the development of stable and miniaturised equipment can bring. This can affect professionals and amateurs alike. The growth of closed-circuit television equipment, cassette audio recorders, industrial, low cost video cameras and recorders, and videocassettes, have allowed the amateur to participate actively in production processes — whether for his own use, or, in the case of local and cable systems, for community distribution. Where money and resources permit, we have reached a stage where even primary school children can confidently handle television cameras, and the result is a most salutary demystification of the profession of the producer.

But the professional broadcaster has benefited equally. Electronic colour cameras, for example, used to be cumbersome, needing three or four tubes, and posing major problems in setting up. Recently, their control has become much more automatic, and new cameras (mainly Japanese) weigh only 9 kg (for a three-tube camera) and 6 kg (for a single tube camera). They are therefore quite comparable with 16 mm film cameras. Solid state developments have had a special impact (a term describing equipment where there are no electrons moving in a gas or vacuum). With digital techniques, and the kind of micro-circuitry already described, extremely small items of equipment, such as cameras, are possible (one prototype, for example, weighs less than half a kilogramme). Liquid crystals, such as are used in electronic calculators and digital wrist watches, may eventually replace the cathode ray tube, making possible a television receiver which can hang on the wall like a picture. Lighting has also been affected. Long-life and lightweight units employing gas discharge tubes, of the tungsten halogen and quartz iodine types, produce several times more light per watt than the old incandescent variety, and television tubes are much more sensitive than hitherto (reducing the amount of ambient light needed to produce usable pictures).

Broadcasting systems are also experimenting with equipment which can superimpose letters and figures on to television transmissions without affecting the normal programme. In the United Kingdom, the BBC and IBA have systems known respectively as SEEFAX and ORACLE, which will allow television receivers to be fitted with special terminal boxes, giving access to numerous channels on which a single frame of information is presented. This can permit the television set to be used as a reference source, and ultimately coupled to a facsimile printed device — meaning that permanent records of information can be kept, or 'television newspapers' introduced.

Distribution

In a congested spectrum, one of the main considerations is to increase channel capacity, whether to transmit simple data or more complex information such as moving pictures. Some of the principal means of doing so which are now developing, or in prototype, are as follows:

(i) By using higher frequencies for broadcasting

In the developing world, there are more opportunities in this direction than in the developed West. Many radio services now use a single side-band system of modulation, which means that they occupy only half the band-width that was previously required, but nevertheless space is already virtually exhausted on medium, high and very high frequency bands. Television broadcasting is well into the UHF band, and although the SHF band is theoretically attractive, it poses considerable technical problems. The only real contribution, apart from laser developments already mentioned, is in a better regulation of existing frequencies, to avoid waste.

(ii) By using multi-channel networks

In the West, in densely populated metropolitan areas, the advantages of cable networks are well appreciated; the inhibiting factor is usually economic, as a large initial outlay is involved, which must either be supported by public funds or by commercial investment. A multi-channel capacity can be provided either by offering separate circuits for each channel, or by modulating each channel's signal on to a slightly different carrier frequency. At the receiver, in the first case, a simple selector switch may be provided, or where more than a dozen channels are involved an elementary exchange can operate in much the same way as a telephone (with a code dialled by the operator). Where a modulated signal is involved, a tuning device rather than a switch is provided.

These systems operate mainly in compact metropolitan areas. But where there is a need to connect widely separated population centres, microwave connections can be provided to join the systems together.

(iii) By using satellites

The use of satellites to broadcast to widely separated areas is now commonplace, particularly for major broadcasts, where the programme is relayed from one broadcasting system to another, and subsequently re-distributed by normal transmission. The progress in satellite design has been very rapid, since the introduction of 'Telstar' in 1962, with only twelve telephone circuits. In 1964, INTELSAT (the International Telecommunications Satellite Consortium) was created, to establish a global communications satellite system. It now has more than eighty member nations, representing 95 per cent of the world's telecommunications traffic. A whole series of satellite launches began with 'Early Bird' (Intelsat 1) in 1965, continuing into the 'seventies, up to the current Intelsat IV series. However, these are all *point-to-point* satellites, requiring large and expensive earth stations. They are not primarily concerned with television transmissions, but with general telecommunications; where television is involved, they are the concern of the broadcasting organisations, who rent time from the consortium and re-transmit the pictures received.

A second generation of satellites (in use in the USSR and in Canada), are *distribution* satellites: medium powered, providing a fairly strong signal over a limited area, within which reception is possible with smaller, less costly earth stations for subsequent re-broadcasting. But the new goal in satellite operation, particularly for countries which cover a wide geographical area and have scattered populations, is the *direct broadcasting* satellite, which can broadcast into local communities. A pilot version is offered by the experimental satellite ATS—6, launched in 1974, and used between 1974 and 1976 for programme experiments in the USA and in India. This permits reception in villages and local communities, using a

2-metre dish at a central reception point. Broadcasting into individual homes is, however, at least a decade away, and will have to await both the results of current experiments and a favourable investment climate.

(iv) By using information compression or injection techniques
Drives to increase channel capacity have produced time or space sharing techniques, where information is compressed into a narrower bandwidth, or additional information is superimposed on to a normal signal. In television, for example, this has included adding audio information to the synchronising pulses which are always part of the transmitted signal.

(v) By making the most of existing systems
Whatever the pressure on space, most systems are — at some time — underused, and with some thought and ingenuity they can be extended. There are often slack hours, during the day or at night, on both national and regional services, which can be used to transmit information for recording and re-use. If automatic recording devices are improved, this practice could be much expanded.

Retrieval and interaction

In recent years, probably the greatest benefit to the user has come about through *recording techniques*. The audio-tape recorder is now familiar in most countries; with the introduction of cassettes, there has been an even greater upsurge in the use of pre-packaged, user-proof audio programmes. The cassette is more lightweight than the gramophone recording and its reproduction equipment less bulky: its advantages in such areas as correspondence education, language teaching or music education are only just being realised. Although hardware costs are considerable, the freedom which the physical distribution of cassettes brings is much valued in an environment where teacher adaptation and control are important, in keeping with modern curriculum trends.

A similar kind of revolution is beginning with video recording. Originally, videotape recorders were all of the transverse scan variety, with the tape passing over four recording heads, using a 2 inch tape width. But the development of helical scan recorders (with narrower tapes wrapping a single helical turn round a central drum) brought the video recording market within reach of consumers other than broadcasting organisations.

The early development of video recorders was hampered by lack of standardisation in tape size, incompatibly between equipment (even within the same range), and both electronic and mechanical problems. Various gauges have been employed, ranging from ¼ inch, through ½ inch and ¾ inch, to 1 inch formats.

It was hoped that the emergence of the videocassette would help to resolve this position (though, already, standardisation seems out of the question, with several formats in use). The videocassette has the same intrinsic advantages as the audio cassette; it can be linked with, and inter-faced with, cameras and normal receivers, and compatibility, at least between models of the same range, is possible.

Other systems which offer replay-only facilities use discs or film bases. One disc system records on to magnetic material; another is similar in principle to gramophone recordings and employs plastic discs, produced from a metal master. Other systems still use laser techniques to produce the master recording, with tracks recorded on film, which is then con-verted photographically on to a glass master, from which photographic transfers can be made to plastic.

In film-based systems, replay is by a miniature telecine system, with the film scanned by an electron beam, such as in the Electronic Video Reproduction system (EVR). Obviously, there are many possibilities using combinations of these techniques, and use is dictated by market demands and manufacturer's interests.

Retrieval

Where channel capacity is adequate, a dial access facility can be incor-porated into a distribution system, to allow for personalised retrieval of materials. Dial access is another portfolio word, which may cover a number of situations, ranging from a simple 'request' facility (in which a user institution telephones the producing organisation, asking them to play a particular programme at a particular time), to more complex systems, where individual channels, and even programmes, may be dialled direct, using a pre-set code. If linked with a computer network the facility can be very sophisticated, though there are substantial economic limitations.

In this, as in other areas, the major obstacle is that of development costs in constructing the network. There are already many kinds of net-work in existence, but it is in the telephone system that the greatest inter-action is possible, with feedback available not simply from the individual subscriber to the exchange, but between subscribers. It is this kind of interface which the adherents of access are seeking, and which is at the moment neither technically nor economically possible for mass media.

The goal, however, is not only to enlarge the feedback potential of individual networks, but also to provide interfaces between different networks (such as occurs, to a very limited extent, between radio and the telephone system, on 'phone in' programmes). Particularly if this involves a widespread computer network, with its great possibilities for information retrieval at speed from a large memory store, with storage on electro-magnetic tape and with slaved audio-visual displays, the potential is large indeed. But the costs involved are also prodigious, and real advances are bound to be very much in the future.

Interaction

The modern trend is towards user access and participation — the encouragement of a dialogue between producers and audiences. This is being attempted in many ways, ranging from the involvement of audience groups in production processes to the pre-testing of programmes with sample audience groups, and increased participation by audiences in actual programming. Technology is of help in several ways. In radio, it can permit direct audience contributions, such as the control units which allow for telephone conversations between studio speakers and the general public, or even, to a limited extent, between telephone subscribers themselves. Video formats, at present, offer fewer possibilities for interaction; after all, there are no videophones available — another example of broadcasting's dependence upon parallel networks and technologies. But there are some simpler feedback possibilities, which allow answers to be given to objective-type questions, by pushing buttons on a display panel. This is really an extension of the 'feedback classroom' already in use in industrial training (students are given a multiple-choice test, and indicate their response by pressing a button. The tutor can not only monitor responses from all of his class, but he can percentage out the results and gauge the overall satisfactoriness of the class's learning). If introduced into cable television systems, the device may be used for a whole range of purposes, from programmed instruction in home study programmes to consumer or political opinion polling.

Perhaps the greatest possibility for interaction occurs, however, in the newer forms of community media, which operate within the confines of a single, local area. Here, the media offer a tool to assist normal processes of social development and interaction, mainly by allowing people to see themselves as they are seen by others.

Appropriate technologies

Since it is the applications of technology which are finally important, far more attention is now being paid to seeking out new, sometimes ingenious and preferably low cost solutions to problem areas, and to matching technology with each country's level of social and economic development. In other words, a better dialogue between technologists and educational and social system planners is being sought.

An example of an ingenious solution to a technological problem is found in the use of balloons as high-altitude platforms to provide economic telecommunications coverage (a poor man's satellite, in fact). Using helium-filled balloons, power is fed to the airborne package via the conductive tethering cable, and at altitudes of 3,000 m to 4,500 m above sea level the line of sight extends to 200 km to 250 km from the earth tether point, giving ground coverage areas of up to 200,000 sq. km. In this way much greater areas are open to broadcasting than would be possible with traditional broadcasting modes. The system was tested in the Bahamas, and is in use in Korea; it is also proposed for parts of Africa. Although considerable difficulty was experienced in Korea, with more than one balloon being lost in the TECOM (tethered communication) system, it is still a classic example of combining old and new technologies.

Other devices such as the 'teleblackboard', pioneered in Indonesia, also combine available and traditional technologies to produce new results. The 'electrowriter', for example, uses two electronic pens linked along regular telephone lines. At the transmission end, the teacher writes or draws along a continuous roll of acetate film on the receiver; this receiver has a built-in overhead projector which projects the writings, diagrams, etc., on to a screen. This device is also being developed within the Technology Faculty of the UK Open University, where telephones are additionally in use for telephone tutorials and tele-conferencing experiments.

The second approach open to us is to make a better, more imaginative use of existing forms and systems. It is not surprising that, in recent years, we have begun to return to simpler tools, such as radio — and to stress the importance of low cost media, traditional media such as folk forms, and the psychological advantages of simply produced materials such as can be devised in a learning resource centre. At least these are forms which are familiar, inexpensive and which can be controlled.

One call that has been made urgently is in favour of 'intermediate technology' — a technology which is adapted to the skills and competences of a country, rather than imposed externally. There are serious economic and social doubts to be raised over media systems which demand the importation of large amounts of foreign equipment, and which have to be operated and maintained by foreign personnel (at great cost and little advantage to the country's own development). Solutions may well be found, not in the creation of new technical systems but in the better exploitation of existing means and a greater reliance on the prime resource — human beings.

One of the solutions may lie in local production and assembly. The scientific equipment produced by one Middle Eastern centre, for example, costs half the price of that produced by a British firm, which in turn is modelled upon American equipment which is three times more costly. Other solutions have taken up the principles of applied technology, without actually employing technical equipment. Thus we have seen micro-teaching without video equipment, programmed instruction without technical displays.

A third solution attempts to exploit technology wholesale, on a standardised pattern, to reduce costs. When user requirements are high enough (as for example with radio and television receivers), local assembly lines can be set up, as has happened by now in many parts of the developing world, though it must be admitted that the challenge of standardisation for educational purposes, proposed many times in the reports of international agencies, has never been properly taken up.

Finally, there have been many attempts, quite randomly distributed, to improvise with local substitutes for machined articles. So we have seen scientific lenses produced from polished bottle tops, home-made epidiascopes solar powered by mirrors, daylight film projectors. These are certainly ingenious and inventive, though it is possible that they suffer from an over self-conscious attempt to ape 'superior' Western models. The intention of educational technology, after all, is not to provide cheap replacements for Western masters, but to devise strategies, and means of execution, which are firmly rooted in their national or local environment. This is why the field of development studies is now much concerned with what it terms 'appropriate technology' — representing what might be called the social and cultural dimension of innovation, believing this to be quite as important as economic viability and technical soundness. It is a pity that, all too often, these conservative and conservationist approaches are rejected by the countries concerned in favour of the more sophisticated, more expensive, and fundamentally less suitable forms (such as television), simply because these have the glamour of living up to Western standards. Hopefully, developing countries will finally be convinced that it is no longer necessary to keep up with the technological Joneses, if other, cheaper, more relevant and more adaptable technologies are at hand.

Chapter 6

Media functions

All the factors described so far — organisational, philosophical and technical — have had their impact upon educational media development. But this impact was felt differently in different places, according to variables of culture, of resources, of human involvement. It should be helpful therefore to continue with a brief résumé of media history and functions.

The pre-war period

Educational mass media had their practical origins in radio, the 'twenties and 'thirties, before the Second World War. It is easy to understand why educators should initially be drawn to the medium (far-sighted educators, that is — many academics considered radio only as a new dimension in vulgarity). For those with vision, the potential was there. Mass media reach large audiences with ease, instantaneously. They enlarge the repertoire of teaching resources and aids. They demand a creative involvement from producers. They are appealing and contemporary.

School broadcasting began in the BBC in 1924; it followed in Japan in 1931, in Australia and New Zealand in 1932. It was, predictably, of the kind which has since become known as 'enrichment': programmes designed to intrigue and enlarge the perception of listeners. They enriched the learning process by offering experiences of the world beyond classroom walls, by taking pupils to other places, other times, other milieux. Even then, there was more than a suspicion that a well-organised broadcast could do much to offset a poorly trained or motivated teacher, but the view was not frequently articulated (it would only upset the teaching profession, and do little to endear educators to the new medium). School broadcast officers were appointed to visit schools and discuss programme use and policy, but in a relatively *ad hoc* way. With the onus for production on the broadcasting organisations, programmes were made with pride: professional, well informed and imaginative.

Adult programming followed, in the extension tradition of the universities and workers' education associations. A number of listening group experiments were started, with discussions centred on the broadcasts. In Australia and New Zealand, radio programmes were used (though only marginally at this time) in support of correspondence education.

In the United States, for reasons already described, the impetus was slower. But in 1938, reservation was made by the FCC for a number of 'curricular' stations, broadcasting on medium wave frequencies (extended to FM in 1941). It was also in 1938 that school broadcasting was introduced into India, always a pioneer in Asia of educational experiment.

The war interrupted this natural growth. But war came later in North America, and in 1941 an initiative was launched in Canada which had major implications for the development of rural broadcasting. At this time the Canadian Broadcasting Corporation launched *Farm Radio Forum*, programmes directed towards the country's scattered farmers, to be heard and discussed in specially formed listening groups.

The 'fifties

The immediate post-war years were preoccupied with economic revival, and it was only in the 'fifties that new patterns of media development were seen. Dominant was the emergence of television in education, both at a national level and in a cluster of closed-circuit experiments. But there were also new ventures in the extension field, including the transfer of rural broadcasting to the developing world and the first systematic experiments with linked broadcasting and correspondence education. Many of these initiatives were tentative; there were no natural models to follow, no empirical traditions on which to draw.

The early enthusiasm for radio produced a natural counter-reaction, based on the sensory limitations of the medium. To some extent this could be, and was, offset by producing a range of accompanying support materials (teachers and pupils booklets, charts, posters, audio-visual materials), but this both increased the cost of the product and made for an ambivalence in programme philosophy — did one assume that support materials were always available, or did one try to devise broadcasts which could stand on their own, regardless of whether the support items were in use? The dilemma generated some experimental work which would bear fruit later, including linked film strips and radio, a preliminary form of 'radio-vision'.

However, television, with its wider range of audio and visual resources, seemed to offer a new solution. Depending upon where, and how, it was introduced, it had two dimensions to offer — one of optimising the teaching force; the other of providing a rich, audio-visual resource. The former, the 'direct teaching' tradition, was particularly characteristic of the USA, where early work with educational television was carried out by educators; the latter of Europe and Japan, where broadcaster control was the norm.

Direct teaching was addressed mostly to a logistical problem — how to make scarce teachers and specialists stretch further. Instructional programmes tended to be replicas of classroom teaching, with pupils sometimes appearing on the screen, and with little in the way of visual illustration beyond the normal resources of a classroom. The broadcasting tradition, an extension of the 'enrichment' principle, started from the medium itself and from the recognised autonomy of the broadcast producer; programmes were fully visualised, though not always relevant in educational terms.

Although there was a later fusion of these two models and a pooling of experience, for some time the debate on the relative merits of each was argued hotly. In the end, this separation of traditions was probably useful. The direct teaching approach explored very fully the role of the teacher/ presenter, the assignment of responsibilities within a planning team, the functions and methods of utilisation in the classroom, as well as of evaluation and research. The enrichment approach stretched the capacity of the medium, producing new and highly imaginative ideas for programme conception. This would hardly have occurred if there had been agreement, from the beginning, on philosophies.

In the United States, the initiative came, as usual, at the local level. Closed circuit systems were developed, operating over wired networks, within individual college campuses and school districts. Broadcast instructional television was also mostly found at the community or State level, working through public broadcasting outlets. Within a decade more than sixty such stations went on the air, serving schools by day and homes by night, and the beginnings of cooperative programming were visible – with a national programme coordination centre in New York, and circulating programme libraries opening in Indiana and Nebraska. Over the same period, the number of closed-circuit institutions approached 300.

A characteristic system was that of Anaheim, a Los Angeles school district of some twenty schools. The introduction of television was as a result of local enthusiasm, both for the possibilities of the medium itself and as a means of improving instruction in science, mathematics, social studies and languages. In 1959, programmes were introduced in five pilot schools, at the elementary fourth and fifth grades; over the next few years, provision extended downwards and to other schools in the district. Comparative evaluations were made of schools with and without television (not surprisingly, if only through a Hawthorne effect, the television schools prospered). Special audio-visual resource classrooms were created for viewing, and staff time saved by the use of television was diverted to allow for 'skills' classrooms, where small group tuition was offered as a bonus to TV classes.

Probably the best known of the American systems is that of Hagerstown in Maryland. In 1956, a five-year experiment began, addressed to 21,000 students throughout the grade system in forty-six schools. At one time, 140 programmes were being broadcast each week, the vast majority of them live. Six channels were in operation, and some 10 per cent of the teaching was offered through television. Not surprisingly this put a considerable strain on reception conditions, and viewings were often with multiple classes, viewing on large screen projectors with numbers approaching 300, though the large group always broke into smaller groups for discussion after the broadcasts.

At a larger level again, at the close of the decade MPATI (Midwest Programme on Airborne Television) began operations. An early move towards satellite reception, transmissions were broadcast from an aeroplane flying in a figure-of-eight pattern over a 322 km radius, offering twenty-four programmes a day to 450,000 students in a complex of States and school districts. Inevitably this led to a rash of coordination problems, with each school offering advice on what kinds of programme would best suit its independent needs. More than anything, the experiment showed the difficulty of providing common media experiences in a country where education was so completely decentralised: a difficulty to be raised again in Europe in the 'sixties.

In Europe and Japan, the broadcasting networks first took up the challenge of instructional television. The BBC began its school television operation in 1957, the Independent Television Authority (representing the commercial companies) shortly afterwards. This introduction followed the same thoughtful pattern as radio, with a gradual build up of output so that today TV broadcasts are available to some 85 per cent of the school population. Within 20 years, the total provision has extended to some sixty radio series and thirty television series each year, the majority of them backed by a range of support materials.

NHK, in Japan, followed suit shortly afterwards in 1959. Japan, since its first experimental work with radio, has had the advantage of easy access to network time, with a channel devoted exclusively to education; in Europe, time has been shared between a number of competing interests, though by and large the schools, in uncompetitive daytime hours, have had as much time as could be afforded. The pattern of most of this network programming, in the 'fifties, again reflected the earlier traditions of radio, with broadcasts of a general, illustrative or enrichment kind, in the fields of drama, social studies, geography, languages, the sciences, but only loosely allied to the curriculum. Although educational representation was well catered for by such bodies as the BBC's Schools Broadcasting Council (which directed overall policy) the tradition of leaving each producer independent was still pursued. The scope of utilisation training was improved, with lectures from education officers often written in to the teacher training schedules, and evaluation became more systematic, with regular viewing reports from education officers and some questionnaire surveys, but the medium was still the prerogative of the broadcasters.

The sequence of instructional mass media development seems to have been very much the same in most countries. The beginnings are in school broadcasting, initially at the secondary level, which is a small sector, with higher funding — important for the acquisition of receivers — and with better trained and often better motivated teachers. This is followed by experiments in the primary sector and in specialist areas, e.g. remedial work, programmes for the school leaver, civics education, technical education and teacher training. Shortly afterwards comes work with adult audiences in a much less formal environment, and with correspondingly less possibility of providing structured learning experiences. The BBC, for example, began experimenting with adult programmes in 1961, and created its Further Education sector in 1963.

But other experiments were also forthcoming with adult audiences. In Japan, TV and radio broadcasts are a regular part of NHK's Correspondence High School, which has provided secondary courses for 100,000 school leavers and working young people since the 'fifties. In 1956, the Chicago Junior College began to transmit programmes for degree students who could not attend regular classes and for other interested adults, using the hired facilities of the local ETV station. In Italy, RAI attempted, from 1958, to cope with the shortage of secondary schools by creating the Centro di Telescuola, transmitting a regular schedule of lessons, complete with course guides, to emergency classrooms where children were placed under the supervision of monitors. This activity developed, in 1960, to the famous series 'It's Never too Late', which used the same techniques with adults to help combat illiteracy. This series at one time claimed 1.5 million viewers, and 55,000 regular students; in examinations pass rates of between 75 and 84 per cent were recorded. In the developing world, ACPO, in Colombia, is one of the earliest and longest lived of pioneer ventures in community development and fundamental education. From headquarters in Bogóta, it broadcasts 19 hours a day, with programmes relayed to three other stations in Colombia; its efforts are reinforced by a widely read weekly newspaper, and a considerable extension network. This is one of the most impressive of all media initiatives, since it grew up from the enthusiasm of one Catholic priest and has now developed into Colombia's largest radio network.

In 1956, the principle of the farm forum, first developed in Canada, was extended to India, beginning with a pilot project in the Poona region involving some 144 specially created listening groups. This pilot experiment was carefully evaluated, though expanding the pilot to wider audiences proved a different matter again. Development plans framed in 1959 called for a phased extension to 200,000 villages (a third of the total number in the country), but in practice by 1965 only 12,000 groups had been formed. Predictably, the care and attention to detail which had been lavished on the pilot phase could not be sustained at this level.

Most of these experiments are very different in character. Some were created purely through personal enthusiasm and were not sustained; others were better planned and lasted longer. But in these early ventures it is possible to see some of the major themes which were to be developed much further in the 'sixties. The question was finally being asked — mass media for what?

The experiments could be categorised, even at this stage, in one of two separate ways. There is firstly the attitude to media which sees them as a tool to remedy some existing deficiency — a shortage of teachers, of schools, of subject specialists. The second sees media as a means of reinforcement or upgrading. Television, radio, audio-visual aids have their own potential, which can make of learning a more demanding and engaging activity, and so improve the quality of educational life.

In general terms, these two approaches mirror the main concern of the 'fifties — the problem of quantity versus quality. It was an antithesis which was seen in many contexts, including that of development. The first need is to provide enough school places, enough teachers, enough materials, to allow an educational system to flourish at whatever performance level has been set. Once this is achieved, there is time to deal with the more sophisticated question of quality. In practice, however, the antithesis is not so very simple. For as quantitative demands are met, new performance goals are created — and once again the system shows a shortfall. Indices of quantity and quality are, in effect, not fixed or immutable; they reflect stages in approaching a shifting norm, and they are bound to be set and re-set continually, opening up afresh with each generation.

The 'sixties

The 'sixties were a time of intense activity and very substantial achievement in media use. The achievement amounted, in the main, to a recognition that media are not panaceas for general problems, but one of a number of answers to specific problem situations. In other words, the systems approach was taking root. Educational television was developed in the Third World, as part of a comprehensive programme of educational reform. The standard formula for closed circuit television (a production centre, a distribution system, and multiple reception points) was queried, and new models were tried out, involving mobile facilities, learning resource centres, media libraries. Problems of research and evaluation were studied in a new way, which tried to come to grips with programme formation, not simply head counting or statistical reviews. The area of non-formal and informal education was a subject of special probing, and multi-media projects were devised, with carefully conceived links between media. Finally, the beginnings of community media were seen in the wider, adult community, in both developed and developing countries.

For the most part, apart from experimental work with television in India, instructional TV development at the national level was in a handful of smaller territories and this situation still pertains. In Singapore, television programmes cater for a total population of 500 schools in a compact city state; its audiences are numbered in thousands. American Samoa, with programmes offered through twelve grades, is addressed to less than 10,000 pupils. El Salvador, in a matter of 3 years, expanded its programming to cover a target audience of 40,000 in three grades, before going on to extend its services to three lower grades, and ultimately to the adult population. Niger — one of the earliest model projects — never expanded its operations beyond twenty classrooms, involving 800 students.

The reason for this limitation is self-evident: in a compact setting, the environment is both organised and controlled, with fewer variables. The system in American Samoa was the first major undertaking of its kind to be conceived from an early planning stage; it was to cover the complete school population of this small territory, throughout its elementary and high school grade system. Six VHF channels were opened, involving the construction of two new transmitter towers; to produce the programme output required, four studios were constructed. Even so, they could barely cope with the volume of output — 6,000 programmes a year at the height of the project. This level dropped later, but it can be seen that the level was far higher than demanded of most other facilities in the world, with little chance for pre-planning and extensive visualisation. The final result of the Samoan project was to show a marked decline in interest in television at the upper educational levels, and there was a general feeling that too much television was being introduced overall. Since the early days, more relaxation has been introduced into the system, so that there are schools (especially at the secondary level) which do not have television programmes at all — and in general the exposure has decreased sharply.

In El Salvador, where television was only one component in an educational reform project, progress was deliberately slower, and systematic evaluation was included from the outset. In 1969, experimental work began with thirty-two pilot classes at the seventh grade; by 1972, this had expanded to 1,179 classes, spread across three grades (seven—nine) in 263 schools. Subsequently, three more grades (four—six) were introduced. The evaluation of this project, systematically conducted throughout the experiment, showed a sharp improvement (of 20 per cent) for students exposed to the whole educational reform package (including teacher training, the benefit of a new curriculum and new teaching materials), but without sharply differentiating the effect of media.

Simultaneously, a period of what might be described as 'in-fill' began. In the mid-'sixties in Europe, local ventures began to take shape — the Glasgow City Schools System, the Inner London Education Authority's ETV service, the Plymouth City Television Service — as educators' challenges to broadcasting autonomy and college and university CCTV systems, already highly developed in the USA, began to proliferate. Conversely in America, where the local scene was one of variety, pressures were felt for greater federal organisation; it was in the late 'sixties that the Carnegie Commission's report on public television was published, leading to the delicate forms of coordination described earlier in this chapter.

More systematic, and more widespread, programmes in multi-media combinations were now produced, particularly those involving study groups and correspondence education. A sequence of broadcasting and correspondence related courses began in the United Kingdom, with the cooperation of the BBC and the National Extension College, as a precursor of the Open University; in Germany, the Bavarian Telekollege offered high school correspondence courses with television support. A multi-media programme was introduced in Senegal; a study group programme in Tanzania. The Senegal experiment, from 1965 onwards, was deliberately diverse, including television programmes for women on health and nutrition, home economics, literacy and youth programming and film documentaries. In Kenya, the Correspondence Course Unit established at the University of Nairobi, which began work in 1968, has achieved a considerable reputation for its combination of correspondence, radio and face-to-face instruction, in the training and upgrading of teachers and adults. But the greatest interest lay in radio, with radio education study groups created which threw up, not for the first time, the political realities of group animation. Once programmes are largely field produced, with extensive contributions from audiences, the voice of criticism is both sharply and personally felt — and can prove disconcerting to Governments.

The 'seventies

Following the dynamism of the 'sixties, the 'seventies have been mostly a time of consolidation, with the shadow of recession in the background. The shift of economic power is making its impact even in the field of media; it is now the developing countries which may have the greatest opportunity to experiment further, especially with large scale systems.

This consolidation has been marked by a growing understanding of systems approaches, including a recognition that systems analysis is a tool, not a mandate. In the Third World, the most sophisticated approach of the decade has been in Korea, where the educational reform project, under the aegis of the newly formed Korean Educational Development Institute, has been in progress since 1972. The main area of activity has been in the Elementary-Middle Schools, although some out-of-school work has been started; the reform package includes new instructional delivery models, teacher training, new curricular and instructional materials and research and evaluation. Radio and television were included from the outset, but over the years, in broadcasting as in other areas, there have been shifts of direction. The original, predominantly economic rationale has veered more towards qualitative considerations; at the same time the broadcasting component has been somewhat reduced, and the delivery system has shifted from an extensive microwave system to a tethered balloon (TECOM) system. Some of this reflects economic astringency; some reflects rethinking and an innovative approach to technology. It is a project well worth monitoring. In the industrialised world, the Open University began its courses in 1971 — after a run-up period of 18 months, barely enough to cope with the sophistication of course planning involved. Programmes were created by course teams, reflecting both academic and media specialisms; initially Foundation courses were directed towards 25,000 students, in faculties of Humanities, Social Sciences, Mathematics and Science, later extended to include Technology and Education. One of the principal problems was to define the extent and composition of the media mix (and especially the relative merits of radio and television, with the latter seen as ten times more expensive than the former). The interest in the outcome of this debate was that it deliberately restricted the role of mass media, basing the main teaching load on correspondence, and using media for motivation and demonstration functions, and set out to create new means for interaction between students and teachers – with a network of local study centres, residential summer schools, tutors and counsellors. It also seized upon radio as a way of providing for regular dialogue with and between students, a role which was quite as important as instruction. Other projects have also benefited from the same kind of approach, such as 'Project Sun' in Nebraska, a carefully planned network of college and local extension courses. The character of this experiment is more relaxed than that of the Open University – based on the establishment of learning resource centres, and the creation of learning packages which include TV (broadcast over the Nebraska ETV station), audio cassettes, texts, community newspapers and learning kits. In the school television field, the most notable new departure was that in the Ivory Coast – a highly structured use of television under French direction. With a new grade being taught with the aid of television annually from the beginning of the project, each involving 20,000 students, the total number included by 1974 was in the region of 100,000 students, and first moves were being made towards adult education.

But the 'seventies are perhaps mostly clearly marked by two almost opposing trends – one at the macro, one at the micro level. The spread of telecommunications satellite systems meant that experiments were possible with more directly educational aims – using the new series of ATS satellites launched by the USA. The first were in audio – involving health education in Alaska, the PEACESAT system of the Pacific, a prototype exchange programme between Brazil and Stanford University. This was followed by more dramatic experiments with direct broadcasting reception – in North America and in India. The satellite, often treated as the ultimate in media technology, has perhaps received more attention than is justifiable; it is only another form of distribution. But it is an unusual form, with new possibilities for interconnecting scattered territories and producing a genuine global dialogue, offering a practical interface between the industrial and the developing world.

Experiments with ATS–6, launched in May 1974, should do more to provide information on the technical and management problems of direct broadcasting by satellite, than to make a contribution to the theory of learning systems, since the experiment was only of short duration. For 9 months, the satellite was used to re-broadcast programmes to more than fifty rural schools in an eight-State area bounded by the Rocky Mountains. The experiment was coordinated by a specially created organisation, and many programmes came from the nation's largest instructional videotape library, the Great Plains National ITV Library. Programming had an emphasis on career education, social and environmental studies. Simultaneously other broadcasts were made to Appalachia and Alaska, in fields including health education and teacher training, and there was some experimentation in two-way audio and video links between production and reception points.

Later, the satellite contributed to Third World development, in India (an exercise which involved changing the satellite's orbital position). World interest focused on SITE, which was designed as a cooperative venture between the two countries (with NASA supplying the satellite, and India supervising ground reception, including technical design and implementation, programming and evaluation). Programmes were produced under the control of All India Radio; they were beamed, for 4 hours a day (using one video and two audio channels) to 2,400 villages in six States. For this programme, under the general supervision of ISRO, the Indian space organisation, extensive preliminary studies were carried out, including the identification of suitable village locations by groups of interdisciplinary teams, and needs assessment research on the selected sites prior to production. Internal coordination problems were considerable, and the mammoth task of software production began very late; moreover 1 year is a very limited time in which to make a detailed evaluation. Nevertheless, as an exercise in management planning for the eventual introduction of an Indian satellite, the programme was invaluable.

At the other end of the spectrum, a growing concern for individualisation of media, and a more meaningful exchange between producers and audiences, has thrown up the new area of community media, using small-format, lower-cost technologies in the interests of 'access and participation'. Beginning in Canada, the spread of local and community radio stations, and action-oriented (often politically oriented) video groups, spread to the USA and then to Europe. These forces have been felt particularly within cable television, which began as a means of providing additional channels, improved reception and enhanced commercial opportunities, but was soon seized upon by community action groups as a means of involving local audiences in programming (so much so that this right is now mandatory with the granting of cable television licences in Canada, and in the prototype United Kingdom stations).

In Canada, 'Challenge for Change' began in 1967; its French counterpart, 'Société Nouvelle' in 1969. It is run by an interdepartmental committee comprised of seven federal government departments, who furnish half of the budget, and the National Film Board, which provides the remainder. Its policy has been deliberately varied; although it began by emphasising local media resource centres, which could produce programmes for the community cable television outlet, it has now moved much more to consider concepts of long-term social change.

A characteristic (and successful) project has been Videographe, in Montreal, which is a store-front production centre and theatre in the city. Anyone with an idea for a project is allowed to present it to the Videographe committee; if it is accepted, equipment is loaned, and editing facilities are available. When it is complete, the material can be shown in the Videographe theatre, and it goes into the permanent cassette library. Similar projects undertaken by the programme have included attempts to improve industrial communications, and work in prisons, with video being used as a prime communication tool.

The Canadian programme undertook what is probably its best known work in Fogo Island, off the coast of Newfoundland, husbanded by the

Extension Department of the Memorial University. The main thrust was to use the media to reflect communities to themselves, as a kind of public introspection out of which new insights and community building forces might emerge, and in the course of this work far more became known of the role of the group 'animator', as neutral observer and stimulus rather than active participant. The first period of Fogo was conducted on film, but after 1971 the advantage of videotape production (cheaper, and with instant replay) was proven, and film was reserved only for items which were to be preserved as records, or shown to wider audiences. The techniques evolved in this long experience have since been spread, not only through North America, but to programmes in Africa, Latin America and the Caribbean.

At all levels, in both the developed and developing countries, there has been a new emphasis in the 'seventies upon using media to provide social and educational opportunities for adults and drop-outs, particularly in informal environments. (In the new terminology, non-formal education implies specific learning programmes which are outside the formal school and college framework; informal education denotes a process of lifelong learning, which occurs by unstructured exposure to outside influences, in the home, at work, in the market place.) In industrialised societies, this is reflected in home study programmes, the development of community resource centres, the creation of public media channels. In the developing world, it appears in the design of new media systems, and in the emphasis which is given to development communication (media used in association with social and economic development, with literacy, with family planning or environmental campaigns). Major new planning designs, such as that undertaken by Unesco of educational mass media in Thailand, and now being carried out by the governments of Indonesia and the Philippines, have as much if not more emphasis on reaching adult, rural populations than on addressing the schools. Everywhere, rising costs, retrenchment, have made for a new interest in lower cost technologies, and the 'rediscovery' of radio, which fell into some disuse in the 'sixties (it suffered from its early association with 'enrichment' broadcasting, and lacked the glamour of television as a resource). Radio's suitability in the field of non-formal education, where institutionalised reception points are few, and where the costs of providing receivers have to be met by individual listeners, is easily demonstrable. Not surprisingly, it is made the focal point of some recent major studies, such as that carried out in Nepal, with the assistance of a consortium of donors.

Where does this leave us at present?

As will be seen in later portions of this handbook, the scope of educational mass media reflects, more sharply than ever before, a constant interplay and friction between the mass character of the media — a means of talking to everyone at once, but with an identical message — and the need and desire of individuals in the audience to be treated independently. Economics demand the former; individuals prefer to pick, choose and browse among the media repertoire. There are no absolute solutions, but technology, ingenuity and objective thinking are producing some partial answers.

Trends are, of course, simply to identify in retrospect. At the time, they are not seen in such a perspective, and the orientation of the 'seventies is not yet in focus. What is well defined, however, is a new caution, in dealing less prescriptively with media, paying less attention to technique, and turning more to individual problem areas, to the solution of which mass media may contribute.

Chapter 7

Media evaluation

The final factor in our equation for media development is that of evaluation — providing measures of performance. We have seen how the functions of media have changed over the years; equally, methods of evaluation and research have also changed. The trend has been for evaluation to be framed, not as a summary appendix to a project, giving a judgement on success or failure (which is likely to be ignored, because it comes too late), but as a part of the formulation process itself.

The need for evaluation has been realised from the beginnings of media history, and especially from the 'fifties, but its development has been hampered by two factors. The first is financial and political; while media researchers, and to a growing extent producers, have sought confirmation, or rejection, of the premises on which they were basing their work, in many cases politicians and financial controllers have not been impressed by the urgency of the research argument, and even when a system plan has included major evaluation components, they have frequently been reduced, or omitted entirely, from the final design. Evaluation is a costly affair, which shows results only over the long term, and even then the returns may not always be positive.

The second factor is more technical. The evolution of tools for media evaluation has been protracted, and is by no means complete; indeed, the modern trend is to admit that the tools available cannot always be precise, and to settle for a process rather than absolute instruments. The situation in which media find themselves is one of shifting variables; it is extremely difficult, particularly in a multi-media system which is part of a comprehensive educational reform process, to determine what, if anything, is due specifically to the media contribution. It was only after early studies in the USA showed, in the majority of cases, inconclusive results that the emphasis in evaluation shifted to less clinical or statistical measures.

Some of the techniques of evaluation which are now being used are reviewed in Part 4 of this handbook, but it is important, at this time, to give some account of current thinking.

The first attempts of evaluation were mostly subjective or statistical. So, education officers or inspectors were appointed to visit schools and report on the way in which broadcasts were utilised, usually according to a pre-arranged formula, so that some measure of comparison between difficult reports could be found. Alternatively, schools were asked to furnish answers to questionnaires, giving their reactions to broadcast series.

This kind of approach depends to a large extent on the centralisation of the system within which it operates, and its degree of control over users. Thus in Singapore, from the very beginnings of the ETV operation, a reliable measure of audience reaction could be secured, because in a small system of approximately 120 schools a rotating random sample could be devised to furnish evaluation data, and missing returns could be pursued without too much effort. The result was a regular commentary on programme content and relevance, which was available to producers to help them plan for new series, or reformulate old series. This kind of reliability was simply not available to schools in the United Kingdom, where questionnaire completion was a voluntary affair, depending on the willingness of teachers (and in any case, not based on a statistical profile of the viewing population).

Certainly, within the system's limitations, the Schools Broadcasting Council produces a reservoir of data for the BBC and its producers. But such data, although useful, is very circumscribed. It gives an index of which programmes are unsuccessful; it does not necessarily indicate why this is the case. Moreover, it has little to say about overall educational improvement.

In the USA, the original impetus for research was more on the efficiency of educational television as a learning channel than on programme evaluation. In this situation, the emphasis on television rather than on multi-media working was a bonus, since it reduced some of the variables experienced in later studies, and allowed TV classes to be compared with non-TV classes. The results were far from dramatic, showing television to be, in general, a teaching medium comparable with normal classroom instruction, but at least they confirmed that the use of media was not, as some had feared, a retrograde step. However, the creation of the newer media systems, such as those of El Salvador and American Samoa, allowed for more comprehensive evaluations to take place. (Earlier experiment in the US had been confined to small instructional systems, and the results were not always comparable.)

The difficulty in interpreting such results is primarily one of defining improvement. Normally it is taken to mean relative superiority in criterion-referenced tests, but it is arguable whether this is a valid base on which to measure. In El Salvador, for example, those pupils who were educated through the new system did better in achievement tests by some 30 per cent than other students; but the question must still be asked – is quality a matter of test scoring, or of more fundamental changes of attitude and motivation? To a subjective observer, the benefits of new structures, new patterns of training and of study, are evidence in themselves, but they are not statistical evidence.

So the result of this work was still very often tentative, particularly where the media were concerned. It showed improvement after the introduction of a total package of educational reform; it did not, however, distinguish between the contribution of individual media and other reform components. As the principal evaluator put it: 'Students . . . will learn from any medium if, on the one hand, the content is not too difficult for them to master, and, on the other hand, the content contains material new and interesting to them.' Additionally, evaluation which was based upon measures of standardised testing was of relatively little use to the producer, who wanted answers to much more specific questions. The producer was more likely to ask: 'If I am going to produce a programme on X, and I can choose between three separate methods of attempting the programme, which of these is more likely to suit educational system objectives?' It is in response to this kind of enquiry that the current, less inflexible and less analytical trend towards formative evaluation has been born. The impact of formative evaluation is not so much to measure system performance after the event (though this is still very necessary), but to build in interfaces between planner, producer and evaluator, and to monitor progress at all stages along the production route.

This kind of emphasis is one in which evaluation really becomes part of programme construction, rather than an annex to the system. As such it is of great importance to this handbook, because it has a critical impact upon programme planning. It began, and has been developed most significantly, in the work of the Children's Television Workshop, where programmes like 'Sesame Street' and 'The Electric Company' were first devised by exchanges between producers and researchers, and where programme piloting and testing continued right through the design. It has continued, somewhat more institutionally, within the instructional system of the Open University, in which whole courses, including far more than media components, are based upon the corporate planning of course teams, with representatives of both academic and production disciplines, and with a leavening of educational technology, curriculum and social science specialists.

In this context, all methods are pertinent. The goal is to involve the evaluator from the very beginning in programme development: to use the best tools and techniques that are available, but never to relinquish a problem simply because a technique cannot be validated; to allow for as many feedback loops as can be devised, and to encourage the cross-fertilisation of disciplines, so that producers can, in the end, undertake a major part of the evaluation process for themselves.

By this time, the main transitions shown in the matrix of Fig. 1.1 should appear much clearer. The move from traditional to innovative approaches has been illustrated in a number of ways, reflecting both structural and philosophical change. On the one hand, there has been a breakdown of rigidity: in the patterns of educational administration, of media control, of curriculum introduction. Conversely, a greater degree of sophistication has evolved in planning mechanisms. Both are necessary, and mutually reinforcing; once there has been an erosion of purely autocratic control, a greater unity of planning is needed, to make sure that the outcome of diversification and increased flexibility is not anarchy.

We have spoken throughout this introductory section as if 'educational mass media' are one thing. Of course, they exist at many levels — local, regional, national. In the parts of this handbook which follow, these separate levels will be recognised, as they assume different organisational models, staffing and training needs, and offer varied possibilities for use and evaluation.

But the trends which have been identified are also general across all levels. A local closed circuit system does not exist in a vacuum; it is part of the total media fabric connecting its users. In the specific planning formulae which follow, this concept of interaction and interdependence should not be forgotten.

Media planning

Chapter 8

The planning process

Part 1 of this handbook began with a matrix of change; Part 2 begins with a network of the media development process (Fig. 8.1). Deliberately simple in outline, it can be read without technical skills. It illustrates the dynamic process with which the rest of this book is concerned.

Several points should be emphasised. Firstly, the network assumes that the planning process is being taken seriously, with a clear and logical transition from planning research, through the setting of objectives, to the controlled evaluation of media performance. As we saw in Part 1, this is by no means always the case — and if we look back for a moment to Fig. 1.1 (p. 3) it is clear that, in what follows, we are opting for innovation in educational philosophy, even though technological innovation may be a long distance ahead. It is the author's belief that, however limited or basic the technical tools available, media planning will always benefit from a systematic approach. Some suggestions will be given in the body of the text for adapting this process to less favourable educational environments, though in the end the reader must make his own adjustments, based on a personal assessment of where he stands in the development cycle.

Secondly, the network does not distinguish between media. It is a generalised tool and as such it is applicable to any medium, or to multi-media combinations. In the pages which follows, where (in particular instances) there are separations — e.g. in distribution, in staffing and training — between media, these are described, but they are matters of technique and detail, not of overall design.

Thirdly, the network does not distinguish between levels of operation. In basic planning, this is unimportant, but again, later in the text, these separations are followed through. At that time, we shall distinguish primarily between *national* media operations, *regional or State* level operations (including large cities and city States), *community or local* operations (e.g. at the level of a small town, or a school district), and *institutional* operations (e.g. a college or community centre). Other distinctions are also made between audiences (school and adult, or sectoral audiences), since these equally affect patterns of organisation and use. But our intention is, throughout, to emphasise the unity of media deployment, while still allowing for practical differentials in various contexts of use.

The pattern adopted for this purpose is simple. At each stage, we begin with the planning process itself, amplifying the general model of Fig. 8.1. Once the main argument has been followed through, we turn to specific

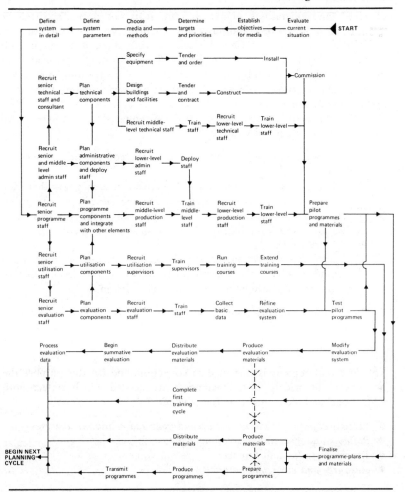

Fig. 8.1 A network for educational media development.

cases — to the media themselves, and to their settings — to see when, and why, the exceptions occur.

Planning research

Before any identification of media can be made, we have to be very sure of the problems with which they are expected to assist. In theory, any educational system, at any level, must have a clear picture of its objectives; in practice (as media planners find out all too quickly) this is usually far from the case. While there is always a body of information available on the character and operations of the system, it is not normally sifted or analysed, and the expression of targets is couched only in general terms.

So the media planner finds himself obliged, if he is to do his job properly, to stimulate a much broader activity in planning for education in general. Ideally, he should motivate others to do this for him; in practice, he may have, tactfully, to do much of it on his own account, drawing on specialist experience.

The sequence of events involved in the planning process (also reflected in the network) is generally as follows:

(a) An examination of educational needs, in the context of overall social development.
(b) Translating these into educational objectives, in such a way that they can be reflected in systems design, and ranking these in priority order.
(c) Assessing the contribution which media can make towards their realisation, and establishing the relationship of media to other innovatory forces.
(d) Measuring this assessment realistically against prevailing conditions, to determine at what point the system is likely to fail or develop inertia.
(e) Elaborating the above into a detailed project design.

Each of these categories implies several levels of activity.

Data collection

The first requirement is one of data collection, and for this purpose the net has to be widely cast. Documents are needed which reflect both educational and media practice; they include:

● *Statistical data, including cost breakdowns and economic analyses*
● *Policy statements and development plans*
● *Research studies and projects*
● *Resource and curricula materials*

It is likely that, as planning continues, these will have to be supplemented by other enquiries, including specially commissioned surveys (e.g. of available media resources) and structured interviews (e.g. with decision makers). But such needs will become apparent only as project outlines become clearer, and the first essential is to establish educational requirements. This is a matter of evaluating the available evidence, and deducing priority needs.

Defining objectives

Volumes have been written on the problem of defining objectives, and little more will be said here, except to emphasise the difficulty of framing them in such a way that they are meaningful to practical educators and producers. Too often they are expressed as vague goals, which might be achieved in any number of ways (and the measurement of which is virtually impossible).

The distinction between a *goal* and an *objective* is, therefore more than academic. A goal is a general, categorical description of a learner's behaviour; it is not concerned with responses to particular stimuli. An objective, on the other hand, *is* specific: it has been defined, very simply, as 'an *intent*, communicated by a statement describing a proposed change in a learner — a statement of what the learner is to be like when he has successfully completed a learning experience'. So, to be useful, the framing of an objective has to (i) be in clear, unambiguous language, reflecting precisely the intentions of its author; (ii) show practical outcomes, changes in behaviour or performance anticipated (a difficult thing when more than practical or motor skills are involved); and (iii) be simple — a complex sequence of responses must be broken down into individual objectives. This is the difference between such a vague formulation as 'to induce habits of creative thinking', or 'to develop a sense of citizenship', and 'to be able to solve a simple linear equation', or 'to be able to operate a television receiver'.

Of course, it is not always possible to be specific in exactly this way. Some kinds of behaviour defy precise definition in terms of performance, as they are concerned with aesthetic, ethical or psychological responses. Furthermore, in the planning process we are concerned with objectives in two different ways. At the macro level, we are dealing with larger concepts, and we cannot expect to be specific in the same way as when framing detailed instructional objectives. When we review the prevailing climate of an educational system and try to determine what are its main goals, both explicit and implicit, we are actually using the technique of specifying objectives as a tool of analysis. We are asking: What does the system believe its main orientations to be? What are its main problems? How many of these are genuine, how many hidden? How many of the policy statements are formal documents, reflecting an 'official' position, and how many genuinely reflect the purposes and priorities of the system?

When we come, later, to deal with programme construction, we shall be on safer and firmer ground. At that time, we need to develop precise instructional objectives, which explain what we hope to achieve by distributing a particular programme, or creating a particular learning experience. In other words, at this time we are constructing, rather than analysing, through objectives.

As a practical illustration of this (and other) principles, we shall draw upon a large-scale planning exercise with which the author was associated. This was a Pre-Investment Study of Educational Mass Media for Thailand — an exercise carried out by Unesco, as a preliminary study on behalf of the Thai Government, prior to negotiations for a World Bank Loan. The purpose of the study was to plan for the coherent development of educational mass media at a national level; it was carried out by a team of some twenty-five consultants, over a period of 7 months. The procedures adopted (described in greater detail below) were along the lines just discussed, beginning with an analysis of the current situation, gradually evolving alternative solutions in which media could feature and finally settling upon a preferred system. But although the study was a large-scale affair, the same principles apply (appropriately scaled down) to other levels of mass media development.

In the following extract from the final report, we see how the team approached the problem of fixing educational objectives in relationship to media.

Educational objectives and media in Thailand

Before a media project can even be contemplated, the most crucial educational objectives have to be identified. This is quite a difficult task, for four main reasons. Firstly, objectives are not always explicitly stated, but are often implicit, 'hidden objectives'. Secondly, there are several different levels of objective, ranging from precise behavioural objectives through enabling objectives to vague statements of intent, and often objectives at one level are inconsistent with those at another. Thirdly, different population groups (for example parents and educational administrators) often have conflicting objectives. And fourthly, objectives are frequently formulated more as post-rationalisations than as guidelines for future policy and action.

We must therefore first discuss some of the different types of overall educational objective identified for both the formal and the out-of-school educational system of Thailand, and then proceed to isolate those objectives that seem to be most critical and most amenable to achievement through the use of mass media. On this basis we can begin to outline a few broad general objectives for the media system as a whole. In the main, as the function of the proposed media system is to affect positively what is taught and learned, only those objectives that are likely to have a considerable impact over a relatively short period of time will be considered.

The various policy documents extant include three main types of objectives. First, there are those objectives that assume that all 'education' is a 'good thing'. Such objectives are usually quantitative (aiming for example at achieving universal seven-year elementary schooling by 1980), though sometimes they are also partly qualitative (for example, improving the qualification structure of the teaching force, or reducing repetition and dropouts). This type of objective does not concern itself either with what is learned, or with the relationship of education to broader social, cultural and economic objectives.

The second type of objective commonly quoted relates to academic theories of child development and often seems like a copy of models developed by liberal Western educators, bearing little relationship either to the realities of Thai society, or to their practicality given the very limited educational resources available. Very often the actual effects of the school system are in complete contradiction to these objectives; for example, the objective 'to develop the ability to work and live in harmony with others in a cooperative manner' is in conflict with the competitive nature of all current schooling.

The third type of objective attempts to relate education and schooling to other social, cultural, political and economic goals. For example, 'secondary and higher education institutions should produce the skilled manpower needed for the country's development'. This type of objective does not assume that education is an end in itself, but that it is a means towards achieving some other end. Apart from a mainly verbal commitment to education's role in promoting democracy, it is only during the last decade or so, since Thailand has become interested in 'development' per se, that this type of objective has begun to occupy a significant position in the various policy statements.

Apart from these three categories of objective as seen by government and educational administrators, the objectives which parents have in sending their children to school, and those of the older students themselves who are motivated to continue their education, cannot be ignored. Parents are interested in their children being educated (as are the older students themselves) not because they are interested in education in its own right, or because they feel that what is learned will turn them into 'whole' men and women, or because they feel that their schooling will help them play a more dynamic role in the development of their country. Their interest is because, in the eyes of parents, schooling helps to discipline children, and more importantly because, in the eyes of both parents and children, the school gives certificates to the successful, which provide them with social status and offer a chance of obtaining a relatively secure and well paid job. Even though school discipline may be declining, and the number of educated unemployed is increasing at an alarming rate, these old expectations are still of crucial importance in most people's minds. Though it is realised that the school system is one of the prime instruments of society for distributing social status and high earnings, and that inevitably, with the present structure of the system, the majority of participants must 'fail', the desire for certification as a powerful motivating factor cannot be ignored.

Because of the nature of the media, and the need to justify the large expense involved in setting up an educational media system, it is felt that the emphasis of any media service should be on the third type of objective (education for social, cultural and economic development). At the same time, one cannot discard either accepted theories of child development and adult psychology, or the demands of potential users and their parents.

The past development of objectives

Historically speaking, Western-style schooling and education was adopted in Thailand about 100 years ago as a response to, and a protection against, imperialistic pressures from the colonial powers in surrounding countries.

At the time it was felt that, if Thailand was successfully to resist colonialisation, modernisation was necessary, and one of the preconditions for such modernisation was the establishment of a Western-style school system.

Thus, despite the fact that Thailand was, and is, a Buddhist country and had, and still has, a mainly peasant economy, a Western protestant, urban materialistic-type school system was grafted on to traditional Thai culture, without any prior attempt being made clearly to define its objectives, both internal and external, or to study carefully whether the stated and hidden objectives of the system were consistent.

The first comprehensive list of educational objectives in Thailand was not prepared until 1895, and from that time onwards there were more than a dozen major changes. In qualitative terms there have been quite wide shifts of emphasis, varying from attempts to use education as a means of maintaining hierarchical stability and agriculture harmony, to attempts to promote democracy, or to develop the 'whole' child according to Western liberal concepts.

Despite these wide variations, there has probably been little change in what has been taught and how it has been taught. However, over the last 40 or 50 years, as people have begun to play greater lip service to democracy, schooling has probably tended to become more academic, less relevant to the existing environment, and seen more as a continuum leading from the first grade of elementary school through to university.

The last major revision of educational objectives took place in 1960. In general terms this is still in force and is likely to remain so until at least 1977.

Though there are a very large number of specific curriculum objectives of each level of schooling, the overall objectives of the 1960 National Scheme for Education can be summarised as follows:

(i) *The Thai people shall be educated according to their individual capacities, so that they can be moral and cultural citizens with discipline and responsibility, with good mental and physical health, and with a democratic outlook. They should be given the knowledge and skills necessary for carrying out an occupation useful both to themselves and to the nation.*

(ii) *Boys and girls should receive full-time education up to the age of 15.*

(iii) *Boys and girls should strive to gain knowledge and experience that will serve a useful purpose in their lives.*

(iv) *Education must serve the needs of individuals as well as those of society. It must also be in harmony with the economic and political system of the country.*

(v) *Four basic types of education should be given to all boys and girls:*

    (a) *Moral education*
    (b) *Physical education*
    (c) *Intellectual education*
    (d) *Practical education*

(vi) The State should educate the population of the country to as great an extent as its economic system will allow.

In these basic objectives no real emphasis was given to using education as a tool either for national development or for rural transformation. Nor was there much emphasis on the role education should play in the equalisation of opportunity. Finally there was no emphasis placed on the need to increase quality per se.

By the time the second Five Year Plan for national development went into operation in 1966, there appeared already to be a distinct change in the character of objectives, despite the fact that there was no significant change in curricula, text books or methods of teacher training.

The second Five Year Plan placed a distinct emphasis on relating education to development, on relating expansion to equality concepts and on improving the tools of education (text books, teachers, buildings, etc.). In addition the idea of education and its standards being ends in themselves was again introduced.

The objectives of the third Five Year Plan (1971) followed the trend of the second plan, except that they were more specific. They can be summarised as follows:

(i) To develop the educational system so that it will play the maximum possible role in the social and economic development of the country.

(ii) To expand lower elementary education to cater for the growth in school age population and to expand upper elementary enrolments as rapidly as possible, so that universal compulsory 7-year education can be achieved by the late 1980s.

(iii) To expand secondary and higher education, particularly in the fields of medicine, technology and teacher education, so that the country's future manpower requirements are met.

(iv) To increase the efficiency of all levels of education by reducing repeater, dropout and failure rates.

(v) To improve and diversify the curriculum at all levels, particularly in rural areas, so that what is learnt is more directly applicable to the future lives which the children will live. It is desired that secondary education courses should provide students with a general academic background, whilst at the same time preparing them either for further education courses or for their future vocation.

(vi) To improve the qualification structure of the teaching force at all levels.

(vii) To expand and improve education for rural development in order to lessen the wide disparities of income between rural and urban areas, and the agricultural and industrial sectors.

(viii) To expand non-formal education rapidly in accordance with the concept of life-long education.

It can be seen that over a short period of a decade or so the overall objectives of the Thai Educational system have shifted significantly away *from a 'theoretical' child-centred orientation, towards a greater emphasis on development, problem solving and other national and social goals. In addition there is a tendency for education to become less equated with schooling and the teaching of academic subjects and for it increasingly to be seen as a lifelong process, aimed at providing the mass of the population with the opportunity to acquire relevant skills, knowledge, attitudes and ideas which will help improve their quality of life.*

Admittedly these significant changes of emphasis and priority have not yet been accompanied by equally significant changes in teaching method, curriculum or the structure of the system, though there has been rapid development of innovative forms of adult and non-formal education, and also preliminary attempts to diversify the curriculum in general education.

However, the fact that the practice in and out of school has not changed as rapidly as the objectives does not mean that any new media service should be used to reinforce existing practices. The contrary should be the case, since it is the bureaucratic inertia of the existing system which is retarding those changes which Thai leaders would like to see occur. Thus any new media service must certainly have as one of its prime functions the implementation of high priority objectives which are presently not being realised, or even attempted to any large extent, by the present system. For example, the new media service, as a minimum, should be used to:

(i) *Help speed up the process of curriculum diversification so that what is taught bears a greater relationship to what the child needs to know.*

(ii) *Make education more an instrument for rural development than it is at the moment.*

(iii) *Help promote deep and lasting democracy and community self reliance.*

(iv) *Help widen the scope of educational opportunity, so that attempts to do so have some chance of counteracting the powerful social, cultural and economic forces which at present ensure that there will be no real equality.*

(v) *Help turn the theory of 'lifelong education' into reality.*

It should be emphasised that the function of the new media service should neither be to improve further those facets of school system which already have a reasonable quality, nor to promote existing poor (but wide ranging) teaching practices which do not involve teacher/pupil dialogue, and which are not of very great relevance to the environment in which the child (or adult) finds himself.

The position is taken generally in this report that education is not an end in itself but a tool for development, which in turn is not an end in itself (or merely an increase in GNP or other statistical indicators), but a way of increasing the sum total of happiness and satisfaction within a given society.

When planning for widespread media use within the social and educational system, great care has to be taken, as must be taken with education itself, to avoid creating expectations and aspirations which cannot be achieved. If such expectations are created the media will, in a Buddhist sense, be leading to 'miseducation' and 'misdevelopment'. A media system is required whose objectives ensure that the values of one population group (which may be out of harmony with the environment of other groups) are not 'universalised'.

This extract has been reproduced at length, because it illustrates quite clearly the importance of educational objectives as a means of analysis. In the first review stages, the character of the educational system has to be assessed, to see what shifts of emphasis have occurred over the years, where priorities lie and in particular where there are gaps between theory and performance. It was significant, for example, in this study, to find that while formally expressed objectives changed, curricular materials did not; this is the kind of discovery which is important to media planning. The weight of hidden or implicit objectives (such as parental assumptions and aspirations) is also significant, since media have a persuasive as well as an instructional role to play. The success of the instructional programme depends largely upon its realism in estimating such factors as teacher or student interest, motivation and capacity to change.

The report went on to distinguish, separately and in detail, between the objectives of education in formal and non-formal settings, and to try to identify the priority interests of all of the groups involved (political, educational, parental, etc.). At each stage, it also tried to distinguish between those objectives which were clearly expressed and could be measured in some way, and those which were too loosely framed to be more than a subjective guide to the planner. It is apparent, even from this brief extract, that many subjective judgements are involved. This can hardly be avoided. The approach through objectives is as a method of analysis, to help put a considerable body of information in order, but in setting priorities, weeding out the important from the unimportant, and translating generalities into specific programmes, a good deal of pragmatism is inevitable.

Chapter 9

Media justification

This chapter looks at media characteristics. In it, we are trying to isolate some special qualities of educational media, so that, in the chapter which follows, we can review the process by which they are assigned to specific tasks.

Educational mass media are complex and multi-dimensional, and we cannot describe their quality in a simple table, or even in a more complex model. A medium like 'television' acts quite differently in one situation from another; television is a portfolio word, covering a technical system rather than its application. And when we combine different technologies (TV plus videorecording, for example), we come up with different possibilities again. We shall have, therefore, to isolate media characteristics in stages.

The first reference frame is that of the *media* themselves: defining the intrinsic qualities of mass media in general, and then individual media. The second is that of *applications* — adopting the perspective of user and audience. Here, we consider such modifying factors as audience size or grouping, audience level and the subject matter of the presentation. Finally, we draw on past *experience*, called from research and evaluation studies. In this way, we should arrive at a cumulative picture.

The discussion is once again summary. There are many books on media selection (some of them listed in the Bibliography). But it is most important to draw this corpus of knowledge together, for the benefit of both planner and practitioner. In doing so, reference will be made (as also in Chapter 10 which follows) to teaching resources will go beyond educational mass media, since the process of media identification is one of discrimination between many strands.

A. Media

Characteristics of media

Generally speaking, audio-visual equipment and materials are of two kinds: those which are used as a *teacher-centred* tool, and those which are *learner-centred*. The former help the teacher present information to a whole class and enrich his professional repertoire (often making up for deficiencies in method and training); the latter help students to work more independently, in small groups, in pairs or individually. These will match different types of curriculum development, and so the type of innovation suggested will affect the selection of media.

The mass media are basically examples of the former. Television and radio offer materials for corporate viewing and discussion, or offer the teacher guidance in a particular field. The same is true of many items of equipment (film projectors, film strip/slide projectors) which are commonly used by whole classes. However, loop projectors, small hand viewers and teaching machines are of a different order, being designed for small group or individual use. The same distinction can be made with print materials. Traditionally, text books have been designed for whole class use, where all the pupils are expected to progress at the same pace. If pupils are, because of individual abilities, backgrounds and aptitudes, to be allowed to develop at their own pace, then a greater variety of materials, packages, topic books, worksheets and workbooks is more appropriate.

Yet this relationship is no longer absolute. Radio combined with audio-cassette recorders in the classroom (allowing the teacher to record programmes and build up a resource library), or television combined with videocassette recorders (and a tape library), radically change the character of the media, making them suitable for small group usage. In other words, radio and television are no longer discrete media.

Preconditions for media use

Media in isolation from their potential audience and their producers have few innate characteristics, either positive or negative. But there are some preconditions, without which no media system is likely to succeed. These include:

(*a*) Good quality production and technical standards and training.
(*b*) A system for ensuring adequate levels of utilisation.
(*c*) Continuing training of field personnel and teachers in utilisation at all levels, and supervision of field or classroom use.
(*d*) An adequate investment in personnel, facilities and materials.
(*e*) Satisfactory coordination between the many different agencies involved in programme planning, production, distribution, utilisation, evaluation and research.
(*f*) Considerable management skills.
(*g*) Flexibility, in the sense that the media system not only keeps abreast of new technological and educational developments, and evaluates its own performance effectively, but also retains the structural capacity to respond to research findings.
(*h*) A suitably developed technical infrastructure to provide the conditions for success.

Benefits of media

If these conditions are met, then media by their very nature (as opposed to the message they carry) are likely to produce several immediate *benefits* in the process of educational reform. For example, they should have the ability to:

(*a*) Provide access for large audiences to interesting and relevant educational materials.

(*b*) Favour particular audiences (e.g. a rural population) by a careful choice of media and reception equipment.

(*c*) Spread scarce talent widely, whether this be of teachers, materials or teaching models.

(*d*) Draw upon a wide range of audio-visual materials, which appeal to different senses and perceptions and which can be related to different aspects of the learning process.

(*e*) Attribute status to particular types of learning (as an overspill from the high status which mass media have in entertainment).

Limitations of media

Conversely, there are also *limitations*. For example:

(*a*) Mass media productions are aimed at large audiences; hence the degree of specificity in their audience is restricted. An economic balance has to be found between the needs of particular audiences and the production costs of the system.

(*b*) With mass media, there is only a limited opportunity for audience participation, involvement and feedback.

(*c*) With mass media, there is only a limited degree of flexibility. The process of interaction which occurs in the classroom, whereby a teacher can modify his role according to pupil response, develops with educational media only over a period of time, particularly as it takes a considerable time to evaluate and then remake poor programmes.

(*d*) With mass media the teacher can have little control over programming, and thus broadcasts may not always be relevant in time and place. With other media the teacher can use the materials when he needs them, but the unit costs are much higher.

Quite apart from the character of mass media as a whole, individual media have their own strengths and weaknesses. It is impossible to list these exhaustively here, but some generic media characteristics which may be considered are as follows:

(*a*) *Radio*
  (i) has a potentially great coverage, and is inexpensive (in absolute as well as relative terms) in unit costs, if extensively deployed;
  (ii) can be received anywhere: in the house, in school, in fields, or whilst travelling;
  (iii) does not require electrification in reception areas;
  (iv) requires a high degree of concentration from the listener, in view of its dependence on the aural sense (advantageous for music programmes);

(v) requires visual support in most instructional areas;

(vi) being free of the limits of time, as long as it can obtain the imaginative involvement of listeners it is suitable for supportive types of learning which benefit from a dramatised presentation.

(b) Television

(i) has potentially a great coverage (once the infrastructure exists). Installation costs are high but once coverage is widespread, unit recurrent costs are lowered;

(ii) can be used both in the school and in the home;

(iii) requires electrification (or a somewhat cumbersome provision of battery supplies or field generators);

(iv) involves both aural and visual senses and employs a wide range of presentation techniques;

(v) is particularly suitable for teaching which requires:

- detailed close-up demonstrations (i.e. laboratory experiments)
- presentation of experiences, places and processes unfamiliar to the viewer
- dramatic presentations
- animated presentations
- complex technical processes
- the demonstration and analysis of teaching models.

(vi) requires relatively expensive reception equipment, which cannot be viewed by large audiences;

(vii) unless skilful animators or teachers are used, it tends to induce a passive reaction on the part of the viewer.

(c) Recorders

Audio and video open-reel or cassette tape recorders can be taken as extensions of radio and television, in that they offer the same kind of material, but with easier access and tutorial flexibility. The addition of a microphone or a camera enables useful skills training, rehearsal, and participatory production to take place.

(d) Film

(i) can be used for many of the same purposes as television (and can indeed be transmitted over television), but because of its better picture definition, its larger size screen and the corporate involvement of audiences it can be more effective for some purposes (when projected) than TV. It is, however, much more expensive in unit costs;

(ii) requires a complex distribution system;

(iii) uses expensive though robust projection equipment, and also requires electrification (or provision of generators);

(iv) can be used most effectively only at night or in darkened rooms;

(v) can cater to large audiences;

(vi) is more flexible than broadcast television in providing documentary materials intended for local use;

(vii) can be more easily slotted into school timetables than TV.

(e) Other projected aids

Their main advantage is that they can be used by the teacher independently, within his own scheme of work, applied to general class programmes, to small group work and to individual use. In many cases, also, the teacher (if trained and motivated) can generate his own materials (slides, film strips, transparencies). The range of projected aids is therefore related to function, i.e.

Film loop projectors can be used to present single and cyclical concepts, and are made with or without sound; *film strip projectors* show programmed sequences of visuals; *slide projectors* show individual slides (which, depending on the type of projector available, can be sequenced at will); *overhead and opaque projectors* show two-dimensional material, which can either be produced by the teacher or drawn from library resources open to him. The potential of these media can also be enlarged through combining two or more forms. Thus audio tapes or cassettes can be combined with film strips and slides (with or without synchronisation).

(f) Non-projected aids

These have been the staple diet of the classroom, and functionally they are very versatile. Thus, books can either be used as general texts, or as individualised workbooks, worksheets, etc.; and materials can be prepared singly, or packaged within a 'kit', related to a particular topic or concept. Their main use within the context of a mass media system is as support materials, to explain the programmes (for the teacher) or to follow up, extend, enrich and test them after use (for the pupils). In most media systems they are invaluable as a means of interpreting a generalised system for use in a specific context; in some cases (e.g. correspondence education) they are at the heart of the system, since they are the main means of dialogue between teacher and learner. There is also a place for newspapers, magazines, posters, etc., in many kinds of community education work.

The mass media paradox

In summary, it can be said that the principal arguments for the use of mass media in education are:

(a) *speed of address*: they can reach large audiences instantaneously

(b) *penetration*: their reach is limited only by their distribution system

(c) *cost effectiveness*: with widespread usage, they can produce low unit costs

(d) *quality*: they can draw on the best teaching and planning resources

(e) *variety*: they can employ a wide range of aural and visual illustrations far beyond the teacher's available repertoire.

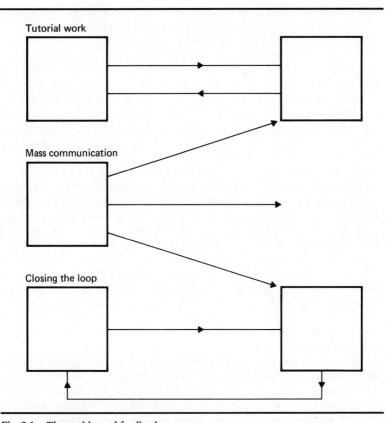

Tutorial work

Mass communication

Closing the loop

Fig. 9.1 The problem of feedback.

Yet as we have noted, each of these strengths has its counterpart weakness. Speed and penetration can be interpreted as indiscriminateness: an average product addressed to an unknown scattered audience. Cost effectiveness can imply appealing to the largest possible audience at all costs, thus reducing relevance. Quality and technique are high cost factors, which demand maximum yield. An equation is necessary to balance pros against cons and this equation is the crux of the media selection process.

We have already seen that the paradox of the mass media − the fact that those very qualities of high distribution which make them so attractive also limit their flexibility and adaptability − has preoccupied producers and educators for a long time, and a number of partial solutions have been found. The problem is illustrated by Fig. 9.1. The traditional, tutorial-centred approach to teaching is built upon a concept of dialogue; teacher and class interact. Mass communication, being detached from its audience, cannot assume a dialogue.

The task is to close the loop − to allow for feedback from audiences, and ultimately for the incorporation into media designs of their needs, preferences and tastes, at a level as close to the individual as possible.

One approach to this problem is founded upon technology: the creation of individual forms of media, which can be used in a classroom situation rather than broadcast over the air waves. In this category are the film projectors, the Super 8 projectors, or more recently audio and video-recorders and cassettes. In some cases, these actually use the same materials as are broadcast, or record them off the air; the increase in versatility comes from their use by a teacher or monitor. A comparable technique, which depends more upon an analysis of the learning process, is found in programmed instruction and in teaching machines. In programmed formats, learning is broken down into component parts which are presented in small steps. Checks are built in upon student performance, and if a student shows that he has not understood a particular step, he is referred back to a revision programme. Programmed instruction can be of many kinds — it can imply simple printed texts, or a composite of many kinds of audio-visual device, including the computer, but the principle of task analysis and sequencing is common to all forms.

A second approach is through systematic planning. This is partly afforded by the techniques of systems analysis and the creation of media systems, such as we have already considered. We attempt in the first place to make our programmes as close to educational objectives as we can; and subsequently, through feedback and evaluation, to improve upon our efforts the next time round. In many ways, this is more than a technique; it is an attitude of mind.

The real attraction of systems planning is that it gives a genuine priority to programme relevance, takes time to consider special problems and needs and to finding ways of working around them. An example can be taken from network planning. Although, to justify its overhead expenditure, the bulk of a radio network must address itself to large audiences, a certain amount of time can be reserved for minority audiences — which will be, as it were, carried by the momentum of the whole system. Although minority, subsidiary channels are best avoided, as they tend to become élitist, programming across dual networks can retain the popular qualities of each, while still allowing plenty of freedom for specialised material. Moreover, intelligently conducted needs assessment research (finding out what audiences actively want to see on their screens) can improve, from the outset, the relevance of programme content and the method of exposure; at a simpler level, surveys of behaviour patterns and social organisation can fix programme timings so that they have a chance of proper utilisation. A programme for farmers is of no use unless it is broadcast when the farmers are available to hear it (posing the supplementary question: do they hear it at home, or on transistors while they are working in the fields?). Equally, a programme on domestic science is of no use unless it mirrors the dietary habits of its audience. These are specific questions, which can be answered concretely by the sociologist, and they can substantially influence a programme's acceptability.

A third approach is through improved utilisation training. Teachers and

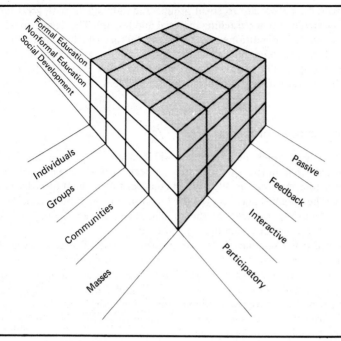

Fig. 9.2   A model of media access.

monitors are given intensive pre- and in-service courses in the functions of
media, and are shown how to apply general materials to their own personal
teaching programme. Such approaches depend upon the motivation and
self-reliance of the teacher; utilisation courses are an essential part of any
media programme, and should involve not only teacher trainers but
evaluators, researchers and producers. The media user needs to have basic
skills at his disposal: where to place equipment, how to operate it, how to
plan for its use, how to prepare for and follow up programmes. But he also
has to develop a rapport with producers and evaluators; he has to feel
involved in the production process, experiencing a common bond with
others in the system.

A measure of all these problems is found in the model (devised by
Bernard Webster) shown in Fig. 9.2. The left hand axis is a direction-
finder: are we engaged in formal or nonformal education, or in
development?

Given these bearings, the current trend is to try to make the media as
individual, and as participatory, *as is appropriate to the functions they are
asked to perform.* General television is, for example, addressed to mass
audiences and is a passive pursuit; many would like to see it linked more
frequently to local communities, and to become more participatory.
Educational media have, in the past, often been equally passive, designed
for large classes; most would prefer to see them more sensitive and

personalised, appropriate to small groups and individuals, with great inter-action between teacher/teaching material and learner. The degree to which this is possible is conditioned by the many factors which we have already noted (technical, economic, structural, psychological and so on). But if we can at least pinpoint a direction in which to move, we shall have gone some way towards fixing parameters to the problem.

B. Applications of media

It is the way in which media are used which is most important, and having established what innate qualities they appear to possess, we should now look at media *applications*. We have to consider (*a*) the kind of tasks which they may be asked to perform; (*b*) the locations in which these tasks are to be carried out; (*c*) the level of the audiences which are to be reached; and (*d*) the subject matter which they are to treat.

The following summary lists twenty differentiated functions of media. Note first of all that it is arranged in order of complexity: simpler tasks come first, more complicated tasks follow. Secondly, it is arranged accord-ing to scale, with local applications preceding more widespread versions. Finally, it makes reference to all mass media (television, radio and support media), even though in some cases (and these are stated) the application is confined to only one or two forms.

This list is not necessarily complete (or if it is, technology will soon make it obsolescent.) But it should provide a basic categorisation for the analysis which follows.

The kinds of tasks

1. *As a teaching tool*
Media are not only received in the classroom; technology can be used *by teachers* within their teaching programme. In other words, they can prepare aural and visual materials, either as complete 'programme' packages or as segments to be encapsulated in a lesson. When team teach-ing is practised, the possibilities for assembling varied audio-visual resources are increased.

There are a number of provisos to be made. Firstly, the teacher will be confined to whatever resources he can lay his hands on — either those he can create for himself, or can distill from local libraries. Secondly, he is limited by the quality and range of his equipment: whether or not he has mixing facilities (to combine audio and visual sources); whether he can assemble and edit materials; whether he has (in television) a monochrome or colour facility. Thirdly, he will be in a better position if he can work across several media formats — an audio system on its own will have little impact, but if combined with other visual forms, it will be improved by more than the sum of its parts. The main advantage to the teacher is that, within the system's limits and within his technical and intellectual capacity, he will have personal control over the sequence, scope and pace of his materials.

2. As a laboratory tool

Except when electronic technology is itself the subject of enquiry, this application is mostly restricted to video forms. Only one student at a time can observe through a microscope: this is a lengthy process and group discussion is difficult. But if a television camera is coupled to a microscope, whole groups can watch the enlargement, and examples can be recorded for future use. The same principle holds for such processes as single frame viewing, speeded up and slow motion processes, all of which are useful for technical analysis (though additional instruments have to be provided, to link or extend the basic system).

3. As a display medium

This is again a basic use of television, in which television monitors are used as a convenient means of projecting audio-visual materials which may have originated in a number of forms. Provided a suitable telecine system is available, films, slides, film strips, film books can all be displayed on a monitor, and they can also be pre-recorded so as to make retrieval and sequencing easier.

4. As an archive

Television and radio recording can preserve material which deserves repeated viewing or hearing. So tapes of visiting speakers, difficult laboratory experiments, public events, case study material, etc., can be stored for future use.

5. As a learning resource

Television and radio archive recordings can also contribute to learner-centred activities. In essence, a library of material is built up, for the student to use either independently, or under teacher control.

Both student direction, and the means of retrieval, may be quite complicated. In a programmed teaching format, the learner is directed to a particular sequence to suit his progress, either by a textual reference, or (in Computer Assisted Instruction — CAI) by a computer program. Equally, retrieval may be physical, or through some kind of 'dial access' device, where materials are extracted from a storage bank by operating a cue code. The horizons are technical and financial, and extend beyond simple institutions.

6. As a means of overspill teaching

In the main this use also involves television. The work of a single teacher can be relayed (limited only by the capacity of the distribution system) to a number of separate locations, either in the form of direct teaching which reproduces an original classroom situation, or in a more completely visualised form.

Because of its sensory limitations, radio is of little use in this context. But in view of the lack of direct interaction between teacher and audience (or limited interaction, if some kind of microphone connection for students to pose questions is provided), audio recordings and other support materials can be a useful bonus.

This use of television is less frequent now than a few years ago, when it was used, especially in American closed circuit systems, to overcome teacher shortages, or to supplement the work of specialist teachers. In a college or university, distribution need not necessarily be to a variety of locations — a single lecturer may address several hundred students in a specially equipped lecture theatre, and the audience can see his teaching in detail (as well as the illustrations which he is using) on monitors strategically placed around the auditorium.

7. *Creative expression*
Whether or not radio and television are considered to be art forms, they are undoubtedly creative media, and at all levels from the primary school upwards it is possible to involve students in the making of programmes, offering a highly satisfying contact with a new discipline. Unlike many creative experiences, the mass media also allow the maker to look independently at his work once it is finished.

8. *As a tool for communication training*
Training in communication techniques, whether for media staff or as part of an orientation programme for those whose jobs will bring them into contact with media, demands practical work with communication technology. Evidently, all media are involved.

9. *Educational technology training*
The same principle holds good for teachers and educators being instructed in the principles of educational technology (either specialists, or as part of a familiarisation programme).

10. *Micro-macro teaching*
Television is once again the main agent. Television and recording systems can be used in the training of teachers, to show individual students and groups their performance before a class. This gives the student a unique opportunity to see how he appears to others, and how successfully he has mastered his instruction.

11. *Observation*
An extension of (10) is in the making of observation recordings for replay and analysis. This is not confined to the educational sector; recordings can be made to assist the psychologist, the surgeon, the sociologist or political scientist. In some cases, audio recordings only may suffice (and these are generally much easier to secure since they produce fewer inhibitions in their subjects).

12. *Social animation*
The role of community media has been mentioned in Part 1, and is explored later in this handbook. In the hands of a community development worker (or without him, for that matter), audio and video recordings give a unique opportunity for individual and group viewpoints to be sought and counter-pointed, or for the views of one community to be transmitted to another. They also offer a new formula for advocacy, assisting minority or pressure groups to plead their case.

13. *As a community service*
In most communities, the principal mass media channels leave many needs unfulfilled. Some kinds of minority programme are not possible, or are not provided; local issues are too parochial to be treated; little dialogue is possible between producers and audiences, or between different audience members. A local community service helps redress some of these imbalances. Technical infrastructures are important − a radio transmitter, a wired distribution network − but these can sometimes be catered for as an extension of an existing service, originally established to serve quite other functions. A university radio station, for example, can act as communications trainer, teaching tool, educational technology centre, component in an open learning system, and also serve as a community focus.

14. *Audience participation*
One important contemporary interest is in access to and participation by users in the media process. This theme is explored later; it involves both the participation of audience representatives in programmes and in programme planning, and the direct handling of media tools by individuals and groups. The process ranges from the 'phone in' radio programme, through the creation of video groups benefiting from low-cost production and recording equipment, to the 'open channel' situation of many cable television systems or network experiments such as the BBC's 'Open Door' series (which gives minority groups the chance to make programmes for national airing). The degree to which participation can be contemplated depends to a large extent on the prevailing structures of broadcasting, union and manpower relationships, and the technical capacity of the system (it is obviously easier for local cable systems than for national open broadcast channels), but some action is possible at all levels.

15. *Training and mobilisation*
Both radio and television (ideally used associatively, with support from other media), can be used for training and mobilisation purposes. Here the media are used to communicate directly, and regularly, with specific groups, usually of professionals. Examples would be a nationally or regionally based teacher-training programme, upgrading and professional courses for professional workers such as doctors or engineers, training and refresher courses for extension workers. The object is not to provide a

structured learning experience leading to formal qualifications, but to introduce new fields of knowledge, techniques and experience, as rapidly and as widely as possible, to key personnel. Subsequently the media can also be used to keep in touch with these groups, to reinforce their work and sustain their interest over the long term.

16. *Development communication*
With development communication we move to highly structured, and often complex, communication systems, where mass media are anchored to specific development goals, planned in close association with extension work. The media system's main task is motivation and reinforcement, and its relationship with other activities — delivery systems, the activities of field workers, etc. — is critical. Obviously, far more elements than mass media are involved, and in many cases media are the least important component of the model.

17. *Enrichment*
In Part 1, this concept was fully explored, as a means of supplementary teaching in situations where media deployment is diffuse (either because the educational system is highly decentralised, or because the level of competence attained is already high enough for the system to be mostly teacher directed). This approach is best attached to an extensive use of recording, so that library resources can be built up at the local and school level.

18. *Curriculum support*
In contrast, a full range of media can be used in a more systematic fashion, where education is centrally administered and planned, to support a major scheme of curriculum renewal or extension. Close planning is needed to coordinate teacher training programmes, curriculum development and media.

19. *Social justice*
Mass media can be planned to help redress social inequalities, and to encourage the development of socially disadvantaged groups. At one level, this principle may imply the deliberate retarding of a medium like television, which is normally urban based, in favour of radio, which can be extended more rapidly to a rural population. At another level it can lead to such series as 'Sesame Street', the American pre-school series directed originally towards children in urban ghettoes, whose whole environment is poverty stricken. It is really more of a planning criterion than a separate application of media. The selection of students for the United Kingdom's Open University, for example, has taken account of social profiles, and the need to favour disadvantaged, working-class groups.

20. *Open learning systems*
The open learning system is the most complex of current media systems, for

which infrastructures are assumed either to be non-existent, or to be only supportive to its particular objectives. An example is again the British Open University, where many media are employed, including interpersonal communication, to create new learning opportunities for subscribers. At times, some existing institutions may be used (for example universities as hosts for summer schools, or college lecturers as part-time tutors or markers), but these external structures are still being specially enlisted, to fulfill a special role dictated by overall system design.

Very often, the open learning system is geared to acquiring qualifications. But it can also support liberal or post-experience courses — in fact any situation where the existing provision seems to be inadequate for large numbers of people.

In this account, we have moved sequentially from simple uses of media to applications which reflect more philosophical concerns. The demands of each upon individual media are shown in Table 9.1 (with special emphasis upon multi-media possibilities). The key employed is as follows:

HP = High Proficiency
PP = Partial Proficiency
 S = Supporting Role Only
MM = Multi-media working desirable

Table 9.1 Applications of educational media

Application	Television	Radio	Other media
1 Teaching tool	HP (MM)	PP (MM)	PP (MM)
2 Laboratory tool	HP	—	—
3 Display medium	HP	—	—
4 Archive	HP	PP	S
5 Learning resource	HP (MM)	HP (MM)	HP (MM)
6 Overspill	HP	S	S
7 Creative expression	HP	HP	HP
8 Communication training	HP	HP	HP
9 Educational technology training	HP (MM)	HP (MM)	HP (MM)
10 Micro/Macro teaching	HP	S	S
11 Observation	HP	PP	S
12 Social animation	HP	HP	S
13 Community service	HP	HP	S
14 Audience participation	PP	HP	S
15 Mobilisation	HP (MM)	HP (MM)	HP (MM)
16 Development communication	PP (MM)	PP (MM)	PP (MM)
17 Enrichment	PP	PP	S
18 Curriculum support	HP (MM)	HP (MM)	HP (MM)
19 Social justice	PP (MM)	PP (MM)	S
20 Open learning system	HP (MM)	HP (MM)	HP (MM)

Location

We have noted in passing that television and radio offer very different possibilities, if they are used as part of a school CCTV system, in a community cable service, or in a major national network. Accordingly, we shall look next at *location*, working from simple to complex settings.

The main contexts to be considered are the *individual institution*, the *community*, the *region or State*, and the *national network*. There are, of course, other permutations between, but these should give a reasonable grasp of the framework within which we are operating.

1. *The institution*

Here, we are not taking account of schools and institutions which receive programmes broadcast by national or regional networks; these are regarded as components of a larger media system. Rather, we are interested in the use, by a school or college, of media as an active tool in teaching, and in consequence, it is necessary first to say something about the nature of the technology involved in the production chain. For television, the basic item is the television camera, which transmits its picture to a television monitor. To provide a choice of pictures, more than one camera has to be used, permitting the producer, once a switcher or mixing unit is added to the system, to cut (or mix, or fade) between cameras, and so to change the image on the viewing monitor. The further addition of a recording device means temporary or permanent records can be made of what is viewed. Subsequently, a telecine chain (consisting of television camera plus film projector and/or slide/strip projector) allows other visual illustrations, from library sources or specially filmed, to be included. Special effects can be created by a special effects generator (allowing for example the insertion of one picture into another), or special attachments coupled to the camera allow for microscopic work, mirror images, negative effects, slow motion or speeded up processes. So the system is modular, its capability controlled only by technical and economic considerations. The same is basically true of other media. In radio, the first need is for a microphone; several microphones, and a mixing unit, allow for the mixing of a number of sources. Gramophone recordings, spot effects, tape recordings open up the field further. Special effects such as reverberation can be generated by electronic means. With an audio recorder, permanent records can be made. In other support media, the quality of print work, the range of visual illustration, the sophistication of film strips, slides or loops are conditioned by equivalent demands. More will be said later about production processes, and for greater detail, reference should be made to the companion volume (*Producing for Educational Mass Media*, Unesco/ Longman, 1976). What is important to recognise at this stage is that the applications of media are delimited by system size and performance, and conversely, systems are best designed after a clear understanding of function has been obtained.

At the level of the single institution, therefore, it is the simpler applications of media which are relevant. In the individual school, where a few classrooms are grouped together, connected by a wired distribution system, the media are being employed to match functions 1 to 7 in Table 9.1.

In the case of teacher-training institutions or institutions of higher learning, more specialised functions come into play. It is here that training functions (8, 9) are most likely to be encountered and those of pedagogical analysis (10, 11).

2. *Community*

The definition of community is rather diffuse, and for this reason the distinction between institutions and community is also diffuse, as institutions — schools, colleges, community centres — can be focal points for community development and action. But we can take as a working definition of community an environment which is large enough to allow for interplay between groups and individuals, but small enough for these to interact physically, and for a sense of involvement and identification to spring up.

Thus we might be considering a village, a small town or a group of villages, but not a State or city conurbation, where loyalties and identifications are found, but physical interaction is restricted.

The interplay of media in the community is mostly described by functions 12 to 14. In other words, the purpose of involving media is to permit an expression, in media terms, of community presence; to offer materials of local interest which for logistical reasons are overlooked by larger networks; to create learning and browsing resource centres; and to offer a genuine means of audience involvement and participation. The environment is large enough to reflect group activity, but not so large that the individual is forgotten.

However, just as local institutions can serve a community, so can the reverse be true, and in practice, all of the functions 1 to 14 may be served by a single media centre operating at two levels. There are advantages in this arrangement; a genuine bond is created between the individual institution and the environment in which it is placed.

3. *The city or State*

The transition from community to State is also gradual, and some of the same kinds of activity may well be reflected in media systems at a larger urban level. In many ways, this is an ideal level for media activity: usually small enough for producers and users to relate physically as well as by correspondence, often compact enough for cable or other multi-channel distribution systems to be economic, and yet rich enough in resources for professional materials to be prepared. Moreover, the environment is controllable enough for a rational evaluation to be made, and it is no surprise that many of the media systems which have been systematically developed and evaluated are either in cities (Hagerstown, London, Glasgow) or in compact States (Singapore, Hong Kong, American Samoa, El Salvador).

The State may operate as an independent unit (especially where, as in India, education is a State subject), or it may work as a subsidiary part of a wider system, making regional adaptions of nationally distributed, and hence less personal, materials.

Its functions may include, in a modified form, each of the categories

12 to 20. But the equation persists; the larger the services are, the less personal materials become, even though more resources are available for their creation.

4. *The nation*

At this level, we reach the widest field of activity (at least until communication by satellite is such that intercontinental and global programmes can be a regular event and not, as at present, periodic contributors to national chains).

It is in the national context that the most ambitious uses of media are contemplated — the mobilisation of teachers or development workers in massive re-training programmes, the total renovation of curricula, extensive open learning systems and the reform of educational structures.

Interaction

This division into distinct locations has been made as a tool for comparison, and should not be taken too literally. If the impact of media is to be felt, different levels of the system — local, national and regional — must be planned together and be mutually reinforcing. In practice, this asks for a degree of coordination which is difficult to arrange, and compromises and partial solutions have to be accepted. Yet if the overall perspective is remembered, then at least the compromises will be made on rational grounds.

A summary of this analysis is given in Table 9.2. The symbol X indicates a main application, S a subsidiary or supporting interest.

Table 9.2   Context of educational media

Application	Institution	Community	State	Nation
1 Teaching tool	X			
2 Laboratory tool	X			
3 Display medium	X	X		
4 Archive	X	X		
5 Learning resource	X	X		
6 Overspill	X	X		
7 Creative expression	X	X		
8 Communication training	X	S		
9 Educational technology training	X	S		
10 Micro/Macro teaching	X			
11 Observation	X			
12 Social animation	S	X		
13 Community service	S	X	S	
14 Audience participation	S	X	X	S
15 Mobilisation	S	S	X	X
16 Development communication	S	X	X	X
17 Enrichment	S	X	X	X
18 Curriculum support	S	S	X	X
19 Social justice	S	X	X	X
20 Open learning system	S	S	X	X

Audience levels and subject areas

The functions considered so far have been contextual; the kinds of service which mass media can be asked to perform, and the environments in which these are likely to be executed. Our final two criteria are of a different kind, referring more directly to traditional educational groupings — that is, educational level and content.

The issue at debate here is what can the media do best, and for whom? For this analysis, a different measure of comparison is proposed, which is illustrated in Table 9.3.

The description of levels follows orthodox lines. *Pre-primary* is taken to include both nursery and kindergarten classes, and preparation for schooling (including efforts directed towards children in the home). *Primary* embraces the American 'elementary', and *secondary* the American high school stage. *Teacher training* covers all structured training programmes. In the *higher education* and *formal adult* sphere, the controlling factor is that learning takes place in formal institutions, or according to structured programmes. (So an open learning system leading to *formal qualifications* would be included in this category.) *Non-formal* education, on the other hand, includes activities outside the recognised infrastructures of school and university, which focus on the improvement of social and occupational capabilities. It is designed more towards satisfying individual needs, and developing problem solving abilities, than towards curriculum content.

The range of *subjects* proposed includes only those to which media are agreed to make a contribution; it is not comprehensive. The key to the grading of *media* proficiency is as before; HP indicates High Proficiency, and PP partial proficiency. The key applies only to television and radio: the role of support media is more difficult to determine and only general indications are given.

Table 9.3   Audiences and subject areas of educational media

Level	Subject matter	Television	Radio	
Pre-primary	Pre-reading	HP	—	Difficult to
	Number	HP	—	co-ordinate,
	Story-telling and fantasy	HP	HP	except as
	Music	PP	HP	spin-off and
	Arts and crafts	HP	PP	follow-up
	Environment	HP	HP	material.
Primary	Drama and story	HP	HP	Learner-centred
	Music	PP	HP	reference and
	Arts and crafts	HP	PP	resource
	Science and environment	HP	PP	materials are
	Mathematics	HP	PP	desirable,
	Language studies	HP	HP	accompanied by
	Geography	HP	PP	teacher guides.
	History	HP	HP	
	Social studies	HP	HP	

Table 9.3 continued on p. 82

Table 9.3 – *continued*

Level	Subject matter	Television	Radio	
Secondary	Drama and literature	HP	HP	Both teacher and
	Science	HP	PP	learner-centred
	Mathematics	HP	PP	materials are
	Language studies	HP	HP	needed (carefully
	History	HP	HP	structured if part
	Geography	HP	PP	of a multi-media
	Social studies	HP	HP	system) with
	Current affairs and			full teacher
	liberal studies	HP	HP	guides.
	Music	PP	HP	
	Arts and crafts	HP	PP	
	Technical and vocational	HP	PP	
Teacher training	Educational method	PP	PP	Reference materials desirable.
	In-service reinforcement	PP	HP	Reference materials useful, and a newsletter.
Higher education and formal adult education	Arts and humanities	HP	HP	Learner-centred
	Social sciences	HP	PP	materials are
	Science and technology	HP	PP	needed,
	Mathematics	HP	PP	especially in
	Education	PP	PP	open learning
	Business and commercial	HP	PP	systems.
Non-formal adult	Literacy	PP	PP	A variety of
	Agriculture	PP	HP	materials is
	Development	PP	HP	needed for
	Industry	HP	PP	penetration and
	Current affairs	HP	HP	reinforcement; a
	Home studies	HP	HP	range of learning
	Science and technology	HP	PP	materials for
	Languages	HP	HP	home students;
	Arts	HP	HP	and training,
	Participatory and			refresher and
	student contact			demonstration
	programmes	PP	HP	materials for field workers.

Which level is best?

Some experiences of media preference are given in the next part of this chapter, derived from research studies, but it cannot be said that *any* level is unsuited, provided that the media are used intelligently. A good producer, with imagination, can turn the most unlikely subject into a stimulating programme, and finding the correct level at which to pitch his production is a matter of experience and familiarity with his audience (going out into the field to meet them, not confining himself to the control room). However, there is evidence that media appeal especially to younger children, who are intrigued by the variety of stimuli offered and who have not been so over-exposed to mass media that they have become resistant to them. It is also true to say that some techniques (e.g. puppets and cartoons) can only be used successfully with young children. It is at the higher educational levels that resistance to media is most generally found, especially in universities, though this often stems from a poor use of the medium as a second-best alternative to personal tuition.

Which subjects are best?

It will be seen at once that those general qualities of educational media which were isolated at the beginning of this chapter are related in Table 9.3 to specific subjects. This relationship comes from a direct matching of means and techniques against content. So diagrams and animations suggest an explanation of concepts and relationships (science, mathematics, sociology); close-ups and special technical effects imply technical and laboratory processes (science, technology, vocational and technical subjects); drama is at once a part of literature and a means of enlivening almost every subject area; location filming opens up the world to students of geography, languages and the social sciences; the opportunity to interview important personalities enlivens current affairs. Music and voice are instruments for fantasy and story telling and language learning. Editing possibilities mean that processes can be compressed and remodelled, which is useful in scientific areas, industrial studies and domestic sciences alike.

In these cases, the creative potential of the media works towards the enrichment of content. In some other areas, the opposite is true. The mass media require selection and juxtaposition; so they usually have to run to a prescribed time span. In other words, they are structured. They are less applicable where case study materials are required raw (in sociology, for example), or where unplanned interaction between audiences is important (as in pedagogy). In such cases the technology may obtrude; it is difficult to plan for the unexpected in such a way that social processes are not affected and subjects are not inhibited by the technical paraphernalia surrounding them. But even here special methods can often be worked out, to help subjects forget the viewing eye.

Which medium is best?

Television, as a full sensory medium, comes out best in most situations (as it will inevitably do, when economic factors are not being emphasised. We are, after all, dealing here with only one facet of the equation upon which media decisions are based).

Radio is shown to be superior especially in the area of music (television can teach skills, develop the idea of programme music, and orchestral practice, but does not focus down on the main auditory sense). Radio potential is also greater in non-formal education, where not only cost, but portability, access to audiences, and immediacy, make it a more flexible instrument. In participatory programmes, too, radio is an easier medium for the amateur to master, employing a simpler technology.

But in areas which have demonstration elements, or which are highly dependent upon visual identification, radio must have a lesser role to play. However, its drawbacks are considerably reduced once other support media are introduced into the system, especially when these are cooperatively planned and produced. Of these, print radio and 'radio vision' are the most important.

Support materials and multi-media working

While support media are desirable in most areas, they are most essential at the secondary and formal adult level. At the pre-primary level, the physical infrastructures do not exist to support a media system even if this were desirable — what is more likely is that programmes will be supported by materials (especially print) which extend basic principles and concepts, but which are not essential to understanding. In the primary school, a variety of materials should be provided, but less rigorously integrated. They are there for pupils to use when they wish, not as a necessary step in a structured learning process.

At the other end of the scale, in non-formal adult education organised learning structures are also not available, and a disciplined relationship between materials is not possible. But a wide variety of support is still needed, both to spread the basic message, by sheer volume and variety of exposure, and to provide tools for the extension agent, who is basing at least part of his work on the mass media stimulus. Coordinated media systems are most likely to be effective at secondary, higher education and formal adult levels, where learning tends to be more compartmentalised and more carefully programmed (at the junior levels it is the unity, rather than the divisibility, of the world which is being emphasised).

The proportions of the multi-media mix will be different in every case, but there are some general considerations to be borne in mind. Firstly, the more complex the mass media system, the more it will need in the way of support. Partly this is because a complex system presupposes a detailed analysis of learning tasks, and therefore a more rigorous analysis of media contributions. But it is also because, in a refined media system, a good deal more is needed to establish links between materials and to guide the teacher in using them. Consequently, print media are especially important.

In open learning systems, the need for variety in the instructional design is greatest of all, since producers and learners have no other structures on which to fall back. They cannot assume an interpreting teacher, or a detailed discussion period after a lesson; they have to try to cover all possible difficulties, hesitations and queries in advance. So an open learning system will include not only audio-visual and print components, but means of interpersonal connection (marked assignments, programmed instruction, telephone tutorials, summer schools, a network of tutors and counsellors).

The relationship between radio and television

Finally, the relationship between radio and television is interesting, and not usually fully exploited. It is not simply a matter of using television, along with support items, to subsidise areas where radio is weak. Rather it is a question of balance, so that each reinforces the other. In language teaching, for example, television can show language being used in real life situations, show lip movements, reproduce printed text, animate sentence structures. Used associatively, radio can provide follow-up drills, examples of conversational practice or question exploratively what has been presented on television.

In music, television can analyse musical behaviour, while radio allows for free, uninterrupted listening. In mathematics, the burden of explaining concepts, relating mathematics to life, showing notations, falls upon television, but radio can burrow into mathematical history, set problem situations for solution, dramatise mathematics so that it intrigues the reluctant child. The same is true of science, technical and vocational subjects.

Radio, in other words, because of its limitations, has the time to do at greater length what the more expensive visual medium is reluctant to do, for fear of being thought irrelevant or wasteful. Radio can call upon the listener's imagination, tell stories, provide subjects for fantasy and creative work, transmit extended discussions where faces and features are less important than content, offer drills and practice. It is also a very useful means of providing links between audiences who do not regularly meet face to face. An open learning system will always have difficulty in retaining the interest and motivation of its students; so will an extension system with its field workers. With radio, they can be kept in touch. Indeed, one of the main features of the use of satellite communication in Alaska is the opportunity which radio connections give for health workers to talk directly with their supervisors, even to secure diagnoses for their patients. In the Pacific, too, one of the most important uses of PEACESAT is to keep educational or agricultural workers from different countries in touch with each other.

C. Experience

Cost

There will be no attempt in this handbook to enter into an exhaustive discussion of costs. On the one hand, any attempt to give a range of costs for equipment purchase or installation would be ill-advised at present, with unpredictable shifts in world conditions: only some general principles are discussed in Part 3 (Chapter 12 — Technical facilities). Equally, a debate on the economics of media, discussing in detail issues of cost-effectiveness, would also be open to error. Even if the author were an economist, which he is not, so many variables enter into communication costings, salary and price charges are so rapid, so many hidden costs are to be taken into account and so many differences stem from local conditions, labour markets, taxes and levies, that comparisons between different situations are always suspect.

What will be offered here is not so much a standard accounting for media, as some illustrations of characteristic costings, on the clear understanding that they are not always comparable. The section (compiled from secondary sources) should demonstrate that media can be afforded, and that, on a reasonable unit or exposure basis, costs are rarely prohibitive.

We shall be discussing the following areas or analyses of expenditure:

(*a*) Capital or development costs;
(*b*) Recurrent costs;
(*c*) Cost breakdowns (into production, transmission and distribution);
(*d*) Unit costs.

In cases where comparative estimates can be given between media-assisted and traditional education (e.g. in open learning systems), some tentative judgement of equivalence will also be made.

Capital costs

In absolute terms, capital costs are naturally variable, ranging from a few thousand dollars for a school installation, to between $50,000 and $150,000 for a closed circuit system, and up to several million dollars for a comprehensive television system ($3.6 million, for example, over a 7-year period in El Salvador, or a projected basic $17 million in Thailand — minus tax and contingencies, and phased over a 6-year period). Such figures perhaps make more sense when they are related to other expenditures. In El Salvador, for example, the capital costs of instructional television amounted at their height (1971) to 17 per cent of the Ministry of Education's capital appropriation; in Thailand, they were projected at 4.6 per cent of the total education budget. Capital expenditure is always likely to be heavy, but it is a single, developmental expenditure and one which is not likely, as some commentators would seem to assume, to consume a dramatic proportion of total educational expenditure.

Recurrent expenditure

To most Ministries of Finance, this is the most disturbing item. Capital expenditure is one-time, and in a developing country is often offset by technical assistance or foreign loans; recurrent expenditure has to be maintained year in, year out. In El Salvador, it has been running at under 2 per cent of the annual total educational recurrent budget (about $500,000); projections in Thailand amounted to 0.5 per cent of total educational expenditure (approximately $3.6 million dollars, once the system was expanded).

Expressed in percentage terms, these expenditures can be viewed more realistically. The drain upon resources has, evidently, to be weighed against potential savings and other advantages to the educational system. But it seems likely that, even in an expanded media system, a maximum of 5 per cent of the total educational recurrent provision will be demanded (and of course the larger the system into which media are being introduced, the lower will that percentage become). In El Salvador, projections over a 25-year period, assuming a future primary school expansion, assume a recurrent annual expenditure of well over $1 million, but the percentage represented is still about 4 per cent.

Cost breakdowns
With capital expenditure, costs are likely to be apportioned fairly equally between the three main components of production, transmission, and reception (including reception equipment). In Thailand, the relative proportions were calculated at 37, 38 and 25 per cent. But much will depend upon the character of the system under consideration. In some countries, for example, educational mass media may be carried on the backs of other, more general media services, with a consequent saving in transmission facilities. In an industrialised country, reception equipment will probably be provided by the users themselves, affording equal savings.

But again, it is the breakdown of recurrent expenditure which will cause the greater concern to financial authorities. In all cases, the largest proportion of the recurrent financial provision will be devoted to staff costs and associated overheads — variable, depending upon local salary levels, but always considerable. In the Open University, a breakdown of recurrent costs showed between 75 and 80 per cent going to staffing and overheads, with 15 to 18 per cent to production direct costs, and 5 to 6 per cent to transmission, the latter mostly absorbed by the BBC's network. In Thailand, where salary levels are much lower, 45 per cent was apportioned to staffing and overheads, 40 per cent to production and 15 per cent to transmission costs.

In a slightly different context, the costs of actual production are of interest. These are again rising, and figures quoted here cannot be taken as specific. But a characteristic figure for a learning system in a developing country is between $1,200 and $2,000 per hour for television. The Chicago TV College costs about $800 per hour; the NHK High School $1,973; the Bavarian Telekolleg $8,700; the BBC Open University about $20,000. At the other end of the spectrum, 'Sesame Street' was absorbing some $42,000 hourly, and 'The Electric Company' $75,000.

A comparison with radio is of the greatest interest. While NHK Gakuen was costing almost $2,000 hourly for television, its radio component averaged $356 (more than five times less). In the BBC, the cost to each student of a television programme in the Open University schedule stood recently at about $3.6, and of a radio programme $0.384 (a ten-times differential). This is a ratio to be borne in mind by the planner.

Unit costs
The economist approaches decisions on cost efficiency through the concept of the unit cost. In other words, the total costs of the system are

totalled, and divided by the number of students exposed: this can be related to a unit of time (unit costs per annum or per hour), to a programme unit, or to a total project. The advantage of this approach is that equivalent unit costs can be calculated for alternative, or traditional, forms of education, and a basis for comparison found. The disadvantage is that, in both calculations, many items of expenditure are likely to be omitted or given a doubtful weighting (how do we reflect, for example, the costs of a transmission system provided by an agency outside of the education ministry?), so that a false perspective may result. Moreover, in many instances, since no alternative solution is proposed, because media are seen as a qualitative supplement to a continuing educational system, little is gained from the calculation bar an expression of whether media represent reasonable value for money. Add to this the fact that every system is different, and unit costs applied to one context are not properly comparable with another, and the limits of the methodology are soon apparent. But it can at least reassure the financial planner, in terms which he understands, that he is embarking upon a rational enterprise.

As an example, some unit costs for earlier television projects are quoted in Table 9.4 (compiled by Wilbur Schramm).

Table 9.4   Sample unit costs for educational television

Medium	Place	Number of students	Per year
ITV	American Samoa (Schramm, 1973)	8,100, ITV carrying core of teaching	$157
ITV	Hagerstown (IIEP, 1967)	21,600, ITV carrying core	$28
ITV	Mexico: Telesecundaria (Klees, 1973)	29,000, ITV carrying core of curriculum	$22
ITV	El Salvador (Speagle, 1970)	25,000–35,000, ITV carrying core	$15
ITV	Colombia (IIEP, 1967)	250,000, ITV carrying core of about one-third of curriculum	$9

Some of the figures are higher (Samoa in particular, where the numbers of students in the system are fewer), but in no case are they prohibitive.

Expanding the system quite dramatically can also leave unit costs relatively untouched, or even reduced. An average cost per student in El Salvador, projected over a 25-year period and assuming primary school television programming through grades 1 to 6, was still $17 (as compared with $15 in the limited high school phase of 1971).

Cost benefits
The economist and treasury official, however, frequently ask for more than a simple demonstration of cheapness; they are looking for proof of efficiency, and preferably of savings.

This is a more difficult undertaking, and it is only when media are asked to provide alternative solutions to educational problems, such as are envisaged in open learning systems, media-assisted correspondence schools and the like, that a valid basis of comparison is found, simply because we are then concerned with true options, not hypothetical cost comparisons. In Mexico, for example, the cost per student per annum of the Telesecundaria project was calculated at $151, compared with an estimated $200 for regular schools at this level. A figure quoted for the Open University of $1,174 per student per annum, compared with $1,666 for regular university courses in campuses without a high post graduate enrolment, and $1,999 for campuses with strong professional schools. In Australia, some years ago, the cost of correspondence education with radio support was given as between $310 and $337 in New South Wales (set against a quoted $265 for regular classroom tuition at the same level). In this context, it was interesting to note that in another State, Victoria, the figure was put much higher at $611, because of a lower enrolment, and the illustration shows quite clearly the importance of student numbers in reducing unit costs (the break even point for this kind of education was calculated to be 10,000 students). A further comparison was made between the 'School of the Air', also in Australia, which uses the Flying Doctor radio service to provide tutorial contact between student and teacher. A figure of between $400 and $450 compared very favourably with the only *possible* alternative solution for a scattered rural population (i.e. boarding schools, at an average cost, at that time, of $600—$1,200 per student per annum).

Most of the studies of distance education, including media support, show the same kind of pattern. The services of the Bavarian Telekolleg, at $122 per student p.a., related favourably to $400—$500 p.a. in an equivalent trade school; in the NHK High School of Japan they stood at $308, to be set against $540 for traditional schooling. However, the comparison may be much less attractive if based upon student success (the graduate cost per student of the NHK Gakuen stood at $2,143). This is why institutions like the Open University have been so concerned with student performance, and why the high pass rate of the University, as already recorded, is especially promising.

Estimates of cost efficiency in other educational areas are far more difficult to make. The Thai study already quoted concluded that, while it was possible to show that unit costs were very reasonable, and could certainly not be considered a drain on educational resources, they could not be assumed to result directly in cost savings, because the system was directed towards qualitative improvement, much of which could not be contemplated by any other means. However, in this study (for the benefit of scrutinising economists) a comparison was made with the cost equivalent of formal schooling. The results are given in Table 9.5 (in US dollars), which reflects unit costs per participant, per programme.

The alternatives presented in Table 9.5 (from highest to lowest) are so framed because the unit costs of various levels of the system were themselves different (television, for example, was to be mainly restricted to

Table 9.5   Comparative unit cost estimates in Thailand

	Lowest	Highest in school	Highest out of school
Radio	0.000135	0.00295	0.02
TV	0.0135	0.0385	0.1635
Cost equivalent	0.008 (Elem.)	0.02225	0.172
Formal education	0.02225 (Sec.)	(Sec.)	(Teacher training)

upper educational levels), and there is therefore a spread of costs as between elementary and secondary or adult education. But the figures demonstrate that at all levels bar one, the costs of media compare very favourably with traditional forms. It is also apparent that in the one case where media could be used as a definite alternative, rather than a supplement, to a formal programme — i.e. post experience teacher training — media are competitive in cost, and if radio is primarily employed, quite considerably cheaper.

Another way of presenting the same argument for Thailand was to show that the unit recurrent costs of the projected system at the elementary level would not be sufficient to purchase even two small elementary school readers per pupil per year. To replace the media system by, for example, an adequate supply of printed and other materials would have been at least *ten times* more expensive.

Analyses in El Salvador (by R. E. Speagle) came to similar conclusions.

Table 9.6   Comparative unit cost estimates in El Salvador

Student enrolment	ITV cost per student ($)	Conventional cost per student (junior high)	Conventional cost per student (elementary)
5,000	0.144	0.032	0.02
10,000	0.072	0.032	0.02
25,000	0.028	0.032	0.02
50,000	0.016	0.032	0.02
100,000	0.008	0.032	0.02

Table 9.6 gives comparative operating costs per student hour, by traditional methods and with media intervention, and it illustrates particularly the rising benefits of media depending upon student numbers. A break even point is indicated at about 20,000 enrolments for junior high school students, and at about 35,000 for the less costly elementary grades.

A further set of calculations is directed towards teacher training. The comparative costs are shown in Table 9.7 of re-training teachers at different levels in the introduction and operation of a new curriculum. The traditional method for junior high school teachers involved a 2-year course of study; the method assumed for primary school teacher training required either a 9-month residential course, or a 3-month crash programme. The ITV method assumed in-service training, a regular schedule of teacher training programmes, and associated work books, guides and other

Table 9.7   Comparative costs of teacher training in El Salvador

Teacher level	Traditional system cost	Short course traditional system	ITV system
Elementary	$29,720,000	$7,520,000	$257,600
Junior high	$4,568,000	$2,284,000	

materials. (The use of television at the junior school level did in fact occur; training for primary teachers is under discussion.)

It will be noted that most of the examples given so far are concerned with television, because it is mostly through television that, to this moment, major educational reforms have been approached. But the examples from Thailand are enough to show that the cost benefits of using radio as an integral part of an instructional system are considerably greater (by as much as ten times). It is to be hoped that some Government in the developing world will have the courage to return to the radio medium as a major reform instrument, rather than as the *ad hoc* tool which it has mostly been to date.

Non-formal and adult education

Little can be said of the cost of media in non-formal and adult education, because very little data is available. Some attempts have been made to quantify the costs of group discussion (the Indian experiment in Poona, for example, put the cost of each discussion group at $4.38 per meeting). But the absence of data is really a reflection both of the amorphous quality of much of the work in this area, and of the way in which adult provision is taken as an extension of the institutionalised school system, resisting attempts at economic separation (except in the specific context of distance learning or open learning systems).

Some unit costs have already been given for Thailand; another projection shown in Table 9.8, again made in El Salvador, compared the cost of reaching adults through the instructional television system with that of a formal adult education provision.

Table 9.8   Comparative costs of reaching adults in El Salvador

Enrolment	Traditional system	ITV system (with TV sets)	ITV system (without TV sets)
200,000	$1,800,000	$1,532,000	$1,132,000
500,000	$4,880,000	$3,652,000	$2,652,000

Cost comparisons between media

We have spoken in this brief section of media in general (as part of a media system), or about specific media such as television, for which economic

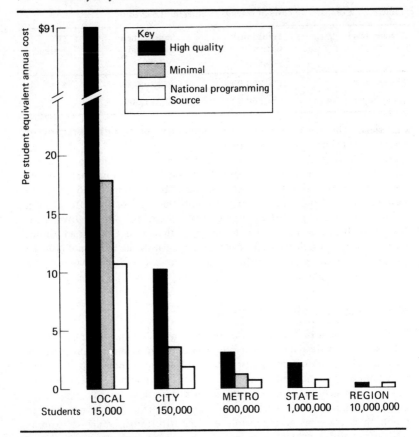

Fig. 9.3   ETV production costs.

information is more readily available. But what of comparisons between media? Which media are cost beneficial in which situations, and how do costs compare as between the different functions of production, distribution and reception?

A survey conducted by the General Learning Corporation in 1968 gave a very complete, although theoretically based, cost comparison. The Corporation produced estimates for five different locations, which they called local, city, metropolitan, State and region, matching populations for media coverage of 15,000, 150,000, 600,000, 1,000,000 and 10,000,000 respectively. Graphical representations of this study are given in Figs. 9.3 to 9.7. Seven types of media are included: ITFS systems (operating on 2.500 megahertz, as local instructional television systems, most commonly encountered in the USA), satellite television, broadcast television on UHF frequencies, closed circuit TV, physical distribution by videotape, physical distribution by film, and finally radio. (The original study included other media which are omitted here.)

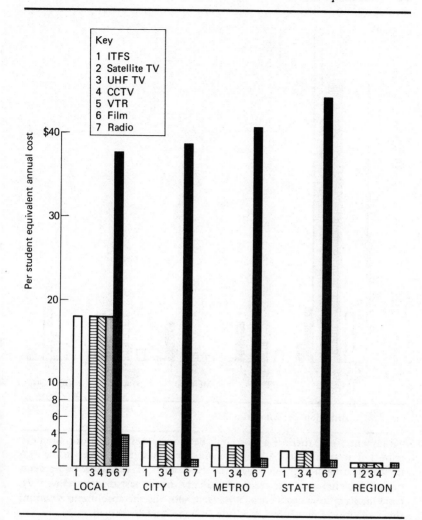

Fig. 9.4　Production cost comparisons.

The first diagram (Fig. 9.3) illustrates production costs per student per annum, at various levels of production quality. It reflects the possible reduction in costs which stems from an acceptance of programming from a central source (in the case of a large national provision, by a factor of up to 100:1). Figure 9.4 compares production costs for a number of media and illustrates differentials both of media character (big media versus little media) and of scale (since mass media costs, such as radio and television, decline as audiences increase, but physically distributed film remains high because print costs do not show such radical reductions).

Distribution costs (which follow in Fig. 9.5) really reflect audience

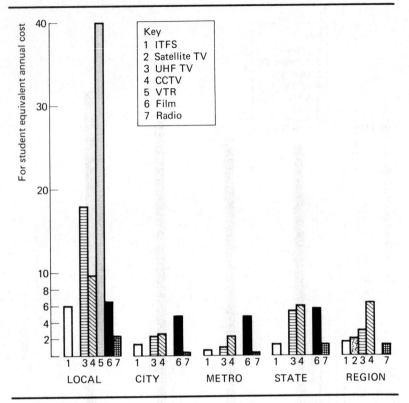

Fig. 9.5   Distribution cost comparison.

catchment areas; there is a close link between coverage and optimum distribution arrangements. A similar economic argument emerges in Fig. 9.6 in considering reception costs (i.e. the cost of receiving equipment, projectors, etc., and user training). Finally, in the last diagram (Fig. 9.7), total media system costs are summarised, showing the absolute necessity in the case of mass media for a sizeable audience to be retained.

The GLC study concluded that costs tend to cluster into two broad bands. Total costs of instructional television 'fall between $30 and $40 per student per year for the local area (5 to 10 per cent of yearly expenditures). They converge on $10 for the city and roughly the same for the metropolitan area. The radio system was about $2.50 per student per year for the metropolitan area and $3.50 and $2.50 for the state and region, the lowest cost for any system'. The estimated cost of doing the same job with films is about $50 per student, with very little change in the case of larger audiences or broader coverage, because of the expense of duplicating and delivering films.

Table 9.9 shows representative estimates from the GLC study.

These estimates were produced some years ago, and they cannot be

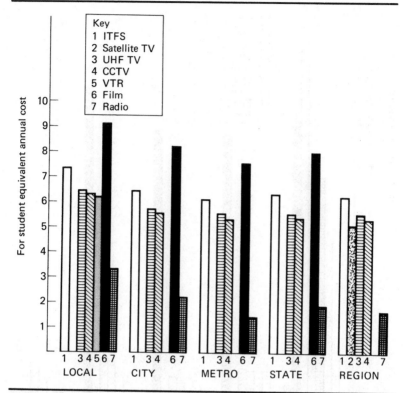

Fig. 9.6   Reception cost comparison.

used as a basis for real cost projections. A number of arguments could also be raised against their method of comparison. The bases for calculation included the assumption that an annual total of 1,000 hours of programming would be required for a local system, and that this would increase gradually to 1,600 hours for a regional or national system. In practice, of course, some media are not ever used in this way. Film production and distribution on such a scale have never been seriously attempted; library systems are more the norm, and films are most often employed for special instructional or motivational tasks.

The estimates for VTR provision are also no longer exact, now that

Table 9.9   Media cost estimates per student per year for carrying a considerable part of the instructional load

	For 15,000 students	150,000	600,000
ITV	$40	$10	$9
Film	$52	$50	$52
Radio	$9	$3	$2.50

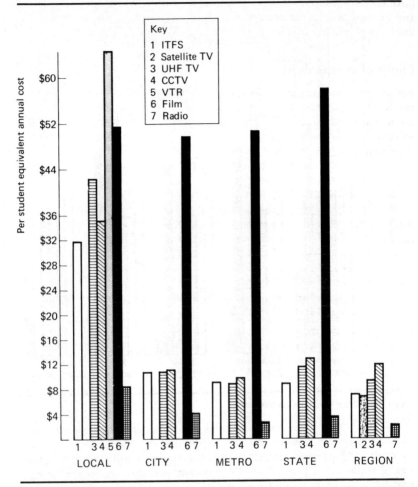

Fig. 9.7   Estimates of total cost of media instruction.

videocassette systems are being marketed in greater numbers. The satellite figures are similarly dated, since no widespread experience of costs was available at that time.

Nevertheless, the sequence illustrates quite clearly the argument of mass distribution which has been stressed on a number of occasions already. It also gives further resource information on whether or not to use a particular medium in a given situation, although the economic argument has to be weighed carefully together with other considerations (expertise, technical factors, production demands). In other words, it is reasonable to use radio at all levels from the local to the national, unreasonable to use a satellite at any but the national. Closed-circuit television may be applicable to any environment; likewise videotape. Open circuit television can be justified from the level of the city upwards. But there is no certainty that any of these will be the correct medium to use in any of these contexts, until a large number of other criteria have been met.

Limits of cost analysis

For an exhaustive analysis of cost analysis issues, the reader is referred to the work of Jamison, Klees and Wells (see Bibliography, p. 363). These authors are well aware of the problems of securing reliable data, of finding suitable criteria for comparison, and of excluding, or interpreting, non-economic variables. In most cases, where comparisons are made between different projects, in the interests of cost comparison, one of the most important criteria of all — relative quality — has to be excluded from the analysis, because it is not measurable in equivalent terms.

More than one writer has queried the validity of cost benefit analyses made in the context of educational technology, and implied either that deficient data has been used, or that the selection and interpretation of data has been such as to underestimate real costs and hence favour the technology being evaluated. The issue was debated at some length in an issue of 'Instructional Science' which appeared in October 1975, and the kind of criticism which was made is characterised in its concluding article (by M. Carnoy and H. M. Levin).

Rather than limiting our analysis of the media's impact on society to narrow cost-cognitive learning studies, we must understand the total role of the media in the educational/social systems which they serve. For it is that total role that will determine whether Governments will accept instructional media or not. Cost effectiveness studies will only service to legitimise these choices on the basis of criteria acceptable to those funding agencies and governments that have a vested interest in avoiding discussion of the larger agenda.

In the past few years, many economists have become uneasy about the rigidity with which their art is sometimes characterised, and a good deal of research is under way to discover social and cultural, as well as economic, indicators of development, which can measure the quality as well as the *per capita* income of life. Unfortunately, the educational media planner, especially in the Third World, is often locked into a more conservative system, which insists upon economic analysis according to the traditional order; however much he suspects that what he is doing is artificial, hypothetical and basically unreliable, he will have, for the moment, to continue the game.

Research

We have seen, in Part 1, how media development has been largely *ad hoc*, paced by the availability of new technologies. This historical process

Table 9.10 Use of mechanical and audio-visual aids

Period	Aid	Sensory channel	Verbal or pictorial?	Who controls rate and repetition?	Group or individual instruction?	Dating from?
Medieval	Chalk, blackboard	Sight-sound	Both	Maker	Group	Earliest times
	Models, charts, maps, etc.	Sight-sound	Chiefly pictorial	User	Either	Earliest times
Renaissance	Books	Sight	Chiefly verbal	User	Either	16th century
First industrial revolution	Photographs, slides, film strips	Sight-sound	Pictorial	User	Group	Late 19th cent.
	Silent motion films	Sight	Pictorial	Maker	Group	Early 20th cent.
	Recordings	Sound	Verbal and musical	Maker	Either	Early 20th cent.
	Radio (school broadcasts)	Sound	Chiefly verbal	Maker	Either	1920s
	Sound-motion films	Sight-sound	Both	Maker	Group	1930s
	Television	Sight-sound	Both	Maker	Either	1950s
Second industrial revolution	Tape recorders	Sound	Chiefly verbal	User	Either	1950s
	Language laboratories	Sound	Verbal	User	Either	1950s
	Programmed texts	Sight	Chiefly verbal	User	Individual	1950s
	Teaching machines	Sight	Chiefly verbal	User	Individual	1950s
	CCTV	Sight-sound	Both	User	Group	1950s/60s
	Computer-assisted instruction	Sight-sound	Both	User	Either	1960s/70s
	Videocassettes	Sight-sound	Both	User	Either	1970s

is illustrated in Table 9.10, which maps the development of media across successive industrial revolutions. We can see from this table the growing sensory range of media, and their increasing emphasis on user control, featuring group and individual applications.

But although subjective experience yields many valuable insights, if possible we would prefer to base our decisions on concrete research and evaluation. Accordingly, in the following pages, we look at the results of some research, mostly carried out over the past 15 years, as it affects the two fundamental issues of efficiency and quality.

Media research

The literature on educational media is considerable, and in a practical handbook of this kind there is no place for more than a cursory summary. For more detail the reader should turn to Wilbur Schramm's book, *Big Media—Little Media*, upon which this chapter draws heavily.

Even the researchers are hesitant about the conclusions which can be drawn from their work. There are well over 500 documented studies comparing educational media (most of them on instructional television, a fair number on film, but relatively few on radio). In most cases, methodological difficulties have been experienced. If we are going to compare televised instruction with traditional face-to-face teaching, how do we arrange to make the comparison? How can we make sure that the subject groups (the television and the control group) are not contaminated (by casual exposure to media, for example, or by variations in teaching quality)?

Instructional television

Table 9.11 summarises 421 comparisons between television-based teaching and traditional teaching; it was drawn up in 1967 by Chu and Schramm. It confirms that students learn well from television, with younger children faring better on the whole. Table 9.12 demonstrates further that the effectiveness of ITV is spread across most subject areas.

Table 9.11   Results of 421 comparisons between ETV and traditional instruction

Level	Number of cases of		
	No significant difference	ITV more effective	TI more effective
Elementary	50	10	4
Secondary	82	24	16
College	152	22	28
Adult	24	7	2
	308	63	50

Table 9.12   Relative effectiveness of ETV and TI by subject matter

Subject	Number of comparisons	Percentage of comparisons in which ITV did as well or better than TI
Mathematics	56	89.2
Science	100	86.0
Social studies	77	89.6
Humanities	45	95.5
Languages	77	88.3
Skills	26	96.1
Miscellaneous	40	75.0

One of the most intensive studies of instructional television in the USA has been of the closed-circuit system in Hagerstown, Maryland, which began operations in 1956. This service has offered very widespread programming, and some of the gains of children in Hagerstown schools over students in other rural schools, over a 4-year period, are summarised in Table 9.13.

But while these figures illustrate well enough that children can learn from television (and this point can now be taken for granted), they do not say that television is radically better than any other medium. The concensus seems to be that, while all children *can* learn from any medium, they do not necessarily *do* so − this will depend upon a number of other conditions (motivation, quality of teaching, etc.). Nor does it say that the mass media of television and radio are necessarily better than smaller audio-visual media; it is a question, as always, of relating medium to function.

Programme research

Not surprisingly, the best results come from the most intelligently planned series. Figure 9.8 shows pre-test and total scores on tests administered after viewings of 'Sesame Street' (the well-known American series for pre-school age groups, produced by the Children's Television Workshop in New York). Here significant learning gains were recorded, which should certainly be expected from a series which deployed so many resources, and was so carefully planned and produced.

Research into 'Sesame Street', by the Educational Testing Service of Princeton, also showed that those children, regardless of age, who watched the most, learned the most (see Fig. 9.9). It demonstrates that the programmes were as effective for black disadvantaged children in the age group (3 to 5) as for white disadvantaged children, that 3-year-old viewers in the audience gained more (if they were among the more frequent viewers) than older children who watched less frequently, ending with a higher test score, and that the programme's format (which set out to compete with fast-moving regular television presentations) did not produce any adverse

Table 9.13 Learning through television in Hagerstown

Grade 8	Hagerstown schools						Rural schools					
	Sept. 1957		May 1958		May 1961		Sept. 1957		May 1958		May 1961	
	Grade equivalent	Percentile	Grade equivalent	Percentile	Grade equivalent	Percentile	Grade equivalent	Percentile	Grade equivalent	Percentile	Grade equivalent	Percentile
Vocabulary	7.59	(23)	8.13	(23)	8.44	(35)	7.06	(10)	7.30	(8)	7.89	(16)
Reading comprehension	7.69	(19)	8.26	(18)	8.46	(24)	7.29	(10)	7.63	(8)	8.08	(14)
Spelling	7.56	(15)	8.18	(22)	8.61	(33)	7.17	(10)	8.05	(15)	8.14	(20)
Capitalisation	8.10	(48)	8.65	(50)	9.18	(72)	7.37	(16)	7.94	(19)	8.38	(37)
Punctuation	7.44	(21)	7.98	(29)	8.60	(55)	6.93	(10)	7.63	(19)	7.82	(24)
Usage	7.37	(17)	7.89	(17)	8.27	(29)	6.67	(7)	7.47	(10)	7.65	(13)
Map reading	7.95	(31)	8.52	(24)	8.86	(44)	7.65	(17)	7.99	(8)	8.49	(23)
Reading graphs and tables	7.79	(28)	8.52	(27)	8.76	(29)	7.51	(16)	7.93	(16)	8.20	(22)
Knowledge and use of reference material	7.97	(39)	8.66	(43)	8.93	(57)	7.55	(18)	8.09	(16)	8.47	(31)

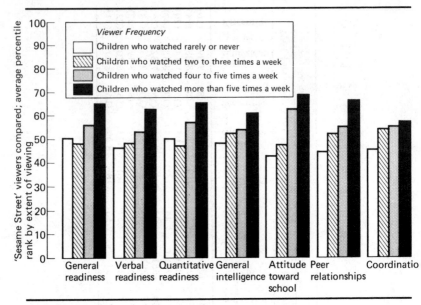

Fig. 9.8   The effects of 'Sesame Street'.

reactions to conventional instruction once the viewers in the audience entered school.

A more recent example comes from the sequel to 'Sesame Street'.

The 'Electric Company' set out to use television to assist in teaching reading skills to young children. Tests administered to school children in first to fourth grades showed significant gains among viewing pupils, as opposed to those who did not see the series; these included children in the bottom range of their classes and extended across a number of curriculum areas featured in the programmes (not only reading). The results showed the programme to be exactly what it set out to be: an effective instructional supplement for children beginning to experience reading difficulty. It won a favourable reaction from teachers, was watched by approximately 2,000,000 pupils (one out of every four second and third graders in large American cities) and penetrated to every region and type of community in the country, with special benefits for pupils from low socio-economic groups and those who had greater than average difficulties with reading. The speed of acceptance of the series was also remarkable, thanks to considerable publicity; within 2 months of its inception in October 1971, it was being used by 23 per cent of all the elementary schools in America.

What makes a good programme?

It is easy enough to show that television is effective, if used in competent hands, but it is much less easy to analyse what makes for a good programme. In general terms, we can say that a successful programme is the

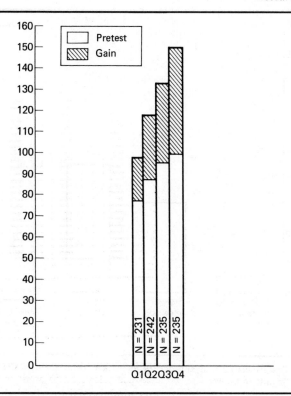

Fig. 9.9   Learning from 'Sesame Street'.

result of careful planning, combined with imaginative and sensitive production. But can we say anything more precise about the elements which make up that programme? Unfortunately, most research findings in this area tend to corroborate the obvious. They show, for example, that picture quality is important, but not *that* important (the main consideration is one of visibility, not meeting technical specifications); that screen size is not a major factor, provided the material displayed can be easily seen (and read, if it includes print); that musical backgrounds, unless relevant, do not contribute to learning; that the speed of information, and of speech delivery, should be on the low rather than the high side (say 150 words a minute); that simplicity and clarity of organisation and presentation are important; that repetition aids understanding, and that 'rest intervals' are useful.

One conclusion of research which should be emphasised is the importance of student participation, in whatever way this can be organised (drills, practice sessions, problem solving elements, etc.). This is illustrated by a unique study in Denver, USA, of a Spanish teaching television language series, which was used together with (and compared with) other

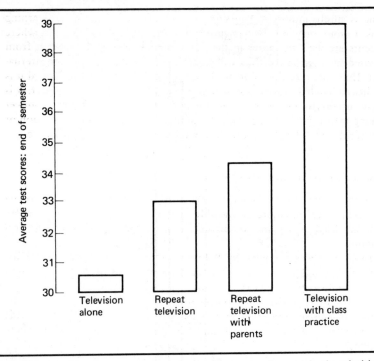

Fig. 9.10   The effects of four approaches to learner involvement in the television teaching of Spanish in Denver.

learning experiences. The study was devoted to repetition and follow up: in the comparison, one group viewed the television programmes once only; a second group viewed them twice, with the second viewing coming immediately after the first; the third group had a second viewing at home, if possible in the company of their parents; and the final group followed their original viewing with a period of oral practice, under the direction of the classroom teacher. This experiment emphasised the overriding importance of classroom follow-up and drills, which were more important than repetition (though repetition clearly helped). The results are shown in Fig. 9.10.

A point of special interest also concerns colour as opposed to monochrome television. There seems to be no special advantage in colour, unless it is colour that is to be learned (e.g. in parts of medicine or chemistry), or unless it affords the best available means of coding some important discriminations.

There is a difference, however, between learning and persuasion, and between learning and liking. Eye contact (where the presenter looks directly at camera, and hence at the viewing audience) seems not to be an important factor in learning, but it may well have an importance in motivating or persuading audiences to listen or accept. And the factor of

iking is surely important, outside of a specific investigation of learning
gains. Colour may not be a significant addition in television, but where
students are used to colour in their own homes, they will expect it from
televised instruction (or they will regard the latter as a second-rate alterna-
ive). Humour, too, does not produce measurable gains, yet provided it is
not heavy handed, but stems naturally from the script and presenter, it is
surely useful to be relaxed and human? It follows that the producer
looking at research findings must be careful to add to his interpretation of
their results what he also knows instinctively, from his own experience.

Research into media systems

While there may not be much research at present into programme formats
and techniques, far more is available on media systems, especially where
these are used as a main component in a major educational reform programme.

Table 9.14 was compiled by Wilbur Schramm for his book *Big Media—
Little Media*; it picks out some of the main characteristics of three important schemes — (*a*) American Samoa; (*b*) El Salvador and (*c*) the Ivory
Coast. There are obvious differences in philosophy and attitudes to media
as part of the reform programme (and indeed in the orientation of the
reform itself). But what results have been seen so far from each of these
systems?

(*a*)   In *American Samoa*, a significant improvement was noted in one of
the system's objectives — the raising of the standard of *oral* English. The
fourth, fifth and sixth grades of non-television schools in a controlled
experiment were inferior, on testing, to the third grade of a village school
which had the benefit of television; this applied to speaking and understanding English. Yet the improvement did not spill over into reading
skills, or into other curriculum areas. There is evidence that Samoan
children do better in questions based on rote learning than in those
requiring abstract reasoning or thinking. This is a phenomenon which they
share with minority 'disadvantaged' groups on the American mainland, and
it has been suggested that one of the main reasons is that, to all intents and
purposes, the Samoan school is conducted in a foreign language (since the
medium of instruction is English, which is not the native tongue and is not
met with at home). It seems that in this kind of situation, television does
not, at present, offer a solution. But still, in the one field where all schools
are competing on equal terms (the learning of English as a foreign
language), television does much more than hold its own.

(*b*)   In *El Salvador* a general ability test, independently administered,
revealed that students who studied with the benefit of ITV and other
elements of the educational reform programme gained from 15 to 25 per
cent more than their peers, who were exposed only to the traditional

Table 9.14   Main characteristics of three educational television systems

	American Samoa	El Salvador	Ivory Coast
Major objectives	Swift improvement and expansion in schools, make curriculum fit Samoan life, concentrate on mastery of English	Greatly expand enrolment in Plan Basico without loss of quality, introduce new curriculum, then turn to other parts of system	Expand enrolment in primary school, train teachers to carry load of new responsibility
Outside support	Assistance through US territorial budget	Assistance (loans, grants plus technical assistance) from USAID, IBRD, UNICEF, Unesco and others	Assistance (grants plus technical assistance from France, IBRD, Canada, UNDF, Unesco
Preparation time	About 3 years	About 9 years general, 2 years specific planning	About 4 years
Use of TV	Core teaching	Core teaching	Core teaching
Support of TV	Classroom materials, feedback, in-service training, curriculum revision	Same	Same
Pace	Twelve grades in 2 years; reached every child in American Samoa in 4 years	One grade at a time; doubled enrolment in Plan Basico in 4 years	One grade at a time; 20,000 pupils first year, 60,000 second year
Classroom teachers	Qualified teachers	Qualified teachers	Qualified teachers
Teacher training	Emphasised in-service training	Full year of retraining for each teacher	Extensive in-service training
Organisation	Integral part of Samoa Department of Education; under US educators and broadcasters at first, administration now Samoan	Integral part of Ministry of Education; used advisers, but project always in Salvadorean hands	Integral part of Ministry of Education; large number of foreign experts
Television facilities	Six open-circuit VHF channels, two transmitter towers on mountain, four studios, ten VTRs	Rented time on air for 4 years, and managed with one studio for 3 years; now has two transmitters of its own and building with three studios	Has building with two TV studios, one radio; national TV network provides time

Table 9.14 – *continued*

	American Samoa	El Salvador	Ivory Coast
Production	6,000 programmes a year (2,000 hours) until 1971; later about 2,200; all subjects in 12-year curriculum, plus pre-school and adult services	13 programmes per grade per week; about 500 per year in five subjects – between 4 and 5 hours a week	7 to 8.5 hours a week; French, maths, basal education

system. This reflected improved scores in mathematics, social studies and natural science and the relative superiority of the ITV students was most marked at the seventh grade. Student attitudes to television remained reasonably favourable to televised instruction throughout the 4 years when attitudes were surveyed, with some decline noticeable as they moved from the seventh through to the ninth grade; slower learners and disadvantaged pupils were in general more attracted to the medium. Teacher attitudes to the television system declined gradually over the same period.

Because ITV was introduced into El Salvador as part of a package of educational reforms, it was often impossible to separate out the specific impact of television, if indeed there was one. For example, the learning advantage of Reform classrooms with ITV over traditional classrooms was roughly equivalent to their advantage over classrooms without ITV. Does this mean that if the Reform programmes had not included television, they would not have produced learning gains significantly greater than those of the traditional system? Or conversely, would ITV alone have led to increased learning? Its evaluators conclude, in general, that specific aspects of the Reform were not independently influential; it was their mutual support and cross-fertilisation within a total system which finally mattered. They also conclude that the impact of ITV in forcing curriculum development at a pace dictated by deadlines imposed by the medium was an important factor. Television within the Reform process, they observed, was significant in helping students to improve general intellectual skills; the most impressive gains in the whole exercise were in general ability rather than subject specific tests. But they also concluded that an evaluation of the *quality* of the television offered was not really made; and they observed that the lack of imaginative, stimulating programming most likely accounted for the gradual decline in ITV's popularity among students and teachers alike in the later years of the Reform.

(c)   In the *Ivory Coast*, where an evaluation system was introduced from the outset, early results showed a new proficiency for ITV pupils in modern mathematics and skills of expression, and a decline in traditional areas of recitation, writing, reading, arithmetic. The evaluation of this system is, however, a long-term undertaking, beginning with an exhaustive study of pupils and learners, which includes tests of cognitive and

psychomotor skills and teacher—pupil interaction analysis; the intention
to introduce and extend a new kind of 'éducation de base', to develo
greater individuality in approaches to teaching and learning.

As previously in our discussion of costs, all the systems cited above de
with television, because it is only through television (of the mass media
that anyone has ever tried to bring about major educational reform. Th
researchers were not in a position to say whether television was the onl
way to embark on such a programme, but they would certainly claim tha
it proved a useful catalyst. It made financial support from the outsid
world easier to secure; it involved people fully and engagingly, and ofte
secured a degree of commitment and whole-hearted participation whicl
would be difficult to secure in any other way. Furthermore, it imposed it
own strict timetable and imparted a sense of urgency to a process which i
not normally associated with deadlines.

The studies of these projects showed other things equally clearly. The
showed that a commitment to a mass medium such as television must b
considerable (with political as well as technical and financial support)
They illustrated that teacher and pupil resistance will be encountered, an
that once the novelty of the medium has worn off, a danger point i
reached. This is one reason why local involvement from the very beginnin
is important. A project such as that in Senegal, founded upon Unesc
assistance, diminished once the assistance was withdrawn; this is the fat
of many pilot projects. On the other hand, the media system in Singapor
never had the benefit of financial assistance from outside, even in its firs
years — and though this produced early difficulties, in the long run it ha
had its benefits. There must be a decision from the outset to consider th
future and to include an adequate budget for the expansion programme (a
happened in El Salvador and in the Ivory Coast).

These observations are based on large-scale media systems. But simila
conclusions are reached by researchers studying the impact of media in
educational systems where they are used as a means of partial, qualitative
improvement. This is evidenced by studies carried out in Japan, India,
Singapore, Thailand, Colombia and Africa.

Media as extensions of the educational system

Media may also be used (as in open learning systems) to extend the opportunities for formal educational programmes outside the physical confines
of the school or higher education system. This seems to be an area in
which the media really do work, at many different levels. Comparable
learning gains are recorded when set against traditional instructional forms
the process is often cheaper; it is sometimes the only way of achieving a
particular end. There may be no other way open of retraining a teaching
force, offering a high school education to students at work, or a university
degree course to adults who have long bypassed formal educational
channels.

Perhaps this is because, instead of relying upon structures originally conceived for other purposes (e.g. the traditional school system), or improvising in areas where no support structures are available (e.g. in general adult and informal education), the media system must itself create a supporting structure which must include both teaching materials and learning environments.

There are many different examples and approaches in view. In Mexico, the 'Radioprimaria' expanded 3-year primary schools to 6 years without new buildings and with minimal additional teachers. In Chicago, the TV College offers complete 2-year junior college courses, and the possibility of transferring to a 4-year university course. In Bavaria, the Telekolleg offers courses preparatory to trade and technical studies, and basic secondary school electives to students who are working and cannot attend full-time education. In Japan, the NHK Gakuen covers a complete high school curriculum for students at work. In Sweden, 'TRU' provides a wide variety of courses, extending from pre-school to adult education.

In Australia, a radio correspondence school offers twelve grades of instruction to children in remote parts of the country (some of them supplemented by use of the 'Flying Doctor' radio, which permits direct contact between student and teacher).

Certain characteristics are shared between all of these options. Most are multi-media, combining correspondence courses and texts with radio and/or television. Most make special arrangements for personal contact, whether this be through summer schools, class meetings on campus, or through a tutor contact and marking system. The trend too, in many cases, is towards 'open-ness', both in learning systems, and in entrance. This is not surprising, as they have frequently been devised to cater for the student deprived of more traditional (and hence qualification-based) opportunities. Adequate data is available on student enrolment, audience composition, success and failure rates; two examples in Table 9.15 relate to the Bavarian Telekolleg and the Japanese NHK Gakuen (derived from research by H. S. Dordick and NHK respectively, compiled for Wilbur Schramm). They show success rates which are generally comparable with more traditional, full-time options. But information on learning and teaching effectiveness is harder to come by. However, in Chicago, comparisons made between TV students and students receiving the same courses face to face showed (in twenty-seven experimental comparisons) twelve cases where significant differences were recorded over a 3-year period, of which ten were in favour of the television group. In Mexico, studies showed at least no special differences between traditional and television classes at the secondary level, and a similar pattern emerged with radio, as used in the 'Radioprimaria' experiments. In India, at the university level, correspondence education achieved comparable results with normal university education; in Bavaria, students of the Telekolleg did marginally better than those taking an orthodox, classroom-based curriculum. The trend seems to be equally applicable to developed and developing countries, similar for both radio and television, and valid at any educational level. Perhaps the

Table 9.15 Two home learning systems compared

Telekolleg

	First class	Second class
Took exam at end of first 10-month term	41 per cent (of original enrollees)	36 per cent
Took exam at end of second 10-month term	31 per cent	30 per cent

NHK Gakuen

Of	Who entered in	After	This proportion had graduated (per cent)
11,721	1963	9 years	25.3
6,673	1964	8 years	30.5
5,779	1965	7 years	30.2
5,327	1966	6 years	27.5
6,188	1967	5 years	26.1
6,162	1968	4 years	20.5

most interesting data comes from the most advanced experiment of all – in the UK Open University.

Original predictions for this project were that only one student in five would graduate; some sceptics put it as low as 10 per cent. But by 1975 42.4 per cent of the students who had originally been accepted in 1971 had graduated, and it is envisaged that this figure will finally reach 50 per cent (since students can take their own time to complete a course, or can try again if they fail). This figure is lower than for conventional universities in the UK, but not very different from State universities with open admission in America, and it is much higher than for other part-time correspondence courses. It appears that the enormous difficulties of home study have been offset by the high motivation of students (and also by the leisurely attitude of the university, which allows students to pace themselves through the curriculum). It is also interesting to note that, of the students graduating in 1974, 21 per cent would not have been eligible for entry to a traditional educational institution, which is some justification of the original premise upon which the Open University was created.

As anticipated, the group which survived least well in practice was the skilled manual worker, though even these did not drop below 50 per cent of their starting group until the end of their third year of studies. Housewives did particularly well, with a survival rate of 64 per cent. Over the years, too, the proportion of those without formal educational qualifications who apply for admission to the university has risen, with those employed in manual or routine non-manual jobs now making up nearly a third of all applicants. Interestingly again, the enthusiasm of applicants has not diminished with the years, and applications for admission in 1975 were at their highest ever at 52,537.

In general, it appears that the Open University has achieved a good academic standard, both in terms of its courses and of its pass rates. It is also cheap when compared with existing universities (cost comparisons are difficult, because of the non-comparability of different situations, but one early assessment put the cost of educating an OU undergraduate at six times lower than an equivalent education in a conventional university; other estimates have appraised the OU financial advantage as 27 per cent at the most, but have argued that the real significance of such comparisons lies in applying a marginal cost concept, so relating the discussion to OU expansion). It is still far, however, from being 'open'. People with little education and those in manual occupations are still heavily under-represented, and once within the system, find greater difficulty than others in progressing. It has already been suggested that the OU in its present form may not be the best method for many of these people.

Adult and informal education

There are relatively few research experiences in the area of non-formal and adult education. This is partly because the research has simply not been done, partly because of difficulty in setting up controlled experiments for informal situations, where contamination is almost inevitable.

What is available often relates to specifics, in an environment where the exact contribution of media cannot be estimated; i.e. its role cannot be divorced from other factors in adult society. So, for example, it is known that in an experiment in Senegal, which involved setting up discussion groups to meet and discuss adult broadcasts, there were information gains by the viewing groups, on the basis of interviews conducted before and after the broadcasts. Before the broadcasts, only 41 per cent of a sample group knew that malaria was caused by a mosquito bite; afterwards, the percentage had risen to 76 per cent. In the first survey no one in the sample knew that quinine and its derivatives were used as a malarial treatment; afterwards 71 per cent had learned this fact.

Similar kinds of information have been recorded in a variety of family planning studies. In Korea and Taiwan, radio was listed as the most important source of information about the family planning programme. In India, in the Meerut district, after a campaign using printed materials, cinema slides and a newsletter, the proportion of urban men and women knowing about the loop increased from 43 to 61, and of rural respondents from 13 to 23. A mass media campaign using radio spot announcements in an Iranian province raised the average number of pill acceptors from 425 to 575 per month.

One series of development campaigns in Africa was (and is still being) mounted in Tanzania. Characteristically, radio broadcasts, printed materials and a network of study groups were employed in intensive, short-term campaigns; the last example was of 12 weeks' duration. Each took a particular orientation (e.g. 'Man in Health' or 'Food is Life'), aiming to promote social awareness of a particular problem, which should lead to action and can also be integrated with educational and literac efforts.

The campaign on 'Man is Health' involved some 2 million peopl planning began 18 months before the first programme went on the air. depended heavily upon a considerable adult education network, whic commands some 2,000 coordinators and supervisors, responsible to som thousands of adult education centres operating from primary school base: A parallel network of health workers is also involved, and both sets wor together in the training of group leaders and in extension and follow-u activities. In fact, 75,000 discussion group leaders were trained in 3½-month period, through a snowball training scheme.

The national average attendance figure at discussion groups linked wit radio programmes was 63 per cent. Two aspects of the programme wer evaluated — information gained, and changes in observable househol health practices. In the survey, significant gains were noted in informatio gain as between the discussion groups and control groups; more impo tantly, in a survey of eight villages before and after the campaign, a seri of eleven observable health practices was measured on a 0—12 point inde and overall a relative increase of 60 per cent was found (a rise of from 3. to 4.8 positive health practices). There were also reports of increase attendance at rural dispensaries, which indicated some continuity o incentive.

Interpersonal factors

These results confirm common-sensical observations, and if they had bee otherwise there would be little point in continuing to use mass media i development campaigns. It is clear from the work carried out that a com bination of media produces better results than single media, and that learn ing is greater where subject matter touches the lives of those exposed t media messages. Acceptance also seems to be greater in younger than olde people.

The most important discoveries in the adult and informal sector, how ever, have related to the intermingling of media with interpersonal com munication. No media message acts entirely on its own; it is passed on filtered, interpreted by discussion and debate. In one survey carried out i Taiwan, it was found that visiting 20 per cent of the homes in a distric was more cost-effective than visiting 30 per cent or 50 per cent, because o the diffusion factor, and in a Pakistan district, during a particular famil planning campaign, 76 per cent of all acceptors during the first 30 month of the campaign came from outside the campaign area (i.e. people who ha heard about the clinics by word of mouth).

Many of the experiments have therefore concentrated upon trying t organise and control the process of diffusion through interpersona channels, especially by creating special listening or viewing, discussion o study groups. A standard pattern for these groups is that they meet to hea or see a broadcast, under the direction of a group leader, who may be trained extension worker, but is just as likely to be a local citizen, working in the target area of the broadcast and having some status and prestige in the community — a farmer, for example, for agricultural broadcasts.

Groups are formed for different reasons. Some are study groups, set up to pursue academic study programmes (e.g. in literacy work). Some are community development groups, set up to promote certain social actions or practical innovatory work. Some are purely discussion groups, based on the premise that public debate will lead to heightened awareness of public problems and a greater motivation towards social action.

An early experiment in Poona, India, studied agricultural listening groups, set up to hear 'Farm Forum' programmes (on the model of the wartime Canadian series). In an intensive research programme, forum villages were compared with non-forum villages, and the result showed significant learning gains for the former and even better gains in non-forum villages if these had access to the radio programmes. The main table (derived from Paul Neurath, as main researcher) is set out in Table 9.16, showing, interestingly, that illiterates gained more than literates.

Table 9.16 Poona learning test results

	Literate members		Illiterate members	
	Forum	Non-forum	Forum	Non-forum
Pretest	7.1	5.3	3.1	2.1
Post-test	12.2	6.5	9.4	3.1

Table 9.17 gives the results of a similar experiment in Ghana, some years later (researched by H. C. Abell for Unesco). It shows some of the practical initiatives taken up after the broadcasts (which were not purely concerned with farming), as evidenced in villages which organised one forum, villages which organised two forums, and villages which either had radio and no forum, or were without the benefit of either. It is clear from these tables that not only did radio help to bring about an orientation towards change, but that when it was mediated through a discussion group, the orientation was significantly more marked.

A further study, again in India, tried to measure the effect of group discussion and decision making in changing attitudes, beliefs and behavioural intentions towards adopting an innovation. In all three of these areas, significant differences were found in listening groups which also included group discussion as a feature. This study (by N. C. Jain) went further, to see if a public commitment by a member of the group to the particular innovation under review was also a significant factor. Again, significant differences were found in changing beliefs and behavioural intentions once such a commitment was made. The importance of this kind of research is that it points the way to improved group organisation.

There is no guarantee, however, that any of the results recorded will continue to prove effective, after the early novelty of group arrangements

Table 9.17   Some results of rural radio forums in Ghana

Question	Percentages by type of village			
	Type A (one forum) N = 89	Type B (two forums) N = 82	Type C (radio, no forum) N = 84	Type D (no radio, no forum) N = 83
Action taken to increase production	60	53	42	35
Production cooperatives planned or formed?	17	13	7	2
Action to improve marketing of crops?	25	23	21	9
Marketing through a group or a cooperative?	19	19	18	7
Action to improve harvesting, storing, transporting crops?	27	24	8	13
Joined a cooperative within 6 months	16	19	5	6
Able to name cooperative started somewhere within 6 months?	55	43	35	28
Correct ages for introducing different protein sources to baby's diet?	51	46	41	36
Now saving on a personal basis?	70	60	57	50
Emphasised young people's needs for general education?	11	11	25	39
Emphasised need of practical training?	87	87	72	61

and of media exposure has worn off, such as was reported in India, where the farm forums were finally discontinued. There is also no guarantee that the results of careful research at a pilot level will be incorporated into subsequent designs, again as happened in India, where the principles of the original research in Poona were not fully carried over into the expansion phase.

Study groups, studying for formal academic programmes, are a somewhat different matter, since some measure of their success is available in examination or test rates. The significance of a carefully planned open learning system has already been recorded in the account of the British Open University. In the developing world, the study group may well be a part of a different kind of academic programme, directed more towards the improvement of literacy standards, such as in Italy's Telescuola. A major initiative in this direction was in Colombia, in the development of Radio Sutatenza. Beginning as the personal concern of a village curate, this has grown into Colombia's largest radio network, serving upwards of 20,000 radio schools and several hundreds of thousands of students, through the organisation 'Acción Cultural Popular'.

Unfortunately, this very large scale enterprise has never been properly evaluated, even though it broadcasts 19 hours a day, feeds much of its output to three other regional stations, publishes the most widely read newspaper in the country, and has a full-time staff of 200 in Bogota, with 130 more in its publishing office, 300 field workers and some 20,000 unpaid auxiliaries who work in the radio schools. The only data on effectiveness is in the diffusion of the programme itself. The number of radio schools has increased from 300 in 1950 to 20,000 in 1970; the number of students stabilised at some 167,000; the newspaper has a paid circulation of 70,000 a week, and a single publication sold 100,000 copies in a single year. Pass rates in literacy examinations are recorded as in the region of 75 per cent, and on attitude scales of modernity, innovativeness and integration into rural society, radio students scored higher than non-students. This last item is reflected in Table 9.18 (derived from S. A. Musto).

Table 9.18 Reported importance of ACPO and other influences in the adoption of innovations

Influencing factors	Students of ACPO (%)	Non-student listeners (%)	Others (%)
ACPO	54.0	25.5	15.0
Other development organisations	9.0	13.5	20.0
Imitation (of neighbours, etc.)	33.0	53.5	58.7
Other influences cited	4.0	7.5	6.3

It is not surprising that the data on media in adult spheres is more sparse, and less hard, than in the school sector. Until recently it has been a Cinderella of educational development, and the research worker finds himself in a difficult position, where evaluation is difficult to conduct with any degree of rigour, and other information is hard to come by. But in general, the importance of media, especially radio and low-cost media, has been amply demonstrated, particularly when this is harnessed to a properly planned extension network.

Conclusion

There are obvious gaps in this research. Most of it is at the in-school level, and even there, the bulk of the work done is concentrated upon television. Moreover, the main thrust of evaluation has been to compare television with classroom based teaching, and to measure learning gains using general ability tests. There is relatively little work on programme structuring and production, far too little on radio and small-format media, and the early research on media deployed within informal settings has not been substantively followed through.

Yet there should at least be, in this picture, an adequate validation of the use of media in education, sufficient to satisfy the planner and administrator that he is not embarking entirely upon uncharted waters.

Chapter 10

Media identification

In this chapter, we review the operations of the media selection process. The account is again summary, for two reasons. Firstly, there is a good deal of literature in existence (some of it included in the Bibliography, p. 363), and secondly, it is the opinion of the author that, particularly where complex media systems are considered, the process is a good deal less disciplined than many educational technologists would like to think. There are certain general characteristics of mass media, which have already been examined and which need to be observed in media planning. There are also a number of useful decision-making models, which can help media producers and users arrive at an objective choice. But all of this amounts to little more than a categorisation of experience; it cannot, by its nature (since media are inseparable from their human environment) be the result of rigorous analyses. There are few situations where we can say with any confidence, or even any hope of concensus, that there is a 'right' or a 'wrong' medium to use. As Schramm observed, 'Most school tasks can be performed by a number of different media, and in most cases quite satisfactorily by a number of media. In fact, the conclusion of many researchers is that the chief variance in instructional media effect is *within* rather than *between* media' — that is, *how* the media are used, rather than *what* media are used, makes the difference.

The difficulty is compounded in the case of production decisions. For the classroom teacher, his selection of media is based upon the range of resources open to him, and since he is in control of his teaching programme, he can modify or improvise as he goes along. The selection of media at the production level carries much higher risks, in the sense that a major investment is being made by the producing organisation, which will often demand the rejection of one medium in favour of another, with little or no possibility of the decision being reversed for a considerable time. Moreover, production decisions — especially in multi-media or open learning systems — are made by groups of people, who have different priorities, different interpretations of resource data, so that the concensus on which decisions are based stems mostly from a process of group interaction and dynamics.

In the end, therefore, it is likely that media selection will reflect subjective measures of agreement and personal compromises. This being said, it is no bad thing to review some of the theoretical processes by which models of decision making have been arrived at, and to use these as an analytical framework.

Decisions are, of course, arrived at at various levels. There are decisions, first of all, about the whole nature of the system (which media are to be emphasised, which rejected). There are decisions, secondly, about the context in which media are to be used — how they fit into an overall teaching programme. And thirdly, there are decisions about which media will suit particular learning tasks, amounting to the creation of sub-systems within the total media framework.

So far, we have been working from the macro level downward — first in isolating the character of planning and systems analysis, and then in describing media characteristics. Here, we shall reverse the process, and begin with the basic problem of allocating media to specific learning tasks, before building up to overall assumptions about media structures.

We can begin, therefore, by looking at some of the theoretical issues attached to the conditions of learning. We shall have to determine, in relation to media, the *types* of learning which comprise the instructional tasks in view, the *content* of this learning, and the *situation* in which learning takes place.

Types of learning

There are many taxonomies of learning, particularly in the area of early learning by children, or the acquisition of simple motor skills. These models have been described as inelegant and unfinished, and they are set mostly at a rather basic level, but in crude terms they help to discriminate between different learning tasks and the different potential of media (all channels, not only mass forms) in contributing to their fulfilment. So, psychologists have distinguished between such tasks as conditioning (learning to respond to a signal or stimulus), rote learning (memorisation), probability learning (choosing a correct alternative from a set of words or objects), the learning of concepts, motor skills, and problem solving.

Figure 10.1 is a classic presentation by W. H. Allen of the suitability of media to different learning tasks. These have been grouped as the learning of facts; making visual identifications; learning principles; learning procedures (a model of how to learn to perform a particular task, or tasks in general); motor functions, and — in a rather different category — the motivation of learning towards a particular set of attitudes or opinions.

The figure attempts a general estimate of media suitability for each of these learning situations. As Schramm has emphasised, it is (*a*) rather a vague indication, especially in its categories of suitability ('low—high—medium'); (*b*) it is debatable on certain points (such as the rating of still pictures as 'low' in the creation of attitudes — surely advertisers would not agree?); and (*c*) it is based on experience, rather than on specific research. It is a kind of graphic summary of rule-of-thumb experience.

A further area of learning theory which affects media is that of the *sequence* of learning, whether this is teacher or learner directed. So learning has been categorised in elements of gaining and controlling attention;

Instructional Media Type	Learning factual information	Learning visual identifications	Learning principles, concepts and rules	Learning procedures	Performing skilled perceptual-motor acts	Developing desirable attitudes, opinions and motivations
Still pictures	Medium	HIGH	Medium	Medium	low	low
Motion pictures	Medium	HIGH	HIGH	HIGH	Medium	Medium
Television	Medium	Medium	HIGH	Medium	low	Medium
3-D objects	low	HIGH	low	low	low	low
Audio recordings	Medium	low	low	Medium	low	Medium
Programmed instruction	Medium	Medium	Medium	HIGH	low	Medium
Demonstration	low	Medium	low	HIGH	Medium	Medium
Printed text books	Medium	low	Medium	Medium	low	Medium
Oral presentation	Medium	low	Medium	Medium	low	Medium

Fig. 10.1   Chart of instructional media in relationship to learning objectives.

stimulating recall; guiding learning; providing feedback opportunities; assisting long term memory; assessing learning outcomes. Other behavioural descriptions distinguish between stages of motivation, providing cues for the learner, eliciting responses from him and reinforcing his efforts with some kind of reward. These distinctions affect mostly the organisation of individual materials, and especially the relationship of these materials to other stimuli (e.g. their use by the teacher, or within programmed instruction). They condition, for example, the way in which a television programme is organised: the way in which it first seeks to attract interest; the speed at which material is introduced; the ways in which questions are posed, or in which the learner's satisfaction is secured. But they also relate to broader considerations of media. Radio and television are good for motivation, for the presentation of stimuli, but less so for eliciting and assessing responses, or indeed for anything interactive.

Content

Another approach is through the classification of subject matter, primarily

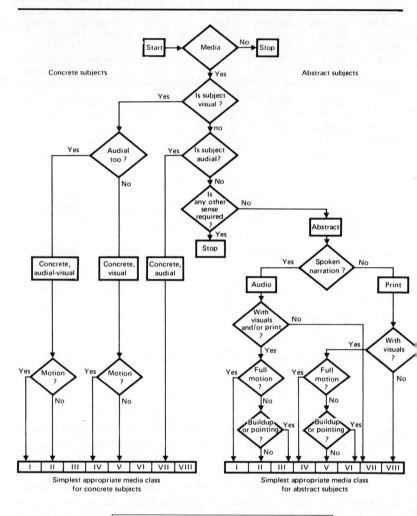

Fig. 10.2   Decision points in selecting appropriate media for a given instructional need.

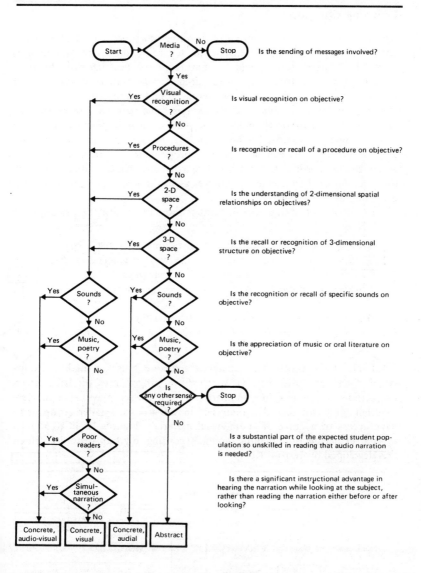

Fig. 10.3 Decision points for distinguishing between concrete and abstract subject matter.

into concrete and abstract forms. Figures 10.2 and 10.3 outline a procedure for relating content to media, developed by Rudy Bretz (in his work for the US Air Force). The model is in two stages — first, a step-by-step programme which distinguishes between concrete and abstract matter, and second, relating this distinction to media choice.

Learning situation

Another factor is the context of learning, the learning *methodology*. Learning may, for example, be achieved, according to the current emphasis of teaching methodology, and the nature of the learning task, by such diverse means as free play, structured (programmed) discovery and enquiry, creative and imaginative work, rote learning, the imitation of teaching models or problem-solving exercises and structured discussion. In each of these situations, media can play a positive role. A television programme can present a model to imitate, or raw material to discuss and analyse. Media tools can be used in a programmed sequence of enquiry, where the learner is directed towards particular visual or audio sources, or they can be used to harness creativity, as in the making of radio and TV programmes by students.

In all cases, learning environment is most important. For example, it can include:

(a) *Groups larger than the class* (lecture sessions; team teaching).

(b) *Working in class* (teacher/class — one way; teacher/class dialogue — two ways; teacher/class discussion — several ways)

(c) *Working in groups* (groups on the same, or on different, work programmes)

(d) *Working in pairs* (teacher/student; student/student)

(e) *Working individually* (pupil directed — free; teacher directed; programmed).

Each of these situations demands a different use of media. Groups larger than the class may view television programmes on large-screen projections or on multiple monitor screens; classes may listen or view together, or (with recorded material) in sub-groups; smaller groups may have access to a range of audio-visual materials. Figures 10.4, 10.5, 10.6 offer a further decision-making model, according to group structure, which was developed by Jerrold Kemp.

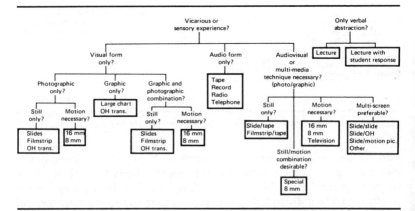

Fig. 10.4   Presentation to regular size class and to large groups.

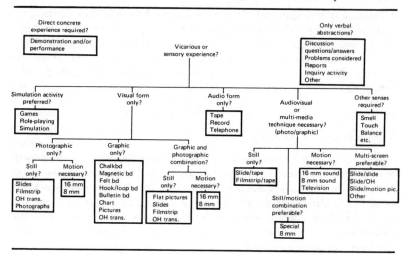

Fig. 10.5   Small group interaction.

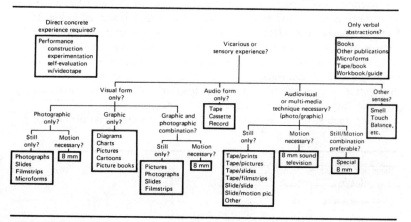

Fig. 10.6   Independent study for independent students.

How far are models useful?

These models are offered with a proviso. They are simple constructions, based on taxonomies of teaching and learning processes. They can be used as guidelines, especially for the novice, but we must not be carried away by their beauty or rectitude. There is a danger in most tools of analysis — whether they are for systems design, learning theory or model building — that we will build absolutely on their premises, when in practice they clearly cannot cover all the factors involved in our choice.

The models supplied so far are also theoretical; they deal with optimal learning conditions, but pay no attention to logistics. Our basic equation was one of setting economic advantage against the teaching proficiency of mass media, and for this other considerations have to be included. We have already discussed (in Chapter 9) some basic factors of media availability, manpower resources, maintenance and reliability of equipment, as well as the overriding factor of cost. These may be plotted on a 'gameboard', comparing vectors of quantitative and qualitative efficiency.

A gameboard for costing

Figures 10.7 to 10.12 provide an example of this approach, as developed by two American researchers, J. K. Lonigro, Jr. and A. J. Eschenbrenner, Jr.

Figure 10.7 gives a general ratio of costs (on a 'low—medium—high' scale) for audio-visual media, assuming reasonable levels of audience return. (It is, in other words, a reflection of unit costs, not of absolute production costs. If a different set of assumptions is used, the scale will have to be adjusted accordingly.)

Figure 10.8 then draws up a gameboard for plotting the cost/proficiency ratio. Using the scale already suggested in Fig. 10.7, we arrive at an optimum area for media consideration, which is shaded in Fig. 10.9. But, as special considerations may apply to some instructional tasks (where high proficiency is obtained at medium to high cost), this is also reflected, in Fig. 10.6, as an area for further consideration. (This is likely to be an area of innovation, where the application of new technologies may, after tests produce an eventual lowering of costs, or where a high cost may be justified because of special aptness.)

The gameboard can, naturally, be varied to accommodate other vectors.

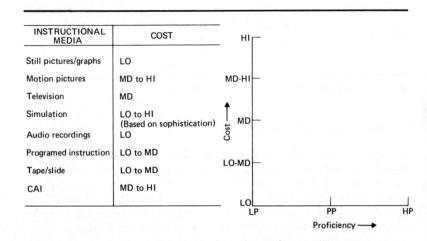

Fig. 10.7 Production cost of instructional media.

Fig. 10.8 Gameboard for media selection.

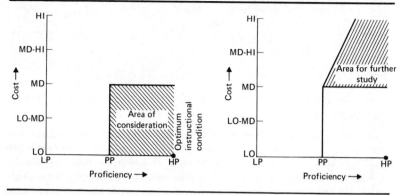

Fig. 10.9   Optimum instructional condition and area of consideration for media.

Fig. 10.10   Area for further study.

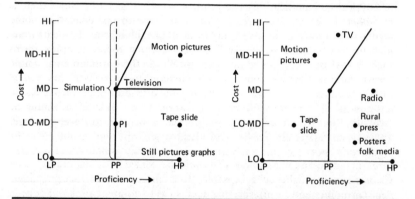

Fig. 10.11   Learning multiple discrimination.

Fig. 10.12   Reaching rural audiences.

But in all cases we must know the objective of the comparison which we are making. At a micro level, Fig. 10.11 uses the board to analyse the recognition of a trigonometric function on an oscilloscope (learning multiple discrimination). The authors conclude:

Initially, we plot proficiency versus cost for each medium; not surprisingly, still pictures and graphs fall at the optimum point. They are inexpensive to make and yield a high degree of proficiency for this type of learning. Slide tape presentations also produce a high degree of proficiency, but a greater expense. Additionally, programmed instruction, television and low to moderate cost simulations fall within the area of consideration. Some media, such as audio recordings, though quite inexpensive, will not allow us to meet previously stated proficiency criterion.

Motion pictures fall in the 'area of further study' where proficiency is high and cost moderate to high. Based on a knowledge of situational variables, one can complete a study or make a decision regarding the desirability of using motion pictures to teach visual identification skills. Recognition of a sine wave on an oscilloscope can be taught with still pictures and graphs; however, teaching adjustment of its amplitude may be most efficiently accomplished using motion pictures. If motion pictures cannot be produced, one would have to utilise sequential stills to show changes in amplitude.

Comparisons of this kind have to be made regularly when we come to programme development, and the technique is useful for helping course team decision making (see Part 3). But at the wider planning level of the original media system, a different kind of plotting would ensue. Suppose, for example, the objective were to reach out to rural adult audiences, in a developing country where radio was partially developed, television not at all, and where considerable difficulties were experienced in physical communication. The result is seen in Fig. 10.12. Since there is no coherent set of structures for adult and non-formal education, some media would have to be ruled out from the beginning (media demanding high literacy rates, a strong, well-trained teaching force, complex forms such as CAI or programmed instruction). Within the optimum area, simple forms (rural newspapers, posters, folk media) show up well, if they can be locally produced, or do not pose insuperable distribution problems. Radio appears as the most useful communication form. Television would be effective, but would be too complex and expensive to develop. Other audio-visual materials create considerable distribution problems. The argument is not that this analysis is correct; it may well not be so. A task force of audio-visual mobile units could be considered; community television viewing might be acceptable. It is an exercise in focusing down decision points and in interpreting data, so as to compare pros and cons in a graphical way.

Multi-media decisions

In the above, we see the genesis of the kinds of decision made in multi-media selection. The account may seem very theoretical — and in many ways this is so. The gameboard is an analytical tool which may work in optimum circumstances, but generally it is best seen as a metaphor of how to approach the problem, rather than as a prescriptive formula.

In most cases, far more considerations enter into the picture than are isolated here. Since media operate within human society, reflecting both individual personality and social organisation, the number of hidden variables is considerable and defies exact analysis. (In fact, the more systematic we make our model, the less exact it is likely to be.) Moreover, decisions on media systems — especially in the developing world — are not always made by professionals, nor are they made after a thorough and exhaustive review of possibilities. To provide a sense of perspective, an account is reproduced below of how two educational technologists, John Tiffin and Peter Combes, evolved an approach to media problems in a more realistic vein, certainly taking account of the theoretical models open to them, but acknowledging the vagaries of the decision-making process. Their account distinguishes between what they call 'master media', 'complementary and supplementary media', 'the media combination', and the 'ratio between media'. In other words, it looks at the media selection problem from the point of view of correspondence between media, rather than a precise identification according to learning functions. It also tries to show who makes which decisions, on what basis and in which sequence.

Master media

Master media may be selected for teaching or for learning. Master media commonly used for teaching are television, radio, correspondence and 'face-to-face' communication. Master media commonly used for learning are books, audio cassettes and discs, programmed instruction. The words 'master medium for teaching' indicate that the medium is used for taking a teaching initiative in a learning situation. It is being used actively to bring about a behaviour change in a specified group of learners.

By contrast, with a master medium for learning the initiative is taken by the learner. The medium is essentially passive. No direct relationship is assumed between the learner and the producer of the instructional material. A student reading a book may pick it up or put it down as he pleases. Dynamic feedback may be missing altogether, or confined to the modifications made to a book from edition to edition, or to the changes made to the programming in a language laboratory from time to time. The learner adjusts to the medium. He can do this because he can pace it as he wishes.

Complementary and supplementary media

In general, master media are versatile. However, each medium has its limitations, and to be capable of a broad spectrum of instruction it may need the 'assistance' of other media. These other media we shall call complementary media.

For example, where either broadcast television or radio are used as master media for teaching, two major deficiencies are quickly noticed — their transitory nature, and the fact that they do not permit the kind of dynamic feedback that a teacher has. To overcome these drawbacks, programmes are usually accompanied by some kind of printed text book or working notes to which the student may refer as frequently as he wishes.

The teacher in the classroom has traditionally used 'face-to-face' techniques as his master medium and blackboards and texts as complementary media ('. . . now read Chapter 6 and then we will talk about it'). In an attempt to bring more of the outside world into the classroom, he may use television (broadcast or cassette/disc), radio films, film strips and so on, as complementary media.

The media combination

The decision as to which media to use as a long term, established and institutionalised system to cover a broad range of curriculum requirements is one made at high policy level as the basis of an educational strategy. For example, a State might decide to use direct broadcast radio to village classrooms with semi-trained helpers assisted by distributed notes. Another might decide on newspaper presentation of adult vocational teaching (e.g. farming or health techniques) with occasional mass meetings. The combination of master media and the complementary media for an instructional system we shall call the media combination.

An effective media combination for an instructional system should be capable of a broad spectrum of instructional tasks. However, when the producer of educational materials is planning to achieve a specific learning outcome he may find that the given media combination is not adequate for the specific task.

Example
A producer is working for a secondary school instructional system. The media combination used by this system is that of television as master medium, classroom monitor and printed texts as complementary media. As part of a series on maps, he wishes pupils to gain actual experience with maps. So he arranges to supply each school with good quality maps of the local area for use in a practical exercise. In this case the maps are a supplementary medium.

In a technologically rich society, the introduction of supplementary media may be simple. In many countries, however, introducing supplementary media may involve too many problems (in the example above, difficulties and delays involved in the postal service) to be worth while.

Ratio between media

By ratio between media we mean the relative quantities of the media used. For example, a media combination might consist of 15 minutes of television, 10 pages of text and 1 hour of monitor. Ideally, the quantity of message carried by each medium should be determined purely by what the producers want each medium to do. However, the constraints on the use of the media often limit this. For example, the teacher might like to use more television, film and slides, but has not sufficient time for all of them. The educational radio producer might like to broadcast for 10 minutes to students who would then use their workbooks for 10 minutes, and repeat this pattern for an hour. However, he has only one 20-minute slot available. In such cases adjustments and compromises must be made. The result is the ratio between media.

Decision-making personnel

We shall classify people in the decision making process into four groups:

Group 1: policy makers
This includes anyone, from a head-master to a Minister of Education, who is responsible for making policy decisions about an instructional system.

Group 2: educational technologists
These are the people responsible for planning the use of instructional media and relating them to the given objectives.

Group 3: producers
These are responsible for making the material to be carried by the medium. They include radio or television scriptwriters or producers, text-book authors and instructional programmers. Teachers are also included when they are responsible for the development of the material, as in the 'face-to-face' situation.

Group 4: users
These are the people at the receiving end of an instructional message, whether students in an institution or the executive who is learning a language by a home study method.
  These groups are not always mutually exclusive. For example, a teacher is, in a sense, both the producer of instructional material and the educational technologist planning which medium shall be used for which message. The producer of a series of television programmes may also be his own educational technologist, making the decision as to which supplementary media are necessary for his series.

The decisions

We suggest that there are five levels of decision made directly or indirectly by these groups of people, and we relate them with the matrix shown in Fig. 10.13.

Which master medium?

This decision is the direct responsibility of the policy maker, though he may base his decision on the advice of an educational technologist. He should be influenced by such factors as:

- *Access of users to a given medium*
- *Attitude of users to a given medium*
- *Whether users can afford a given medium*

  Failure to consider these matters may mean that at a later date the user

Decision makers → / Decisions ↓	Policy makers	Educational technologists	Producers	Users
Which master medium?	Directly responsible	Advise		Indirect
Which media combination?	Directly responsible	Advise		Indirect
What is the ratio between the media?	Possibly	Possibly	Possibly	
Which part of the instructional message goes in which media?		Direct		
Which supplementary media are needed?	Indirect	Direct	Direct	
Which media to USE or whether to use a media combination				Direct

Fig. 10.13   Who makes which decision?

will — consciously or unconsciously — decide not to use a selected medium. Feedback on utilisation will show that the selection of the master medium was wrong and may necessitate the choice of a new master medium.

To make his decision, the policy maker should be aware of the financial resources available and the political context. The factors he must consider are wide ranging. However, he can simplify his task by a process of elimination as follows:

1. Does he need the master medium for learning or for teaching? This decision may halve the alternatives.
2. Are any of the possible choices clearly unsuitable in terms of the educational context or the learner? (for example, correspondence courses would hardly be suitable for a literacy campaign). A preliminary consideration of possible media combinations might be needed here.
3. For each remaining master medium, we suggest the application of the model shown in Fig. 10.14.

This model establishes a short list of possible master media. A final decision must take into account:

(a) The possible media combinations.
(b) Cost effectiveness.
(c) Urgency.
(d) Where a new technology has to be introduced, possible further applications and long-term viability.

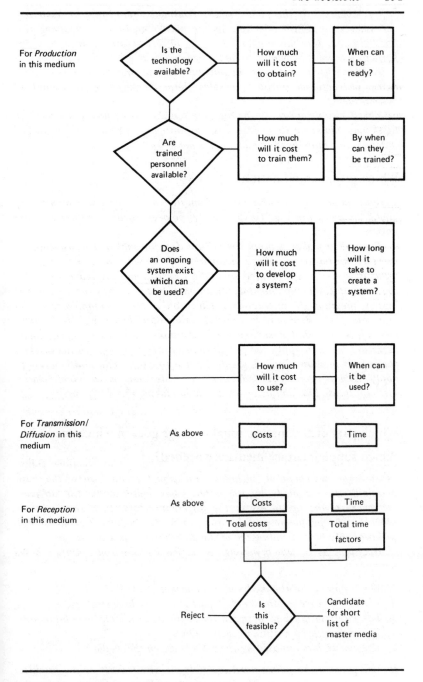

Fig. 10.14   Choosing a master medium.

For example, if the policy maker considers committing the resources necessary to establish television as the master medium — involving as it does studios, transmission facilities, an infrastructure of reception and perhaps hundreds of people to be trained and paid — he must consider it as a resource with a wide range of possibilities, and one that can be used for many instructional purposes besides those envisaged at the point of commitment.

The decisions are those for the policy maker. An educational technologist may advise on these decisions, but normally a producer does not and indeed is not hired until the decision is made.

Which media combination?

Various common combinations of master media and complementary media are shown in Fig. 10.15. Clearly, however, other combinations are possible.

The policy maker is again the critical decision maker, because complementary media are usually a major item of expenditure. For example, if radio is to be complemented by audio cassettes and printed workbooks, the cost of the complementary media may be more than the cost of the master medium. If instructional television is to be complemented by monitors, then there may be a major training problem as well as the question of salaries and a structure of supervisors. The policy maker may, therefore, have to apply the practicability criteria as used for deciding on the master medium. Indeed, the decision as to what media combination to apply is not necessarily sequential to a decision as to which master medium to use but may be instrumental in making this decision.

Which part of the instructional message goes in which media?

Which supplementary media are needed?

In a large system that includes educational technologists, the basic decisions will be made by the latter. They will allocate the different messages to the producers in the different media. In a small system, however, the people responsible for producing the educational materials will probably be controlling the media combination as a whole.

Decisions as to which message is carried by which medium are based on:

1. *The suitability of the medium to the message.*
2. *The role of each medium and its part in the teaching strategy.*
3. *The interrelationships between the elements of the media combination.*
4. *The style of presentation in each medium.*
5. *The constraints imposed by the ratio between the media.*

In this process the educational technologist, the teacher or the producer may decide that for a specific instructional task he needs a supplementary

Complementary media ↓	Master media for teaching				Master media for learning			
	TV	Radio	Corresp.	F/Face	Books	Audio Cass./Discs	Video Cass./Discs	P.I. Teaching machines
Correspondence	Yes	Yes		Yes				
Face/face	Yes	Yes	Yes					
Radio			Yes	Yes				
TV			Yes	Yes				Yes
Print (words and pictures)	Yes	Yes	Yes	Yes		Yes	Yes	Yes
Blackboard/whiteboard				Yes				
Wall visuals (charts, posters, maps, etc.)		Yes		Yes				
Practical materials	Yes	Yes	Yes	Yes	Yes	Yes	Yes	Yes
Film strips/slides	Yes	Yes		Yes		Yes		Yes
Film	Yes	Yes		Yes		Yes		Yes
Video cassettes	Yes	Yes	Yes	Yes	Yes			Yes
Audio cassettes	Yes	Yes	Yes	Yes	Yes			Yes
Telephone	Yes	Yes	Yes					

Fig. 10.15 Media combinations.

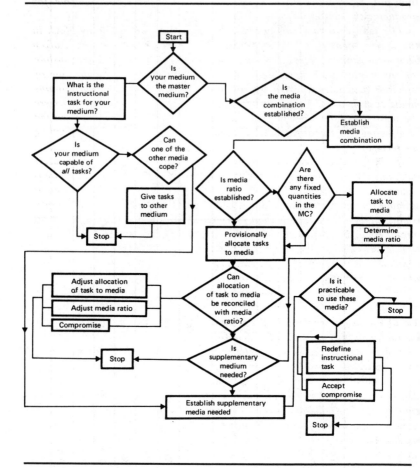

Fig. 10.16   Model for media decision-making process by producer or teacher.

medium. The need should be a clear cut one arising from the inadequacy of the institutionalised media combination. For example, when the media combination of teacher, blackboard, text books, overhead projectors and radio is insufficient for a lesson on a famous composer, the teacher could bring in his own equipment and records for the specific lesson. However, where the master medium is a mass medium, the complications and expense of introducing a supplementary medium may need a decision from the policy makers as to whether it is economically possible.

The model shown in Fig. 10.16 is a basis for the decisions that face a teacher or producer in a particular medium.

The model includes the item 'Is your medium the master medium?' If it is, then the producer/teacher is going to accept responsibility for allocating the tasks to the other media in the media combination. If not, he needs to find out what his particular task is from whoever is responsible for producing the master medium.

The failure to face this question has been a major stumbling block in the development of schools television. Television programmes have often been made without reference to the teachers who were, in fact, responsible for the master medium ('face-to-face' communication). Since the role of television was not allocated by the teachers there was not a harmonious media combination. Television was approaching the situation as if it were the master medium when in fact it was a complementary medium. This led to a feeling of competition with the teachers, who responded by switching the receiver off.

If the producer/teacher has established that his is not the master medium, the next step is to identify the instructional task for which he is responsible, and then to decide whether the task he has been given is suitable for his particular medium. It is possible that all or part of the task is not suitable. He will then want to know if the task can be undertaken by one of the other media in the media combination. If the media combination is not capable of dealing effectively with the task, then the need for a supplementary medium is apparent. The problem may equally apply to the producer/teacher responsible for the master medium.

In both these cases, the supplementary media must be established and a decision obtained — probably from the policy maker — as to whether the use of the supplementary media is practicable. If it is not, then either the instructional task must be redefined, or some compromise accepted.

The producer/teacher who is faced with a given media ratio must bear the constraints involved in mind when deciding which instructional message shall be carried by which medium. If, however, he is able to decide his own media ratio, then he first proceeds to a provisional allocation of instructional messages to instructional media. This allocation is done on the basis of professional judgement of the characteristics of the media involved. These characteristics change rapidly with technical advances and may not be constant in world wide use of the medium (e.g. one radio station's stereo FM channel may be capable of transmitting information that cannot be handled by a small receiver in the fringe reception area). Figure 10.17 is a simplified analysis of the state of the art in various media and is intended more to show how such a matrix can be constructed than to give definitive information.

Notes on media selection matrix (Fig. 10.17)

A. These media are essentially transitory in nature. Recall is possible but not easy. Most of the media so marked are teacher controlled, and the recall depends on the rate of learning.

B. It is possible for the learner to pace these, but not easy. The good teacher will respond to the desire of the majority of his students that he go more slowly or quickly, but the teacher has to set the same pace for everyone.

C. As far as the learner is concerned, there is no response to feedback. A

A blank = no; / = yes Key to letters (A–L) follows	Radio	TV	Film	Face to face	Correspondence	Print	Filmstrips and slides	Overhead projector	Audio cassette	Video cassette	Black/white board	Wall visuals	Telephone	Teaching machine	3-D materials
The message can be recalled		A	A	/	/	A	A	/	/	A	/	/	A	/	/
The message can be learner paced	Not directly		B	/	/	B	B	/	/	B	/	/	/	/	/
The message can be adjusted to feedback	D	D	C	/	/	C	C	D	C	C	/	C	/	/	C
Dynamic interaction is possible (see Note E)	F	F	/							/			/	F	
Words/Nos. can be shown		/	/		/	/	/	/		/	/	/		/	/
Simple still pictures can be shown		/	/		/	/	/	/		/	/	/		/	/
Complex still pictures and diagrams can be shown		G	/		/	/	/	/			G	/		/	/
Information can be shown in colour		H	/		/	H	/	/		/	/				
Moving pictures can be shown		/	/					I						I	
Spoken words		/	/	/					/	/			/		
Complex sound (music)	/	J	/						/	J					
Complex drama	/	/	/	/	/				/	/					
Simple drama (K)	/	/	/	/	/				/	/					
Complex things		/	/	L		L	L	L		L	L			L	L
Simple things		/	/	/		/	/	/		/	/	/		/	/

Fig. 10.17   A media selection matrix.

reprint of a book or a new version of a video cassette might embody changes as a result of criticism, but this is a slow process and does not affect the learner who provided the criticism.

D. *Possible, but not immediate.*

E. *All media can pose questions. Here we mean the capacity for question and answer.*

F. *This is possible, but not easy. A television lesson could ask a question and receive telephoned or written responses upon which to base the next programme.*

G. *Yes, but not easily. Although the television screen can show simple pictures, such as a diagram to illustrate Pythagoras' Theorem or an outline map of South America, it cannot show a detailed diagram of a diesel engine or map of the world without dealing with the details sequentially, such as by intercutting various shots or by camera or lens movements.*

H. *This depends very much on the state of the art in the area being covered. Not all colour television systems can guarantee that the colour seen by the viewer is exactly the same as that seen by the producer, for example.*

I. *'Quasi motion.'*

J. *These media can transmit music, but with restricted quality.*

K. *The distinction is between a teacher dramatically telling a story and the production of a serious play, between an illustrative piece of drama designed to teach a grammatical rule in a foreign language and a re-enactment of part of a country's history.*

L. *The distinction between a 'complex' and a 'simple' object is subtle. An aeroplane (to an engineer) is complex, a paper dart is simple. A cloud (to a meteorologist) is complex, a cup of water is simple.*

This paper has been quoted extensively, because it tries to go beyond theory — based on its authors' Latin American experience — to come to grips with practical media problems. Planning for educational media represents a balance, as stable as possible, between two approaches. At the micro level, there is the relationship of media to characteristic learning tasks — the kind of analysis which has just been described. At the macro level, there are broader considerations — which media can be afforded, which structures are already well developed, which approaches best suit the level of development of a particular country or institution. We should therefore apply what we have described at the micro level to a broader national canvas, and we will again take the example of Thailand. We have already seen (in Chapter 9) how educational objectives were derived for the system. Now we shall see how these were translated, by the planning team, into medium-term proposals. The following pages are taken directly from the final report.

An example from Thailand

For this purpose, the priority objectives of education in Thailand in relation to media were grouped under four thematic headings of access, optimisation, participation *and* orientation.

Under access *may be included objectives such as: making education available to wider audiences; increasing equality of educational opportunity (particularly between rural and urban areas); promoting new programmes and speeding up the implementation of new curricula and other innovations.*

Under optimisation *may be included objectives such as: emphasising relevant subjects; improving pre-service teacher training; reducing wastage; improving the effectiveness of field development personnel through in-service training; and promoting functional, problem-solving education.*

Under participation *may be included objectives such as: encouraging participation in community activities; creating communication flow between different segments of society; promoting two-way communication between administrators and teachers; stimulating a dialogue between the mass of the population and government officials; and moulding curriculum development into a dynamic, continuous process.*

Finally under orientation *may be included objectives such as: improving attitudes of parents, administrators and the general public towards education; developing a sense of national and community identity and pride; discouraging rural—urban migration; narrowing the gap between expectations and reality; and fostering positive attitudes towards the development process.*

The above categories are not, of course, mutually exclusive. For example, 'to create a two-way flow of information within the classroom' is likely not only to lead to an increase in efficiency in learning and thus 'optimisation', but should also lead to greater 'participation' of students in their own education.

These categories (used for simplification) have particular implications for media use. Firstly, in relation to access, *the electronic mass media (especially radio) have a prime role to play in widening the range and accessibility of educational experience. Electronic media can reach large audiences (at relatively low unit cost), and by selecting between media it is possible to favour underprivileged groups. Thus, where a major objective is to increase the provision for rural audiences, an emphasis on radio programming for the rural population might be adopted (since radios are common in the villages). Equally, a particular educational level can be stressed, by making equipment and materials available most generously at that level.*

If it is desired to reach the poorest segments of the population, most of whom live in the more inaccessible regions of the country (and many of whom are illiterate) the mass media may offer the only practical tool. Given the fact that the majority of these areas are not electrified, and are outside TV reception areas, maximum reliance will have to be put on radio.

Secondly, in terms of optimisation, *film and audio-visual aids are probably the most effective media, as they not only make an appeal to more than one sense, but can also be more easily fitted into the learning patterns of different individuals or groups. Students (and adults) learn in different ways, and for optimal learning variety is necessary; at the same time different concepts and subject areas addressed to different audiences are suited to differing formats. However, economic considerations often force a choice between mass media and other media. For example, language teaching and music require audio presentation, so that depending on the size of the audience (i.e. economic considerations) and the sophistication of teachers, either radio or audio tapes could be used. Similarly in science teaching either some form of projected aids or TV could be used.*

A further need is to optimise those resources already in existence, both material and human. In this task, media again have a role to play. On the one hand, proven resources — good teachers, good programmes, good teaching models — can be disseminated through radio or TV to large groups of students and learners. Secondly, the media can help provide training in utilisation and methodology, with radio and TV programmes supporting in-service and pre-service teacher training, offering samples of good classroom practice and necessary skills and knowledge, and providing micro teaching and macro teaching experiences.

Although less structured, the same opportunity occurs in non-formal education and in development work. Extension workers also need training in the use of professional and communication techniques, and both the mass media and other audio-visual media (including video recorders and projectors) can be used. Once trained, professional involvement will depend upon continuing contact and support. Mass media (especially radio) can offer this support; individualised media, especially low-cost printed materials, can assist in field work. In addition, for both in-school and out-of-school education, visual media, either television or film or film-strips (depending on the size of the audience), can be extremely useful in providing skill training models.

Thirdly, a new potential for media (particularly radio, TV and audio and video recorders) exists in the field of community involvement and participation. Traditionally, the mass media have been used for communication along hierarchical lines — for administrators and planners to talk to practitioners, for Governments to talk to electorates. New formats, and new models of programming and programme organisation, allow for a greater two-way dialogue; they include discussion and question-and-answer programmes, phone-in programmes, participatory programmes (in which audiences themselves produce, or direct production) and local uses of broadcasting and of video techniques. They provide a means for audiences to talk back to producers, to communicate directly with administrators, for communities to identify themselves and their neighbours. Certainly some of these techniques, as developed in the West, might be too complex to work effectively in Thailand, in conflict with traditional concepts, or impossible to implement because of political considerations, but equally the team felt that some attempt should be made to envisage two-way systems of communication using the media.

Finally, in the context of orientation, *all media (particularly radio, TV and film) can be and have been (often unintentionally) used to promote attitude change. This may involve creating expectations, aspirations and motivation in the area of development work (e.g. health and nutrition schemes, and family planning programmes), or changing the attitudes of the general public to education. Such uses demand a high cooperative effort between development agencies (each with a somewhat different veiw of the development process), between different media and between the media and field workers, whose responsibility it is to interpret and build upon the overall message. In addition judicious use of the mass media may reduce the existing wide gap between expectations and reality, by providing realistic vocational and career guidance, and emphasising the problems faced by new migrants to the towns.*

The following table, outlining possible media strategies for meeting some selected general objectives (which together cover most of the more detailed objectives already elicited), summarises the above discussion.

Objectives	Means of attaining objective using media strategies
A. Access	
1. *To make education available to wider audiences.*	*Use electronic media to transmit high quality materials and to increase audience range.*
2. *To help redress the balance between rural and urban communities.*	*Emphasise those media (i.e. radio) which are or can be, made available to rural audiences and direct programming towards these audiences.*
B. Optimisation	
1. *To make optimum use of educational materials.*	*Produce coordinated range of electronic media programmes and other AV materials in support of curriculum change, including teaching utilisation models.*
2. *To reduce wastage.*	*Produce stimulating, attractive materials, using all available media which encourage the learner to make the most of educational opportunities. For adult education make programmes entertaining and relevant.*
3. *To make optimum use of human resources.*	*Support training programmes for teachers, development and extension workers, using in particular radio, film and video tape.*
4. *To relate education to life and to society in general.*	*Provide relevant programming, on radio and TV, support vocational training through the use of selected visual materials.*
C. Participation	
1. *To improve communication flow within the educational and social system.*	*Devise programme formats using radio (perhaps also TV and video recorders) which increase participation by audiences and dialogue between planners and audiences.*
2. *To increase individual involvement and participation in community development.*	*Devise new formats, using new technologies (particularly video recorders) which allow for community expression and participation.*
D. Orientation	
1. *To develop positive attitudes to the development process.*	*Use electronic media in support of development programmes, and the coordination of all development activities.*
2. *To develop a sense of national and community identity and pride.*	*Produce programmes for the electronic mass media, film and other materials, for both children and adults, which stress Thai cultural traditions and nation-building activities.*

)bjectives — *continued*	**Means of attaining objective using media strategies** — *continued*
3. *To improve attitudes of parents and the general public towards education.*	*Devise special radio programmes for parents and the general public, and include similar items in general programme formats.*
4. *To lessen the gap between expectations and reality.*	*Devise special radio (and to a lesser extent film and TV programmes) providing realistic career guidance, realistic views on the standard of life in towns and information on the potential and the importance of rural areas.*

Some specific uses of educational media in Thailand

Having isolated general media strategies it was possible to deal more specifically with the role media could play in Thailand, at both in-school and out-of-school levels.

The same categorisation of objectives (into access, optimisation, participation *and* orientation*) has been retained.*

(I) The role of media in in-school education

Media used in-school enjoy a considerable advantage in that they are deployed within a familiar environment, whose structures and infrastructures have been developed over a period of time. A good deal of information is therefore available both on audiences and on audience characteristics.

At the same time, if only the present situation is considered, this can generate problems. If media are unfamiliar, they may be resisted; if accepted, they may be wrongly used. While in the adult field a good deal of effort has to be directed towards building up audiences, in the in-school field, where audiences are captive, an equal effort has to be directed towards changing practices which are outmoded, working against the development of the individual child or against his assimilation into society. The main impetus of media provision at the in-school level should therefore be directed towards supporting innovative forms which are being contemplated, and introduced, in related fields (curriculum renewal, teacher training, etc.). It is of the greatest importance to coordinate media programming with curriculum development, and as new curricula are prepared to produce materials in support of these for both pupils and teachers.

(a) Access   *Firstly, there is the major problem of inequalities of educational opportunity, both in resource allocation and in enrolment provision as between regions, between rural and urban areas and between different population groups. There is also the problem of ensuring adequate levels of education to meet the social demand. The objective 'to increase equality of opportunity' can only be met if priority is given to those areas of the educational system which are less well-endowed (i.e. the elementary schools and the rural population). The choice of media here is primarily determined by logistical factors; it is clear that radio is of particular importance, because of the prohibitive cost of creating an educational television network or making extensive use of other AV media, or even in providing sufficient textbooks to all students. Equally, the media survey specially conducted for this study already shows a high utilisation of school radio programmes at the elementary level, with much less use at the secondary level. (It should nevertheless be noted that considerably more programmes are produced for elementary schools.) Finally, the fact that radio can be received in non-electrified locations is of importance in the elementary schools, which are worst off in electrification progress. The use of radio also puts a premium on the development of support materials (especially print). These must be well produced, relevant and available in quantity if radio is to achieve more than nominal efficiency.*

(b) Optimisation   *A large number of problem areas have been identified under this heading, including authoritarian methods of teaching, the irrelevance of much of what is taught, over-emphasis on examinations, shortage of resources, high rates of pupil wastage and poor pre-service teacher training. Related to these problems, several objectives for media have been identified, the most important of which are: 'to encourage creativity and dialogue within the classroom', 'to improve methods of teaching' and 'to emphasise relevant subjects'. Obviously all of these should be seen in a dynamic context.*

In relation to the first of these major objectives, not only is a change in teacher and parent attitudes required (see below), but also media formats which insist upon dialogue and which leave room for both teacher and pupil initiative. Though classroom-based projectors and recorders may be theoretically the most useful tools in this respect (and increasing use should be made of such equipment), because of economic and access problems the greatest reliance will still have to be placed on electronic mass media. For these to be effective the production of printed support materials for both teachers and pupils is again of great importance.

For pre-service teacher training a wide range of AV materials should be used, with particular emphasis on showing 'good teaching models', and on using video recorders to record teaching practice. For in-service teacher training, because of access problems radio should be used, accompanied by printed support materials and residential courses during summer vacations.

To emphasise the principle of relevance, the greatest possible use should be made of projected AV aids, but in addition radio and/or TV can be used to give status to subjects that are under-emphasised in normal teaching. It is essential in this context to accompany media use by a change in the examination process.

Finally it should be stressed that great care must be taken when preparing media programmes not only to make them entertaining for children, but also to relate what is taught to the existing background and environment of the audience.

(c) Participation   *It is important not only to make the curriculum more flexible, so that pupils have some say in what they learn, but also to improve communication lines between administrators and teachers (and between parents and teachers). Here media by themselves can do very little, for unless the teacher is given some freedom in determining what is taught and how, and unless administrators are aware of the importance of dialogue with teachers, little can be achieved. Given a more flexible curriculum, and a change of attitude in administrators and teachers, the media then have a viable role to play. In response to the first objective, if simple projected aids (which can be pupil-operated) are available, with adequate software, pupils can be motivated to pursue their own particular lines of enquiry, particularly if the mass media are used to create new and wide-ranging interests in parallel, well-documented fields. In response to the second objective, there is no reason why administrators should not appear on radio and television to explain the reasons behind Government decisions; they will gain all the more by being seen as human beings as well as signatories to policy documents. Equally, teachers should themselves be encouraged to appear on programmes, to ask questions, to give opinions and to discuss professional matters with colleagues. For meaningful exchange, the development of regional programming (in radio especially) will be crucially important.*

In this context, the mass media are not the only potential vehicle. A media service should have its own newsletter or magazine; it should open its doors to visitors (especially to school children); it should reflect the feelings of its users in articles, letters, personal statements. Communication demands a breakdown of 'us' and 'them' attitudes.

(d) Orientation   *Two possibilities are open. Firstly, the attitudes of parents, older children and administrators towards education have to be changed, if the innovations which many leading policy makers would like to see introduced are to be effectively framed. Secondly, children must be helped to assume a positive attitude towards their communities (mostly rural) and towards the nation, to ensure that their expectations are realistic.*

There are two ways of achieving these objectives (both of them linked with other reforms). The first is to include 'hidden messages' in general TV, radio and film programming; the second is to prepare specific radio and TV programmes (and to a much lesser extent films) on the role of the school, of the parent in his child's education, on the problems of Thai society, and on career guidance. A mixture of both approaches is indicated.

To conclude, the main media emphasis at the elementary level *should be upon radio (for economic and logistical reasons), with the thrust of programming being on attitude change, pupil involvement and the broadening of the child's horizons, rather than on the transmission of facts.*

Other media should be made available in the most economically effective way to those schools which are ready (or can be ready) to use them, and should deal more with transmitting relevant facts and concepts, and encouraging pupil participation.

At the secondary level *radio, TV and other media could all be used effectively. Radio may be oriented in roughly the same way as in elementary schools; television for increasing understanding of the practical application of scientific and mathematical theory, and for skill training (also to some extent attitude change); and other media for skill training and individual learning of facts and concepts.*

In teacher training *a wide range of AV materials should be used to demonstrate teaching models, as well as for individualised learning. In addition video recorders can be used to make teaching practice more effective.*

Finally the mass media can both directly and indirectly play a special role in creating more positive attitudes towards education.

(II) The role of media in out-of-school education and development

Adult and non-formal educational activities are very diverse; they also include a large number of initiatives which work outside an institutional framework. The potential for media is therefore equally varied. Some provision can be made for special groups, in much the same way as at the school level (materials for accompanying adult classes, or designed for specially formed groups). Other materials can be produced in support of training programmes (much as for teacher training). But the vast majority of programmes at the adult level are likely to be heard by individuals, within their own homes or in the fields, and this trend has been vastly reinforced by the spread of the transistor radio. The adult listener is not part of a captive audience. In a country like Thailand, with a crowded broadcasting spectrum, the amount, if not the quality, of competition is very high. Programming, whatever its objectives, must be intriguing, challenging, entertaining — attractive in its own right. In much of the adult education area the initial listener motivation is only minimal and so educational radio must woo its public before it can be confident of any audience at all.

This is not to say that it must not also be relevant and specific. But a programme, if it is to succeed, has to do so largely in its own right, without the considerable assistance that may be expected of a teacher in the classroom.

(a) Access   *Perhaps the most significant problem identified in the field of adult and non-formal education is that of access. Very limited (and uncoordinated) resources are available for providing the huge quantities of knowledge, skills, attitudes and ideas needed by the mass of the population if they are significantly and rapidly to increase their quality of life.*

It is here perhaps that electronic media have the greatest advantage, for they can spread learning opportunities widely and, in the case of some media, equally. For this purpose, radio is the obvious tool, in a country where the medium is already well developed. The receivers exist; it is the programming which is deficient. Consequently, a broad range of programmes is required both for general audiences and for minority groups. Some of these programmes will be of a composite kind, including local music, culture, history, current affairs, drama, etc. Others may deal with specific skills — simple engine repairs, household management, gardening and smallholding — or introduce concepts and information — on economics, social science, mathematics — in a simple and informal way. Finally a most important category will deal with attitude and behavioural change — family planning, health, hygiene, nutrition, child care, marketing, etc.

The main prerequisite is that the programmes should be relevant, interesting and entertaining. They must be related to local and regional situations (hence the importance of audience research, and of regional programme development as soon as is possible within the system) and adapt their scheduling to the pattern of life and activity of the listener.

The same observations can be made of television, though opportunity is much more restricted. Television is a more costly medium, and at present its availability in Thailand is limited (as is set ownership). Programming for television must therefore be geared to its growth, and at present the majority of television receivers are in the towns. Perhaps one of the greatest services which television can provide is to show the town dweller something of the country life which he has either left, or has never known, and attempt to enhance its status.

As far as other media are concerned, in an unstructured situation their disciplined use is impossible to organise. But it is important that print and newspaper channels should be used to publicise programme schedules, as well as to support programmes. It might also be possible to encourage independent film producers to make feature films with a specific development message.

b) Optimisation   *If this group of objectives for out-of-school education is to be met then a varied use of media is implied. If teachers and other field agents are to be given continuous in-service training, then radio, and various projected aids, should be used. If learners are to be provided with relevant practical skills then film and TV have a useful role to play. If functional education programmes are to be rapidly expanded to cater for their potential audience, then radio will have to be used.*

It is in this context, therefore, that some specific educational activities should be discussed. One example is functional literacy. Classes meet in the villages in the evenings and base their work on specially prepared relevant texts. The media can help keep wastage to a minimum by creating special radio programmes and simple supporting print and audio-visual materials, not only to assist the learner in his studies, but also to enhance his sense of importance and self-respect. This is crucial, as there is in Thailand a certain degree of social stigma attached to being illiterate, and the present literacy classes only enrol an insignificant proportion of illiterates.

A similar situation exists with respect to adult 'second chance' classes, where tuition is at present often based on school materials (which inhibit the adult learner). This programme is currently being functionalised, and support is needed both in materials and in tutor training for the new, problem-solving curriculum. Broadcasting assistance could be arranged both during class meetings (which would require scheduling at a specific time) and for home-based activities (which would be more flexible in timing). However, since utilisation levels of home-based broadcasts are likely to be poor, and as special training is not generally given to adult teachers, class support programmes would certainly seem to be needed.

It would also be possible to dispense entirely with classroom teaching and to mount a programme of correspondence education, with or without mass media support (because of economic considerations, among the mass media probably only radio could be used). Individuals living far from existing 'second-chance' classes could take the course partly by listening to programmes for formal classes, and partly through correspondence; alternatively it would be possible for special radio programmes to be transmitted late at night for correspondence students. It should be noted however that correspondence education is costly (even though part of the cost can be financed from fees) and administratively complex.

A further media possibility is in training. In some ways, all educational broadcasts can be seen as a means of teacher or field agent training; the programmes are not only addressed to the adult learner, but can also offer guidance and teaching models. Training can nonetheless be much more specific. Special programmes can be directed towards teachers and development workers, designed to teach them something of communication techniques, or professional disciplines. Additionally radio can be used as a means of keeping regularly in touch with extension workers, to keep them informed and updated, and to retain their interest and motivation in a field where isolation is common. Other materials can also be produced in support of training programmes — tapes, films, print and audio-visual materials, with an emphasis on low cost technologies.

One final possibility which is built around the use of mobile AV vans. Such units are run by a number of development agencies; concentrating on projected AV aids (some with videotape recorders), they can be most important as a resource base for local training programmes, particularly those which must take place in rural surroundings. They must however be accompanied by trained personnel (to lead discussions) and printed support materials. Equally, they could be used in support of vocational training programmes. It should be emphasised that in terrain where television is unavailable, or economically unfeasible, the mobile AV unit is the only integrated delivery system available for visual demonstration.

(c) Participation   *Three of the objectives for non-formal education are extremely important. These are 'to encourage real dialogue between the people and officials . . .', 'to improve the communication flow between different segments of society . . .', and to make people aware that their 'participation in development activities is an essential precondition for their success'.*

In recent years, some new approaches to community media have been devised, which are now being seen to have a particular relevance to the developing world.

Fundamental to these experiments is the location of a field worker, or 'animator', within the community. His continued presence is imperative; he cannot simply appear from the outside, record material and then depart to an editing channel. He must know, understand and sympathise with development objectives, as they appear at the village level. The use of technology in such situations is open-ended. In practice there are few limits on what community videotape facilities can be used for, as they can do all that the written word can do, but more powerfully, and can be used by illiterates and uneducated people as much as by the educated. The community can record its own folk forms; it can send messages to the authorities; it can greet neighbouring communities; it can argue through village problems at length and in depth. Some experimentation in Thailand could provide considerable guidance for future social and political development, and help create a really vital and live democracy.

Radio listening groups offer a formula for participation in development-oriented broadcasting which has been used in many less developed countries. The idea of listening groups is simple; programmes are generated in order to lead to discussion (and subsequent follow up) by specially devised groups, under a local leader. At times training is given in group animation, and at other times, extension workers can serve as group leaders. However with the advent of transistor radios (which exist in 65 per cent of households in Thailand) it is very difficult to form groups merely to listen and discuss radio programmes (this is why the Indian farm forum experiment was discontinued). The same may not be true, however, where programming is devised for groups which have already proved their viability. These may be professional groups (e.g. Young Farmers' Clubs), or they may reflect traditional society practices (i.e. a habit of meeting in the evenings in the shadow of the temple or in an adult reading centre). In such cases, a new outlet is created for an existing pattern of social behaviour, and where examples exist in Thailand the addition of radio programmes and some simple printed support materials may well direct a passive institution into something with more positive social utility.

It should be emphasised that whatever media system is used audience involvement should be encouraged. For example, the regional centre producer can act as animator, relying upon local talent and interest to construct many of this programmes, Programming can be based upon written, spoken or recorded interviews; comments and reactions can be invited and aired. Audience involvement is not only an asset in programming, but also community development can be intensified by a judicious airing of activities. A community which sees itself on television, or hears itself on the radio, will be more inclined to continue its efforts towards self-development.

(d) Orientation   *Finally, a more direct use of media in the development process is for orientation, and specifically for attitude change. Many of the objectives for out-of-school education require a change in attitudes for their achievement. For example: 'to encourage people to live in harmony with their environment . . .'; 'to promote . . . a feeling of Thainess'; 'to improve attitudes of the general population to development'; and 'to help people realise that education . . . is something that must take place throughout their lives'. In some cases general attitude changes are needed, in others specific changes (i.e. attitudes towards family size).*

From the experience of other developing countries it seems that mass media can be used initially to introduce new themes and to motivate audiences to explore new experiences. Once motivation is aroused, they have temporarily a reduced role to play, but if a trial is made, and an adoption results, they can again be used to remind, to repeat and to reinforce. In this way, they are intimately linked with the machinery of extension work, which relies upon personal agents to interpret media messages, to localise and make them relevant to particular communities, and above all to make the services or processes available which the media are introducing. If, once the audience has been motivated through radio messages, reinforcement is provided by using other AV materials, the attitude change is likely to be more lasting. Thus a coordinated approach to attitude change is essential.

A radio network such as the one being proposed in this project should be open to development communication in the broadest sense. It should, first of all, be prepared to carry development messages in its own programmes; equally importantly, it should be prepared to offer its facilities to other sectors and Ministries.

This will make considerable coordination demands on all the agencies concerned. It is suggested that, at all costs, the creation of special production units in other Ministries be avoided; what are required are small resource units, which can provide script ideas or drafts, background information, suggestions on resource speakers and generate supporting print materials, leaving the producers of the Ministry of Education to carry out the technical aspects of programme production.

The specific proposals in this quotation are, of course, applicable to one country only, at a particular point of time. But implicit in the passage is an attempt − critical in media planning − to come to grips with social and political realities, while still arguing from a sound theoretical base. It is this process which is transferable; and for that reason alone, the extract is worth detailed study.

Chapter 11

System design

We have now decided upon the main objectives of the educational system, and considered the principal ways in which mass media can help achieve them.

The next critical step is to match what has gone before against the ability of a country or institution to sustain media growth. There are no theoretical solutions to media problems: whatever the 'ideal' combination of media may appear to be (and the conclusion of most research is that there is no such thing), for media development to be successful it has to be fed with trained technical and production talent, regular supplies of materials and adequate technical infrastructures. This is where a realistic appraisal of the environment is crucial — not only of what exists on the ground, but the capacity of institutions to train for new disciplines, the interest and adaptability of users, the scope of plans for further technical support.

The planning team

This matching process is best carried out by an operational planning team, reflecting whatever skills are necessary both to appraise current conditions and to plan the outlines of the new system. The composition of the team will naturally vary from place to place (it may be no more than a single person drawing on specialist advice as he needs it), but it will always be engaged in a sequence approximately as follows:

(a) evaluating current and future media potential;
(b) setting this potential against an 'ideal' media pattern;
(c) evolving and presenting alternative propositions to put to decision makers, with balanced arguments for and against each;
(d) elaborating, once a decision on the preferred system has been taken, a detailed plan for the system.

Whatever the size of the team involved, it is likely that the disciplines below will have to be represented in some way, even if they are combined in fewer persons.

1. *Education.* Educational planning, curriculum, teacher training, adult and extension work.

2. *Administration and Management.* Educational and media administration, economics, finance, systems analysis.
3. *Media.* Educational technology, production disciplines (radio, TV, audio-visual).
4. *Technical.* Engineering (network and studio), power, maintenance.
5. *Utilisation.* Urban and rural sociology, in-school and out-of-school utilisation, development communication.
6. *Evaluation.* Evaluation method, research design, statistical method.

There is no ideal way of selecting a planning team, as there is no ideal number. The work should be dictated by the magnitude of the problem, though more often than not it is determined by the resources available. Few media systems have been allocated adequate resources at the planning stage, and a good deal of *ad hoc* activity has usually to be undertaken — persuading specialists in other fields to help provide background data, encouraging local institutions to cooperate in mounting surveys, involving research students or interested teachers in data collection and analysis. For this reason, the character of the team leader is important: he has to be, primarily, a good manager and administrator, capable of drawing the best from specialists with very different viewpoints and philosophies, and able to synthesise, from their findings, a coherent result.

Pre-planning is obviously essential. A good deal of organisational work can be done in advance, saving time and energy at the time when the pressure is at its greatest (the time of report writing), and the time of experts, in visiting institutions, holding conferences, etc., can be optimised if a proper schedule is drawn up.

A special word needs to be said about foreign specialists working, as planners, in developing countries. Unless they have a good deal of experience, they are likely to suffer in adapting themselves to a local culture, and will often respond by insisting that only those structures with which they are familiar are satisfactory. A visiting planning team can become almost inbred in its way of working, detached from the realities which they have been asked to evaluate. In an area like media technology, foreign experts are often necessary, because they possess rare skills, but they have to be carefully nurtured by their leader, and their opinions have to be sifted for bias.

In any case, this handbook is not intended as a guide to the deployment of overseas specialists; insofar as it constitutes a reference source, it is designed to help people work out their own futures on their own behalf. The modes of technical assistance have changed, and today, if experts cannot integrate their efforts within a local team situation, they are likely to be rapidly removed from the planning scene.

Evaluating current conditions

The survey of current conditions which begins the media planning process is not haphazard; it is more a matter of finding answers to key questions.

Among the most important (here given with an explanatory commentary) are the following check points.

Social structure

Is the level of development of the country such that it can assimilate a media system?
Media are technology based, and for their creation and maintenance need a ready supply of trained manpower, equipment, competent servicing, routine replacement of parts. Even more so, they require acceptance. If the society is unused to media technology and to its demands, progress will be slower. If the above are not available, they will have to be created, and the pace of development must be adjusted accordingly. The question must also be asked — are the chances of success high enough to risk the initial investment?

What is the current media provision, with what kind of purpose?
There is little point in replicating existing and expensive infrastructures (e.g. transmitter networks). As far as possible technical services, even production services, should be planned conjointly. But there will be cases when the existing provision is too fragmented or commercially oriented, with little interest in or commitment to development programming, and here separate technical arrangements may finally be necessary.

What is the present pattern of distribution and of use of media?
It is obviously important to know who owns or has access to radio and television receivers, what are their patterns of viewing and listening, to what extent these are individual or communal, how quickly usage is growing (and within which social sectors). This is particularly true of the out-of-school area, where educational media are usually in direct competition with other formats.

What is the attitude of particular social groups (social leaders, political and religious organisations, etc.) to media?
Influential groups may affect educational media in two ways. They can inhibit its development, through innate antagonism; or they can assist, even promote its use, by encouraging their followers to participate, and by taking it upon themselves to help with programme preparation and utilisation. This is usually a question of motivation.

What are the existing patterns of social organisation, especially at the community level, in both urban and rural environments?
Viewing and listening will depend upon satisfactory integration with the dominant life style. If group viewing is contemplated, for example, such factors as timing, or the placement of receivers, will be affected by local cultural habits, and sociological advice is necessary for the planner.

What is the attitude of Government, and of educational and other authorities, to the use of media in education and development?
Unless there is a strong commitment at these levels, media cannot succeed.

Education

What are the goals, objectives and priorities of the social system as a whole and of the educational system in particular?
This is the crux of the problem, which has already been discussed extensively.

What changes in educational structures are required for educational media to operate effectively?
Media used innovatively cannot often be grafted on to existing structures. (They could of course be used to support an antiquated and traditionalist system, but this is hardly a valid reason for their use.) Not only must the implications for educational organisation be considered; an estimate must be made, on realistic premises, of the possibility of the new structures being accepted.

Is the primary need in education one of quantity or of quality?
This is a broad question of objectives, but one which is fundamental to the choice, range and deployment of media. Put at its simplest, it is a choice of whether media are needed as a permanent or interim alternative to a school system (e.g. where there are too few teachers or schools), or as an additional tool for qualitative improvement. The former choice is less frequently adopted today; if adopted, the majority of educational processes are mediated, and direct cost comparisons can be made between media based and traditional school systems. In the latter case, media are part of a comprehensive set of resources at the teacher's disposal. This question will certainly dictate the form of any feasibility study (a quantitative emphasis allows for cost efficiency analyses).

Can the objectives specified be attained more easily, more cheaply, more efficiently or more quickly using forms other than media?
This kind of comparison must be taken seriously, and backed up by realistic arguments (there are certain cases, for example, where an alternative to media might be an extended crash programme of teacher training). Planning should include a proper justification of media, not serve as a proselytising force.

Is the introduction of educational media likely to be backed by the majority of educational opinion?
It is relatively easy to sound the attitude of planners and administrators, but more difficult to determine the reaction of potential users. If possible, special surveys should be undertaken. It is unlikely that all teachers and educators will welcome media, which they may feel will threaten their role in the classroom, or produce an additional workload, but it will be diffi-

cult to proceed if an overwhelming majority of the teaching force is resistant to change. A continuing public relations and training programme will help, but cannot be expected to produce miracles. There is, for most innovative forms, an optimum climate, and when circumstances are weighted in their favour, it is sometimes necessary to allow a few years' breathing space before embarking on an ambitious programme.

Is coordination possible between all the agencies likely to be involved in the use of media?

Like most innovatory forms, media have a ripple effect. They tend to spotlight deficiencies in performance and coordination, and the fact that they have a material end product makes this spotlight that much more dramatic. A successful media project may bring to light weaknesses in the curriculum which have not previously been articulated, simply because there may not have been, in the traditional educational structure, a means of evaluating, or vocalising, discontent. The educational system has to be secure and flexible enough to accept such disclosures, and modify itself when necessary.

The difficulty is worse for out-of-school education. Adult and development programming involves many ministries and agencies, with separate command structures; coordination cannot be imposed, but has to be worked for and mutually agreed. This assumes at the very least an absence of overt hostility between agencies.

Media

Is there a ready supply of creative and production talent available to service a media system?

If not, adequate training arrangements will have to be made. Educational media are only as good as their producers.

Should production be in the hands of educators or media specialists (i.e. broadcasters)?

This issue (debated in Part 1) is still live, and needs sensitive local analysis.

Technical factors

What is the current level of engineering and technology, in terms of manpower, resources, plant, etc.?

The phasing of operations, and their reliability, will always be dependent upon the prevailing technical climate. At the planning stage, in particular, experienced engineers, architects, etc., are essential.

What attitude is taken towards the maintenance and servicing of equipment?

This has proved a genuine stumbling block in some societies, where preventive maintenance is unknown. The habit of running machinery until it breaks down is a difficult one to eradicate.

Who has control of media distribution and to what extent is cooperative working possible?
This question will determine not only how distribution processes are organised, but also the extent to which an educational media service is called upon to provide its own engineering staff. It is assumed that, in the majority of cases, production engineering and technical operations will be a function of the service, but distribution can be considered a separate aspect, and one which is far better handled by broadcasting and tele-communications authorities. This having been said, if there are overriding reasons why such cooperation is not possible, the issue should be squarely faced, and a decision taken as to whether it is best to make a special investment in a separate distribution chain, or to abandon the project altogether.

How easy is it to obtain technical equipment locally, or, failing this, what is the import situation?
Mass media cannot evolve without equipment: if there are heavy duties on imports, and special exceptions cannot be arranged, then the additional cost must be realistically assessed. Where high tariffs are the rule, and foreign exchange is not readily available, projects will be subject to considerable delays in implementation.

Utilisation

What arrangements are already in existence to train teacher/users in the use of media?
It is likely that these arrangements, if they exist, will be minimal, but the infrastructure must be open for them to be introduced. This means, at a minimum, the introduction of media utilisation as a component (prefer-ably compulsory) in pre-service education courses, the mounting of extensive in-service courses, and the training of other groups (e.g. extension workers, community development workers) in utilisation techniques.

Can existing training institutions and their staff handle the anticipated volume of utilisation training?
While experts and consultants can be imported to help train teachers, they cannot handle this work alone. Facilities and premises must be available, and some kind of snowball pattern will almost certainly have to be arranged for in-service courses (with experts training a few local trainers, who in turn run subsidiary courses, and so on).

Evaluation and research

Are there adequate institutions, services and manpower to handle evaluation and research requirements?
In the main, evaluation and research staff with specific media experience

will not be found and will have to be trained. Consequently, there must be a commitment on the part of the administration to the need for evaluation (which is demanding in staff and resources), and there must be some means of ensuring that returns to questionnaires, surveys, etc., are made. Sometimes, this can be demanded, in an authoritarian system, but more often it has to be wooed.

Furthermore, there should at the very least be research and higher level institutions which can sustain these newly trained personnel and offer adequate services and facilities for their work.

Finance

Is adequate finance available to provide the necessary minimum of development expenditure?
Few planners are ever given access to the funds which they would like, but there is a basic minimum beyond which it is pointless, even dangerous, to proceed. All too often in the past, services have begun on a less than minimal provision, simply to get started; so-called 'pilot' experiments have begun without any real commitment to their continuance, and what evaluation has been done has simply confirmed the inadequacy of the basic provision. This is a self-defeating exercise.

Is adequate finance available to provide the necessary minimum of recurrent expenditure?
This is a most important criterion. Basic expenditures can often be met under technical assistance or loan arrangements, but recurrent expenditure (for staff, materials and supplies) is a permanent commitment, which must be assured from the outset. Again, there are basic levels, without which a service cannot effectively meet its terms of reference.

Are adequate amounts of foreign exchange available, to meet basic commitments?
Unless a country is in a very fortunate position, a foreign exchange component in a media project is indispensable.

The operational plan

The answers to these questions should reveal some basic truths: namely —
1. Whether the time is ripe for the introduction of media technology.
2. The rate at which media can be introduced.
3. The infrastructure which will have to be developed, both before and during the project's lifetime.
4. The availability of trained personnel and resources, and the ways in which they can be built up and reinforced.
5. The main institutions and agencies upon which the system can depend.

6. The major inhibiting factors in introducing media, and the main areas of attack necessary to ensure the project's viability.

Based upon these insights, a specific operational plan can be prepared, describing in clear and unambiguous terms the outlines of the system. At its fullest, it should include the elements in the following list, though in some cases (e.g. at the school or college level) much of the detailed economic analysis will not be required, particularly cost–benefit analyses.

(a) Detailed instructional objectives, both for the whole system and for individual media and media combinations.

(b) A clear account of the systemic relationship of media.

(c) Detailed projections of audiences to be covered, specific media uses in relations to specific audiences, subject areas, grades and levels.

(d) Detailed accounts of specific programme series (across all media, individually and collectively), with an elaboration down to the individual programme level.

(e) Audience size projections for all subjects and media combinations.

(f) Production facilities required, and equipment and building specifications with sketch plans for building works including space utilisation data.

(g) Detailed descriptions and technical specifications for the distribution system, including indications of equipment available locally.

(h) Detailed specifications for reception equipment, including indications of local supply.

(i) A clear description of the relationships and communication pattern between cooperating agencies.

(j) A complete description of organisational structures proposed.

(k) A complete description of the planning process for the generation of media programmes.

(l) Detailed projections of supporting print and audio-visual items.

(m) Electrification and power data.

(n) Production, technical and administrative manpower requirements.

(o)˙ Training requirements and programmes.

(p) Utilisation training patterns (both full-time and in-service).

(q) Evaluation system requirements (including both conceptual and logistical elements).

(r) Associated research designs.

(s) Detailed costing—capital and development costs, foreign exchange and local.

(t) Detailed recurrent costing, broken down into production, distribution and utilisation subsections.

(u) Unit costs per student per annum, capital and recurrent by level.

(v) Unit costs per student exposure, capital and recurrent by level.

(w) Detailed phasing, showing the development and interrelationship of all items listed above.

(x) A breakdown of costings according to this phasing.

These are basic, logistical items. But a good plan should also have other qualities. It should, first of all, show the thought processes which have led to its crystallisation — the various options which were examined and discarded, and the reasoning behind critical decisions taken en route. It should, secondly, carry within it an account of the means by which it can be implemented: a blueprint for the system's developers who will follow. It is also useful to provide a summary (for reference purposes, and for those — probably the majority, including some decision makers — who will not or cannot find the time to review the whole document), and to isolate supporting data in separate annexes. A possible arrangement, broken down for ease of reference into separate volumes might be:

1. Summary

2. Educational, social and media objectives

(*a*) A survey of educational goals, objectives, priorities and targets, framed according to the social structure of the country or institution concerned, and its overall development programme.
(*b*) A description, and analysis, of the overall strategy by which these objectives are being realised.
(*c*) An analysis of the means by which media can assist in the realisation of these objectives.
(*d*) A comparison, where appropriate, between media solutions, and alternative solutions.

3. The current situation

A critical and analytical description of present structures (including media structures), in which present performance and promise is related to targets and goals.

4. The media project

A clear statement of the proposed media approved including:

(*a*) Objectives — long range and short range;
(*b*) Historical evolution;
(*c*) Justification (including economic, educational and strategic arguments, and where appropriate cost—benefit and cost efficiency analyses, related to projected audience sizes);
(*d*) A basic description of the project;
(*e*) Organisational and institutional framework;
(*f*) Programme preparation and production processes;
(*g*) Staffing, recruitment and training needs and provision;
(*h*) Utilisation (broken down into appropriate levels, and including training and preparation needs as well as methodology);

(*i*) Technical needs, maintenance and servicing arrangements;
(*j*) Evaluation needs and methods;
(*k*) Research needs and methods;
(*l*) Operational plans (including networks and systems diagrams, where appropriate);
(*m*) Technical assistance and aid requirements;
(*n*) Costs and financing.

5. Annexes

(*a*) Educational enrolment figures, audience sizes, projections, etc;
(*b*) Cost breakdown (capital and recurrent);
(*c*) Cost analyses (unit costs, cost benefit and cost efficiency studies, as required);
(*d*) Equipment specifications;
(*e*) Building and architectural requirements and plans;
(*f*) Summaries of relevant background documentation, research results, etc.;
(*g*) Bibliographical and reference sources.

The presentation of alternatives

In the previous section we used the word 'insights'. This is because, although we have worked from as rational a base as possible (specifying alternatives, working out an ideal media strategy, evaluating current strengths and weaknesses, measuring vested interest), the production of a plan to match these requirements involves, ultimately, a set of judgements. While we can say with some confidence that certain approaches will not meet our objectives, or are unlikely to work in prevailing media conditions, there is still room for dispute on positive recommendations. There are few planning teams which reach unanimity; a consensus is the best that can be hoped for. Moreover, there are always fashions in media use, and the best of planners will be swayed both by these and by the conditioning of his own experience.

So there is room for more than one proposition to be put forward. Even more importantly, we should recognise that ultimate decisions on whether or not to adopt a specific design will be taken by decision makers who do not have the same technical background as the planning team, who have not covered the ground with the same thoroughness and who are likely to give their main emphasis to political or economic considerations, which may well operate over the short rather than the long term.

It is therefore important to present these decision makers with some degree of choice. Firstly, this allows them to make judgements according to reference frames which are not exclusively political; they are weighing up pros and cons, and drawing conclusions. This in itself militates against snap political judgements.

Secondly, it draws them into the planning process and gives them a feeling of identity and involvement. At best, this will encourage them to give the project a special weighting; at worst, it will make it impossible for them to say, once the design is complete, that they have not been consulted (and so to reject it out of hand). A planning formula in which the final version is arrived at in stages, with decision points placed strategically en route (and with alternative strategies gradually narrowed down to an agreed design) is the most realistic option.

An example

As a concrete illustration, the example of the Thai study can again be taken. The account below was written by an educational economist and planner, who acted as deputy team leader (Nicholas Bennett).

The preinvestment study was divided into two phases, the first in December 1973–January 1974, and the second in April–May 1974. The gap between the two phases was designed to provide Government with an opportunity to comment on the team's proposals and to answer specific questions raised by the team before the detailed design of a specific project. In order to maintain continuity a small core group of specialists was employed throughout the period December 1973 to May 1974. During the first phase of the study three major activities were carried out. First a great deal of relevant information was gathered and analysed on the educational system, its problems and objectives; the media system and its educational uses; the social, cultural and economic situations in different regions of the country; the administration of educational projects and the mechanisms for interdepartmental cooperation (particularly at the district and village level); and the spread of reception equipment and the coverage of alternative schemes for the expansion of TV and radio transmission. All previous research relating to educational media in Thailand, their production, distribution, utilisation and evaluation, was identified and analysed.

Secondly, the characteristics of various types of media and their applicability to the Thai situation were studied. From this study, combined with an analysis of the existing problems and objectives of education and the curriculum reform process, objectives of the educational media system for both in and out of school purposes were identified and elaborated, including details of the most effective media for specific types of education and fields of study.

Thirdly, on the basis of this analysis of the existing situation, the setting of objectives and the general policy guidelines from the Ministry of Education, seven alternative approaches proposed by the Government were analysed and evaluated. The most promising was identified and revised to take account of the finding of the team.

During February and March the Ministry of Education studied the proposal for an educational media project recommended by the team and accepted it with some minor alterations. The Ministry commented on many of the other questions raised by the team, thus providing a sufficiently solid foundation for a detailed project. The team was therefore able to concentrate its attention throughout April and May on the preparation of a specific main project and associated sub-projects. Complete project details were formulated, including:

(a) *Objectives and justification*
(b) *Staffing and training*
(c) *Programme and programme preparation schedules*
(d) *Technical specification*
(e) *Details of buildings (including draft plans) and equipment (including draft specifications)*
(f) *Description of utilisation procedures*
(g) *Full recurrent and capital cost information*
(h) *Foreign aid and technical assistance requirements*
(i) *Evaluation and research procedures*
(j) *An operational plan, including details of project component phasing.*

All the background information collected throughout the study, especially that which led to the selection of the project and that which would be needed for its evaluation and implementation, was edited and included in a Final Report. This Final Report thus had two main functions, first to act as a project request document to be presented to foreign aid donors, and secondly as a handbook for project implementation to be used by the relevant Thai Government officials.

On the positive side the conclusions of the study did justify the Government's decision to carry out a detailed enquiry before embarking on a large scale media project. At the outset the Ministry was mainly interested in mounting an in-school TV project, but as the study progressed it became clear that this was neither feasible nor particularly cost-effective and thus the emphasis moved towards radio (with multi-media support) with a concentration on adult and out-of-school audiences. If the study had not taken place Thailand might have found itself with a high cost ETV system catering for urban children who already have considerably greater educational opportunity than children and adults in other parts of the country.

A crucial aspect of the study was the continuous consultation with high Ministry of Education officials. Before each phase of the study the team checked with the Ministry (and the steering committee) that the study was progressing in a direction that was both feasible and acceptable to the government. Without this continuous seeking of policy guidance and approval it is likely that the study would have resulted in a project which was not consistent with the requirements of the authorities.

The account is not complete, and other parts describe quite frankly some of the problems which were encountered in the exercise. It was short of time; it was not always possible to recruit the exact specialists needed; not all Government departments were as interested as the sponsoring authority (the Ministry of Education). There were also those cultural problems already cited, inevitable when a group of foreign experts visits a developing country. But the study does show the importance, not only of corporate planning, but of frequent interaction between the specialists who are carrying out the planning and those in authority who are taking the decisions. This is true, whether the system being designed is at the level of a single school or of a nation State; planning is not only logic, fore-thought and systems analysis — it is also public relations, persuasion, motivation and involvement.

The importance of flexibility

In this section, we have shown how a project can be elaborated which is both rational and realistic. But any system will, in the end, be a com-promise, picking its way among alternate propositions and opposing forces, and this means that the final design must, above all, be flexible. It must be able to modify itself, to respond to changed circumstances, to accommodate differences of emphasis. Any institution tends, over the long term, towards rigidity and the system proposed should do everything within its power to work against this tendency. No set of educational objectives, however carefully formulated, will remain static. If the purpose of an educational media system is to improve quality, in the teaching force or in the classroom, and if it is successful, then that very success will change the nature of its objectives. Initially, at the point of introduction, strongly directed, centrally produced materials will probably be needed, which make the most of the distribution potential of electronic systems. Over a period of time, as innovative forces make inroads on established attitudes and produce better qualified, better motivated, more resourceful and more confident teachers, the system must allow for materials organised in a less structured way, thus returning to the teacher a greater freedom of choice. It is a principle which is important enough to put last in this section, and one which is assumed throughout all the chapters which follow.

Media programming

With Part 3 we turn to the practical business of operational planning. Reverting for a moment to the network diagram reproduced in Fig. 1.1, we have reached the activity 'Define system in detail'. It is at this point that the network branches into components of building and equipment, recruitment, training and programme development, with associated activities of utilisation training and evaluation.

We have now to consider three aspects of operational planning: the *structures* which are to be created, to fulfil the system's objectives; the *process* with which these structures are engaged; and the *phasing* of their construction.

Put simply, the structures are the institutions (buildings, facilities, staff) which are needed to produce the kinds of material envisaged. The way in which these are framed, the planning and production models adopted, make up the process of media realisation. And the sequence in which different parts of the process are introduced constitutes the phasing.

Chapter 12

Technical facilities

Structures

We begin with a production facility. Any media service, from the simplest level upwards, will contain elements of *technical and engineering services, production services* (graphics, film, design and creative programme sections), and *administration*, even though these may well be represented by only one or two people.

The media facility, therefore, has to match a production process which is, in principle, as shown in Fig. 12.1. In this diagram, we see the marriage, at a technical level, between electronic and physical production and distribution forms, with some common services pooled between them. A more specific description of the production process will be found in Chapter 13.

In assessing demands, consequently, we have six separate areas to consider:

1. *Studios*
2. *Control rooms*
3. *Other technical area*: film or telecine area, recording and editing channels, photographic services, art and design services, etc.

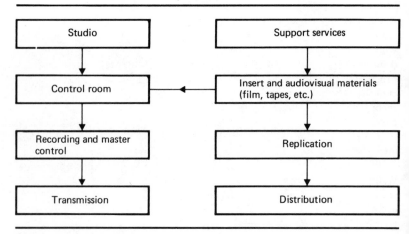

Fig. 12.1 Production sequence.

4. *Workshops, maintenance areas, house services*: air conditioning, electricity, etc.
5. *Storage space*: for scenery, film, tapes, materials, etc.
6. *Other accommodation*: offices, libraries, viewing theatres, rehearsal rooms, lecture rooms, committee rooms, make-up and wardrobe, etc.

Depending upon the location and upon the size of the service, these will operate at vastly different levels. But in concept, the same functions apply throughout (even if a service is operating from a mobile vehicle, it still has a control room, and the location in which it is working becomes the 'studio').

The account which follows is based on a medium-sized facility, at the level of a State system. Any special requirements, which arise at other levels, are dealt with later.

Studios and control rooms

We can take these two together, as they are closely associated. The studio is the equivalent of the theatrical stage, where the actual programme is performed. The control room, adjacent to the studio, is the nerve centre of the operation; from this point, technical instructions are given, and the different aural or visual sources are selected and 'mixed' into a composite whole.

In principle, therefore, radio and television studios serve much the same purpose. It is in technical operation that differences arise, which lead in turn to variations in design and construction.

1. Radio

Studios
Radio studios are designed very much according to function. Thus, larger studios are constructed to accommodate drama and music productions, where a number of performers are involved and several microphones, of different types and characteristics, are in use; smaller studios handle talks programmes or limited discussions. Modern design has tended to concentrate operational functions as far as possible, especially when pre-recorded tapes and records are employed, and in commercial radio in particular, the 'self-operated' studio (where the announcer plays in recordings, cartridges and cassettes, as well as handling continuity announcements) has become commonplace.

With radio, sound quality is obviously the overriding consideration. Walls and ceilings are acoustically treated, to produce (in a drama/music studio) reverberation times of approximately 0.55—0.65 seconds, with an even diffusion of sound across the spectrum. In a talks studio, a reverberation time of 0.35—0.55 seconds is adequate.

Thus, a medium-sized drama studio might be 7 m x 8 m, with a finished acoustic ceiling height of about 4 m, while a talks or continuity studio might be 4–5 m x 6 m, with a ceiling height of approximately 3 m. In a music or drama studio, far more microphone outlets are required, with panels on each wall providing for three to four microphone connectors, two headphone outlets and one cue light outlet. Monitor and talkback loadspeakers are wall-mounted above control room windows, and the studio floor should be separated from both the floor slab and the walls to ensure isolation from structure-borne impact noises. The most frequent causes of noise penetration are structural vibration and sound carried by pipes and steelwork, through internal doors, through walls, windows and ceilings. Sound locks are needed at the studio entrance, and an acoustically sealed window communicating with the control room. It is common to arrange for different acoustic properties in different parts of the studio (to distinguish between 'indoor' and 'outdoor' acoustics); these can be achieved partly with curtain drapes, drawn across as required, and partly by arrangements of acoustic screens.

In talks studios such requirements are reduced (perhaps one-half of the microphone outlets would be needed), and acoustic isolation is less critical. Floors can therefore be of a cork or mastic type, with the spring-type isolators used in drama studios (expensive to install) unnecessary.

In talks and continuity studios, it is also usual to install interview tables, acoustically treated and secure, often with a suspended microphone above (placed in the viewline of the announcer operator).

Continuity suites
These are small talks studio combinations, which are used for network presentation (distributing the final programme output of the station), for announcer-controlled operations, and as standby studios for talks, commentary and interview programmes.

Control rooms
The same general principles apply to control rooms, where operational functions are carried out (i.e. the balancing and mixing of various sound sources — live performances, music, tapes, discs, etc. — and recording on to tape).

The technical facilities required include audio mixing consoles (up to twelve channels for smaller studios, up to sixteen or beyond for larger studios), discs playback units for gramophone recordings, reel-to-reel audio recorders for programme inserts and final programme recording, and in smaller or commercial stations cartridge and cassette playback recorders (these are very useful for effects, spot announcements, commercials, or for continuity purposes).

Monitoring and talkback loudspeakers are also required, both to review programme sound and to communicate with studio personnel.

Master Control
Master Control is a centralised technical control area, where a number of

technical functions are pooled, and where network operations are carried out (the linking of different programmes in a transmission schedule, with continuity either pre-recorded or, more commonly, coming from a continuity suite).

As far as possible, therefore, Master Control areas should be designed for operation by a minimum number of staff. However, this does not mean that one can skimp on space. They have to provide room for equipment racks, jackfields, amplifiers and so on, as well as for control consoles, and there must always be space left over to allow for future expansion. This is one area where improvisation is very difficult, once a service expands; the freedom to move, and to have access to equipment for maintenance, is critical.

The Master Control area will include the following facilities:

(*a*) control consoles for networking;
(*b*) jackfields, distribution amplifiers, line amplifiers and other items of distribution equipment (both internally, within the studio complex, and routes into and out of the studio centre);
(*c*) 'off-air' monitoring equipment;
(*d*) technical telephone system (for internal communication between technical areas);
(*e*) a master clock system, slaved to all studios and technical areas;
(*f*) test facilities (for generating test signals);
(*g*) a reverberation unit which can be patched to individual studios as required.

2. Television

Studios

In appearance, television studios are similar to radio studios, but more complex in facilities to cater for the visual element.

Sets are arranged around the studios; cameras operate in front of, and frequently within, these settings. The cameras themselves have long cables, which are run from wall boxes. (Making sure that cables do not cross, or become entangled, in the course of studio productions is one of the producer's prime concerns when he plans his shots.) Above is the lighting grid, where the studio lights are suspended.

The television studio must give room for manoeuvre; drama, for example, cannot be properly mounted in a studio less than 15 m x 10 m. It must be sufficiently high to take a lighting grid and to allow for air-conditioning and ventilation (a good height would be 12 m).

A smaller studio might be 9 m x 7 m, with a ceiling height slightly lower (though in a complex with studios of varying sizes, ceiling height is likely to remain constant, for obvious architectural reasons). This is not to say that studios of a smaller size cannot produce effective programmes, especially in converted premises, or that drama cannot be produced in a more limited environment. In television, especially, improvisation has to, and does, occur. But it will involve some compromises, and will probably mean recording scenes out of sequence, with sets struck and re-set in between recording segments to compensate for the reduced space.

Consequently there are, in a television studio, three separate zones of activity. The floor is taken up by cameras; microphones and sound booms occupy a thin layer between 2m and 3 m from floor level, and above that is the lighting area. The actual volume of space required for lighting is variable, depending upon the form of suspension system employed; as much as 3—4 m of headroom is sometimes needed.

Even the most primitive studio has to be *proofed* but acoustic treatment is far more of a compromise in television than in radio. Television studios have to accommodate a good deal of equipment and must be multipurpose in design. For a studio of 15,000 cubic feet (approximately 425 cubic metres), a reverberation time of 0.5 seconds will be satisfactory, and this can usually be achieved by treating the walls, and sometimes the ceiling above the grid, with acoustic tiling and/or cabots quilting.

Air-conditioning is essential, especially in tropical countries. Humidity must be kept down or the equipment will degenerate rapidly, and television equipment, especially lighting, generates a good deal of heat. Every kilowatt of light generates a kilowatt of heat, which will raise the temperature of 3,000 cubic feet of air (approximately 90 cubic metres) by $-17.2°$ C per minute. A good, silent air-conditioning system is required: room conditioners will not suffice, as they make far too much noise and are underpowered. Ideally, in hot damp countries, air-conditioning should be run on a 24-hour basis, but if this is economically impossible dehumidifiers can be installed to be operated when the studio is not in use.

A regulated *power supply* is needed to operate camera and videotape equipment, and voltage stabilisers are required. The power consumption of this equipment is negligible, but stability is most important. Each stabiliser should be capable of stabilising all the power required for the technical equipment of a particular studio or technical area. For lighting, approximately 40 watts per sq. foot of power will be required for Image Orthicon and Plumbicon cameras, and 100 watts per sq. foot for Vidicons. If an extra 2.5 kW is added for each camera in use, plus an extra 3 kW for each telecine machine, and a final 5 kW for good measure, this will make a reasonable rule-of-thumb assessment of demands, good enough at least for a check with the electricity authorities as to its availability. A three-phase supply is needed, but, if possible, all technical equipment in a particular area should be on a single phase. Connector sockets are needed throughout the studio for connecting cameras, microphones, television monitors, loudspeakers and so on. Vision and sound connectors are best isolated from the mains cables, with a separate 'technical earth' provided; if this isolation is not secured, a mains fault can easily damage sensitive vision equipment, or cause interference.

Studio floors, except in the most basic installations, must be accurately level (in the better studios, to a flatness of plus or minus, 1.25 mm in 3 metres). This is to allow for smooth camera movements and is not just a question of finesse: irregular tracking will be visually disconcerting and will interfere with the viewer's concentration. Laying floors is a job for the expert; they must be properly joined and quiet to walk on. Heavy duty lino is the most usual surface in use, though hardboard, rubber composition and other composition substances are sometimes used. The subfloor is also important; it must be stable, usually made of a thin layer of asphalt on concrete.

In a film studio, many of the *lights* in use are placed on stands on the floor; they are moved to a new position for each successive shot or sequence. In television this arrangement is not possible, as the programme is shot continuously, with cameras moving to new positions whenever they are not 'on the air'. For this reason, studio space is at a premium, and lighting has to be kept off the floor, with lamps mounted above the working area. The method of suspension used inevitably affects basic questions of studio design. The simplest method is to clamp them to a lighting grid (an arrangement of metal pipes in the form of scaffolding, with a mesh of 1−2 m across each section). This is secured to the studio walls and ceiling, and has to be substantial enough to take the full weight of the lamps themselves. Light alloy tube is normally employed, able to take the standard 1.1/8 inch (28.5 mm) spud or spigot which is used for TV lighting fitments.

In more complex lighting systems, lights may be fixed on 'barrels', which are raised and lowered mechanically or manually, or on movable ceiling tracks: for such an installation expert advice is necessary. If the grid is mounted fairly high, and a reasonable volume of lighting is available, lights may be left permanently in position and their height adjusted by using pipes, telescopic hangers or pantographs. The principal reason for such an arrangement is to economise on time. Lighting can be very time-consuming when it is done properly, and any system which reduces the manual labour involved is welcome. Some typical methods of suspension are illustrated in Fig. 12.2.

A note should also be added at this point on *camera types*, or more specifically on *camera tubes*, as these are the mainstay of the television studio. Nowadays, camera tubes for studio applications are of two kinds, called the *photo-emissive* type (of which the long established image orthicon is one) or the *photo-conductive* type. The *vidicon* was at one time the most common photo-conductive tube in general use, but a decade ago the *lead oxide vidicon* (or as it is more widely known by its trade names − the *Plumbicon* or *Leddicon*) came upon the scene, and particularly for colour television applications has virtually replaced the older vidicon. Vidicons remain in use, however, in many closed-circuit television installations, because of their relative cheapness.

The *image orthicon* has, for many years, been standard for high quality monochrome studio pictures, but creates many problems if required to be used in colour television applications. It is also more bulky and is considerably more expensive than vidicon or Plumbicon type camera tubes.

Colour television raises some different problems again. In the original

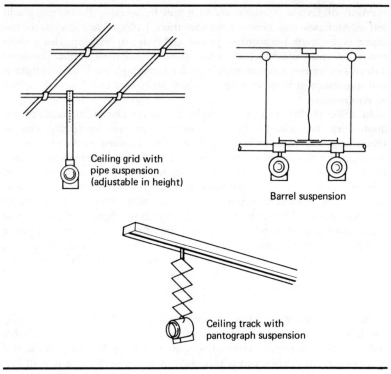

Ceiling grid with
pipe suspension
(adjustable in height)

Barrel suspension

Ceiling track with
pantograph suspension

Fig. 12.2   Typical methods of lighting suspension.

version of this handbook, *Planning for ETV* (1971), there was little discussion of colour; at that time the majority of educational television
operations were monochrome, and the concensus of research was that, in
most cases, colour capacity added little of instructional value. But the
situation has been changed, at least in broadcast applications (CCTV issues
are dealt with later), simply because colour has become so much more
widespread. Instructional relevance loses its force as an argument, once
students are used to colour in their general viewing: if it is not introduced,
then ETV becomes, necessarily, a poor relation. The Open University, for
example, began operations in monochrome, but has been compelled to
colourise gradually, and its new premises, now under construction, will
have a full colour facility.

In colour television, the camera is required to separate the light from a
scene into red, green, and blue components and this (based on mirrors and
prisms) requires three (sometimes four) camera tubes. The modern colour
camera, therefore, is usually equipped with photoconductive Plumbicon
tubes, which have good resolution and generally good performance characteristics. Thus the modern colour camera may be made, if not smaller,
then at least no bigger than the old monochrome image orthicon camera.

Much discussion is also heard of alternative *colour television systems*, but in fact this is a problem of transmission, not of production. Of the many systems of transmission proposed over the years, virtually three remain, NTSC, SECAM and PAL. Chronologically, the NTSC (National Television Systems Committee — USA) was the earliest successful system and is in use in such countries as the USA, Japan and Canada.

Atmospheric disturbances, reflections (ghosts) and receiver design inadequacies resulted in variable quality colour reception, and subsequent modifications to the basic NTSC system produced the French SECAM (Sequence and Memory) system and later the German PAL (Phase Alternate Line) system — each claiming improvements in the reception of colour television signals. These do not, however, imply that the NTSC system is obsolete. Subsequent design improvements in transmission equipment and receiver circuitry have resulted in three fiercely competitive transmission systems, each professing certain advantages over the other in various aspects of colour television signal generation, processing, transmission and reception.

Control rooms

Like radio, a television studio has a separate control room, cut off from the studio proper by a soundproof window.

In smaller studios, it is better to have the control room at ground level (although the larger studio complexes have their control rooms at least half a floor above, to provide a bird's eye view of the studio). In educational media, where amateur performers are so often used, it is preferable to site the control room so as to allow easy access to the studio. The value of panoramic studio observation is in any case much exaggerated.

Sound-proofing between control rooms and studios is of particular importance: otherwise technical instructions will filter through into the studio and may be picked up by the studio microphones. For this reason the control room window is normally made up of a double glass panel, vacuum-sealed, and set at an angle to cut down reflections. To ensure insulation, at least 25 cm between panels is required. The layout of control rooms is also a matter of some debate, though a characteristic example is given in Fig. 12.3. Within the control room, a line of monitors or TV screens, each showing the output of a different camera or other visual source (e.g. film) is set in front of the director, allowing him to make a choice between alternative pictures at different stages of the programme. The monitors need to be placed fairly close together, so that they can be seen without too much head movement; they should be set just below the horizontal line of sight (for comfortable viewing), at a distance from the director of between six and eight times the picture diagonal (see Fig. 12.4).

Originally, this line of monitors was usually placed above or below the control room observation window, allowing the director to look into the studio as well as at his monitoring screens. Often, however, the view into the studio was obscured by settings or by a cyclorama, and there was a

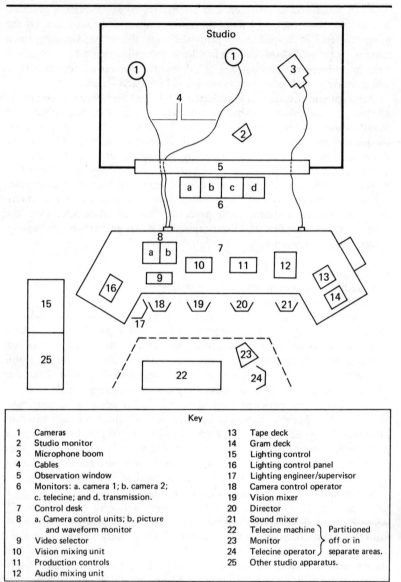

Fig. 12.3   Simplified control room layout.

Key

1	Cameras	13	Tape deck
2	Studio monitor	14	Gram deck
3	Microphone boom	15	Lighting control
4	Cables	16	Lighting control panel
5	Observation window	17	Lighting engineer/supervisor
6	Monitors: a. camera 1; b. camera 2; c. telecine; and d. transmission.	18	Camera control operator
		19	Vision mixer
7	Control desk	20	Director
8	a. Camera control units; b. picture and waveform monitor	21	Sound mixer
		22	Telecine machine ⎫ Partitioned
9	Video selector	23	Monitor ⎬ off or in
10	Vision mixing unit	24	Telecine operator ⎭ separate areas.
11	Production controls	25	Other studio apparatus.
12	Audio mixing unit		

problem of glare from the studio lights. Moreover, in practice, directors found that they rarely, if ever, needed to look into the studio itself: the monitors were far more important. As a result two other control room layouts became possible, as well as the normal frontal layout; the sideways

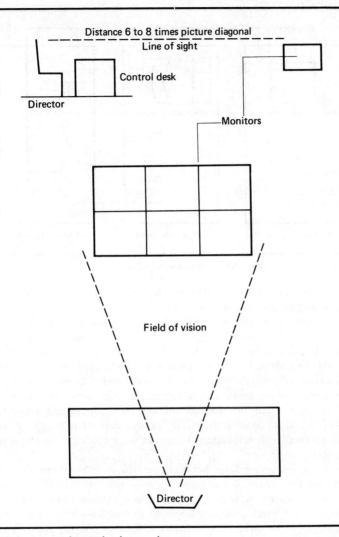

Fig. 12.4 Layout for production monitors.

layout, and the backwards layout. In the first, control rooms were placed at an angle of 90° to the main studio; in the second, the director was actually looking in the opposite direction, away from the studio. These positions are shown in Fig. 12.5.

The choice is a matter of preference, though the sideways layout seems particularly appropriate to ETV. With the observation window at an angle, there is no temptation for the director to look constantly into the studio; at the same time he can check on difficult sequences without too much trouble. The main point to be stressed is that a traditional frontal layout is

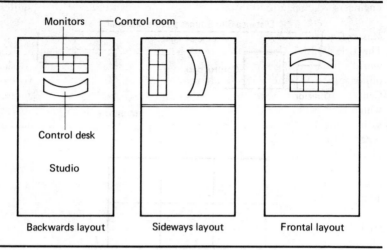

Fig. 12.5   Three approaches to control room layout.

by no means necessary in a TV studio, and there is no point in modifying a building specifically to achieve it.

The lighting arrangements in control rooms are also important. Monitors should be seen against a low level of background illumination, but a concentrated working light will be needed on the control desk, to allow the director and other technical operators to read their scripts easily. The location of controls is also worth a good deal of attention; if they are sensibly placed (and some remote control facilities added) the number of operators can often be reduced for a simple educational programme. Remote 'joystick' controls for CCU (camera control unit) operators are always preferable. A solid control desk is always needed, with ample space for scripts.

Access is important both between control areas and between control rooms and the studio. Other technical areas (and such facilities as wardrobe and make-up, scenery storage and preparation rooms) should be located close at hand; given a thoughtful approach to design, a lot of time and energy can be saved. The architect will not necessarily appreciate this unless it is emphasised.

In the larger studios, there will be separate control rooms for vision and sound, and often for lighting and camera control. At a smaller level this will not usually be possible, but the separation of vision and sound control areas at least is rewarding. Sound engineers require to work with loudspeakers at an uncomfortably high level, and often acoustic modifications are desirable for audio control purposes which are not required in the vision control room. It is possible for sound engineers to use the same monitors as vision control, even when working from a separate cubicle, if their control desk is raised high enough, so that they can see through an observation window over the heads of the director and the vision engineers. A separate transmission monitor will, however, be required.

Master Control
The title 'Master Control' is a term falling from favour in many of the world's broadcasting stations, mainly because of changes in system design philosophies. Whether the modern terminology remains Master Control, or Central Apparatus Area, or any other title, it generally refers to an area which acts as the 'heart' of the system. As such it serves the same purposes as in radio, and though radio and television Master Control areas should be separated even in a service dealing with both media, it will help if they are placed adjacent (easing problems of maintenance and operations).

The same kinds of technical equipment will be found in television Master Control as were previously described for radio, but with some additions. In modern studios, camera control units (CCUs) are housed here, rather than in sub-control rooms (where only remote control 'joy-sticks' are found, for adjustments to be made during a production session). Master Control also houses the synchronising pulse generators (SPGs). All studio equipment from which vision signals originate (cameras, videotape recorders, test signal generators, etc.) rely on the SPGs to produce vision signals which are synchronised, so that it becomes possible to cut between various studio vision signals without disturbance, to 'dissolve' from one picture to another, and to perform special effects on the various signals.

The Master Control area is therefore a technical as distinct from a programme production area, although in some smaller studio centres programme switching and presentation can also be carried out from a suitable control desk.

This means that some presentation equipment (a simple vision mixing unit, slide projection facilities and a tape/cartridge/cassette audio system) may have to be provided. By doing so, of course, instead of employing a separate continuity/presentation suite, both space and money are saved, as well as operators' time.

Other technical areas

In an integrated media service these will be of two kinds: those which act as support services to the broadcasting media; and those which cater for separate production of audio-visual and print materials.

In operation, however, this division of functions may well not be so clear. While a telecine area (to project film inserts for television programmes) is clearly a supporting technical facility to the television process, film and photographic services are not (they can produce both insert materials, and independent films, strips and slides). When the same tools and materials are used, a degree of pooling of resources and personnel is obviously desirable, provided that it does not interfere with operational efficiency. We will begin, however, with those facilities which are demonstrably part of the electronic production process.

Broadcasting support facilities

Telecine
Telecine applies to the area or the equipment used for converting a film image (whether movie or still) into a television signal.

Fortunately the television industry, virtually world wide, has adopted 16 mm film with an image format 4 units wide by 3 units high as 'standard'. (Many film companies still use 35 mm film, necessitating at least one telecine projector capable of handling this size of film in professional installations, but not normally required for educational broadcasting.) Of the other grades of film available, only super 8 mm is creating interest as a further contender for television utilisation at this stage, but the position is still complicated by rapid technological change.

The basic telecine principle is to project an image on to the face of a television camera tube, virtually using the camera tube face as a 'screen'. This type of telecine usually uses photo-conductive camera tubes because of their size, relatively low cost and very satisfactory performance characteristics under controlled conditions.

High-quality telecine pictures are possible with much more sophisticated (and hence expensive) equipment utilising the 'flying spot' technique. This is a very complex system requiring absolute synchronisation between the film movement and the television signal. The flying spot technique differs from the conventional camera tube principle, in that the image is broken down into elements optically, before being converted into an electrical signal.

Telecine equipment would normally comprise at least two 16 mm movie projectors to enable change-over of programme between reels, and one 35 mm slide projector. The three projectors can 'feed' one photo-conductive television camera, normally using a system of mirrors or prisms mechanically operated (in a *multiplexer*) to select the required light path.

Telecine equipment may also comprise a caption scanner for televising graphics, test patterns, titles or a clock, all of which are conventional requirements in television programming. These may be placed in master control, or in a presentation/continuity area, if used.

Audio recording and dubbing
The recording of radio programmes on to magnetic ¼ inch tape (usually recorded at 7½ inches or, with higher quality, 15 inches per second) is now so commonplace that live transmissions are reserved for news, outside broadcast and special topical programmes (such as 'phone-in' programmes).

But in radio (unlike television), audio recording is normally carried out in the radio control room. Special areas are provided however, for audio editing, and for the dubbing and duplication of tapes, so as not to interfere with studio procedures.

An editing suite includes basic facilities for editing tapes (audio recorders and editing blocks), for assembling taped inserts and for adding simple narration to a sequence of pre-recorded tapes.

The process of dubbing or duplicating tapes is a straightforward copying process, and if these are required in bulk high-speed copiers are available.

Videotape recording

Perhaps the greatest single contribution to revolutionise television studio operations has been the development of the videotape recorder. Until this became a practical proposition, all recorded television programmes were made on film as 'kinescopes', by the kine-recording (or tele-recording) process. This technique resulted in loss of quality when compared to the original studio pictures and took a considerable time for processing.

One of the novel features of a videotape recorder is the use of a rotating video head. It was realised early in development work that to record video frequencies (much higher than audio) would necessitate moving the tape past the recording head at a very high speed. To avoid using vast quantities of magnetic tape, it was therefore proposed to move the head, as well as the tape. Thus a very high 'writing' rate was achieved by virtue of the video head recording many tracks across the width of the tape, as it progressed longitudinally at a reasonable speed of about 15 inches per second, (i.e. at a speed consistent with current audio tape requirements).

Further innovations in videotape equipment have included the ability to edit videotape by wholly electronic means, similar to the techniques employed in film production but without the necessity of cutting the tape. Whole programmes may be assembled in segments giving the appearance of a continuous production. Additions or improvements can be made to existing programmes by inserting new segments into an unrequired section without any visible disturbances. Even animation is now possible under automatic control.

Slow and fast motion and 'frozen frames' are available using a rotating magnetic video-disc in full colour, and even tape duplication is possible by a magnetic printing method similar to contact printing in photography.

The standard, broadcast transverse scan videotape recorder takes a 2 inch videotape. However, the once 'domestic' quality helical scan videotape recorder has been developed enormously in technical quality and reliability, and 1 inch machines, with editing facilities, have become quite common in broadcast studios (and standard in CCTV installations). In India, the 1 inch machine is being generally adopted, having benefited greatly from experimentation during the SITE project, where not only were 1 inch machines adopted as the basic standard, but smaller-gauge machines were also used for insert purposes. For such functions, a facility for time-base correction is preferred (though in India, synchronisation problems were avoided by replaying the original tape on to a high-quality television monitor, and subsequently photographing it via a high quality studio camera, while recording on to a standard machine. The loss of quality was thought to be marginal). Further information on these issues is provided in the sections that follow, in the discussion of technical facilities for community media.

Mobile units

Not everything in broadcasting takes place in the studio, and not all location work can be handled by film (especially if live presentation is needed, or simultaneous coverage by a number of cameras). For these purposes, mobile outside broadcasting units are used, which take both cameras and control room into the field.

Outside broadcast equipment traditionally duplicates studio facilities, only in a much more confined space. With the exception of a slide or caption scanner, the telecine component is usually omitted. A characteristic two-camera layout is shown in Fig. 12.6.

Thanks to the use of solid-state transistorised equipment, a vast amount of equipment can nowadays be crammed into a modern outside broadcast vehicle, enabling complex productions to be made off-site. In educational applications, two to three cameras are normally used, and production facilities extend to versatile vision mixing equipment. Traditionally, cameras are cabled back to the control vehicle, but thanks to greater miniaturisation of electronic equipment, portable cameras can now also be carried with back packs, allowing a cameraman to move independently, either recording his pictures on an integral unit, or transmitting them back to the recording van. Mobile videotape equipment is often used so that recordings may be made on the OB site; this was more difficult when only 2 inch videotape recorders were in use for broadcasting, but the advent of smaller format link machines has again helped to reduce bulk.

If the programme is a live presentation (as happens with news or sport presentations) it is necessary to 'link' back to the studio. This is usually done with microwave transmitting and receiving equipment (being in the ultra high-frequency spectrum microwaves travel in narrow beams, virtually in line of sight, which allows transmission without interference to other people). Today, field recordings via small, portapak units are increasingly common. These are carried on the cameraman's back; the scene photographed may either be recorded on a portable video-recorder, or a microwave link may be maintained with a mobile unit or permanent studio. The use of portapak equipment was originally confined to local media systems, because of its dependence upon small-gauge recording, but it is now a common feature of many broadcasting services, especially news services, in America and Europe. During the SITE experiment, the system was widely used, to offset the cost and greater unwieldiness of film.

Common technical services

The remaining facilities to be described are of a more general kind, contributing to both mass media and support services.

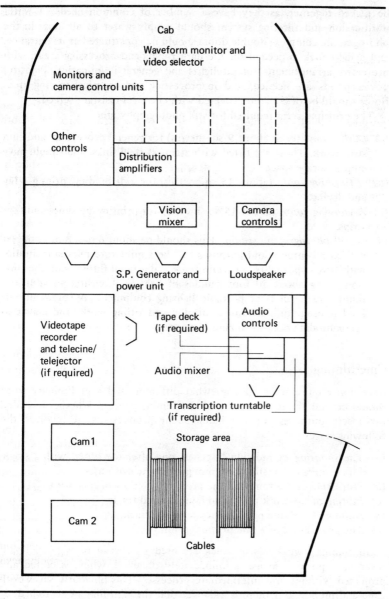

Fig. 12.6 A mobile unit.

Film and photographic areas

As far as possible facilities for still film, film strip and motion picture film work should be integrated, and operational functions combined even though they may serve somewhat different ends. All film facilities should be placed together, as they have a number of common needs. A water purification and filtering system should supply water to all areas in the photographic complex; double doors should be constructed at its entrance, and a light lock is needed for the dark rooms and processing areas, with protective arrangements for safelights and general illumination. Plentiful power points are needed, and in processing and chemical mixing areas floors should be of concrete, covered with chemical-resistant screed.

The principal areas required for still photography are:

(a) *Dark rooms* (each about 9 sq. metres) for general processing, and film strip work. These are fitted with stainless steel sinks, and should have ample storage space.

(b) *A finishing room* (about 15 sq. metres) for slide binding, print glazing and drying.

(c) *A copying room* (about 15 sq. metres) for printing up slides and film strips.

(d) *A still photographic studio.* This should be about 6 m x 8 m in size; it will to all intents and purposes be like a miniature television studio, with fitted spotlights, a curtain track and general fluorescent illumination giving about 50 foot candles of lighting intensity. In addition, points are needed for portable lighting equipment. A studio of this kind is used for portraiture, display and titling work, and may also accommodate occasional cine film inserts.

Cine filming

Cine film requirements are somewhat different, and a preliminary word should be said about the nature of the filming process. Whether intended for insert purposes, or for independent productions, it involves the following stages.

(a) The *shooting* of individual scenes, one after the other, with a single film camera (normally of 16 mm gauge in television).

(b) *Processing* of the film, and the production of a working print.

(c) *Editing* of the work print, and laying sound tracks.

(d) *Dubbing* — producing a composite sound track.

(e) The production of a *fine* or *show print*.

In filming, two kinds of stock are used — *reversal* or *negative*. With reversal, a positive image is immediately obtained, which is edited and projected without any intermediate processes. This obviously saves both time and money, but there is a danger that the film may be scratched, or wrongly cut, and reversal is used mostly for news or for insert film sequences in smaller services, where the volume of film is not great, money is in short supply and materials are not generally stored for re-use in a film library. With negative filming, after the negative has been processed, a print is struck, which is used for editing. When the various shots have been assembled in order, this work print or cutting copy is matched against the negative from which it is taken, shot by shot, using key numbers (printed along each strip of film) to aid identification of the correct portion of the negative. The cut negative is then used to produce another 'fine' print or 'show' print, which is used for transmission. This show print is therefore of high quality, having been graded in the laboratory and not having suffered at the hands of editor or projector; in television it will usually only be projected during a final rehearsal and for the actual recording (for earlier rehearsals the cutting copy is used as a production guide).

If possible, negative should always be employed: it is difficult enough for film projected via telecine to match studio quality, without having to contend with projector scratches and dirt as well. Reversal is best confined to training and news purposes.

Another complication arises with the shooting of sound. Many film sequences are shot silent, or 'mute', but sound adds a valuable extra dimension, reproducing more of the genuine quality of a location. Sound may be 'synchronised' (i.e. picture and sound are taken together, at the same time), or 'wild' (recorded separately).

There are several methods of sound recording. Two of these record the sound optically – the first, *comopt* (combined optical), records on to the same piece of film as photographs the picture, and the second, *sepopt*, (separate optical), on to a separate optical track. Alternatively, if sound is recorded magnetically, this may either be *commag* (combined magnetic, with the sound track printed alongside the film image, on a narrow band of magnetic tape), or *sepmag* (separate magnetic, with sound recorded independently on to ¼ inch magnetic tape, but with film camera and audio recorder synchronised by electronic means, so that both camera and recorder are locked to a pulse signal).

In television, the most common form of recording is sepmag – with film camera and synchronised audio recorder providing independent picture and sound tracks. Commag is sometimes used for newsreel purposes, though there are obvious difficulties in editing, as sound and picture cannot be cut independently, unless the sound track is first transferred on to a new track for editing. Comopt is the usual form for projecting film (with the sound track placed optically alongside the picture image), but the production of comopt prints is usually done in the laboratory. Sepopt is rarely encountered.

The filming process is at once more protracted and more complex than television, but offers much greater control at each of its stages (unlike television, which is assembled in a simple studio recording, the film producer has a number of opportunities to change his mind and make adjustments). Cinema film facilities will therefore include:

(a) A *Camera room* for the storage of cameras and accessories.
(b) *Editing rooms* (each about 10–12 sq. metres) for film editing.
(c) *Review rooms* for individual producers and technicians to review film sequences.
(d) *Chemical mixing rooms and processing rooms* (separate but adjacent),

to house chemicals and film processing equipment, if processing is being done on site and not on contract to a laboratory.

(e) *Review theatres* for film materials to be projected for evaluation. Apart from a general theatre (for use during public screenings and training courses), at least one smaller theatre for production team use is required. It should be able to project film slides and strips as well as cine film, so as to make it possible for multi-media materials to be seen together. These smaller theatres will be about 4 m x 5 m; the main theatre should be much larger, to seat up to fifty people at a time.

(f) A *dubbing suite* (made up of studio, audio control room and equipment room) to handle film dubbing. The dimensions of this area will depend upon the kind of dubbing system installed, but acoustic treatment and insulation is essential.

Finally, apart from *film storage rooms* (which should be in the same general area), an *animation room* may also be required for rostrum camera work. Film animation provides for cartoon work, animated diagrams, etc., with greater sophistication and with greater control than in the electronic studios. In most educational media services, full professional equipment, involving a sizeable animation stand and requiring an enlarged ceiling height, is not needed, and a simpler, low-cost assembly, allowing for multi-cel photography, simple camera movement (using a zoom lens and pantograph) and superimpositions and simple optical effects (mixes, dissolves, etc.) will be ample.

Print areas

In a multi-media service, facilities are required for composition, and for various kinds of *printing* (e.g. photocopying, duplicating, offset or even typographical printing), as well as for processes of cutting, collating and binding.

The dimensions of this area will depend entirely on the volume of work to be handled, and it is likely that a good deal will be subcontracted to external printers. But in-house printing needs must, in any case, be met. These involve considerable photocopying (preferably with a high-speed copier), large amounts of duplicating, dye-line printing for design drawings and some offset printing for small runs of teacher's notes, wall charts, etc. While subcontracting is an attractive solution for complex print work, or for very large print runs, it will not be economical for routine needs (and even more important, delays with these routine materials may hold back expensive production services).

The biggest problem of all in print areas is that of layout, to assist the flow of traffic (between composing, printing, collating and binding areas) and especially to ease storage and distribution problems.

Art services

Comprehensive facilities are needed for designers and graphic artists to produce set designs, caption and animation materials, illustrated materials for use in books and audio-visual items. Apart from these, provision for enlarging and reducing art work photographically should also be available in the same area, including process camera work.

The two most important requirements for design and graphics areas are space and even illumination. If possible, the art room itself should be on an outside wall, so that natural light is available, and the remaining lighting fitments are normally fluorescent (plus individual working lights at artists' desks). A light level of at least 75-foot candles is needed at drawing board height.

Workshop and maintenance areas, house services

Workshops are needed to serve each of the technical functions associated with the media: electronic maintenance, electrical maintenance and carpentry and metalwork. Each of these areas should be placed as close as possible to its main users, and in some cases (e.g. model making) a special area should be provided, if a large volume of work is envisaged.

Advice on the range of maintenance and test equipment needed should come from expert engineers; the requirements will differ in every installation. The expert will undoubtedly insist upon a full range of test items and of equipment spares, and he will be right. It should be a routine part of any storekeeper's duties to check regularly on the technical stores position and to order replacements. Nowadays, in particular, deliveries of spares can be very delayed.

House services are usually best provided from a service block placed apart from the main production centre, to cut down noise and vibration. They include an electrical substation, if required; air conditioning compressors; such services as a general water purification plant; and often the noisier workshops (e.g. for carpentry or metalwork). Useful storage areas can also be provided here (e.g. for large scenery not in regular use).

Storage space

A basic division should be made between storage areas associated with a particular technical function (film, art work, graphics, etc.), and the storage of materials intended for distribution (e.g. audio-visual materials, print materials). The saving in staff which might be expected to come from combining these storage areas will soon be eliminated by the administrative chaos which is bound to follow.

Storage areas, like maintenance areas, must be located in close proximity to the technical functions which they serve. Calculated requirements for storage always seem to be underestimated, and room for expansion is important.

Other accommodation

Offices

It is unnecessary to elaborate on routine office accommodation, which is no different from other spheres. It is always useful, however, to provide a number of small, multi-purpose committee rooms, which can act as shifting bases for particular activities; pressures tend to be seasonal in educational media.

In theory, media are very well suited to open-plan office layouts, though these are often resisted by production staff. Since the whole intention of media planning is to ensure a team approach, any geographical layout which encourages such a dialogue is worth considering.

Library areas

Here a distinction should be made, in terms of layout and administrative procedures, between library reference materials for *producers*, and library services which are part of a materials *loan* service. Production materials should be held separately and never issued to general borrowers. This is especially true in the case of audio-visual support materials which may be used in programmes (e.g. films used as inserts for television programmes), since these must be kept in top quality condition.

Lectures theatres and rehearsal rooms

In most cases, a media service will be used as a base for at least some utilisation training, and it is particularly important for the users of the service to be involved in its day-to-day operations. This means that space and facilities have to be provided for them to see what is going on, attend orientation courses, undertake training programmes, etc. It is always a good idea to build in observation facilities for at least one of the studios in both radio and television, so that visitors can see what is happening without disturbing production. (That facility can also be useful in training courses, where more students are often involved than can be accommodated in a control room at any one time.)

If rehearsal rooms can be fitted into a centre, they will help a good deal to free studios from routine rehearsal commitments. Educational media make a good deal of use of amateur or semi-professional talent, and as far as possible facilities should be designed to cater for their special needs (such as needing more rehearsal with actual properties to hand, or being made to feel at ease in new and tense situation).

Special layout considerations

Educational media make certain demands which are not shared by normal television, and these will not necessarily be remembered by technical consultants unless they are specially emphasised. For example, ETV programmes are very large users of graphic art, and an abnormally large workshop may be required; they also require substantial film and video-tape storage areas, as complete film libraries may be kept and programmes may be stored over a period of years for repeat transmissions.

When science programmes figure largely in the output, a small laboratory and science preparation room are necessary, close to the studio. For science too a water supply in the studio is usually required (with adequate drainage), and sometimes gas, though this can be fed from bottles. Extra electrical points are also needed.

In other areas, the demands of ETV may be less than for general television Make-up and wardrobe do not usually figure largely in ETV programming, and the staffing ratios allowed for an ETV service may be smaller overall, which means that where possible technical and other controls should be centralised.

As an illustration, Fig. 12.7, 12.8 and 12.9 show basic *schematic* relationships involved in planning facilities for radio production, television production and for coordinated media production. In other words, while they make no attempt to show the full range of accommodation required,

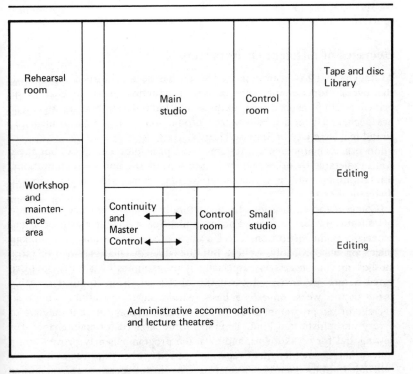

Fig. 12.7 Simple layout for radio production centre.

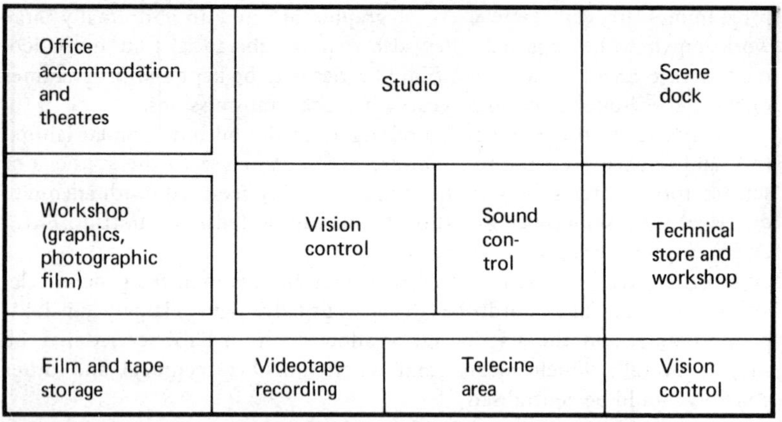

Office accommodation and theatres	Studio		Scene dock
Workshop (graphics, photographic film)	Vision control	Sound con- trol	Technical store and workshop
Film and tape storage	Videotape recording	Telecine area	Vision control

Fig. 12.8   Simple layout for television production centre.

or the dimensions, they illustrate the relationships between technical services which must be taken into account in planning for an efficient traffic flow.

Demands of different environments

Although what has been described so far has been concerned mainly with the overall function of technical and production areas, to elicit basic principles about their design, purpose and interrelationship, the argument has been based on a medium-sized production facility, such as might be found in a large city or State service.

In other environments, the same basic principles will apply, but these will be dictated by other factors — special purposes, budgetary limitations, limitations of audience. In other words, there will be considerable differences of *scale*.

Some of the implications follow naturally enough from a consideration of output, or of finance. For example, for a small-scale installation, especially at the institutional level, a single production studio for radio and television will probably suffice. But for larger installations, two or more studios may be necessary, especially if programmes of a fairly sophisticated nature are envisaged. Assuming that a television studio is available for 5 days a week, on a 9—5 basis (with a single operational crew), an average of ten programmes can be recorded, or perhaps more if they are of a very unsophisticated kind. Time has to be allowed for maintenance, for setting and for breakdowns, and even ten programmes may prove a strain unless there are lengthy vacation periods when no recordings are scheduled. Consequently, an increase in output means a corresponding increase in studios.

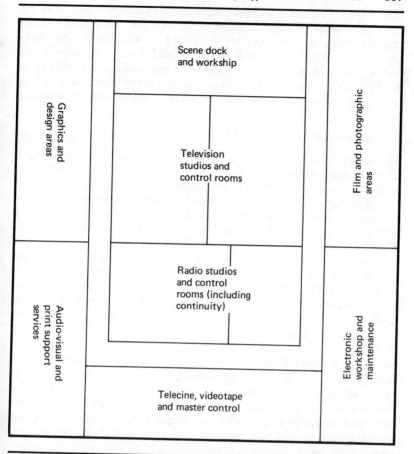

Fig. 12.9 Schematic for multi-media service (administrative accommodation and theatres on floor above).

Such constraints can easily be taken account of by the reader, if he uses his basic common sense, his knowledge of his own situation and its special problems, and whatever technical advice is to hand locally. The position will also be clarified by reference to the Appendix 'Characteristic media installations' at the end of this volume.

But there are other differences which derive more from philosophical principles, relating to the purpose for which media are wanted in the first place. Mostly these arise from a desire for media to help fulfil some specific objective, which is very much linked to social and geographical context, or to the character of a particular institution. So, for example, a teacher-training college may be preoccupied with using media to help in pedagogical work; or a community media service may be most anxious to involve audiences in production processes. These factors will have their special impact on studio and equipment design philosophies (including the question of whether a studio is necessary at all — is a mobile facility better suited?). They are questions which do not so much affect the larger services, constructed at the level of the *regional* or *national* system, where the facilities as described have merely to be rationalised, and scaled up or down, to arrive at the correct proportion. But at the smaller levels of the *institution* and of the *community*, more radical differences are apparent.

1. The institution

The reader who comes from a simple institutional background, say a school or small college, may already be shaking his head at the discussion of studios, control rooms, telecine equipment and so on. He may well be the single representative of all technical departments, working in one or two rooms which are, for him, the production complex. Yet even in the most basic case of a single school fitted with CCTV equipment, the same design philosophies occur, at however rudimentary a level.

Take the case of a simple classroom layout for a single camera, being used to show technical processes to a class seated in front. The situation is shown in Fig. 12.10. The forward teaching area becomes the studio; there is a producer (the teacher himself), a production process (selection of items for illustration or microscopic observation), a distribution system (via the display monitor).

At this level, of course, we are dealing with a technical and visual aid, not a mass medium. Probably the minimum arrangement which we would consider here as a 'television' application is the one reproduced in Fig. 12.11, which shows an improvised classroom studio, distributing to other classes in the same building, by a video cable system. This is a relatively basic level of closed circuit television, but it provides for both live and recorded elements, and a reasonable variety of visual and aural illustration, such as make up a composite 'programme'.

The question becomes: at what level is CCTV (or radio, for that matter) a viable form, and something distinct from a simple laboratory tool? Is it true that CCTV demands a certain minimum of equipment, personnel and resources below which its value is negligible? As usual it is a question of economics. For the initial cost of a television system to be repaid, however limited the system, a reasonably high proportion of use must be assured, and the only way of assessing this is on a cost-per-head basis.

This is not said in any way to disparage the work carried out by many schools, on a minimum budget and with scant equipment; or to criticise the teaching which results. It goes without saying that when a teacher decides to use television within his scheme of work and to assemble, with its help, a variety of visual accompaniments to his teaching, the result is likely to be as good as any carefully planned piece of instruction. But the amount of money available for education is itself limited, and the use of an expensive medium on too small a scale cannot easily be validated.

Some ingenious low-cost studio arrangements have been developed

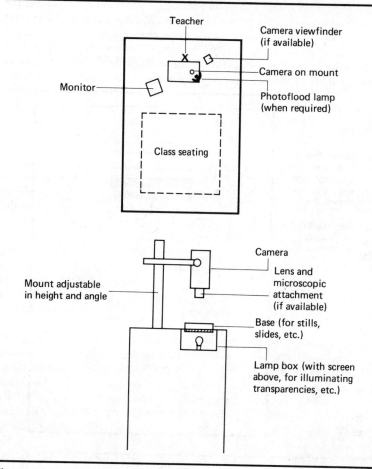

Fig. 12.10 Classroom layout for single camera.

which cut equipment costs to a basic level and reduce staffing (especially technical and production staff) to one or two people. In the 'mini' and 'micro' studios, a single cameraman may carry out a variety of technical functions which are normally shared: the TV presenter may even do everything himself (as well as teach).

The layout of the 'mini' studio is also illustrated in Fig. 12.12. Essentially its characteristics are the restriction of studio space, the confining of the presenter or TV teacher to set positions, and the elimination of a separate control room. All visual sources (film, captions, etc.) are centralised; usually remotely controlled and operated either by a cameraman or by the teacher himself. Alternative angles, close-up demonstrations and so on can be secured by a careful placement of cameras in advance, or by the use of mirrors.

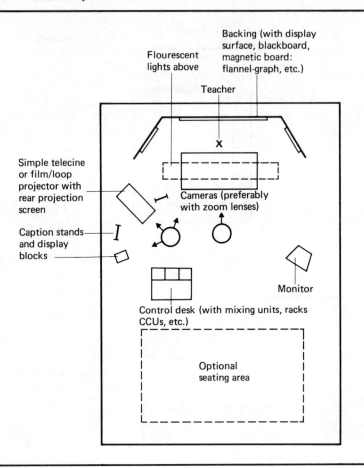

Fig. 12.11   Two cameras in use in school studio.

The system is certainly ingenious, but it is open to several objections. A variety of visual illustration is available, but the teacher himself is often rooted to the spot – which is restricting both to him and to the medium. Moreover it is doubtful whether many teachers can teach and operate technical controls simultaneously; either they will need to rehearse extensively in advance, or the result will be jerky and disjointed.

The fact remains that the 'mini' studio (first developed by Tony Gibson) was a serious attempt to bring ETV within the reach of smaller institutions. For limited school applications, classroom observation (restricted in numbers, and with additional lighting) or for overspill teaching, it is perfectly suitable; it can be experimented with by teachers and pupils alike, and it is an excellent training tool. It could also be used most effectively to try out programmes in advance; these could be put together

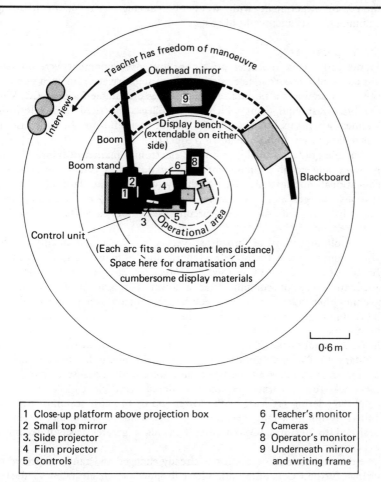

1 Close-up platform above projection box
2 Small top mirror
3. Slide projector
4 Film projector
5 Controls
6 Teacher's monitor
7 Cameras
8 Operator's monitor
9 Underneath mirror
  and writing frame

Fig. 12.12 The mini-studio.

roughly, and assessed, without going to the expense of a full studio record-ing. Like most tools, the mini studio is valuable when it is used with discretion; the danger with television is that to an uninformed user (or financial authority) all 'cameras' will appear alike, all installations multi-purpose. And manufacturers often seem ready to perpetuate this illusion.

There is a basic dilemma here, which has long resisted adequate solution. Many teachers have seen that the mass media are not fine enough tools to suit their needs (or they have wanted to experiment personally with media forms), and they have tried to find methods of using what are essentially high-cost media applications in situations which do not have the unit-cost advantages of widespread distribution. Since the basic economic factor is not a variable (the audience is of a fixed size), the have been forced to experiment with ways of reducing staff, or of reducing equipment costs and overhead costs.

CCTV equipment

In the early days, the attempts to use low-cost equipment were notably unsuccessful. Industrial television equipment (derived from such applications as scanning traffic intersections) was as unsuitable for early CCTV as the broadcast equipment which some colleges inherited from television stations, when this had reached the end of its useful life. In both cases it was bulky, heavy and broke down frequently.

But the gradual availability on the electronics market of transistorised, portable and reliable equipment of good quality, specially designed for educational applications, has gradually changed the face of ETV in schools, colleges and universities. We can now see, in fact, equipment specially designed for closed-circuit uses, not cast-offs from other functions.

The old argument, of 'broadcast' versus 'non-broadcast' quality in television equipment, is therefore no longer valid for many institutional users. Broadcasting equipment is used for *broadcasting*; provided there is an adequate range of equipment at a lower standard for CCTV, which assumes that video signals will not be transmitted over the air (with the inevitable degeneration in quality which results), lower-cost solutions can be found. (It is important to note, however, that equipment of non-broadcast quality can still use broadcast technical *standards*.)

Many CCTV installations are still monochrome, either because colour equipment was not available when they were built, because colour equipment was too expensive, or was considered insufficiently accurate in its colour rendering (at least at the lower end of the cost scale), or because colour is not generally necessary for the kind of work the system is designed to perform. Colour also demands a greater level of technical expertise.

Nevertheless, this situation has already changed and can be expected to change further. Cost differentials have dropped, as the electronics industry has developed; reliability and fidelity have improved. Less technical expertise is needed for automated equipment. A great deal of general broadcasting now takes place in colour, and students have become accustomed to its greater information content. Some ETV subjects demand it, such as medicine, parts of the chemistry syllabus, geology, cartography or biology. Research has shown, certainly, that increased information content may not always be an advantage, and for many applications black-and-white CCTV continues to be entirely adequate. But when the normal milieu for television is one of colour, pressure is difficult to resist.

The prime need is to relate the CCTV provisions to the educational objectives which the installation is required to fulfill. The absence of this relationship can lead to one of two familiar questions being asked: 'We have CCTV facilities; what shall we do with them?' or, alternatively, 'How can we possibly carry out all the work we are asked to do, with these inadequate means?'.

If a school or college only wants to show pictures from a workshop as inserts into lectures, a full-blown studio installation is, for example, quite unnecessary. If children are to be brought into a studio for the observation of lessons, a mobile CCTV provision may not be required, and so on.

Studio or mobile facilities?

A studio permits controlled use of technical factors such as lighting, acoustics and freedom from noise, and therefore allows a product of higher technical quality to be attained. In particular, complex productions can be made involving many media such as film, gramophone records, captions, audio tape, slides, interviews and science experiments or demonstrations. It can also be used for recording teaching skills, for example in a micro-teaching situation, and in this case it may be termed a 'studio-classroom'.

The advantages are clear: inside a television studio, the technical aspects of the operation are most closely under control, there is freedom to work and to manoeuvre, and any complications or breakdowns can be more easily settled. The drawbacks are almost entirely psychological, affecting the television subjects themselves. Since both class and teacher have been taken out of their normal environment this may result in an unnatural presentation, which is in turn self-defeating as far as educational objectives are concerned. Some variations have been proposed to help solve this problem. Hidden or remotely-controlled cameras may be used, or a class may be brought in for a number of 'pilot' visits before any real attempt at recording is made; in this way inhibitions are reduced. However, if a recording schedule is to be maintained, there is an early limit to the amount of acclimatisation that can take place. It has to be accepted that to use a studio centre as both studio and television classroom invites a degree of unnaturalness. The effect of this unnaturalness will vary from place to place, and can only be established by sustained experiment and research.

Portable or mobile facilities, ranging from a battery-portable kit, via a trolley with control equipment to, at the upper of the scale, a fully equipped mobile control room, may be required for bringing outside material into the educational institution. This may be especially important in a teacher-training context. In using a mobile unit to work on location away from the studio there are gains in verisimilitude, in naturalness, which are usually matched by technical losses. There is always a degree of technical improvisation about location work; conditions are more cramped, audio quality is necessarily rougher, most situations are less controllable. The benefits lie almost entirely in the fact that the subjects are working on home ground, and will not only be freer of restraint, but will be able to make use of their normal environment in the teaching process.

Another possibility allows the same cameras and control equipment to be used for outside recordings as for a studio. In the latter context, a van,

Studio   Garage

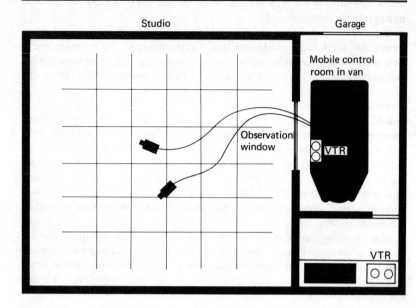

Fig. 12.13   The drive-in studio.

fitted out as a mobile control room, is parked in a garage next to a studio which is in one sense another 'outside' location (see Fig. 12.13) and may be called a 'drive-in studio'. The cameras, previously used for recording remote situations, are now placed in the studio and plugged into the van in the garage. There may be a telecine facility for showing film and slides permanently based in the building which would also need videotape play-back equipment for showing tapes when the van is making fresh material on location. A window in the van corresponding to another window in the wall of the garage permits observation of the studio from the van. The only permanently installed equipment in the studio itself consists of a set of lights.

The drive-in studio allows for the provision of both studio and mobile facilities of high quality for approximately the cost of either one, excluding building costs. It is well suited to an installation for which a new building is available or where the ground floor of an existing building can be easily converted. The 'garage' will however need air-conditioning in hot climates or central heating in cold ones.

Flexibility
Which of these solutions is preferable? The modern trend is to recommend against fixed alternatives, but to design a facility which can match all the stated needs of the institution. There are not, after all, many functions of CCTV which can only be carried out in one way.

As an example we may take the functions of *micro* and *macro teaching* in a teacher-training institution.

Television can enable students and staff to see themselves teach a lesson, see good and bad aspects and discuss their mistakes. Teaching can be with small groups using only segments of lessons — so compressing time and helping students to gain an insight into teaching practice. This is the essence of *micro-teaching.*

Macro-teaching is used to show part of interaction analysis, and to enable a group to see a complete class at work in a teaching/learning situation.

All that may be required, in both cases, is a television camera, a video-tape recorder, a monitor and a microphone. The principle of micro teaching is that the student/teacher who has previously seen a model of, or an aspect of, teaching such as narration, chalk-board skills or questioning, gives a short lesson to a small group of children, and while doing so is recorded on videotape. This requires little technical skill, and ordinary lighting is adequate in most cases. The tape is later replayed in whole or part, so that a discussion may be held on the effectiveness of the lesson and the skill being learned. Generally, only one particular teaching skill will be developed during the short lesson segment given, and after the teacher has had the opportunity to re-draft his material, following a critique, he will again present his lesson to another group of children or peers. This will again be videotaped and replayed for further evaluation.

Another of the ways in which this type of teaching can be used, employing a television camera and videotape equipment is in the 'example situation'. Here, an experienced teacher will present an ideal lesson, skill or objective, so that it can be replayed to students to give them an example of the correct methods, response or behaviour which are essential for the mastering of the skill. The student can then try a similar pattern of teaching and compare the results.

A few moments' thought will show that these functions can be provided either through a studio facility (used as a studio classroom), or through a mobile facility (which records, *in situ*, in an actual school). Some of the micro-teaching functions can in fact be provided by a simple combination of camera/microphone/recorder/monitor which can be set up virtually anywhere (simple recordings of teacher performance, for subsequent analysis). A general principle, however, is that modern opinion is against the construction of elaborate *distribution* systems in educational institutions, unless the authorities are very sure of media potential. A cable distribution system attached to a studio production complex is an expensive undertaking, and it represents a considerable commitment to the future. It means that production is assumed to be in fixed locations, likewise viewing. It demands a high concentration of usage, and allows relatively little freedom for experiment with the unknown. At a time when there is a much greater emphasis on individual uses of media, this could well prove, in the long run, to be a mistaken investment. The one new exception might be when a production studio constructed in a college or university is used as the main base for a *community* cable distribution system, since at such times usage is much wider, more varied and more likely to see continuing and changing demands. On the other hand, a campus radio distribution network, which is much less costly, can be a very useful vehicle for student contact in a diffuse campus.

In summary, the present concensus seems to be as follows. A careful approach to planning can reduce staff needs and overheads, by centralising technical functions and maximising facilities. Modern technology has produced equipment ranges which are perfectly adequate for institutional uses, provided that more is not expected of them than they claim to perform. Considered educational planning can reduce surplus elements from an installation (so that studios are not constructed if they are not necessary for the task in hand, or full broadcast facilities are not insisted upon when open broadcasting is not even in view). But planning and foresight will only reduce costs to a minimum level, beyond which it is not advisable to proceed. The final criterion is whether the facility does the job efficiently, in an economic way which compares favourably with other strategies. Planning has to be matched by a sense of reality in expectations.

2. The community

More than any other field, community media are in a state of flux. The emphasis on extending lifelong education, reflecting community interests and pressures, involving audiences in planning and production, has led to a new call for versatility which makes the most exacting demands upon facilities. In effect, community users have been asking for all of the image-creating and manipulating facilities previously associated only with professional broadcasting, and this has had its impact on production arrangements, organisational and technical facilities alike.

In radio, the pressures have been somewhat easier to satisfy. The radio medium is simpler than television, and community radio services, operating on low power, have been able to open their doors to audiences, not simply to participate in programmes, but also to make their own programmes (if necessary under technical guidance). Cassette recorders are a standard item in many households, which means that recordings can be made by amateurs and used in programmes. The more dedicated amateurs can soon deal with the intricacies of tape editing, and with access to relatively cheap reel-to-reel recorders can put together edited actuality programmes. The telephone has become a routine part of broadcasting, since a simple device was introduced which made it possible for calls to be routed from the public telephone system to the radio control room, so that the studio presenter could speak directly to his audience (and have this dialogue relayed to listeners — if necessary with a 7-second delay incorporated, to avoid libels or profanities over the air). But it is in the video area that community media have now become most active, thanks to improvements in video technology.

The first ½-inch video recorders appeared commercially in 1965–6, but the real beginning for small-gauge video technology came in 1966 and 1967 with the advent of the portable, battery-operated video recorder/camera combination which has since come to be referred to as the *Port-a-pak*.

The Port-a-pak received a warm welcome from experimental and documentary film makers, for its value as an instant replay tool and as a low-cost medium for experimentation. But the difficulties of exchanging tapes, due to the very small number of machines in circulation, and a conflict of standards between manufacturers, produced a situation in which video activities were limited almost exclusively to the production of local tapes for specialised local audiences.

However, by 1970 many owners of Port-a-pak, both private and institutional, had begun to seek means of extending the distribution possibilities of small-gauge videotape, and the emergence of uniform standards among hardware manufacturers made possible videotape exchange networks.

In this same period, film makers and television producers alike were developing an interest in tools for production which were less cumbersome to carry, which required fewer operators, which could cut production costs and which, when used on location, did not exert such a technological presence that they radically altered the situation or event which they had set out to capture.

It was finally the coming of community cable television in North America which made large-scale broadcasting of ½-inch videotape information a reality. The cablecaster's need for low-cost, locally-originated material for distribution to a local audience (combined with the fact that cable transmission does not demand the high technical standard required for radio frequency transmission), suggested two areas for experimentation: super-8 film and/or ½-inch videotape. Super-8 technology has not made such major strides, as applied to broadcasting, though it now appears to be moving ahead again; even so, manufacturers have not been so ready to exploit this area (e.g. for low-cost super-8 telecines). In video work, however, the introduction of time-base correctors has made possible the conversion of ½-inch videotape signals into broadcast standard signals, thereby permitting ½-inch tape to be either broadcast directly or transferred to 2-inch or other broadcast-standard formats.

Basically speaking, a ½-inch video system is a small-scale imitation of a television production studio; it is only a question of the purpose for which the equipment is to be used with determine the technical details of the hardware. The simplest system one could describe would probably be a Port-a-pak with its camera or a recorder connected to a TV receiver/ monitor for the purpose of copying television broadcasts or replaying tapes. There are also ½-inch editing systems which can interface with more sophisticated editing systems utilising 1-inch and 2-inch video-recorders and ¾-inch videocassette. A number of small engineering companies have sprung up which offer specialised accessories for portable video equipment, including 3- to 5-hour batteries, switchers which permit two cameras to be recorded on one Port-a-pak via a unit the size of a cigarette pack and units which permit mixing of images from tape and camera.

A combination of factors also led to the forming of cooperatives in which groups of people pool their equipment and talents to extend their production capabilities. While one person with one machine can produce tapes, editing or more complex production require a number of video-recorders and/or cameras and multiple operators, so that this cooperative evolution benefits all parties. Many of these cooperatives have grown into community service cablecasting, while others have set up community access centres to create programming for broadcast television channels.

Similar to such community information projects are the uses of small-gauge video equipment by political pressure groups, ranging from parent-teacher organisations who use videotapes to bring living examples of problems into meetings, to political activists who use videotapes to create 'newreels'.

This kind of development should help media to become the property of community organisations, not purely of media professionals. But it can also improve the forms of interaction between audiences and professional producers, allowing groups to make contributions to broadcast programmes (made entirely on their own, not in a professional studio, with the intervention of 'technical assistance'). Perhaps most important of all, it can permit, in time, the emergence of much lower cost community services, with a full range of production and distribution facilities, so that the inevitable comparison between 'professional' and 'amateur' programming is not made so often.

The most recent hardware appearing on the market is aimed at eliminating problems which limit the widespread distribution of video-tapes. The development of the time base corrector (TBC) was long awaited and is already changing the face of news production. Several small stations are entirely dependent on ½-inch videotape for the production of local news material and every major network is currently engaged in research in this field. There have been national colour broadcasts of productions originated on ½-inch videotape and in several developing countries broad-casting of national television is done entirely from ¾-inch videocassettes. Whereas previously a television studio for broadcast purposes was unthink-able for less than a quarter of a million dollars, there are on the air today complete stations set up on $50,000.

However, it should be emphasised that community services are by no means always associated with distribution systems. It is true that many local resource centres in North America were originally set up with access to cable television channels in mind, but some of these groups found that so much of their energy was going into routine production on behalf of the cable companies that they had little time left for the experimental activity which had originally intrigued them. So, while materials are often offered to local stations, many centres (like Videographe in Montreal) con-centrate on production, which is then viewed in their own community theatre, and placed, in cassetted form, in a resource library. This approach, they feel, gives them a greater flexibility, and frees them from formats distated by external sponsors.

Equipment needs and technical advice

It remains only to add some notes on equipment needs and some as to advice. The intention of this section is to give planners and users a sufficient grasp of fundamental principles to be able to carry on a dialogue with technical experts (not so much to avoid being misled by salesmen — though this can happen — as to lay the foundations for a corporate planning approach).

Technical advice should always be sought; it may be expensive, but it will save considerably in the end. There is relatively little expertise available in design for media installations: the fact that an architect is trained does not mean that he can plan a radio or television complex, unless he has already had practical experience of doing so. It is a point which has to be argued vehemently with administrators.

At the same time, this should not be seen as a means of shrugging off responsibility for the technical component of a project. Clearly, independent advice is best — manufacturers exist to sell their equipment, and the claims which they make may not always work out so advantageously in practice. A descriptive brochure on technical equipment needs objective interpretation and comparison with other products. Even in the simplest of operations, this can be secured — from other media services, other broadcast engineers and so on.

We saw, in Chapter 11, the kind of functional analysis which is involved in systems design, in which technical matters are only one component. The technical consultant will be of only limited assistance unless he knows precisely what the system is required to be — which means that he, too, must be involved in a group planning exercise, to design an ideal technical instrument for a particular job. This is a formula which not only educators, but also engineers, are sometimes resistant to adopt; as specialists they are often anxious to compartmentalise their work .

For example, levels of programme output and phasing will affect the building programme, conditioning the number of studios and the speed of construction. The kind of production envisaged will determine the character and size of studios, and their equipment range. If regional as well as national production is in view, equipment compatibility becomes a factor. The numbers of staff available, and their level of training, are the most critical consideration in facilities and systems design, especially if on-the-job training seems to be necessary. The problem is not simply one of providing the engineer with information on which to base his work; he can often demonstrate how, with some technical ingenuity, a higher or better quality output may be secured.

Fees

As a general rule, consultants are paid on a percentage basis, calculated according to the total cost of their particular component of the project. Thus:

(*a*) *Architects* are paid 6¼ to 7 per cent of the total cost of building works (with two-thirds of this being taken to represent the stage up to tendering).

(*b*) *Structural engineers'* fees are calculated at 7 per cent of the total of structural works.

(*c*) *Mechanical/electrical engineers'* fees are calculated at 6 per cent of the total of mechanical/electrical works.

(*d*) *Broadcasting systems engineering* fees are calculated at 6 per cent of the total cost of all technical facilities and installation.

(*e*) *Acoustic engineers'* fees are calculated at 6 per cent of the cost of building works requiring acoustical treatment.

These fees are paid at negotiated intervals during the project, and are finally based on *actual* costs.

Before embarking on any project, it is as well to consider very carefully what kinds of expertise are available locally, and what must be sought from outside; it is not an area where petty savings are justified. A special word should be said on broadcasting systems design, and on so-called 'turnkey' operations. It is not uncommon to find a media system awarded to a single manufacturer, on the understanding that he will provide all the equipment necessary, as a single package. (If he does not manufacture a particular item, then he undertakes to secure it from another source.) In return, no consultancy fees are charged, and in theory the client has a trouble-free system provided at a lower cost with minimal effort on his own part.

In fact, this may not necessarily be the case. If independent consultants are used, then the client has the advantage of a system tailor-made to suit his requirements. Tenders are sought competitively for all categories of equipment, and it is up to the consultant to evolve a suitable combination, to issue exact specifications, to evaluate tenders and to ensure that equipment as delivered meets what has been demanded. There are advantages in this approach, both in efficiency and in cost. On the one hand, an exact system should result (not something close to the client's intentions, but modified by what the manufacturer who is handling the turnkey operation has available in his range). On the other hand, 'marked up' prices are avoided, such as always occur if the main manufacturer has to go to a competitor to supply specific items. In broadcasting, in particular, few manufacturers cover the complete field of equipment, and some items will certainly have to be bought in. If carefully handled, savings achieved by use of independent consultants should exceed consultancy fees, and also lead to a more efficient system. The point should be considered carefully.

Costs

The earlier volume, *Planning for ETV*, made some attempt to quote price ranges for equipment, but this is no longer a possibility. In recent years there have been spectacular and unpredictable rises in prices of equipment, especially in construction works, which make any kind of forecasting impossible; an estimate would be out of date even before it was printed. In 1971–2, annual price rises stood at 5 per cent; in 1973 at 15 per cent. Moreover, this is an average figure – there is a considerable variety in the range of individual price increases. While some items, benefiting from new and miniaturised technologies, have remained at a constant price or even become cheaper (some reception equipment, for example), other items have increased by over 50 per cent.

The position is further complicated by world shortages in fuel and steel, which make both construction and delivery times difficult to guarantee. Today, one element in the final choice of equipment must be the reliability with which delivery dates can be met, or the kinds of sanction which are written into contracts for non-completion.

This being said, there are certain areas of costing which are often forgotten in original calculations, and some appreciation of these must be given.

Freight charges will have to be faced: they can be calculated at between 10 and 15 per cent of the total capital expenditure on equipment (depending upon the distance of the manufacturer from the installation). For this reason, when asking for quotations, it is better to ask for delivery to be included, rather than taking ex-factory prices (CIF, rather than FOB).

Installation costs can normally be estimated at about 15 per cent of capital expenditure, for a reasonably large installation. Smaller installations may cost less, perhaps as little as 5 per cent. The bulk of this item, apart from materials, will be made up of engineering and labour expenses, and these will again depend upon the distance and time involved. Engineering charges may be in the region of $70–$120 per day, but at a considerable distance air fares, subsistence and other incidental expenses must be added. Where possible, for economy, local labour should be employed, and it is as well to bring up this point with the manufacturer in early discussions.

An adequate range of spares is most essential, at a cost of about 10 to 15 per cent of the total. Manufacturers will advise on the appropriate range; much will depend upon local availability of spare parts.

Finally, *amortisation*. Electronic equipment has a limited life, and a proportion of recurrent expenditure should be set aside annually for its eventual replacement. Renewal over a 5- to 10-year period is a fair estimate (at the lower end of the scale for CCTV equipment); in practice, everything will not fail at once, but this allowance is for an average over the whole range.

It is evident that, in the present world position, estimates for media projects must be continually updated, and any savings which can be realised through bulk orders (especially of reception equipment) should be maximised. There should also be the minimum possible interval between tendering, the awarding of tenders and the signing of contracts. Most tenders state clearly their period of offer, and if a new tender becomes necessary, it will certainly result in a higher cost proposition.

Chapter 13

Organisation and programme development

In the introduction to Part 3, we made a distinction between structures and processes. This distinction is important in any discussion of organisation, because all too often the departmental structures of an institution are stressed, to the exclusion of what they are meant to be performing. A media service is more than its buildings and organisational forms; it is an instrument for realising a policy (laid down by a policy-making body) to the satisfaction of its users (who must also be given the means of expressing their satisfaction or condemnation of its efforts).

We can understand this distinction better if we consider educational media provision as a particular kind of system.

Strictly speaking there is only one universal system of which we ourselves and every thing and person to which we relate are components. However, in practice we can isolate any part of the whole system which we wish to consider. Such a sub-system will have numerous outputs to and inputs from other sub-systems.

For example, the educational system of a country can be divided into many sub-systems such as central and regional education authorities and individual schools. Each school has numerous external connections, a few of which are illustrated in Fig. 13.1.

If we wished to study, for example, the financial operation of a school,

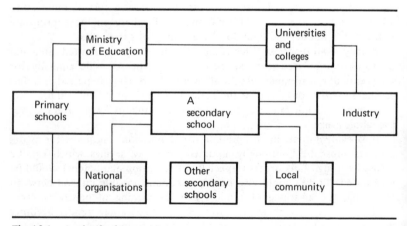

Fig. 13.1   A school sub-system.

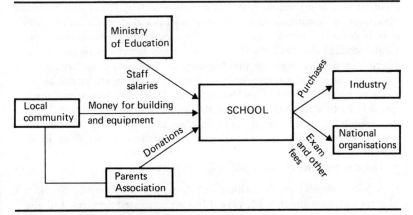

Fig. 13.2 A school financial system.

then the system could perhaps be reduced to a simpler but still valid network with inputs and outputs as shown in Fig. 13.2.

If, on the other hand we wished to see an educational media service as part of a system we might devise something like Fig. 13.3.

This kind of crude representation does not attempt to show everything

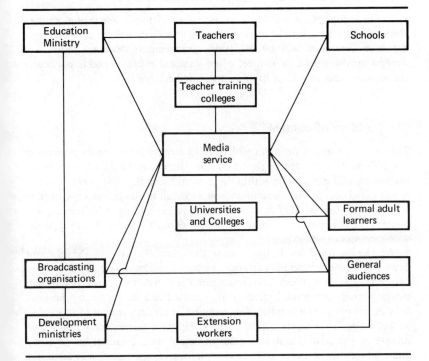

Fig. 13.3 An educational media system.

involved in a relationship; it is deliberately selective. It is looking for the viewpoint of communication, and it is apparent that, for a service which goes beyond the school system (as, if for economic reasons alone, most media services do these days), there are many interfaces to account for. There are policy links to the Ministry of Education, to broadcasting organisations and to other interested Ministries. There are user links to all kinds of audiences, formal and non-formal. There are training and institutional links to universities, colleges and teachers. Our organisational model has, therefore, to reflect all these links so as to allow for a satisfactory dialogue between all concerned, and to facilitate rather than impede coordination.

The components of our model will therefore be:

1. A *policy-making model*, which lays down broad objectives, provides a means of coordination between different interested agencies, and also a means of high-level arbitration where conflicting representations are made.
2. A *programme and materials development model*, which translates these broad objectives into practice, providing a forum for corporate planning involving all production and user agencies.
3. A *utilisation and evaluation model*, which involves users as active participants, not merely as sources of outside opinion.

These components will exist at any level of media operation, though obviously the broader the system the more sectors will be involved, and the more complex will coordination arrangements become. Much will depend on the nature of control of educational media − and in particular the relative responsibilities of educators and broadcasters.

The problem of control

This is, of course, a problem which bulks large only in media systems at the national level. In the single institution, there may be difficulty over the placement of a media unit within the general hierarchy, but overall control is not in debate. In the community, even though media initiatives can stem from a number of different sources, not necessarily educational, the context of operations should be small enough for local coordinating arrangements to be devised.

At the national level, this is not the case. We saw, in Part 1, how historically many different patterns of educational media deployment have emerged, and how these have been modified over the years. Is any particular pattern preferable? Here we are exposed to a dangerous temptation. It is as tempting as it is misleading to think of all educational broadcasting as belonging to a single genre. In fact the term covers programming as diverse as material aimed at formal in-school uses, material for informal adult education purposes or even short informational items embedded in a basically entertainment channel.

However, one basic audience categorisation — into adult and school broadcasting — is helpful, because the two show certain basic differences in planning and execution.

Control of in-school broadcasting

Programmes for in-school use are generally intended as a supplement to a teacher's activities within an institution and are normally subject to prescription by the Ministry of Education or whatever body is in charge of schools. There is, for the producer, a ready-made and predetermined framework, and indeed a ready-made and predetermined timetable for the preparation and utilisation of programmes. Equally there is at his disposal an existing infrastructure which can be used to provide schools with information, support material and publicity — and in reverse, as it were, it can provide him with a ready-made feedback and evaluation mechanism.

The issue of control over school broadcasting is therefore not so problematic, since, while it may be vested in either broadcasters or educators (as far as production is concerned), at least the nature of the audience is fixed, and the conditions of access relatively well known. The issue therefore resolves itself to a simple question: Should an education ministry delegate responsibility to the broadcasting organisation (though, naturally, providing it with detailed directives), or should it provide at least the personnel for a production unit, to act within the broadcast framework?

The ideal solution, historical precedents apart, is for a separate production centre to be created by and for the educators. This may, for the sake of economy, be located within the studio complex of the broadcasting organisation, and almost inevitably the mechanical business of transmission will be carried out by the broadcasters, using their own networks. But educational control of programming can only be properly secured if control of production is also assumed: in this medium, educational function and technique are inextricably bound up with each other. Again, the demands, the inconveniences, the risks are increased; a complete training programme has to be initiated for educators working in an unfamiliar medium.

The usual compromise is for a limited number of educators to work as producers within the broadcasting framework, drawing on pool resources. They are put, inevitably, at the mercy of the broadcasters; they cannot operate at all without sympathetic support, but at least they can interpret the medium in specifically educational terms, relying on their own teaching experience. (It may be better, incidentally, for them to remain a part of the educational establishment, with their responsibilities clearly defined, and promotional avenues retained, than to become part of the broadcasting machine, even though this can produce administrative and industrial complications.)

If neither of these alternatives is adopted, then we are thrown back on consultative machinery, and on the conscience of the broadcasters. We should not put this too bleakly; the arrangement can work well enough, as in the BBC or in NHK, but there are many cases where it does not work, and as a matter of principle it is better to legislate against such difficulties.

Controls are most easily introduced at the planning stage, when the media service is on the drawing board. An education authority has to stake its claims early. It will not always find broadcasters, or even governments, enthusiastic about devoting profitable television time to the cause of the biggest ministerial spender. It is particularly important for a Ministry of Education in a country where a commercial TV service is contemplated to insist that rights to educational transmissions should be written into the contract. They are unlikely to be refused where there is competition for a franchise, and they need not be taken up immediately.

Once the pattern of broadcasting is fixed within a country it is unlikely to be radically changed, and any plans for educational media must take the existing structure into account.

Whatever arrangements is decided the following practical points should be agreed:

1. Educational 'policy' must be left to the professional educators.
2. All scripts and programme materials must be written by, or at the very least vetted by, educationists.
3. A schedule of programme timings must be agreed by the Education Ministry.
4. Either educational production personnel should come from the teaching force or, failing this, education advisers should be appointed to work with the production teams, with acknowledged responsibility for educational aspects of programmes.
5. A realistic consultative machinery should be established between broadcast and education authorities.
6. Teacher consultation, utilisation training and evaluation machinery should be in the hands of the Education Ministry.
7. A guarantee should be given by the broadcasting authority that transmission times will not be interfered with unnecessarily.
8. Full logistical support must be given by the Education Ministry, and adequate supplementary materials provided by them.
9. Adequate funds and resources must be voted by both educationists and broadcasters to carry out stated objectives.
10. Education objectives, channels of communication and areas of responsibility need to be agreed together by all agencies concerned.
11. The educational system *as a whole* must be committed to the use of the medium, in the most positive way attainable.

Control of out-of-school broadcasting

Programming for adults, on the other hand, is for the most part governed by quite different, and in many cases much less clear cut, parameters. Firstly, there are those which derive from the nature of the audience. In most countries school age children are compelled by law to go to school; they provide, by definition, a captive audience. Certainly, teachers have to be persuaded to listen, but quite often even that decision is taken for them by other authorities. Almost all adult audiences, although commonly fairly highly motivated, need to be wooed — to be attracted and held. Secondly, although most school broadcasts will entail cooperation with only few Ministries — perhaps the Ministry of Information and Broadcasting will need to collaborate with the Ministry of Education alone — in the adult sphere the possible combination is legion. It may include the Ministries of Agriculture, Health, Community Development, Education, Information, Family Planning and so on, and this presents formidable planning problems. Thirdly, school broadcasts happen during the day, when pressure for air time is usually less than in the evening; adult programming mostly requires peak listening time, and this is difficult to arrange — particularly in those cases when air time means revenue because of the commercial basis of the operation as a whole. Fourthly, educational broadcasting is frequently slow to produce results, and those which are available are difficult if not impossible to quantify with any certainty. This often weakens still further its position within any cost-conscious organisa-tion, where immediate results are usually demanded to justify the continued expenditure of funds.

The issue of control therefore becomes inseparable from that of co-ordination. Control, in fact, normally rests upon historical precedent; it is more common for patterns of school broadcasting to be set first, and structures for out-of-school broadcasting to be grafted on to these. In practice, educational media for adults tend to take their organisation and methodology from the schools operation, sometimes completely slavishly. And it is here that the difficulties occur.

When a planner talks of what 'broadcasting can do' he is talking of a range of techniques which basically have in common only one thing — that they will be transmitted over similar transmitters and received on tech-nically similar receivers. But as well as having a method of transmission in common it is likely that these tools will be used from within a common organisational framework. For both cost and political reasons many countries have one single broadcasting organisation. Where this is not the case it is very common indeed for the Government to have a monopoly — either by design or default — of 'public service broadcasting', which will include educational broadcasting. There are, of course, a number of incidental advantages. It is an advantage for the country in simple cost terms; many transmission systems make for wasteful duplication of equipment. It is an advantage in production terms, in that there is likely to be within a single organisation a cross-fertilisation of experience — both of production and of planning — together with a shared feedback system and the means to disseminate the results of this feedback in a helpful and useful manner.

Whatever organisation is in fact in control, it is therefore usual for all educational broadcasting activities, at least, to be grouped together. But however sensible such an arrangement may be it suffers from one disadvantage. This is that 'educational broadcasting' then tends to acquire a life and organisation of its own — it exists apart from its uses. Here there are dangers. If the control is with broadcasters, there is a tendency for broadcasting to adult audiences to take its cue far too specifically from the tenets of general broadcasting, and produce merely another range of programmes. If it is with educators, there is an equal tendency for the formal 'educational' applications of broadcasting to be exaggerated, and the special situation of adult broadcasts to be ignored. So, not only may the spirit of such broadcasts often tend to be over-academic, but essential links with the wider world of development — reflecting interests outside both education and mass media — may be forgotten.

The key to the avoidance of this situation must lie in the creation of functional links between all agencies interested in both planning and operation, a task much easier said than done. The problems of cooperation between, for example, different Ministries are well known to anyone who has worked in this field. Even cooperation between academies and broadcasters is fraught with problems, each believing that he knows best and what should go into a programme.

Such problems of cooperation may well, of course, not be simply, or indeed mainly, to do with broadcasting. In a large development scheme broadcasting may only be a small component. But it is nevertheless true that in most schemes involving media the media aspect is either the most important part or given pride of place because of the complex organisational problems inherent in its working.

This cooperation must obviously continue at various levels, if it is to be more than nominal. It relates both to levels of *decision making* (overall policy, programme planning, etc.), and to levels of *operation* (national, regional and local). While agreement at a political level is always required (since without it, nothing will follow), for this is to be reflected in materials and in practical working arrangements, a similar apparatus for coordination has to be created in more local settings.

A model for coordination

Figure 13.4 offers a general model for coordination, covering both the in-school and out-of-school sectors. It is, of course, a generalised model, which will be modified in different circumstances (for example, if a broadcasting organisation itself contains educational media facilities and materials, the two strands of broadcasting and educational media will be fused).

We should emphasise that the horizontal lines are just as important as the vertical. Vertical structures reflect a compartmentalisation of various educational and developmental responsibilities, supervised by the central economic planning unit or its equivalent, and ultimately by Government. The central strand covers the main hierarchy of educational media, beginning with an overall advisory body, and continuing from national to

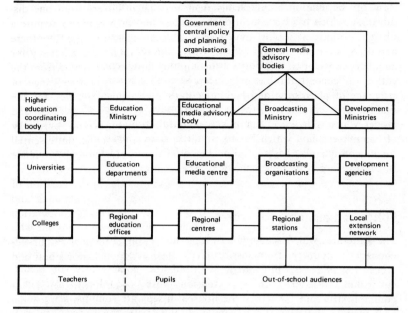

Fig. 13.4 A model for coordination.

local production and distribution arrangements. (The dotted line from the central planning agency shows that, while no direct control is envisaged, membership of the advisory body by the planning unit will be advantageous.)

At the horizontal level, a coordinating structure (probably of committees) ensures: (i) policies and strategies; (ii) programme development, production and distribution arrangements — both national and regional; (iii) cooperative patterns of utilisation (especially important in the adult sphere, where much depends on extension agents). The position of universities and colleges is somewhat different, as these may or may not be a direct responsibility of an education ministry, but in either case, links are important, both for academic and specialist advice and for the integration of media with the teacher training programme.

Finally, the most important aspect of control is not that it should be, axiomatically, in the hands of a particular agency, but that its structural forms should permit interaction. In fact, if any single sector — broadcasting or education, or development — assumes absolute authority, there will be a loss involved, for the truth about educational media is shared between many parties. This was the principal benefit of the Open University, which set up a new kind of cooperative arrangement with the BBC, and provided a forum for the pooling of talent and experience in such a way that confrontations (although these happened) were generally avoided, and in any case an acceptable form of arbitration was evolved. It is to this end that patterns of authority and coordination should be directed. A significant form of cooperation occurs in the Agency for Instructional Television in the USA, which has been mentioned earlier. This operates purely as a consortium project, with only a small Secretariat, and has devised a process of corporate decision-making which works towards a concensus of what members consider to be priority programming. Production also takes place within the consortium, but relevance and quality control are assured by a sequence of pre-testing and formative evaluation, which ensures that the final product conforms to the original formula. This kind of participatory model, which is dependent upon actual consultation, not a formal network of committees, and which has to compete in an educational market-place for its continuance, has a good deal to offer those for whom coordination is still seen largely as a mechanistic process.

Policy and planning structures

The structures which accommodate this model (Fig. 13.4) will vary from country to country, from institution to institution. Planning for media innovation may be integrated, with all the components (of media, curriculum, teacher training, extension work, etc.) located within a common structure, or it may be housed in separate administrative units, with planning links. In theory, obviously the greater the degree of integration the better, since this will lead to a common appreciation of goals, commonly understood objectives and in the end produce a more or less intuitive sharing of attitudes to learning and development processes. But it has to be recognised that, for a variety of political, practical and cultural reasons, such integration cannot always be achieved, and a form of 'task force' planning, with groups of interlocking working committees, will have to suffice.

In most cases, therefore, planning will be undertaken by a hierarchy of committees or working groups, dealing with different facets of policy. At the top of this hierarchy will be policy-making organs. Underneath, there will be a number of working groups, specifically entrusted with planning for specific subject areas, series, or functions.

Figure 13.5 illustrates a characteristic committee structure for media planning. At the apex is whichever body is responsible for *overall broadcasting, media and communications policy* in a country; educational media personnel will be members of this committee, and their presence is important if they are to retain a voice in fundamental decisions concerning frequency allocation, channel space and so on. Educational media frequently have to lobby for their rights.

The next level, determining *educational media policy*, is of a different order. This is the main policy-making organ for the general planning of educational media; it decides goals, priorities, phasing, but only in broad terms. It will undertake such basic decisions as who is to control media production and distribution, what volume of production in anticipated, what funding will be available. It will therefore include representatives at a

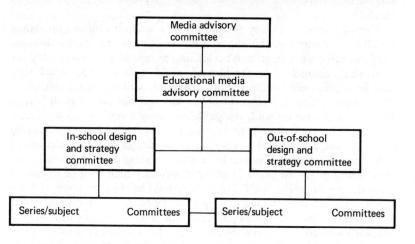

Fig. 13.5 Media planning structure.

senior civil service or (if possible) ministerial level, drawn from all ministries and agencies interested in the system's development. Apart from the Ministry of Education these will include ministries of Information, Telecommunication and various development ministries active in the adult, non-formal and informal areas. Representatives of the Ministry of Finance, the Treasury and of ministries concerned with personnel appointments may also attend. This committee will not meet too often; probably only annually.

At the level below, *design and strategy committees,* for both in-school and out-of-school areas, also meet infrequently (perhaps annually or bi-annually) to review strategies for their particular fields. What subject areas will be emphasised? Which audiences? What forms of association will be introduced between media? Or between media and other innovative programmes? What arrangements for utilisation are envisaged? What means of evaluation?

Finally, there is the level of the *individual series.* Here the number of committees is open ended, and committees may be arranged according to subject, level, or function — whichever seems most appropriate.

Policy-making guidelines

A quasi-committee structure seems inevitable, simply because the interest and attention of a number of people and agencies is required, none of whom is wholly involved with media. As a general rule, a high-ranking and responsible representative is needed from any agency which is likely to make use of media, and the committee, taken as a whole, should reflect the total needs of the educational environment. It goes without saying that the media service itself should be properly represented, normally by its Head.

Even so, there are many limitations to a committee-based operation, which can seriously inhibit the validity of its decisions. Its members are likely to serve on a large number of similar committees; unless they are particularly committed to the idea of media as an educational aid, they may be neither well briefed nor fully involved. A committee is unlikely to frame a convincing and coherent policy unless it has proper guidelines to follow. On the other hand, the guidelines should not be too specific; if they are, the committee may become no more than a rubber-stamping machine, and a good deal of relevant experience in different educational fields may be wasted. Essentially, a policy-making body needs to work from a well produced paper or set of proposals, which must be originated from the media service itself. The paper should not be concerned with too much detail; if it is too long, it may never be read. The media representative has a delicate role in policy meetings; he is there to make sure that the decisions arrived at are sensible, and can be implemented. This is his opportunity to convince members of the potential of the media service; interest from the top of any agency will certainly be followed through by subordinates. At the same time, he must remain open to conviction, ready to modify his own proposals as a result of the attitudes expressed in discussion.

Most of this is obvious. But the policy meeting, while it may only take place once or twice a year, will have an enormous effect on the operations of the service. It will define general objectives and determine the importance of media within the educational system. It will make influential friends or enemies.

As a practical note — a committee of this kind should not be too large, and is best restricted to a dozen or so people. Its role will be generally as follows: to specify the areas of programming, the levels to which programmes are to be addressed, their frequency, their relationship to other educational agencies and to other media, and, most important, their function within the educational system or institution. It is this final point which needs to be spelled out most precisely.

Series development guidelines

Design and strategy planning
This intermediate stage between policy formulation and the planning of specific series has to be handled at a media level of representation. The main advisory committee will concern itself only with broad proposals and objectives; before producers and programme planners are involved, these have to be translated into timetables or broadcasting strands, into separate responsibilities (if more than one broadcasting or production agency is concerned) and into specific objectives for separate audiences of subject areas. If non-formal and informal education is envisaged, discussions can become quite controversial, and it is likely that some matters will have to

be referred back to the main advisory body for arbitration. Design and strategy committees have to develop plans covering:

(a) specific series with associated objectives (including precise audience descriptions);
(b) a detailed account of the contribution of each production agency;
(c) timetables and distribution details;
(d) a proportional allocation of resources, including resources for evaluation;
(e) a broad statement of utilisation assumptions (including training).

It will probably be necessary, to accommodate numbers, to hold separate meetings for design and strategy committees in the in-school and out-of-school sectors, but at least one joint session should be envisaged, to ensure a dialogue between the two. The main advisory body should cover both sectors, since it is concerned with balancing overall output.

On timetabling matters, there will be few problems for the in-school sector. Series will be planned to coincide with school timetables (and in a diffuse educational system, it may be necessary to conduct a sample survey of school timetables, to select optimal transmission times). In the timetable, repeat transmissions should not be ignored; repeats make the problems of school utilisation less acute, or accommodate numbers of classes at the same level, by offering multiple opportunities to hear and view programmes. When production capacity grows, repeating programmes can be difficult, but in the early stages at least there is adequate opportunity, and it is often less expensive to keep transmitters running, than to switch them intermittently on and off.

In the out-of-school sector, where there are more demands for what are often peak viewing or listening hours, different educational and development interests are more difficult to reconcile. But what must be blocked out at this stage is a broad allocation of programmes which match audience viewing patterns and social conditions. Again, this may be a matter for social survey work, to be carried out by an evaluation unit or on subcontract. For programmes addressed to farmers, it is important to know at what times these can most readily be heard (and whether they are normally heard in the home or in the field). Adult education programmes have to be linked to study programmes in a variety of educational institutions; development programmes must take account of the pattern of work of extension agents, agricultural and industrial production cycles, and so on. A sample approach is given in Fig. 13.6. It is, at this stage, very general, but it can serve as a basis for further negotiation.

Programme planning arrangements

Again, some form of task force is required for the planning of specific series, but this will be a far more *ad hoc,* flexible affair. The composition of each working group should be determined by talent, qualifications and experience, not by official status. In order to plan individual series, a good

Time	Programme strand
06.00–07.00	Agricultural programmes
07.00–08.30	General programmes including news, development items, women's items, etc., set in broad entertainment format for the general listener
08.30–13.00	In-school programmes
13.00–14.00	Women's programmes
14.00–16.00	In-school programmes
16.00–17.00	Programmes for teachers
17.00–18.30	General programmes (as for 07.00–08.30)
18.30–19.30	Programmes for home study
19.30–21.00	Programmes for formal adult education and adult extension groups
21.00–22.30	General programmes (as for 07.00–08.30)
22.30–24.00	Programmes for home study

Fig. 13.6   Scheduling considerations for out-of-school audiences.

deal of detailed work is necessary, and specific expertise is required including, in particular, the following elements:

(a) The *executive producer* of the programme strand.
(b) *Individual producers* for each medium.
(c) A practising *teacher* (if possible, the scheduled presenter of the series).
(d) A *specialist* in the subject area under review (intimately concerned with curriculum development, methodology, etc.).
(e) An *evaluation specialist.*
(f) A *curriculum specialist* and *educational technologist.*

To this nucleus, a number of other members may be added on an occasional basis. These can include: an educational psychologist (with experience in learning theory and strategy); several ETV users in the field; a member of the educational inspectorate; a representative of other media-producing agencies (if a cooperative approach is being designed). Altogether the group should comprise some six to eight people.

In this context the word 'committee', with its characteristic overtones, is best avoided. This is a task force which is expected to meet regularly and to produce concrete results. Its role is clear: to design the overall format for each series, in which the contents of individual materials are laid down precisely, their objectives spelled out, utilisation patterns developed and the contributions of specific media crystallised. Meetings should be casually conducted. It is inevitable that group dynamics will come into play, and a natural leader will emerge, but as a starting point it is useful for the supervising producer to present a hypothetical arrangement of programmes for the group to consider. If a multi-media approach is in force this original presentation should be drafted by representatives of all the media strands, and some preliminary meetings will be required. Systems approaches are more complex to operate, and the demands of media used in combination are greater than those of individual media.

The creation of links with users will be discussed later in Part 4, but some user representation has to be assumed even at the planning stage. It is important for teacher/users to be invited to join the planning group (and there should be a regular change of representatives). Similarly, in the design of programme series, the question of user reactions must be borne continually in mind. While it is ultimately the producer's responsibility to make sure that his programmes are two-way communications, it is at the planning stage that the possibility of a two-way process will be made or marred. This is why the presence of an evaluator at the earliest opportunity is important.

The above remarks apply most directly to in-school programming. For adult and general audiences, the same principles are relevant, but there are other considerations to take into account. These amount to some special guidelines concerning the audience.

The first has to do with the educational aims of the exercise. They include truisms such as the need for credibility (this is particularly true for adults — it is no good, for example, telling a farmer to plant new seed if he knows from experience or hearsay that such a crop entails real risks which the broadcast fails to mention); the need to prepare and follow-up a broadcast, to contextualise it within the listeners' experience, and so on. The second concerns the nature of the society in which the listener lives and the expectations which this gives him about broadcasting in general. This is a principle which is frequently ignored but it is of great importance in educational programming. In most countries adults are now used to sophisticated and varied programming — from pop music to news broadcasts. They have come to expect a certain level of production and a certain style of address. Educational broadcasting is very vulnerable to unflattering comparison if it ignores this and provides a diet which is seriously at odds with the rest of the output — or worse still, with what is available, at the same time, on other channels.

The third concerns difficulties of coordination and the need — in development broadcasting in particular — to avoid delivery systems which are too complicated, especially in matters of timing.

A family planning programme which relied for its effectiveness on a booklet arriving in a village a week before the programme, on a group leader having a poster and being willing to display it at the relevant time, on another person taking the radio from his house to the school, on the health worker visiting the village a day after the broadcast and finally on the community development worker arriving a week later to provide follow-up would have so many chances of going astray that it is highly likely it would do so. It is certainly good advice either to begin simply or to pilot the productions — and preferably both.

A further set of considerations stems from the need for advocacy and publicity in the adult programme area.

Public relations are necessary firstly because people from senior civil servants to ordinary housewives need education in what broadcasting can and cannot do, and secondly because the potential audience has to be told what the producer and his organisation are trying to do. People accept broadcasting for schools and for news and for entertainment; it is surprising how few people accept broadcasting for adult education. So the publicity aspect of the media service's work has two facets: general publicity to help persuade people that it is normal to turn to the media for education, and special publicity for particular series or programmes.

In terms of the second type, media producers will do well to exploit their own medium. It is quite possible to feed into the general programming stream material about specific series in the educational broadcasting output, and indeed to feed explicit educational matter into mainstream programming. This is all too frequently neglected even within broadcast organisations. If educational broadcasters are part of a larger broadcasting organisation, or alternatively if those planning educational broadcasting or its uses can have access to such an organisation, then in theory the whole range of facilities will be at their disposal — even though, as educational broadcasters will know, they may have to fight for them. There is no reason for instance why, as with the long-running 'Archers' in England (a daily serial about a farming community), educational material cannot be a normal part of the output. The obverse is also true, and educational broadcasters can gain a great deal from being part of, or at least in close contact with, a larger broadcasting system and thus in contact with people using a wide range of techniques which may be useful to their needs.

Control at other levels of organisation

In progressing from national to smaller media networks, we must first revert to the question of control. In a college or university, rather different problems arise. The first question is whether the media unit, or learning resources unit, should be an independent entity, whether it should be attached to the library or some such central service department, or whether it should be linked to a particular faculty.

The second question is whether media resources should be centralised, or whether, quite apart from a central facility of some kind, faculty units should be retained.

The third question is one of function: should media resource units be regarded as exclusively production or service units, or should they also engage in teaching?

There is no simple answer to any of these questions, and as usual much depends upon precedent and tradition. For logistical reasons, and those of cost efficiency, it is clearly better to have a media service operating as an autonomous unit, but there is a danger that, in doing so, it can become divorced from college life, and unless its director is a senior person in the hierarchy he may not be in a position to command either adequate finance or lecturers' time.

These difficulties will be diminished if the service is faculty-based, but on the other hand this alternative can lead either to a proliferation of small specialised units (with no consolidation of resources, and probably no media professionalism), or to an integrated service being based upon a single faculty, which it serves virtually exclusively to the detriment of other users (who will have to take their turn, and will soon lose interest in media as a result).

Probably the most viable model is that of a centralised facility, either independent or attached to such an authority as the Vice-Chancellor's or Principal's office, directed by an officer with relatively high status, who is represented on university consultative bodies. The worst alternative would seem to be both a central facility, and satellite faculty units which can only lead to ambivalence in control and to a wasteful spread of resources.

One of the main functions of the media service will clearly be production or the provision of technical services (such as recording on technical facilities for micro- and macro-teaching, etc.). It will depend upon local needs whether the production of specific programme materials is also undertaken (and no service should be allowed, in its enthusiasm for independent production, to forget that library materials are often available which will do some jobs quite as well, or better, than it can itself). Teaching is another matter. If a college or university has a communication teaching programme, or an active educational technology programme, the facilities of the centre can be utilised for practical work, and not only will specific teaching assistance be needed from the centre's members, but this will help keep the centre in better contact with the remaining teaching and student body. Until recently, there has been a lot of resistance to the idea of combining facilities for work in communication and educational technology training under one roof, but in an age of financial astringency this is obviously necessary, and experiments already carried out have shown that it is perfectly possible, bringing about a useful exchange between the two sectors.

A simple model is proposed in Fig. 13.7 for a centralised media service.

At other community levels, the problems which arise are not so much who controls activities, as how this control is formally articulated. In a single school or school district, for example, control is vested in the sponsoring authority, and a community service is in much the same position. However, particularly in the community service, informality may be placed at a premium, and the main concern is to see that participation from audiences and users occurs at all levels, from management to programming.

Some of the smallest of the community media groups do not have this problem, because they are small enough to consult easily among

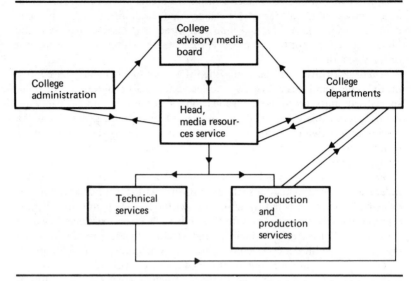

Fig. 13.7   A college system.

themselves. The notion of formal channels is, in any case, likely to be unacceptable. Conversely, in the single school or school district control patterns are not debated because they follow the normal management lines of the parent institution.

In other contexts, however, there is a more delicate balance to be struck. And it is best to find some means of working as a group, rather than as a collection of individuals, partly because this allows for a more effective approach to funding agencies, other civic or community associations or local authorities, but equally because this does permit concensus to be reached on both major and minor policy questions.

The trend towards informality has often expressed itself as a reaction against any kind of committee structure, against the appointment of a chairperson, and the avoidance of an agenda. But there is a danger that, when such simple procedures are omitted, the more timid or inarticulate members of a group will be discriminated against, and conclusions will be difficult to reach. The same cautionary note should be struck in dealing with experts, or with official bodies (such as media organisations). Any community group wants to make up its own mind on policy issues, and to avoid being dominated by professional outsiders, but there are many regulations associated with media, and expert advice — if asked for purely as advice — can be very useful. In other words, community media, while obviously stressing personal and informal relationships between members, need on the one hand to make the most of expert resources in their own community, and on the other hand to ensure that they do not become inbred.

Figure 13.8 gives a simple model of organisation, which emphasises user

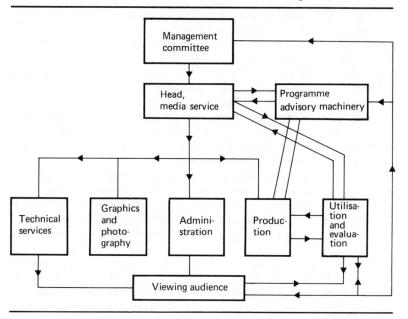

Fig. 13.8   A community system.

representation and gives a minimum of supporting structures for a community service.

Administrative organisation

Having considered organisational relationships, and the sequence of strategic and operational planning, we can now turn to administrative organisation (i.e. the structuring of the media service itself).

At the simplest level, administrative organisation will present few problems: it is most likely to be grafted on to an existing structure. The media system may be run by one or two people, on a full or part-time basis, and ancillary services provided by a common pool.

But as soon as even a moderate level of sophistication develops, and the service becomes a separate unit, an independent administrative structure is advisable. At this stage, a departmental form of organisation is preferable, to allow for growth; it is a virtue of the departmental structure that additional numbers can be grafted on to it without disturbing the basic pattern.

The Appendix ('Characteristic media installations', p. 338) shows this approach applied to a variety of contexts. In the larger installations, of course, the media service may well have to accommodate several existing patterns, and in such cases it is most likely to be built upon a cellular structure, with each production unit working independently, drawing upon a service pool for technical and other resources. This is a frequent pattern within national broadcasting services. Admittedly, there are disadvantages to departmental organisation: principally the insulation which it sometimes encourages. All too often there is a gulf between production and technical services, and the informal, personal links which spring up between producers and engineers, cameramen, graphic artists and so on, are important: they are the more effective for being spontaneous. The criterion is one of efficiency; while a service is small enough to work effectively without any clearly demarcated organisational pattern being imposed, this is all to the good, but above that level lines of communication have to be established and channels of responsibility.

The storm warning usually comes with the emergence of tensions: no one (least of all a technician) can serve two masters. If a number of producers are competing for technical services, priorities have to be established and adhered to. Informality is valuable, but above a basic level of service (with the city system as an absolute watershed) it will obey the law of diminishing returns.

The best form of departmental structure is likely to be the simplest, and 'departments' only exist where demarcations can be clearly made. For example, engineering, graphics, film services, production are all self-defining, and can easily be kept separate. The purpose of such demarcation is to allow for effective management, not to insulate, and the coordination between them is all important. For this reason, an appointment of coordinator or programme supervisor is recommended whose job is to correlate all aspects of the service, to establish priorities and to arbitrate where necessary. This is most certainly not the function of a Head of Service, who should be sufficiently free from routine responsibilities to apply himself to policy matters and to such questions as programme quality or external relations. The coordinator is primarily an administrator, at the level of an assistant head (though not necessarily with that title); he has responsibilities across a number of departments and is therefore detached from the Administrative Department as such. For the sake of illustration, we can take the organisational pattern shown in Fig. 13.9.

The role of each department is clear: in most cases they are service agencies. Depending on the size of the establishment, they may be further

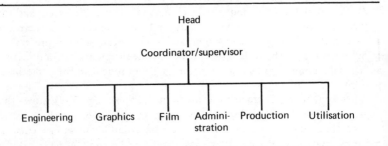

Fig. 13.9   Departmental structure for media development.

subdivided (e.g. engineering and technical operations would be separate in the larger establishments), but each unit has its own hierarchy, and in each there is an ostensible chief.

The overall head is an educationalist and policy-maker; he represents the service externally and monitors the quality of its output as objectively as possible. (In a large establishment he may also have an assistant head, who shares his responsibilities.)

The function of the coordinator (or whatever he is called) is to ensure the clarity of all lines of communication. If a producer requires a certain volume of services, the coordinator will decide whether the services are available, establish the priority of the request, assess its implications (financial and logistical) in relation to total output. ('He' may well be several people, even a separate unit, in a service with a large programme, but the principle remains the same.) In this way, since all requests are channelled through him, the chances of friction among producers competing for limited services are substantially reduced; if they do arise, as they do in even the best-regulated establishments, he will also arbitrate. He will not, however, be concerned with general routine: this belongs properly to the administrative unit, which has its own separate place in the chain and its own supervisor.

From this point on, basic principles are extended according to the logic of each situation. Figures 13.10, 13.11 and 13.12 reflect different, and

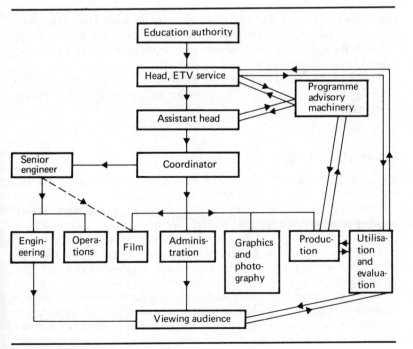

Fig. 13.10   A city or State service.

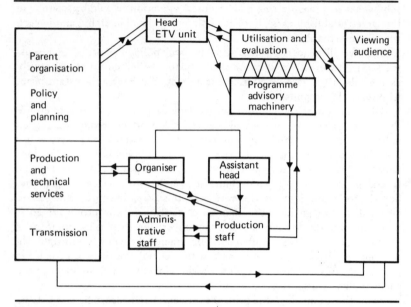

Fig. 13.11   Educational media within a broadcasting organisation.

larger, lines of activity. The first might apply to the work of a city or State system; the second illustrates a more complex situation, where an educational media unit, or educational television department, is housed within a general broadcasting service.

Finally, the most complex model of all illustrates arrangements for a fully fledged multi-media service, at a major national level (evolved for the Thailand project).

Financial planning

Every establishment will have its own methods of financial control and ways of accounting. The main difficulties will arise where the demands of broadcasting are different from the educational norm, and where special pleading and justification are required. We have already mentioned the problem of equipment, and the financial provisions which have to be made to allow for depreciation, spares and installation charges. There are many other areas where the practices of educational television may differ from those of education.

At the planning stage, two points are of special importance. First, it is likely that equipment purchase at least will have to be made according to normal tendering procedures. Quotations or tenders will be invited, manufacturers' submissions assessed by a delegated authority and the results published. This is a part of normal television and educational practice, and

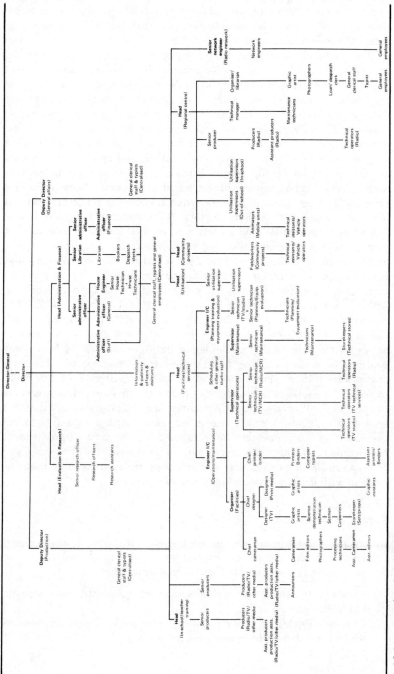

Fig. 13.12 A national multi-media service.

should cause no difficulty, provided whoever is scrutinising the tenders is willing to take advice on unfamiliar technical matters, and not merely to accept the lowest submission.

Routine purchases may be more complicated. Spare parts, for example, cannot be tendered for, as they have to match an existing piece of equipment; the same is true of many items of specialist equipment which are only manufactured by one agency. This is not an unfamiliar situation, but there is in television an element of pressure which may cause difficulty. However carefully programmes are planned, there are bound to be last-minute requirements, items which have to be purchased urgently; a programme is bound by its recording deadline, and in such cases normal procedures cannot be adhered to. The same is true of overtime requirements: they cannot usually be estimated in advance. Items of studio furniture and set dressings are not requisitionable; selection depends on both educational and aesthetic factors. It is important that contingency funds (more substantial than a petty cash reserve) should be available for such items, and discretion allocated to the service to cover the demands — within reason — as they arise. It is a point which is best established early, as it may run quite contrary to existing practices.

Second, there is question of salary structures. Unless a service is located within a national broadcasting organisation, it will be bound by current educational salary levels, and these may well be very different from broadcasting scales. Allowance must be made at the outset to compensate personnel for their additional burden of duties (which will be heavy, not confined to normal teaching hours), the loss of other sources of income (e.g. private tuition) and fewer holidays, and some attempt must be made to relate their salaries to broadcasting practice. Otherwise, even if teachers can be recruited initially they will not stay, and the programmes will suffer accordingly. This is especially true in the case of engineering and technical personnel, who will probably be recruited from the ranks of professional broadcasters and will expect to be paid commensurately.

As an index of expenditures, the following tables are a guide to major items in both *development* and recurrent *expenditure.*

Capital costs

In general, capital costs should be divided into central and regional development components and expenditure should be phased across the period of capital development. They include items of:

1. *Buildings* (including air conditioning, heating, ventilation, acoustic treatment, etc).
2. *Furniture* (including office furniture and items used in technical areas which are not specifically equipment needs).
3. *Equipment*
   (*a*) production equipment
   (*b*) transmission equipment

(*c*) reception equipment (receivers, cassettes, recorders, etc).

(*d*) other items (e.g. audio-visual equipment for review or library use)

4. *Installation costs* (see Ch. 12 ('Technical facilities') for details).

5. *Freight costs* (see Ch. 12 ('Technical facilities') for details).

6. *Consultancy costs* (see Ch. 12 ('Technical facilities') for details).

7. *Basic materials* (an initial supply of production materials is needed at the time of capital development, to build up a stock for production, create a materials resource library, etc.).

8. *Spares* (a basic stock of spares is required for all technical equipment).

9. *Taxes, import duties, etc.* (In the case of materials required for educational uses, these are sometimes waived, but it is also common for duty to be levied, and to be subsequently reclaimed by the education authorities.)

10. *Contingency* (in days of rapid price increases, a 15 per cent contingency allocation is essential).

Recurrent costs

The breakdown of these items will have to reflect the usual budgetary practices of the supporting organisation, and phasing will be according to the financial year employed. As much detail as possible should be provided, especially in the area of personal emoluments.

A. Personal emoluments (staff costs)
(Including special allowances, increments, etc.) A *contingency* allocation should also be made, to cover salary increases.

B. Services and materials

1. General administration (including stationery and supplies, postage and communications, transport and travel, in-house utilities, hospitality).

2. Production materials (broken down into radio, television, print, other media).

3. Library materials (broken down into books, films, audio-visual materials, etc.)

4. Utilisation training courses.

5. Production and technical training courses.

6. Evaluation (including data processing) and research.

7. Transmission (including power costs for transmitter services).

8. Loan services and materials distribution (both library distribution and physical distribution of support materials broken down into separate categories).

9. Technical spares and replacements.

10. Amortisation (according to the replacement period calculated for major technical systems).

11. Information and publicity.

12. Contingency (at 15 per cent).

Phasing

We have already raised the question of phasing in the original systems diagram (Fig. 1.1) which emphasised, above all, the interrelationship of activities in educational media planning. If we confine ourselves, for a moment, to strategic and operational planning, we can see from Fig. 1.1 that the main stages involved are as follows:

1. General survey and feasibility study.
2. Overall planning (educational, technical and administrative).
3. Building works equipment selection and installation.
4. Staffing and recruitment.
5. Training.
6. Production.
7. Utilisation training.
8. Transmission.
9. Evaluation and research.

It will be apparent that many of these stages are interdependent. Without 1, for example, none of the other stages can proceed; 3 cannot proceed until the completion of 2: 6 to 9 are dependent upon the completion of 3, 4 and 5.

At the same time, none of the operations is complete in itself. Production can only begin after a satisfactory training programme has been initiated, but once started, it continues while successive stages are being introduced. It is unlikely that recruitment will be a once-for-all affair: producers will be required, at an early stage, to plan series, but technicians (unless they are to be specially trained) will not be needed until the studio complex is ready for installation and use. For this reason a phased development programme is required, in which links and relationships are clearly stated, their implications followed through.

A simple, graphical way of expressing this sequence might be as shown in Fig. 13.13 (the symbol TX indicates *transmission*).

Deliberately, the diagram gives no precise indication of timing, or of the duration of activities. These will differ from service to service; a simple system can proceed from planning to active operation in a matter of months, while a major service may take several years to become operational. It is unlikely, however that any system can be envisaged, even at the simplest level, in less than 6 months, and with present delays in equipment delivery a year is more likely, say, for a CCTV system. A national service is unlikely to be completed in less than 2 years, and 3 is a more probable period.

Finally, there is *budgetary phasing*. The approaches discussed so far have been concerned with sequence and interrelationship; this is why they are conveniently expressed in network form (provided that the audience for which they are intended can fathom the mysteries of networks — in most cases a bar chart, less sophisticated as an instrument, but more comprehensible in format, will also be required).

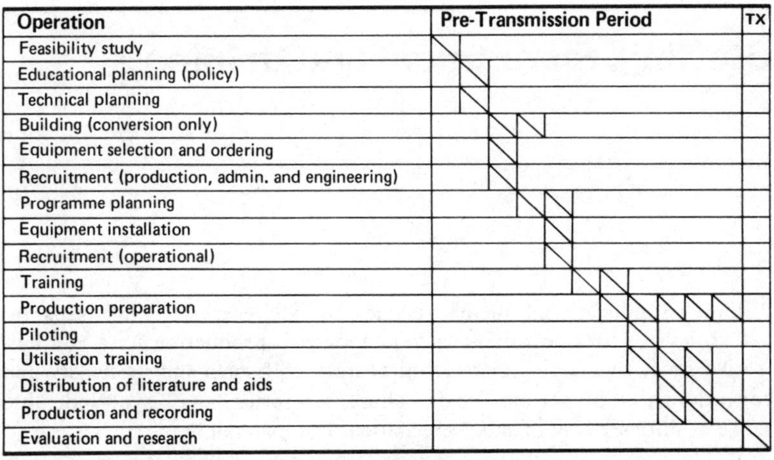

Operation	Pre-Transmission Period	TX
Feasibility study		
Educational planning (policy)		
Technical planning		
Building (conversion only)		
Equipment selection and ordering		
Recruitment (production, admin. and engineering)		
Programme planning		
Equipment installation		
Recruitment (operational)		
Training		
Production preparation		
Piloting		
Utilisation training		
Distribution of literature and aids		
Production and recording		
Evaluation and research		

Fig. 13.13   Duration and interrelationship of operations.

For budgeting, however, a breakdown of expenditures into financial years, and possibly even financial quarters (to take account of such factors as the phased introduction of staff, or scheduled payments on equipment deliveries), will also be needed.

Chapter 14

Staffing, recruitment and training

Within an educational media service, of whatever size, five separate categories of personnel are likely to be required: production staff; administrative staff; engineering and technical staff; craftsmen and specialists; and educationalists of various kinds. These categories cover a considerable range of duties, many of them specialised. For example:

Production staff include producers (who shape the programme overall), directors (who supervise studio operations), presenters or performers. scriptwriters, production assistants (PAs, or assistant producers), research and script assistants (production secretaries or producers' assistants).

Engineering and operational staff include lighting, sound and technical supervisors, maintenance technicians and technical operators.

Specialists and craftsmen include designers, graphic artists, photographers, model-makers, film cameramen and film editors, carpenters, laboratory technicians and scene-painters.

Administrative staff include section heads, executive officers, clerks, librarians, messengers and typists.

Educational staff include subject and curriculum specialists, resource experts, evaluation staff, educational technologists and utilisation officers.

Not all of these will be found in every installation; much will depend upon size, and sample staffing patterns will be found in the Appendix (Characteristic media installations) p. 338.

The production team

Of all these categories, production staff will be the most difficult to secure, simply because an unusual combination of disciplines is needed, and almost certainly special training will be required.

The producer is the keystone of the production unit. He is in overall charge of the series; he supervises the planning of programmes and the preparation of scripts, works with the educational groups responsible for programme planning, controls the selection of aural and visual resources, rehearses artists and supervises (and frequently directs) studio recordings. It is essential, therefore, for him to have a clear knowledge both of the media and of the learning situation.

No one would pretend that a potential producer can be identified in a single interview, but it is quite possible to list the range of qualities which a candidate should exhibit. They include:

(a) teaching experience and an informed interest in education;
(b) a developed sense of aural and visual potential;
(c) a capacity for quick thought and action;
(d) a talent for forming good human relationships;
(e) executive ability and a talent for organisation;
(f) imaginative flair;
(g) good intelligence.

It is unlikely that any candidate will command all these qualities, but he must demonstrate a fair number. Unfortunately, some of them will not show up in interview, and it is advisable, when selecting producers, to make their initial appointments temporary, subject to confirmation. Some special procedures can be devised if time is available, to test such qualities as creative imagination (for example, asking candidates to write sample scripts), and a candidate's leisure interests, as well as his teaching history, are valuable pointers. It is most likely that candidates will come from within the educational system; they must be familiar with the teaching situation, and conditions of service may make it necessary for teachers to be selected rather than external candidates. The most satisfactory means of selection is to run a trial production course for interested candidates, to watch them at work in the studio preparing for experimental programmes and to select them by empirical means.

What of the other members of the production staff? Essentially, programmes are produced by a production team, a small cell of people working in unison on a common project.

The numbers of people to be found in the production unit, or production team, will vary according to the size of the service, the media which are being considered, the resources available and the sophistication of programme formats. They can range from a single person to half a dozen or more. But the main functions of the production team are as follows:

(a) *Directors* oversee the translation of script and resource material into an actual programme. They deal with the cast in rehearsal and during recording, and supervise the *production team* in the studio.
(b) *Presenters* or *Anchormen* perform the actual teaching in the studio, using a variety of illustrations; in radio, narrators have the same function.
(c) *Scriptwriters* write the scripts of the programmes (with full dialogue, and an indication of the forms of illustration to be used, but without technical instructions).
(d) *Production assistants* (PAs or assistant producers) assist the producer in programme preparation, and in television frequency direct both film sequences and studio recordings. They are often junior, or trainee, producers.
(e) *Script assistant* (production secretaries) look after the administration of the production unit, and assist the director during recording. They

keep a full record of the production's history (including the budget), book artists, prepare scripts, arrange planning meetings and rehearsals and book all studio services.

(*f*) *Research assistants* (RAs) carry out basic research for programmes, including materials research.

Some of these roles may, in a smaller service, be conflated or eliminated altogether. In *television* more people are normally required, and in a large national service all the above roles may be provided. But even in quite large services, producers often double as directors. Presenters often write their own scripts, and it is only a lavishly financed operation which can afford independent researchers or script assistants.

For *radio* the unit may well be reduced to a single person — a producer who scripts, records and narrates his own material, though again, when more complex productions are the norm (especially drama), personnel requirements are greater.

Other *audio-visual media* have a different organisational base. While an overall producer/editor will work on multi-media planning teams, and act as general editor for both print and audio-visual materials, their actual execution is much more in the hands of craftsmen — film workers, graphic artists and so on. Since these materials are produced in stages, not on a single occasion as with the electronic media, the editor is more of a coordinating figure, determining content (with the advice of specialists), but then relying on others to translate it into practical material. Thus, though the element of team work is present, it does not require the same degree of physical interaction as the electronic media.

Community media again show a rather different pattern. In community groupings, professionals are either excluded altogether, or are a small nucleus whose main concern is communicating their skills to others. The community media producer is therefore an all-rounder, always with a good operational familiarity with equipment; his craft is inseparable from its tools.

Recruitment of producers

There is, however, more to the allocation of functions than simply economy. A question of philosophy is also involved. It arises from two causes — the form and sophistication of production; and the mode of development of a particular service (i.e. its history, and its context).

The *form of production* is a matter of scale; at a very simple level (e.g. a piece of overspill teaching) there will be no script as such, and no need for elaborate, sustained planning. Some of the functions listed above may then cease to exist at all. There will be no scriptwriter, and no assistants will be necessary. Yet at the level of a national multi-media service, all the roles will be fully played, and may still need further support.

The *mode of development* is a more difficult factor to pinpoint. It arises partly from the educational emphasis laid by a media service partly from the context in which the service is found, and, as was noted in Part

1, there is often what amounts to a cultural split between European and American tradition. (By now, of course, this is a split which has spread throughout the developing world.)

In Europe (and in Japan) services tended to be producer-oriented. Following the pattern of the parent service, the producer would be expected to have a good command of broadcasting techniques, to supervise the entire production operation and to call upon the services of presenters and scriptwriters who would be fully competent, but would nevertheless occupy subordinate roles.

In the United States, where programmes were originally the creation of an education authority, it was natural for a teacher to take overall charge of the production, and to continue his teaching role right into the studio, bringing in a production expert, in a subordinate capacity, to undertake routine direction.

In practice, this can lead to a number of configurations, in which the functions of the production team are differently arranged. We are not so much concerned with research assistants and assistant producers (who are basically extensions, or subdivisions, of existing roles) as with the basic functions of producer, director, presenter (or narrator) and scriptwriter. Some of the principal permutations are expressed in Fig. 14.1, assuming producers with four distinct backgrounds. Likely combinations will be found by following through the connecting lines. The table is expressed primarily in terms of television, but in general the same considerations apply to radio.

Today, whatever the original background of a producer, presenter or scriptwriter, some cross-fertilisation of educational and broadcasting disciplines is essential. The final allocation of functions is a matter of personal choice; many of them can be fused, or omitted, without loss of programme quality at *certain levels of programming*. But ideally, in all cases, personnel carrying out the functions of producer, director, presenter and scriptwriter should stem from the backgrounds outlined in Table 14.1. It is also worth saying at this point that any programme above a basic level of complexity should be scripted (whoever writes the script); even if it is little more than a running order, a written guide is needed to ensure fluency in a programme's technical arrangements.

Recruitment of other production staff

If separate directors are required, they may well come from broadcasting backgrounds: production assistants should also spend a good deal of their trainee life directing programmes (mostly, PAs will be junior producers, undergoing an extended, on-the-job training).

Research assistants are primarily chosen for their academic skills; they may assist, or reinforce, the contribution of scriptwriters and resource experts. *Script assistants*, when available, are high-grade secretarial appointments; they will often progress in time to higher appointment levels.

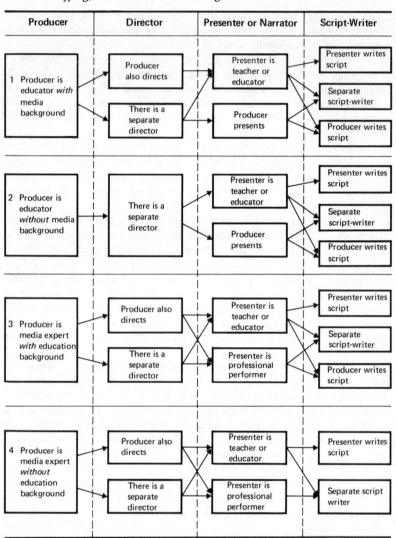

Fig. 14.1   Functions of producer, director, presenter and script-writer.

Scriptwriters, if employed, will normally be part-time or contract appointments, paid on a pro-rata basis. Depending on the kind of script required, they will either be professional writers or teachers (a professional writer is often required, for example, to provide dramatised work).

Presenters, in television, will in most cases be practising teachers, competent in the classroom and on the television screen (the two are by no means the same), and able to handle the technical demands of the medium. This last point is important: when providing film commentaries,

Table 14.1 Qualifications of personnel

Producer	Director	Presenter or narrator	Scriptwriter
1. Excellent educational background and teaching experience	1. Excellent knowledge of media techniques	1. Excellent teacher	1. Developed writing talent
2. Excellent knowledge of media techniques	2. Informed knowledge of education (teaching experience an advantage)	2. Competent in subject area of programmes	2. Excellent educational background (preferably with teaching experience)
3. Broad knowledge of modern communications theory and teaching methodology		3. Excellent performer	3. Informed knowledge of media processes
4. Good knowledge of subject specialisms		4. Informed knowledge of media processes	4. Excellent knowledge of media scripting techniques
		5. Up-to-date in teaching methodology	5. Complete familiarity with subject area of programmes
Notes	Notes Direction may be undertaken by producer, or by assistant producer (PA)	Notes For radio, is not so important	Notes Scripting may be undertaken by presenter, producer or programme adviser (resource expert)

or handling a demonstration, accurate timing is needed and the ability to play to more than one camera — both of which require a certain measure of detachment and calculation.

Presenters may be full-time or part-time appointments, depending on the traditions of the service. A full-time appointee has the advantage of being permanently available for script conferences, pre-filming or rehearsal, but there are certain dangers inherent in this approach. In the first place, contact with the classroom situation is quickly lost by the teacher who performs only on television; furthermore, it is difficult to be rid of an unsuccessful television teacher, if he is recruited on a permanent basis. Certainly, all full-time appointees should be contract appointments, preferably seconded from the classroom (and paid an incentive bonus for television work), but recruited on the clear understanding that the contract will be terminated if results are unsatisfactory, and that in any case the secondment will run for 2 or 3 years at maximum.

Many services will have to rely on part-time presenters, who will be paid a pro-rata fee for work done. In such cases, it should be clearly understood that adequate rehearsal time is needed for the presenter, apart from studio appearances, and there must be a real attempt to involve him in the planning stages of the programme (if he does not actually prepare the script), so as to ensure a real identification with its educational objectives.

The position is similar for *radio narrators*, though neither the pros nor the cons of using amateur as opposed to professional performers are so distinct. The radio narrator is less intimately involved with content; he does not appear in vision, does not handle apparatus in view, can use a script throughout. A good professional narrator can often achieve, on radio, with a short rehearsal and recording period, what would take an amateur unused to dealing with the medium far more time to master. Yet again, there are advantages in having a narrator who can write his own script, and contribute to planning meetings, with the authority which comes from a practising teacher, in full knowledge of both his subject matter and his audience.

At times, *professional actors* will be used in programmes. Drama is an obvious example: indeed, most programmes with a dramatised element will benefit from a professional cast. Current affairs programmes are also possible areas for the practised TV performer, and arts programmes of the general 'enrichment' kind. The advantages of using professional performers lie in the ease which they bring to the medium; when complex production demands are being made, it is preferable, if not essential, to have talent who know the medium well and are at home in the studio.

Engineering and operational staff

Depending upon the organisational pattern adopted for a media service, engineers and technicians may be part of the establishment, or may be obtained through cooperative arrangements with a general broadcasting service. In the case of transmitter and network engineers and technicians, it is most likely that these will be on secondment, or that distribution will be handled directly by the broadcasting channel.

The difficulty occurs mostly in the case of supporting technical personnel for production purposes. We have already explored the arguments which lead, in many cases, to the creation of separate production arrangements for educational media services. While educationally satisfactory, this solution is not always so advantageous to technical personnel themselves, who may lose promotional avenues if they are confined to a small media system. It is probably better, if secondments can be made, to borrow technical staff (for reasonably sustained periods of 2 to 3 years) from a parent broadcasting service, so that promotional aspects are maintained, and links with the larger technical cadre are not broken.

In case direct recruitment and appointment is necessary, an educational authority may not have experience in recruiting engineers and technicians, and competent advice should be sought. In making basic selections for interview, the only satisfactory criterion is professional qualification. There are, of course, many excellent engineers and technicians who do not have such qualifications, but only a technical expert is in a position to assess their value. A senior engineer, in an installation of more than moderate size, should be in possession of a university degree or equivalent professional qualification, as well as broadcasting experience. With technicians and technical operators, experience is the most important asset.

Craftsmen and specialists: administrative staff and educationists

Recruiting craftsmen and specialist staff poses the same problems as the selection of technicians, except that it is likely to be more familiar to an educational establishment — many of the disciplines are already known to audio-visual work. Administrative staff, and educational specialists, present few problems. Even when specialist qualifications or training are required (e.g. in statistical techniques), they should be readily available through traditional academic channels.

Training

Training is one of the most significant needs in educational media planning. It is unlikely, except in highly developed countries, that a ready-made reservoir of trained talent will be available, and special arrangements have to be made.

The kinds of training to be envisaged are:

(*a*) Production training.
(*b*) Technical training.
(*c*) Specialist training (of evaluators, utilisation officers, research workers, media administrators, etc.).
(*d*) User training (the training of teachers and monitors in how to make the most of media).

In this chapter only the first three forms are considered; the training of users is described later, in the discussion of utilisation problems.

Basic training

In the past, there has been a tendency for *basic* training either to be overlooked, or for trainees to be sent routinely abroad to institutions in the developed countries (especially those of donor governments as part of a technical assistance programme). There is certainly a place for such training, but it should be very carefully examined. The formula which has now been arrived at, after lengthy discussions and international conferences, is one of progressive training programmes, according to the level of complexity involved. So it is argued that *basic* training is best carried out in indigenous surroundings; it is difficult enough for trainees to respond to a new set of techniques and disciplines, without at the same time having to adjust to unfamiliar cultural surroundings, and often to language difficulties. The trainee who, at a basic level, goes abroad to learn a new craft often finds himself bewildered and alienated; moreover, he is often learning to cope with problems, equipment and procedures which are poorly related to his home environment. There have been too many cases of trainees learning to produce programmes in a European or American training environment, with resource specialists and services to hand, who return to their own homes to find facilities differently ordered and organised, with fewer support staff, and who then experience a kind of paralysis. If possible, basic programmes should be arranged *in situ*, if necessary with expert assistance from outside.

This in itself poses some problems. If experts are brought in, they must be carefully selected; they should be people who, while knowledgeable in their own specialisms, also have experience of working in other cultures, and especially developing country environments. They must be able to analyse needs and find appropriate solutions, not merely impose the procedures which they know best. Human qualities of sympathy, tact and patience are quite as important as technical skills.

A further problem arises with facilities. It is sometimes possible to borrow existing national studios for training programmes, or to find a suitable resource in a university or technical college, but it may be necessary to phase a development programme so that studios, newly constructed to serve a new media service, are made available well in advance of transmission dates, to allow for a preparatory training programme. However, these are problems which can be accounted for by competent planning: they are not insoluble.

Intermediate training

At an *intermediate* level, training can often be provided by regional institutions, serving a number of countries (such as the Asian Institute of Broadcasting Development, in Malaysia, which serves Asian broadcasters; or the Kenya Institute of Mass Communication in East Africa). Such institutions profit from their regional character to consolidate resources, both material and human, and specialised courses can sometimes be offered beyond the range of national institutions.

International training

International training, on the other hand, is best reserved for specialised work, given in areas where no national or regional provision is available (e.g. in some research and evaluation fields), or as advanced training for people who have been working with educational media for some time. If trainees already have a background of practical work in educational media, they can put the new experiences which they secure in a proper perspective, and make the psychological adjustments necessary to translate their new found knowledge to the advantage of their own country.

Lifelong training

Training should, after all, not be regarded as a one-time activity, necessary only to create the conditions on which a media service is based. It is a continuing, lifelong process. As techniques alter, so personnel need updating and refresher courses; it is likely, too, that staff will change their roles several times in a lifetime, and will need retraining and reorientation courses. As staff responsibilities increase, new instruction in the areas of management and administration are needed. Training should be handled as a planning activity in its own right, with a Head of Training, a nucleus of training staff (who are well versed in training techniques), and in larger environments, a separate training institution. Again, some consolidation is possible; a single institution can, for example, serve the varied training needs of many different kinds of broadcasting, quite apart from educational media, thus saving on facilities and staffing.

Training techniques

It is especially important that the techniques of instruction itself are not forgotten — the *training* of *trainers*. There is now an increasing recognition that instructional programmes have a discipline of their own, comprising the systematic planning of training curricula, due consideration of group dynamics, an emphasis on practical work by individuals and groups, the application of programmed techniques and the use of audio-visual aids. Many of the points emphasised in our discussion of educational planning in Part 2 also apply to training programmes; skills training depends to a great extent on the careful analysis of objectives, the setting of patterns of terminal behaviour, the planning of multi-media strategies by which this behaviour can be achieved.

One illustration is the so-called 'modular' approach. This is really no more than the breaking down of a basic training programme (e.g. production training) into specific component parts — of direction, vision mixing, camera work, lighting and so on. Each unit is described in terms of its terminal objectives, and instructional materials are expressly designed to match this sequence. Practical activities are designed, as exercises, and the student is continuously tested on his mastery of the unit. This kind of activity helps trainee and trainer alike, as it requires the tutor to analyse precisely what production needs are, and to list the basic elements in the production process.

In this process the needs of the trainee must be considered. He must be encouraged to make decisions in his own right, to be given measures to evaluate his own performance and to have some freedom of choice. Where possible, options should be provided — allowing the trainee to take on further work in areas where he feels a particular interest or where he feels weak. While he should have an overall grasp of techniques, he would also be allowed to indulge his natural inclination towards those specific areas which intrigue him.

The use of audio-visual media as training tools is valuable. This is not simply a matter of varying the lecturer's presentation, or illustrating graphically what can be better shown than explained. Audio-visual media are learner-centred as well as teacher-centred tools, and can be used within training in a number of different ways. Loop films, for example, can show technical operations processes; they can be viewed privately, by individuals and groups, over and over again until a particular sequence of skills is mastered. Programmed texts permit the trainee to work through practical and conceptual problems alike, at a speed suited to individual capacity and temperament. Closed circuit television can show a student how he is faring, playing back to him the programmes he has created, his own performance as a presenter. The linking of media to materials, in training as in production itself, becomes a relatively concrete matter, once objectives are clear.

Room must be found in training programmes for experiment. There is no foolproof set of rules and procedures for the production of educational materials, and the training environment — insulated as it is from the pressures of a transmission schedule — may be the only one in which the new, or indeed the old, producer has the freedom to try out new ideas, without running professional risks of failure. Tutors and trainers must be careful to commend experimental forms which show promise, even though they may be at times technically crude; technique is an instrument with which to create programmes, not an end in itself.

Finally, the situation of training as part of a complete media system should never be forgotten. While the emphasis may be on production training, or on engineering training, their place within the system should be continually emphasised. There should be regular interchange between producers and engineers, utilisers and evaluators, with some common sessions in which mutual problems are explored and the characteristics of each discipline are explained to other, parallel disciplines. As part of the training programme, producers should work in teams with other educational personnel, mirroring the whole planning process; they should also review their programmes in the field, discussing them with teachers and users. In a multi-media system, this implies, in particular, that production experience of more than one discipline should be offered, even if (in the final service) there will be a specialist breakdown into production for radio, television and other media.

Production training

As an illustration of the above, we can take production training, which is probably the most important training area for educational media.

A basic training course has to achieve a number of objectives. In particular, it must:

(a) Give the producer a good theoretical grounding in the techniques of media planning and productions, so that he both understands the media process, and has a practical experience of course planning teams, working through an analysis of objectives;

(b) Expose him to the whole media field, in general terms, so that he knows something of disciplines in which he will never work intimately — such as graphics work, photography and camera control, as well as the theoretical problems of utilisation and evaluation.

(c) Give him a practical experience of production — allow him to produce a variety of different programmes, of different styles, and at least one sustained production requiring his full powers of invention.

(d) Give him a practical experience of technical roles outside his normal province — e.g. cameraman, vision mixer or sound engineer — so that he will be able to temper his demands according to what is actually possible.

To do this thoroughly a good deal of time is required: a minimum of 3 months, followed by practical assignments. However, in the nature of things, so much time is not always available and only a shorter course may be practicable — less satisfactory, but certainly better than nothing. Tables 14.2 and 14.3 offer two characteristic training programmes — one of 12 weeks' duration, the other a shorter, 3 to 4 week programme. The number of students on each course should be severely restricted, to allow for maximum practical work — twenty is an outside limit. The character of training should be as varied as possible. The term 'demonstration' has been employed, rather than 'lecture', to show that it is much more than a straightforward presentation of information by a single expert. Some of the teaching may be done with the use of film or videotape materials, some can be done in groups or individually, using resource materials or programmed texts. It is better for students to find out about such matters as shot composition by experimenting with framing on camera, and deducing basic principles, than by having these presented to them in rote form. More abstract principles (the functions of media in different educational contexts, for example) can evolve gradually from group discussion. And while some questions will not be resolved in this way, or at least not in the time available, predetermined exercises can direct the trainee towards appropriate solutions, while still permitting him to find out for himself.

It is assumed, throughout these two programmes, that teachers or educators have been recruited and are being trained in broadcast disciplines. The reverse approach is, of course, possible, though less satisfactory; broadcasters may be recruited, and the particular idiosyncrasies of educational media explained to them. This is a viable approach, provided the broadcaster has sufficient imagination and interest in education, but it is more difficult to achieve success in this way. Educational

Table 14.2   Twelve-week production training programme (multi-media)

Week	Demonstrations (production technique)	Practical studio and workshop exercises	Education and communications theory
1	Basic studio layout equipment, staff and duties	Basic studio familiarisation exercises	Principles of media, types of operation, characteristic uses (with examples), Programme analysis
2	Graphics, vision-mixing, scripting and script layout	Basic vision-mixing exercises/ Graphics workshop	
3	Presentation and elements of studio production	Presentation exercises/graphics workshop	Preconditions for learning, elementary communication and learning theory, applications of educational media
4	Elements of lighting, sound, design camera control, production and administrative routines	Interviews and discussion programme exercises (unscripted)	
5		Five-minute programme exercises (scripted by students)	
6	Mid-course observation attachments to media services		
7	Use of film, filming and editing (at basic level only)	Production of pre-scripted 20 minute programme exercises	Utilisation evaluation and research
8	Further consideration of lighting, sound, design and graphics, and technical processes, including special effects, outside broadcasts, working with videotape, problems of larger productions		
9		Preparation and rehearsal for 20 minute programme exercises (scripted by students)	Planning and organisation of media services and multi-media systems
10–12	Individual tutorials for students	Twenty-minute programme exercises (scripted by students)	General analysis and discussion

strategy cannot be taught in the same way as production technique; it is too full of personal experience and imponderables. If this procedure is adopted, then the broadcaster should be given the opportunity to teach for a period within the educational system. Without first-hand contact he will never understand properly the demands of pace, clarity, pupil response and involvement.

Table 14.3 Short (3 week) production training programme (television)

Week	Session	Period	Monday	Tuesday	Wednesday	Thursday	Friday
1	AM	1	Introduction to ETV D	Principles of shot composition D	The presenter D	The discussion programme D	The scripted programme D
		2, 3	The ETV studio P	Shot composition and vision mixing P	Presentation exercise P	Discussion exercise P	Production demonstration P
	PM	4	The production process (1) D	The production process (2) D	The script (1) D	The script (2) D	Tutorial and group sessions G
2	AM	1	Group exercises P	Group exercises P	Use of film D	Sound D	Project tutorials
		2			Design D	Lighting D	
		3			Graphics D	Utilisation and evaluation D	and G
	PM	4	Group work session G	Group work session G	Group work session G	Group work session G	Group work sessions G
3	AM	1	Group project 1 P	Group project 2 P	Group project 3 P	Group project 4 P	Playback and analysis D
		2					
		3					
	PM	4	Group project 1 P	Group project 2 P	Group project 3 P	Group project 4 P	Question and answer session D

Key: **D** = Lecture demonstration; **P** = Practical work; **G** = Group preparation.

All these observations have been limited to producers, directors and trainee producers, but presenters and scriptwriters also require specific training. They do not, however, demand such an extensive programme, and shorter versions of the courses described can be prepared to suit their needs. Both should be given a general familiarity with the media, and extended practice in their particular field of work. Their training programme may be tied in with that arranged for producers (so that they take part in the practical programme exercises), but in any case, it should precede actual production engagements.

Other forms of training

The training of engineering and technical personnel is a different matter. The chief engineer in an ETV service must have broadcast experience, and the same is preferable with technicians and operators. If this is not possible, technicians must be brought into the service in adequate time for the senior engineer to work intensively with them. As with producers, learning on the job leaves its mark on programme quality.

At times, a local television company may be able to arrange technical attachments for a short period, which will be profitable provided they are working attachments. Some technical colleges arrange operational and maintenance courses for TV technicians; if not, local experts may mount *ad hoc* courses.

Training opportunities abroad

It is impossible, in a brief survey, to list the many opportunities for training which are open throughout the world. Reference should be made to the local offices of Unesco, of the British Council, of the United States Information Agency and of other local embassies and high commissions. Many governments will supply experts for short- or long-term on-the-spot training, and at times private foundations, such as the Ford Foundation, are willing to assist. Production training courses are run in Britain (by the British Council and the BBC, as well as the Thomson Foundation), in the Netherlands, in the Federal Republic of Germany, in Australia, and in Japan by national broadcasting organisations; many university and college campuses in Europe and the USA also run communication and educational technology courses. In some cases, these can be tailor-made to order (often with planning assistance from such agencies as Unesco, the British Council, or the Academy for Educational Development in the USA). In every case, enquiries should be made as early as possible in the planning process. But the tendency to go straight to the donor agency, and to forget that many opportunities are often already available locally, should be resisted. There are often programmes in technical colleges, teacher-training colleges and universities, which may be perfectly adequate. If so, the local version is usually the best, even if it does lack the cachet of a foreign location.

Training and education

It has been remarked that training is for animals, education for humans, and the principle is worth enshrining in planning for media training programmes. Techniques of manpower planning have produced a somewhat mechanistic formula, in which specialist needs are calculated, and training schemes subsequently manufactured to fill the needs. Training should be focused primarily on the trainee, rather than on the specialist slot, and devised with long-term human satisfaction in mind. A media service will benefit in the long run if it extends its educational programmes beyond the bare bones of technical necessity; its personnel will not mature unless horizons are stretched. Whatever the context or content of training, the first criterion ought to be human development.

Chapter 15

Production

This chapter is designed to achieve two ends: to describe the production process overall, omitting technical detail; and to say something about production administration, as it affects both the planner and the individual producer. It is not concerned with media production techniques, which are covered extensively in the companion volume (*Producing for Educational Mass Media*, Unesco/Longman, 1976). However, for the sake of continuity of argument, some passages of the text are common to both volumes.

The production process

To emphasise the continuity of production planning, the discussion is prefaced by a general network (Fig. 15.1), which shows essential activities involved in production across all media. The diagram is subdivided into five phases. Phase 1 is that of *programme planning*, after the curriculum development process is complete, the relative roles of different media have been agreed and series and programme objectives specified. Phases 2—4 are those of *programme preparation*: script and materials development, the compilation of inserts and illustrations and preliminary assemblies. Phase 5 is that of final assembly, *production or recording* of programmes.

We shall begin with *television*, as the most complex form. In many instances, what is said of television is true of other media, certainly in organisational method. Accordingly, the sequence of operations required for television will be described in some detail; in the discussion of radio and audio-visual media which follows, only the main strands of difference will be explored.

Television

The programme outline (Phase 1)

The preparation of a *programme outline* will vary from service to service; there is no standard format. But its function is always the same — it is a means of bringing together the thoughts of the producer in a coherent way, and of indicating to him and to others what means and methods he expects to choose to realise the programme's objectives.

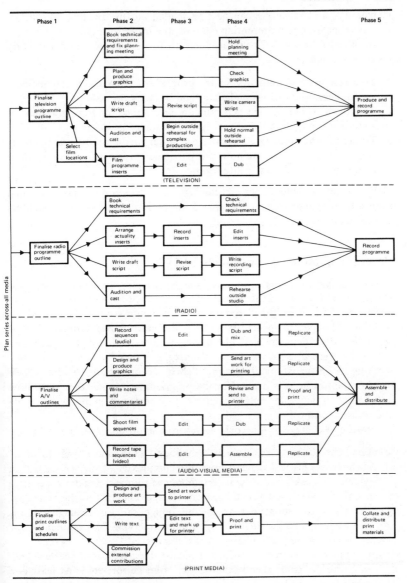

Fig. 15.1 The production process.

So, the outline is a brief statement of intent. It should include, firstly, the programme's objectives: its target audience; its duration; its relationship to other media; and its relationship to previous or subsequent programmes. Secondly, it should summarise the main arguments or contents of the programme, and the means of illustration. A division into studio and film sequences will be very useful (from the technical planning viewpoint), and resources can best be spelled out by dividing the outline into two halves, one representing content, the other format.

In practice, it will help the producer to focus on some necessary early tasks, in particular:

1. To assess his requirements for the programme (financial and logistical), and to begin the various budgetary and booking procedures.
2. To inform other service departments (e.g. those for film, graphics, or administration) of the load anticipated of the programme.
3. To allow other interested agents (e.g. other media producers, planning committees, etc.) to see how this particular programme fits into their own plans, or fulfils their intentions.

Where multi-media series are envisaged, outlines for the various media should be prepared together, so that common intentions and requirements can be deduced.

Programme preparation (Phases 2–4)

Part of the art of media production lies in doing many different things at the same time, without losing track of the whole process of which they are a part. We have already isolated a number of major strands, each of which will involve separate specialists and (in the case of larger organisations) separate service departments. The principal items with which we are concerned here are those of *technical planning, graphics and design, scripting*, working with *artists* and *filming*. Their contribution to the whole programme has been expressed in the programme outline; they must now be allowed to take their separate paths before coming together again in the studio production.

For the next stage of his work, therefore, the producer has to:

(*a*) Cost out the *resources* which he wishes to use, and obtain financial authority. This will depend upon the complexity of the service within which he works, but he will certainly have to match his desires against a known resource level, or against a fixed budget for the series. Of course, if the series has an overall budget he can average out his requirements across all the programmes, reserving film sequences, for example, for only a few important elements.
(*b*) Fix meetings with the various specialist departments concerned (e.g. with the designer, technical manager, film editor, etc.). At least one meeting should be a *joint planning meeting*, where various specialists discuss the programme design with the producer and his staff and each has the benefit of the others' reactions. It is important that, at this early stage, the final production is still seen, thought of and discussed as a totality.
(*c*) *Book ahead* for various services, and issue contracts as required. Film crews have to be reserved in advance; so do studios and studio personnel. It may well be that certain special effects (e.g. back projec-

tion) will need special booking. Such complex processes as film animation have to be negotiated in advance; similarily actors need to be auditioned and contracted.

(d) Draw up an overall *schedule* for the weeks ahead, in which main activities are correlated. This not only serves as a reference point for everyone on the production, but also allows the producer to determine where his critical path lies. Thus, for example, his film editing must be finished in time for the dubbing of film inserts to take place and for the laboratories to produce final prints in advance of the studio production; the same is true of other design and technical areas.

(e) Allocate *responsibilities* fairly and squarely among his production team, so that each person knows what is expected of him and can proceed independently.

Phasing

It is important to note that there is no constant time interval for any programme; everything will depend upon the character of the production, and on the deadlines involved. In a current affairs production, there may be only a few days between the stage of the programme outline and the actual recording or transmission day; this in turn will have its impact upon the resources available. Other programmes may be planned a year in advance, and considerable time may be available for preparation, for testing and so on. So the actual phases of production are constant in their inter-relationship, but the duration of each event is a very different matter.

A possible pro-forma for the producer to use to organise his requirements might be as shown in Table 15.1.

Budgeting

Budgeting, and the procurement of resource materials, are areas which have to be taken specially into account from the earliest planning stage.

Even in the smallest of media services, it is advisable to make producers directly responsible for at least a proportion of the finances of their programmes. There are many items (e.g. scenery, graphics, film, artists' fees) which can be directly attributed to a particular programme or series of programmes, and the producer will often feel freer to manoeuvre if he is allocated a precise sum of money to cover all such costs, which he can then manipulate as he thinks fit. We have, therefore, to distinguish between two kinds of cost, and two methods of costing: between 'above the line' and 'below the line' costs; and between *direct* or total costing, and *indirect* costing.

The items to which we have already referred, which are immediately attributable to a particular programme, are usually known as 'above the line' costs, because they are clearly identifiable as being incurred by that programme. Each production, however, draws upon a considerable range of support services, such as technical and film services, the use of studios and studio equipment, which may come out of a common pool and are therefore less easy to apportion, but which are nevertheless costly to

Table 15.1 Production scheduling

	Scheduled date							
Script								
Outline	X							
Draft script		X						
Revised script				X				
Final script						X		
Camera script							X	
Artists								
Audition		X						
Book			X					
Pre-filming				X				
Outside rehearsal							X	
Camera rehearsal								X
Design and graphics								
Planning meeting		X						
Booking			X					
Sketches			X					
Review							X	
Camera rehearsal								X
Technical planning								
Planning meeting		X						
Book special services			X					
Outside rehearsal visit							X	
Camera rehearsal								X
Filming								
Planning meeting		X						
Book film requirements			X					
Film crew needed				X				
Editing					X			
Dubbing						X		
Print to laboratories							X	
Show print returned								X
Camera rehearsal								X

(In the final version as used by the producer, actual dates would be inserted. In the illustration above, the crosses show the characteristic position of each activity in relation to other activities.)

provide (often far more costly than the other, above the line items). These are therefore termed 'below the line' costs.

We may choose to allocate a limited amount of money to a producer, to cover above-the-line items, and to pay for indirect services through a general departmental or service vote: this limits the degree of financial responsibility of the producer, and is the basis of indirect costing. Alternatively, we may attempt to make each producer pay for every service which he receives, and allocate to him a proportionally larger sum of money: this is the method of direct costing. This second method is, of course, much more difficult to devise; it involves setting a rate for every service provided, and charging each producer according to his use of the service. In the case of a television studio, for example, we might set a fixed rate for the use of the studio, with standard equipment, for a standard unit of time. If the producer required additional facilities, or wished to use the studio for a longer period, the rate would be adjusted accordingly, in line with a published tariff. In the case of an item of graphics, two separate charges would be incurred: one an above-the-line cost, representing the cost of materials used, the other a facilities or service charge, covering the use of personnel and technical equipment.

There are advantages and disadvantages to each method of costing, and ultimately questions of scale are involved. A small media service, with limited personnel and resources, is best advised to apply indirect costing; the range of facilities available is small enough for these to be deployed efficiently using relatively unsophisticated administrative and accountancy methods. Direct costing calls for more complex accounting, and often for data processing; it makes heavier demands on its producers and its supervising staff, in that both have to estimate their needs and deploy their resources far more precisely. But at a certain level of operation (say at that of a State or national service) it can yield dividends in cost effectiveness. It helps to ensure that all technical services and facilities are being used efficiently; financial responsibility is placed firmly on the shoulders of producers on the one hand, and on service departments on the other, and a healthy element of comparative exchange is introduced. There is a continual pressure on both sides to examine what they are getting, or providing, for their money. Producers are less inclined, under a system of direct costing, to use resources gratuitously; they may also have the advantage of financial transferability across a wide range of resources, facilities and services, which can often, with some ingenuity, help them produce exactly the kind of programme they want at the sort of budget they can afford.

Direct costing is beyond the range of many services. Yet, at whatever level a service operates, it is useful to give a degree of financial responsibility to producers, and to hold them strictly accountable for such expenditure. (If possible, some degree of convertibility should also be offered − i.e. producers should be able to trade in some facilities or services against others which they require more, insofar as this can be managed within the administrative structure of the service.) All this involves a three-stage process, beginning with the submission of programme budget estimates at an early stage of planning, revising and updating these estimates as planning develops, and finally comparing the actual costs incurred with those estimated, after the recording or transmission is complete. The process naturally involves a regular dialogue between the producer and whoever in the service is responsible for overall financial arrangements (the same person who has made the original allocation, or who has made a budgetary allocation). It also calls for a reality adjustment. Any producer who consistently exceeds his budget, without adequate justification, has at least to understand that later productions may be under-financed, and at worst that his post is in jeopardy.

As an illustration of the foregoing, some characteristic areas of direct and indirect costing are given in Table 15.2.

Table 15.2　Direct and indirect costing

ETV organisation	
Indirect (below the line) costs (staff, facilities and resources)	Direct (above the line) costs (fees and materials)
Production staff	Artists' fees
Design staff	Repeat fees
Graphics staff	Walk-ons
Visual effects and model building staff	Copyright
Scenic projection (still or moving)	Music
Scenic construction staff	Hiring of premises and locations
Costume staff	Photographs
Make-up staff	Scenic construction materials
Floor managers, studio assistants	Graphics materials
Rehearsal rooms	Visual effects materials
Film shooting (SYNC)	Costume
Film shooting (silent)	Make-up
Film editing	Hired technical equipment
Film dubbing	Film purchase
Film lighting	Film stock and processing
Studios	Film lighting equipment
Studio cameras	Transport
Outside broadcasting requirements	Videotape
Videotape recording	Hospitality
Videotape editing	Travel and subsistence expenses
Telecine	Miscellaneous
Other services	

Resource materials
Availability of source materials is another limiting factor. Most services will want to use a good deal of material which they cannot be expected to provide for themselves: particular areas being film, photographs, music and the use of literary and dramatic works. Film can be taken as a characteristic example. This has not only to be secured (often from abroad), prints made and edited, but copyright clearance and payment have also to be negotiated.

In the main, films, like other materials, are protected by copyright laws, and any use of them for television purposes incurs two obligations: first, to secure permission to use the film material (which may not always be forthcoming, especially if only sequences or extracts are required), and second, to negotiate, and pay for the right to broadcast, the material.

It is impossible to give a general breakdown of copyright problems, as they vary enormously from country to country. Some countries have their own copyright laws (especially the developed countries, where media industries are more vocal); others have none. Some countries subscribe generally to the various international copyright conventions and subsequent agreements which cover both copyright and materials distribution. But others do not recognise their validity.

Moreover, the problem has been compounded by the progress of educational technology. Some *ad hoc* agreements have been secured (e.g. in the United Kingdom, for the recording and institutional use of educational television and radio programmes), but these include conditions which are difficult to regulate, such as the destruction of recordings after a specific period of time. In the case of open learning systems, such as the Open University, new agreements again have to be negotiated, because materials are being distributed and used in a far more extensive and systematic manner. It is a situation which is bound to worsen. In pioneer days, people are more interested in the challenge of new methods and materials than they are in 'rights'. Later these considerations become much more important.

The best solution is to approach the producers or distributors of any material required independently, as early as possible, and to state the precise way in which it is to be used. Often, educational media services can secure favourable rates if they state clearly that they will be using the film in an instructional context. New services, too, can sometimes secure 'pioneer' status, which reduces the scale of payment until a service has had time to build up its resources. When writing to a distributor, however, be careful to state the way in which material is to be used (e.g. whether it is the whole item or an extract; what length of extract is to be used; how many transmissions are contemplated; whether further transmissions or alternative distribution of the finished programme are contemplated; whether any sequence may be reproduced in another form; whether credits can be given to the producer or distributor). Each of these factors can affect the final payment; some distributors, for example, will waive fees in return for a credit.

Clearance of copyright and the payment of fees for permission to use material are technically necessary in many areas. Photographic stills, if acquired from news or other agencies, are also liable (normally irrespective of the length of time for which they are shown on a television screen), and these payments, or a proportion of them, will normally be due for each transmission of a programme. Music performances, and especially gramophone recordings, are also protected; so are literary, dramatic and artistic works. While short literary excerpts may be used free of charge, under the heading of 'fair dealing', any lengthier example incurs a fee. Paintings, sculptures and drawings are in the same position, unless they are permanently exhibited in public or are only used as background.

There is also the question of performers appearing in programmes. Performers naturally have rights in their material, and any sizeable media service needs to appoint a contractual representative, to negotiate contracts in which the rights both of the service and of the performer are clearly formulated. It is becoming increasingly difficult to secure an 'all rights' contract for any kind of work. The number of transmissions envisaged, the scale of payment for each repeat performance, the right to distribute material after an original transmission have to be clearly spelled out.

Production preparation

If we now return to the systems diagram (Fig. 15.1), we can see that for television (as for the other media illustrated), a number of activities interlock in the programme preparation phase, coming together in actual production. They are separate strands of activity, but they are actually coexistant.

Technical discussions are held with the Technical Manager and the Lighting Supervisor, to book special facilities and to review the technical requirements of the production in such a way that likely problems can be ironed out in advance.

Consultations are held with the set designer and with the graphic artist. Settings in educational television are usually simple, and designers may be working with very limited financial resources. This does not make their role any the easier; backgrounds are needed which, while not obtrusive, can set off models, laboratory items, displays and so on to maximum advantage (the plain, evenly lit cyclorama is all too often taken as the hallmark of an educational programme). Graphics are particularly important, as much more than aesthetic appeal is required. Information has to be presented with discretion, so that it can be assimilated easily and read without difficulty by a viewing class.

The script outline is developed into a first full draft, meant for further discussion and some (limited) modification.

Decisions are made about casting; if actors are involved, auditions are held, so that artists can be available for pre-filming. In many programmes, only a single presenter will be required, but the programme script should ideally be written by the person who presents it, and at the very least, he should translate it into his own words and idiom.

Film preparations are also begun. Film in ETV programmes takes two forms: library film, which is excerpted from existing material, and specially shot film. In the case of the latter, even before filming begins, suitable locations have to be found, and arrangements made for their use. Subsequently, graphics and photographic materials go into production, specially commissioned photographs are taken, and art work is begun, to be checked back at each stage with the producer. A revised script is prepared; pre-filming begins; a film crew goes out to photograph each scene shot by shot. This can be a protracted affair, as a single camera is employed, with the individual shots being taken in sequence. The film sequences, after processing, are edited together.

Rehearsals are also begun, outside the studio, for more complex productions. Many problems can be anticipated at this point, and as far as possible a production should enter the electronic studio with all its moves, demonstrations, etc., sorted out, and all words learned. At the end of this period, technical staff may also wish to attend an outside rehearsal to see how things are progressing. Outside rehearsals come to an end; graphics and photographic materials are checked; the set is completed. Camera plans showing the disposition of cameras and sound booms are issued, and the film sequences, after final editing, are dubbed (i.e. the various sound tracks, of commentary, dialogue, music and effects are mixed together, and balanced, into a single, composite track). The camera script is prepared: a guide to the production, distributed to all studio personnel, which includes not only the dialogue of the programme, but also full technical instructions, listing the sequences of shots for each camera, the points at which between cameras will be made, sound sources, the arrangement of film sequences and so on. It is, in effect, a blueprint for the finished production, and tells the experienced reader, at a glance, exactly what will be seen on the screen, and heard at any given moment.

Production and recording (Phase 5)

The performers now move into the studio proper, working inside scenic settings and displays, with cameras operating around them; all film and other materials are to hand, and the director is ready to supervise the process of fitting all components together into an integrated 'programme'.

The process of studio recording is time-consuming and sometimes elaborate, but its principles are clear. We have to remember that two areas are in use: the studio, where the programme is taking place, and the control room, where the production is being supervised, and the many visual and audio sources available are being married together. At this time, the director is in charge of operations, but in many instances the producer will also be directing the programme.

The director is at work in the control room, together with the engineers and technical operators who control sound levels (the sound mixer), manipulate lighting changes (the lighting engineer or supervisor), play in film sequences (the telecine operator), and make sure that camera pictures are satisfactory (the camera control operator). A vision mixer is also present, who is able to select, from the variety of visual sources displayed in front of him on television screens or monitors, any desired picture. At any time in the production he can see the output of each camera in the studio, together with other sources such as film (telecine) and videotape inserts, or outside broadcast pick-ups. Programmes are, of course, of differing complexity. In the simplest form of programme (for example, a piece of classroom observation), there will be a relatively limited pictorial selection to be made, perhaps from two cameras, one focused on the teacher, the other on students in the class, and the technical process will be correspondingly simple. For a more sophisticated programme (for example, a language teaching programme which makes use of a number of dramatised inserts), the process of direction will be more demanding: a full camera script is certainly needed, and some rehearsal will be needed to ensure fluency in the finished version. After all, a polished production is essential for educational as well as professional reasons; otherwise the viewing audience will be distracted by aesthetic clumsiness, or simply not be able to follow what is going on.

Assuming we have a relatively complex production on our hands, a number of rehearsals or 'run throughs', will be needed in the studio, with cameras available — at least two rehearsals before the final recording is made. At each stage, the programme will become more fluent, more identifiable as a whole, and the director will be able, as the rehearsal progresses, to detach himself more from the mechanical operation in order to look at the shape of the finished programme. It is for this reason that, when adequate staff are available, it is better to appoint a separate 'director' for each production, thus leaving the producer free to observe objectively.

Finally the recording or transmission is made. A few services still have to transmit some programmes live, but with the availability of cheaper and improved video recording techniques, they are very small in number.

Other media

The same process is essentially true of other media and further reference to the systems diagram (Fig. 15.1) should make any differences clear. In *radio*, the graphic and visual element is missing, so that the process appears as a reduced version of the television production cycle, allowing for actuality inserts and dramatised sequences. For *print media*, the cycle is confined to writing, graphic and layout design, and to technical print processes. The situation with other *audio-visual media* is rather more complex. In compiling this handbook, which is concerned with educational mass media systems, it has been assumed that audio-visual media will be produced in support of the total system and not as isolated materials; nevertheless the range of media to be covered, especially if they are to be retained in local circuit libraries and used as resource materials, may be very wide. At the same time, production costs are high, and distribution costs even higher, and a judicious selection has to be made.

The principal use of audio-visual media in a mass media system is to provide teacher guidance or a supporting element of richness, of detail, of learning resource and of flexibility. Audio-visual media may, for example, be offered in specific subject areas where more detailed assistance is needed; so in a science or a mathematics series 8 mm loops may be provided to illustrate particular concepts, or a general purpose social studies series may be reinforced by film strips produced on local subjects. Thus, from the production planning viewpoint, the range of support media to be offered may consist of individual items (slides, tapes, etc.), series, or multi-media packages. This requires sophisticated production control, and excellent coordination in the design stage. Moreover, the assembly of audio-visual media is usually carried out in the laboratory, over a period of time, not instantaneously (in a single recording session) as with the broadcast media. The process of creation is therefore at once more protracted and more deliberate; changes can be made to the final format relatively late in the production cycle, even, if necessary, after a finished product has been evaluated.

One final point should be emphasised. If we assume that all media are being produced within a coherent system, with correlations and cross-referencing between materials, then the relationship between broadcast and physically distributed materials is crucial, since they are meant to converge at the point of utilisation. In other words, the physically distributed products (books, notes, film strips, tapes, etc.) which are to be used in the classroom or reception centre must be available at the time of the broadcast transmission. This means in turn that time must be allowed in the production network for them to be created far enough in advance to allow for their physical distribution (often, in large, poorly connected countries, a time-consuming exercise). It is a requirement which poses great problems to producers, especially to audio-visual and print producers, who often need decisions on the content of associated broadcast programmes much earlier than broadcast producers are inclined to commit themselves. Such a situation calls for sympathetic mutual understanding.

Chapter 16

Distribution

For radio and televison, two modes of distribution are available: by electronic means, i.e. by open broadcasting, via the air waves, or through a cable system; or by physical means, i.e. by distributing materials in recorded form, on audio or videotape, disc or film.

The most widespread method is evidently open broadcasting, since this was the basis upon which the electronic mass media were first introduced.

Open broadcasting

As the total quantity of information has increased, so has the demand for frequency space in which to transmit it. Whether for broadcasting or conducted transmission along some sort of predetermined path the demand is always for more bandwidth. As the lower frequencies in the elctromagnetic wave spectrum are used up the required bandwith can only be found by continually moving further up the frequency spectrum. As the spectrum diagram (Fig. 16.1) illustrates, electromagnetic waves, which all have the same characteristics apart from their frequency or wavelength, are commonly divided into discrete bands.

The use of the radio frequency spectrum is governed by international agreement, which is regulated by the International Telecommunications

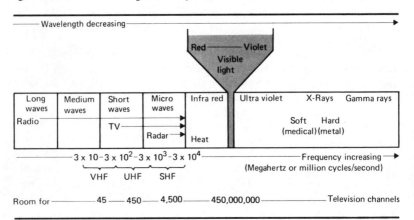

Fig. 16.1   The electromagnetic wave spectrum.

Union. Blocks of spectrum space are allocated for specific services, which include such things as marine radio communications and radio beacons for guiding ships and aircraft as well as broadcasting and fixed services. Each country has to decide the purposes to which its allocation of frequencies is put and then ensure that this use is rigorously controlled.

Frequency usage

If we look at Fig. 15.1, we will see that *Very High Frequencies* (VHF 30—300 MHz) are generally used for direct broadcasting for both radio and television (the latter occupying up to thirteen channels in Europe). Frequencies in the VHF band are also used for trunk telephone coaxial cable links; these use a system called Frequency Division Multiplexing (FDM), which allows groups of channels to be combined into progressively larger groups (e.g. twelve up to 2,700 audio channels) before transmission over the main routes.

The *Ultra High Frequency* (UHF 300—3,000 MHz) band is now extensively used for television broadcasting (e.g. in the UK it provides a nationwide four-channel capability, although due to the limited range of these frequencies hundreds of low-power repeater transmitters are needed to provide more than 96 per cent coverage of the population).

Because of the comparatively narrow bandwidth required large numbers of sound radio stations can be accommodated on the medium and high frequency bands. However, television requires far more bandwidth, and even in the VHF part of the spectrum the bands allocated to television permit only a very limited number of transmitters to operate. Moreover, the higher the definition of the picture (i.e. the number of lines — 405, 525, 625, or more) the greater will be the bandwidth occupied. The UHF part of the spectrum provides greater bandwidth and can therefore support more channels, but its propagation is more sensitive to geographical contours than VHF, and the normal range of reception of 40 to 60 km radius around a transmitting station relies on good line-of-sight paths. Consequently, for 100 per cent coverage of an area many 'fill-in' repeater stations may be necessary.

Beyond the UHF band, there are *Super High Frequencies* (SHF above 3,000 MHz). Waves of these frequencies are also known as *microwaves*, and their use in broadcasting is mostly for providing natural connections (e.g. between a studio complex and a transmitter, or between an outside broadcast vehicle and the studios).

Moving up to higher frequencies still, the development of *lasers* (which are coherent light-emitting sources) and the means of modulating their output, has opened up new possibilities of very wide band transmission paths. For example, a recently announced laser modulator is capable of modulating on to a single laser beam of red light 25,000 radio or twenty television programmes. Since light beams can be completely cut by fog or snow, development has concentrated on guiding these light waves along optical fibre cables. By the use of ultra-pure glass or low-loss liquids inside fine glass tubes the attenuation of the transmitted signal can now be kept very low (a complete cable having fifty conductors with all the necessary padding and protection is only 1 cm in diameter). But in considering distribution forms involving visible light frequencies we are still, clearly, dealing with the future.

Educational transmissions

The costs of operating VHF and UHF transmitters are considerable and well beyond the reach of any but regional or national bodies.

The number of channels for open broadcast work is also limited, and only the richest of organisations could ever contemplate setting up a VHF or UHF network exclusively for educational broadcasts (as was done in American Samoa). For this reason, even if a service decides to create its own studio centre, it will normally have to rely upon national broadcasting transmitters to distribute its programmes. Eventually, a channel may be reserved entirely for education, as is the case in Japan. Educational transmission therefore is not usually separated from other forms, except in the case of an allocation in the 2.5 GHz (microwave) band for instructional television services in America. The microwave frequencies have a limited line-of-sight range, usually highly directional, which makes them unsuitable for general broadcasting. However, all-round transmissions for a few miles are possible, and well over 100 school districts and other educational institutions in the United States are currently operating in the 2.5 to 2.69 GHz band. They provide a four-channel Instructional Television Fixed Service (ITFS). The transmitter power is regulated to a maximum of 10 watts, which produces a service range of about 30 km. At each receiving point there is a dish aerial and a frequency converter which enables a normal broadcast receiver to be used to receive the signals.

Cable systems

An alternative to open broadcasting in smaller locations is by *cable*. Here, the simplest form of distribution is as a direct video and audio signal. *Video systems* are unsuitable for any but the smallest CCTV installations, as their range is extremely limited (about 200 m at maximum), but more complex cable systems, known as carrier systems (in which the broadcast information is modulated and passed along a cable or set of cables), do not have the same limitation. Video distribution is therefore used only within a small group of classrooms or a school, but carrier systems are the norm in most CCTV installations. They can offer better reception than broadcast distribution and are less subject to interference.

Carrier systems are of several kinds. *VHF systems* are multi-channel carrier systems using several (a stack of) different carrier frequencies. The signals, up to a normal maximum of nine, are all transmitted together down a single coaxial cable. So the *VHF stacked carrier* is in essence an extension of an aerial feeder, and merely conveys the broadcast signal, after amplification, to many standard receivers (i.e. those designed expressly to receive broadcast signals from aerials). The carriers used normally correspond in frequency to channels allocated for very high frequency broadcasting.

HF multiplier systems are different in conception. They are designed as a complete system; the receivers are not expected to carry out so many functions, and are therefore both simple to operate and less expensive (e.g. they do not have separate tuners). In these systems each signal is modulated on to a high frequency carrier which is conveyed to the user via a twisted pair of conductors in a special cable. A separate circuit is provided for each channel or programme; sound is carried at audio frequencies on the vision circuit and filtered out at the receiver. Domestic installations of this type are already found in a number of cities throughout the world.

When the number of channels on an HF system rises above fifteen to eighteen it becomes uneconomic to carry every channel to every subscriber. Instead a dial-access system can be used in which each subscriber has only two pairs of wires connected to his outlet. One pair enables him to dial a number to a local programme exchange which connects his selected programme (combined vision and sound) to the second pair of wires which feed his receiver. Exchanges are situated at intervals of 2 to 3 km along the main cable trunk routes. Currently experimental systems of this type have a thirty-six channel capacity, but theoretically there is no upper limit.

Other variations on these two approaches have also been developed, but the economics of each system depend primarily on the number of users. With the HF multipair system the receivers are simpler and cheaper, but the central station equipment is more complex and costly. Morever, these receivers have to be especially designed, while with the VHF stacked carrier system normal broadcast receivers can be used. Several of the larger CCTV installations in the UK employ the HF multipair system, but it is not economic unless the audience is of a reasonable density and a number of channels are required.

In theory, cable distribution is much preferable to open broadcasting for educational purposes. Sooner or later, any service operating on a broadcast channel, especially if it is shared with other users (as on a national network), finds itself short of time and space.

A cable network has greater capacity and a far greater audience involvement and feedback potential; when more channels are available some can be offered for amateur production, or can provide return paths to allow audiences to respond. At first this is done by simple means, such as answering multiple choice questions by signalling a response code. Later on, once the cable networks are better developed, new kinds of interconnection can be provided (e.g. voice connections), and more important still, different networks may ultimately be joined together (e.g. the telephone system, computer networks).

Yet, as we have stressed before, this kind of provision must await better economic conditions. For the moment, the promise of cable lies more in networks which serve individual institutions (schools, colleges, universities), or local areas (school districts, local communities), towns and small cities. In many ways this is as well, as it allows for more experiment with human interaction (often bypassed by technology) before national levels of distribution are reached.

Satellite transmission

Of the many man-made satellites that have been or still are in orbit round the earth a considerable number are communications satellites. The function of such satellites is to act as a repeater of signals sent to them from transmitting stations on the earth. Satellites may be put into one of a number of different orbiting patterns, but for communication purposes synchronous orbits (i.e. those in which the satellite's velocity matches that of a point on the earth's equator and the satellite remains at a height of approximately 36,000 km above it) are generally the most useful, although the USSR gains from using an elliptical non-synchronous orbit because of its particular location on the earth's surface.

A communication satellite requires positioning and orientation controls and a telemetry system which provides position information to the earth and responds to command signals from the earth. It also requires receiving and transmitting aerials and the receiver/amplifier/transmitter which forms the repeater. To drive this it needs electrical energy produced by the solar panels which form its 'battery'.

Communications satellites can be either:

(a) *Point to point* – using relatively low-powered satellites with large and expensive earth stations. They are suitable for data, telephone and television signal links between widely separated countries that have well developed internal communication networks.

(b) *Distribution* – using medium-powered satellites providing a fairly strong signal over a limited area within which reception is possible by earth stations costing about $100,000 from which distribution by rebroadcasting to a limited area is possible. Such systems are in use in the USSR and Canada and under active consideration in a number of other countries.

(c) *Broadcasting* – using a high-powered satellite providing a strong signal over a wide area, which can be received by inexpensive earth terminals located at community viewing centres. Such a system is possible now (as in the ATS–6 satellite used experimentally for North America and India), but increasing the power of the satellite to a level sufficient to relay a television signal directly to an individual home receiver is beyond capabilities of satellites existing or planned for the next decade.

Distribution type satellites may, as in Canada now, make access to television programmes produced at some distant centre an added attraction to individuals connected to a local cable network. The latest Canadian satellite, CTS, has a number of experimental functions: it uses a new frequency allocated for satellite broadcasting by the ITU (in the 12 to 14 GHz bands); and it integrates a number of experimental strands in the community, including two-way voice transmissions to and between small, transportable earth stations, digital communications, remote TV transmissions, and broadcasts to small and remote communities. However, it is the broadcast satellite which finally has the potential to give direct access to information to millions of people in both developed and developing countries. If current trends continue it will eventually also be possible to use cheap terminal receivers for data, computer links, radio and television.

Presentation and continuity

One aspect remains in our survey of broadcasting distribution problems. Whether or not a service is operating its own transmission network, it will have to pay some attention to the problem of presentation. Programmes are not transmitted as and when the producing organisation decides; they have to adhere to strict timings and patterns of distribution. In the case of educational media this is specially important, since groups of listeners and viewers are likely to have come together for the specific purpose of receiving a broadcast.

This means that not only must timings be exact (implying that programmes must start on time, and must run to an agreed length, met exactly by the producer), but they must also follow a regular presentation routine, worked out to serve the best interests of users and explained fully to them on utilisation courses and in support literature. The needs of this routine are simple, and they will inevitably include for television: (i) a station or channel identification in advance of the programme; (ii) a programme and series title displayed in advance on a caption; (iii) a 'count down' probably on a 'schools clock' face, measuring the final minute before a programme. Other refinements are possible (e.g. special continuity announcements to teachers). The presentation routine must not be undervalued; it is a useful way of keeping in touch, in a personal way, with audiences, and the precision with which it is carried out will often decide the reputation of the service for efficiency. In radio, similar routines are employed, with music and continuity/identification announcements following a pre-set routine.

If a service has to handle its own presentation, then continuity studios are necessary, or at the least a continuity desk in the master control area, with access (for television) to a caption scanner or slide projector, and with audio tape, cassette or cartridge provision for both television and radio. It is not always necessary to keep a presentation announcer permanently on hand to provide for continuity; announcements can be pre-recorded, together with captions, and a technical operator can switch them in and out as necessary. For this purpose he must have, in the case of radio, a simple audio mixer, and in the case of television, a simple mixing unit or transmission switcher. If the service pre-records its programmes for transmission by another agency, then it may be a good idea also to pre-record, on the same tape as the programme, the desired presentation routine, including station identification signal, announcement and music.

Physical distribution

Traditionally, physical distribution has been reserved for print materials, or for audio-visual items (films, film strips, film slides, audio tapes, records, etc.) which are either purchased by individual schools and colleges, or are borrowed from a library. Such libraries may be national or regional in scope, though in a large country, if only for logistical reasons, regional libraries are preferable (they can concentrate on popular local materials, provide a better lending and return service, chase up missing and non-returned items more easily, and mount exhibitions and training programmes to promote their services and materials). An interesting development in the United States has been the emergence of the Agency for Instructional Television, which grew out of an earlier experiment with both regional and national instructional television libraries. The AIT is a consortium of users and producers at the State level in the USA and Canada; new series are produced to order by members of the consortium (responding to a concensus of all members), and production is financed collectively. The programmes are subsequently available for use over State networks. AIT came into existence only in 1973 (as a successor to National Instructional Television), and it is already exhibiting both financial and creative success. Not only does it function in the market-place of education, but it adopts a novel cooperative approach to both the production and distribution of educational materials.

Audio-visual resource centres

If considered conjointly with a mass media system, the role of such libraries is usually supportive; they provide additional resources for both teachers and learners and for reference. Mostly, more expensive materials are involved. A *16 mm film* lending library (divided usually into two sections, one expressly for schools and the other for general borrowing) is a first requirement in any progressive centre. The library should provide multiple copies of teaching films and single copies of general films. It is generally better to buy films over a narrow spectrum, but with multiple copies, than to purchase a single copy only of a title if it is to be used in a large number of schools. When too few copies are available interest in the schools will wane, if they cannot obtain the titles requested for the periods needed. This is especially true when materials are serving a common curriculum, or are linked with a media system, as all the pressures on library materials will inevitably coincide. The same position is true of *videotapes* in sophisticated media systems, but while *film strips* and *slides* may be produced and distributed from a central audio-visual centre, it is far better if, once issued, they can be retained by the schools to be used as and when needed. As far as possible, they should be sold or issued free of charge; they are simply not valuable enough to justify the administrative work involved in lending libraries.

Another possibility is to operate a service on a 'film-return' basis. Many newer centres copy material for schools, if the schools provide the basic stock and then return the processed material. In this way, the facilities of the centre are put to full use, with minimal staff requirements.

Loop films can certainly be produced, but they should not be made available for loan from a central audio-visual media centre. It has been found time and again that damage to loops occurring both from transportation and inept use negates any value that the loop might have. It must be remembered that most loop films are produced for showing as a segment in a lesson, or for a student doing individual work. Where there is a highly structured teaching programme, a loop film cannot be brought in casually from an outside source, but has to be available as and when required.

Generally, the same principle applies for any audio-visual medium whose production cost, or life expectancy, is insufficient to warrant a library return system. Further examples would be *charts* and *project materials* (topic books and kits, class packs), which may well be used by a number of classes over a period of months or even years. At the level of the local *community*, although materials are loaned to community groups, the main provision is for individual users. The library therefore becomes a kind of audio-visual reference library, with some materials (preferably on cassettes, for easy use) on the shelves, with replay booths provided, and a theatre for showings of special programmes or compilations.

Print support materials

Obviously, the position also holds true for *print materials* produced in support of broadcasts. In most cases, print support materials, at least for networked programmes, have to be produced and distributed from a central source, to ensure the savings without which they would probably not exist at all. (Regional programmes can of course be covered by lower quality materials, produced in regional centres in simple offset or mimeographed form, but these supplement rather than direct the overall provision.) Whether these are sold to schools or issued free, they are distributed one-way only, not to be returned.

Distribution problems

A one-way system, while it cuts down administrative costs (no central registry of borrowers has to be maintained), still leaves the problem of distribution open. In developed countries this is not particularly difficult, since the postal services can be used. In the developing world, these may be both skeletal and unreliable, and other alternatives must be found. One solution is to deliver materials in bulk to a regional centre, which then makes deliveries by its own van to local centres, or directly to schools. In a large country a distribution chain can be constructed, with packages passed down the line, first to regional centres, then to local, with a further sorting at each level. Ultimately, materials can be picked up by teachers as they come to draw their monthly salaries. (Questionnaire returns can also be distributed, and collected, in the same way, to feed an evaluation system.) In many countries carrier services are available for bulk distribution, which can be much cheaper, and sometimes more reliable, than the post, and this permits at least the initial distribution to regional centres to take place.

It is important to consolidate various services which all require transport. For example, materials distribution can be linked with equipment maintenance services; if the latter undertake a regular run of schools, to carry out routine work on television sets, the same vans can take along with them broadcast support materials. Alternatively, utilisation officers, visiting schools to view programmes and to report on their success, can contribute to the same chain. Consolidation of this kind saves time and money, but it does require careful liaison, especially between different administrative sectors.

Mobile units

A brief note should be added on mobile audio-visual units, which have been used for many years in remote and inaccessible areas (originally devised as cinema vans, but later extended to cover other audio-visual equipment). The typical audio-visual mobile unit will be equipped with film projector, videocassette recorder, monitors and accessories, slide and film strip projectors, and project display items. It can therefore be used to show audio-visual materials to remote villages (either as an *ad hoc* programme, or 'narrated' by an animator); it can be used as a travelling exhibition; or it can be used as a training aid — as in the on-site training of field and extension workers.

Both the design of the vehicles, and the uses to which they are put, depend on a careful appreciation of their function. A mobile unit may be little more than a travelling cinema or display vehicle, in which case it will try to cover as many locations as possible in its circuit. If, on the other hand, it is used to reinforce training programmes, its route will be dictated by the programme itself, and it is likely to stay in one place for extended periods. Finally, if it is seen as an element in a community development programme, then it will be primarily a means of transporting equipment for use by a resident social worker.

In all cases, there are some basic preconditions. Adequate maintenance facilities must be provided for the vehicles, and a supply of spare parts held at their base. Adminstration should be decentralised as far as possible, so that the units are not left to their own devices. Utilisation should not be left to a driver or a technician; unless they are no more than mobile cinemas, this should be handled by a competent development worker. It must be admitted that the history of mobile units has not been particularly auspicious; they have a record of poor utilisation, frequent breakdown and are starved of new, up-to-date materials. In fact, if they are to be effective, they must be used within a disciplined programme where advance publicity is given to their arrival, where the stimulus they offer is followed up adequately after each showing, and where showings are linked with parallel efforts in both mass media and development. They must, above all, be given a regular supply of software, and sufficient resources to keep running. All too frequently, such units are provided by donor governments, but once the donation is made no allocation is made for running expenses.

Interaction between physical and electronic distribution

The ideal media system presupposes a good deal of interaction, at two levels. Firstly, there is cooperative planning in the production, distribution and scheduling of both broadcast and non-broadcast materials, in which both are seen to serve common curriculum objectives. Although it is most critical in the case of materials (especially print materials) which are produced directly in support of broadcasts, it should extend further, to more *ad hoc* productions.

If there is a definite spirit of cooperation between audio-visual libraries and the electronic mass media system the former can be very valuable. They help to provide the flexibility often absent from the electronic media — the possibility for teachers and learners to follow up special areas of interest, or to vary the pace of the standardised mass media presentation. All too often, however, there is virtually no dialogue between the two. This is a pity, not only for the user, but also for the audio-visual service, which is very likely, in the long run, to find itself ignored by schools, starved of funds, and ultimately phased out of existence.

The second level of interaction is one of technology. Given recording equipment (both audio and video) in the schools and colleges, programmes may be recorded off air, and stored in an institutional library. It is this approach which gives most freedom to the mass media system, freeing it from the constraints of rigid timetabling, but still avoiding physical diffusion problems. Not only do schools have repeated access to materials, at times which are controlled by users rather than producers, but the problem of original transmission is also solved, since any hour can be chosen, demanding only the presence in the receiving institution of someone to record the programme for future use.

More refinements are now possible to assist with this process (and others are technically feasible, but are awaiting more widespread development for them to become commonplace). The most important is the automatic recording of materials, by using a time clock coupled to the recorder, switching it on and off when required. This means that even night hours can be used for transmissions, and everyone at the receiving end can then be freed from the chore of recording. The system can be refined further, so that a cue tone, or some similar energising device, switches the recorder on or off — or even, if a simple code is available, switches on only a limited number of recorders in the system. So, in theory, if recorders are permanently switched into a network, specific groups of schools, or certain classes, can have programmes directed exclusively at them, and only those recorders responding to the code employed will actually take the programme. Later, it may be possible for high-speed recordings, both audio and video, to be made in the schools, saving more transmission time still. The limits are both technical and systemic — they can only be contemplated where there are explicit relationships between users, and agreed patterns of working. But in the end they should bring even closer the goal of mass distribution coupled with personal attention.

Part 4

Media utilisation, evaluation and research

Having traced through the outlines of the delivery system which produces mass media materials, the remaining part of this handbook deals with their use, evaluation and recycling. Returning once again to the network of Fig. 1.1, the first point to emphasise is that, although the physical activities associated with these strands only begin once programmes are distributed, planning and preparation have to come much earlier, and are actually a part of the production process.

Training also has to be arranged early − not simply for evaluation and utilisation officers, but a widespread programme of orientation for the media users themselves. Consequently, the discussion in the next chapter will consist of three separate elements: the physical environment for mass media use (including consideration of reception and replay equipment); the way in which materials are used within different educational settings; and the kind of training sequence which is needed for successful usage.

The final chapter will look more specifically at evaluation forms and processes, and at basic research needs.

Chapter 17

The physical environment

However inspired a programme may be, it will be of little use unless it can be seen and heard properly. And seeing and hearing are, in turn, governed by a number of factors — the viewing or listening room, the television or radio receiver, seating arrangements, timetabling and so on.

In an ideal world, all media resource areas would be designed specifically for their purpose. On occasions this actually happens: but all too rarely (an example is given in Fig. 17.1).

In this chapter, therefore, we have to operate on two levels simultaneously — the theoretical, and the pragmatic. Much of the specific technical discussion will be directed towards quasi-ideal conditions, where teachers and users have control over their environment. At the same time, it is acknowledged quite frankly that even adaptations of this theoretical approach will often be impossible, and when events dictate a radical departure from theory, only creative solutions can be found. Improvisation, provided it is carried out in a context of understanding, is a very necessary quality in planning for educational media.

We shall begin, however, with the kind of controlled situation which is usually identified with industrialised countries, where educational resources have a reasonable pre-history and where supporting technical infrastructures exist.

It is certainly advantageous to plan for media from the outset, as acoustic and distribution problems will be more easily solved. But in most locations, this kind of lavishness is simply not possible, and the best that can be anticipated is some modification of existing classroom space. For this more restricted purpose, the two plans are shown in Fig. 17.2 — one showing a flexible seating arrangement focused on projected materials and upon the teacher, the other illustrating how the same room can be subdivided for small group and individual work. Both are proposed at the elementary level.

The receiving room

Apart from layouts, what other factors are important to ensure satisfactory viewing or listening conditions?

In the case of radio, radio receivers and increasingly audio recorders or cassette players, are cheap enough to be bought in bulk; in any case, they

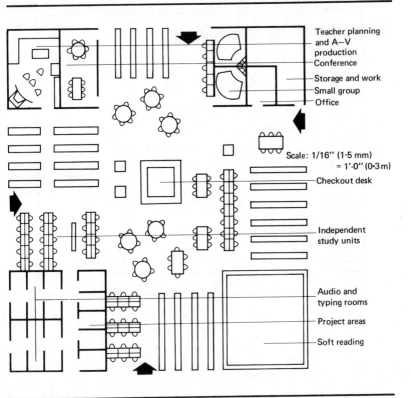

Teacher planning
and A—V
production
Conference
Storage and work
Small group
Office

Scale: 1/16″ (1·5 mm)
= 1′·0″ (0·3 m)

Checkout desk

Independent
study units

Audio and
typing rooms

Project areas

Soft reading

Fig. 17.1   Media resource area.

are portable and can be taken from class to class. So for radio reception it is unlikely that a special room will be reserved: it is simpler to move the receiver than to disturb the class.

It is important, nevertheless, for listening to be in good acoustic conditions, which may mean making some minor modifications to class-rooms — the addition of curtains, perhaps some portable screening. And connection to an external aerial is important in areas of weak signal strength.

It may also be that, where acoustic conditions are difficult, or rooms or classes larger than usual, a mains radio with external loudspeaker and increased power output will be needed.

Television reception is more difficult, because of the relative bulk of the receiver and the need to plan for picture as well as sound quality. In some locations it may be possible to equip the majority of classrooms in a school or college with television receivers, and to feed them all with signals via some form of community relay system. More commonly the number of receivers will be restricted, and only one or two rooms can be utilised. This

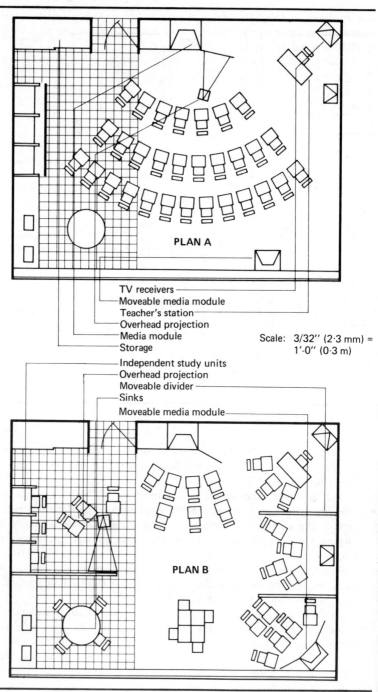

PLAN A

TV receivers
Moveable media module
Teacher's station
Overhead projection
Media module
Storage

Scale: 3/32″ (2·3 mm) =
1′-0″ (0·3 m)

Independent study units
Overhead projection
Moveable divider
Sinks
Moveable media module

PLAN B

can at times be an advantage; it is difficult to modify all existing class-rooms, but one or two rooms can more easily be converted to television and audio-visual display.

A viewing room should be neither too large nor too small; it needs enough space to accommodate its usual audience, with a little to spare. Equal depth and width are preferable, both for acoustical reasons and for seating purposes, and regular boxlike structures are best avoided. The room should not be too reverberant – reverberancy can be checked by clapping the hands smartly, and listening to the echo time, or even more practically by importing a transistor radio and listening to the results when the room is full. It should be well away from extraneous sounds such as traffic, air routes, workshops and noisy stairways or corridors. Some modifications can be made to a room by adding carpets, or acoustic tiling, but the results obtained will be limited. Carpeting, for example, can cut noise levels by as much as 50 per cent (this was checked in an American study); it can absorb the scraping of chairs, or the dropping of pencils, and as a decor it has proven psychological advantages. But it can do nothing to prevent the transmission of noise from one wall to another, or through ceilings.

Lighting is less of a problem with television than with other forms of audio-visual display, though if a television room is serving as an AV centre in general, this advantage may be lost. A light level of something between 37 and 70 foot candles is required for close classroom work; television can be viewed successfully at a light level of about 30 foot candles, so that the slight drop required can be catered for by a dimmer switch or, more cheaply, by switching off one or two lights.

The receiver itself needs placing to avoid glare or reflection; this can be achieved by a slight tilting and, in tropical areas, by incorporating sun-blinds or louvres into the classroom. In many cases non-glare screens are available, with specially tinted facings. The lighting in the area immediate-ly surrounding the television receiver should be at a level slightly lower than that of the picture, to avoid excessive contrast. The face plate surrounding the picture tube on the receiver itself should also be light and matt.

Ventilation is particularly important; fresh air circulation is essential for concentration. Remember that if this means opening windows it may pose an additional noise problem.

The assumption so far has been that television viewing will take place in a single classroom. Later in this section the optimum numbers of students who can be accommodated in front of screens of different sizes is expressed in table form.

There is, in many schools, a temptation to bring several classes together to view programmes, either by cramming them into a classroom meant for half the number, or by locating the receiver in a school hall or auditorium.

Fig. 17.2   Renovated elementary classroom – two layouts.

For a variety of reasons, this should be discouraged whenever possible. Proper introductory or follow-up work is impossible for a teacher dealing with so many students, and the physical conditions for viewing are poor: students will neither see nor hear properly. On the whole it is far better for fewer students to view an ETV programme in favourable surroundings, than for double the number to half-see it.

However, there is one context in which multiple viewing is commonplace: at the college or university level, when television is being used for overspill lecturing or as a lecturing aid. In such cases viewing may take place in a large auditorium or lecture theatre, and the problem of visibility can be dealt with in two ways. Either a large projector model is installed in the auditorium (providing a video display on a giant screen); or a number of receivers are installed at strategic points throughout the hall, to allow for comfortable and close viewing throughout. A loudspeaker system is also installed for sound distribution.

Such systems need to be planned carefully. They raise a number of acoustic problems, and which system to adopt is a matter of preference; the projection system at least means that students are looking at a common screen, and their attention is concentrated in one place, though the pictures produced are coarser. Probably the most satisfactory application of the multiple-receiver system is during a lecture/demonstration which calls for close-up viewing; students may follow the lecturer himself, if he is lecturing 'live', for generalised argument, and turn to the nearest monitor to inspect close-up detail. Once the whole of a student's viewing is concentrated on a smaller monitor, then the receiver is better placed in a smaller room, with a corresponding reduction in viewing group size.

Reception equipment

In selecting equipment, some basic criteria apply to all items and must be evaluated. They can be summarised in note form as follows:

1. *Quality of performance.* Does the equipment do what is expected of it?
2. *Cost.* Technical specifications and performance apart, is the price reasonable and competitive?
3. *Portability.* If necessary, can the equipment be moved easily from room to room, or from place to place?
4. *Ruggedness.* Will the equipment stand up to hard use?
5. *Design.* Is the equipment both attractive and functional?
6. *Ease of operation.* Is the equipment simple and easy to operate?
7. *Maintenance.* Is the equipment easy to maintain, and are repair services available locally?
8. *Reputability.* Does the manufacturer have a good reputation locally?
9. *Reliability.* Does the equipment have a good record for reliability, and has it been used well beyond the prototype stage?
10. *Educational function.* Many items have a dual function — for general

and for educational purposes. Does the particular equipment under consideration answer all the instructional functions which will be demanded of it (which may be quite different from other market uses)?

Some of this information can be drawn from technical literature (preferably from independent evaluations by technical journals, not from manufacturers' literature). Consultation with other media users will be helpful, and in any case, before bulk purchases are envisaged, field tests should be made, comparing different models under offer. For bulk orders, prices are always negotiable, as are other important spin-offs (such as warranty periods, supplies of spare parts, service arrangements and the like). On more technical matters, engineering advice should be secured.

It will help when making an evaluation if a table is drawn up, to show the relative performance of different models. An illustration is given in Table 17.1 (for audio recorders, but easily applicable to other items).

Radio receivers

In the majority of situations, a portable radio receiver will be required (battery-powered, or mains/battery operated). With a battery model, an output of at least 1 watt should be delivered from the integral speaker (for medium group listening, preferably more). An integral aerial should also be fitted, which should be retractable and telescopic, and also capable of being set horizontally or vertically, or at 45°, and rotated through 360°.

In all models there should be sockets available for the fitment of an external aerial, and an output socket for feeding a tape recorder. The latter should preferably be fed directly from the tuner section, with the volume and tone controls having no effect upon the output signal. The replacement of batteries should be simple and quick, with non-interchangeable connections which clip on rather than relying on simple pressure. (If non-rechargeable batteries are used, they should be of high capacity, and there must be good protection against leakage from the battery compartment to the main body of the receiver.)

Mains/battery models should be fitted with an on/off switch which controls both the battery and the mains supply to the receiver. A separate switch, rather than one shared with the volume or any other control, is preferable, and when operating from the mains there should be no current drawn from the batteries.

Choice of wavelength will clearly depend upon local transmissions. There is no point in making provision for frequencies which are not in use for educational broadcasts, and while in some countries a combination of medium and certain short waves may be necessary, in others, medium wave and VHF will be the basic norm. But whatever combination is required, tests of reception should be carried out on sample models of receivers, in actual classroom conditions. A good deal depends upon the standard of loudspeaker fitted, and the case in which it is housed, as well

Table 17.1   Chart for selection of a tape recorder

Qualities	Tape recorder no. 1	Tape recorder no. 2	Tape recorder no. 3
Portability			
Weight	------------------ kg	------------------ kg	------------------ kg
Size	------ x ------	------ x ------	------ x ------
Contained	------ Yes ------ No	------ Yes ------ No	------ Yes ------ No
Construction			
Sturdy	------ Yes ------ No	------ Yes ------ No	------ Yes ------ No
Good carrying handle	------ Yes ------ No	------ Yes ------ No	------ Yes ------ No
Ease of maintenance	------ Yes ------ No	------ Yes ------ No	------ Yes ------ No
Versatility			
Speeds	---- ips ---- ips ---- ips	---- ips ---- ips ---- ips	---- ips ---- ips ---- ips
Trackage	---- 1 ---- 2 ---- 4	---- 1 ---- 2 ---- 4	---- 1 ---- 2 ---- 4
Monaural or stereo	------ mon ------ st.	------ mon ------ st.	------ mon ------ st.
Size of reels	------------------ max.	------------------ max.	------------------ max.

Table 17.1 — *continued*

Qualities	Tape recorder no. 1	Tape recorder no. 2	Tape recorder no. 3
Performance			
Constancy of speed	------ Yes ------ No	------ Yes ------ No	------ Yes ------ No
Signal-to-noise ratio	------ db	------ db	------ db
Wow and flutter	Less than ------ %	Less than ------ %	Less than ------ %
Frequency response	------ to ------ cps	------ to ------ cps	------ to ------ cps
Recording level meter	------ Yes ------ No	------ Yes ------ No	------ Yes ------ No
Fast forward	------ Seconds	------ Seconds	------ Seconds
Rewind speed for 900-ft tape	------ Seconds	------ Seconds	------ Seconds
Automatic shut off	------ Yes ------ No	------ Yes ------ No	------ Yes ------ No
Pause control	------ Yes ------ No	------ Yes ------ No	------ Yes ------ No
Footage indicator	------ Yes ------ No	------ Yes ------ No	------ Yes ------ No
Simplicity			
Ease of operation	------ Yes ------ No	------ Yes ------ No	------ Yes ------ No
Controls labelled	------ Good ------ Poor	------ Good ------ Poor	------ Good ------ Poor
Price	£ ------	£ ------	£ ------

as acoustic conditions, and the final criterion should be aural, once technical standards have been met. When making a test of this kind it will probably be useful to have a radio receiver, recorder or record player of known performance at hand, so that a comparison of standards and suitability can be made. In the case of a VHF receiver, tests should also be made with non-VHF (medium wave) receivers; in areas of good signal strength a noticeable improvement should be obtained.

Other criteria have to do with technical standards and are best evaluated by engineers (as they depend upon a comparison of the various models offered, and of their technical specifications). Battery models will clearly have lower performance characteristics than mains models, since in order to achieve miniaturisation some sacrifices have to be made. In the case of mains models, the power output from a low impedance amplifier (intended for one loudspeaker only) should be at least 2 watts, and in cases where a 'hi-fi' loudspeaker is to be used, higher powers still will be required, since these units are relatively insensitive (6 or more watts should be specified). If portability is not so essential, a separate loud speaker is to be preferred.

Cassette recorder and playback units

These units are increasingly popular in education, as they allow for recording and replay of both transmitted and physically distributed materials. They should first of all be robust, with clear warning lights showing when the unit is in operation, and play at standard tape speed ($1\frac{7}{8}$ ips, correct to plus or minus 2 per cent). A visual indication of the state of the batteries should be incorporated, and there should be some form of tape position indicator (preferably digital, with a three-digit display). The cassette should operate with the equipment in any position; the braking mechanism should also be arranged to avoid tape stretch or breakage, and an 'auto stop' facility should be fitted, so that the equipment switches itself off at the end of each cassette. Play, fast forward and fast rewind controls are necessary, preferably of the latched piano key variety.

If a recording facility is also offered, the system should prevent accidental erasure, and the record key should be clearly marked in red. A means of adjusting recording level should also be given, this level being indicated by a meter, with the scale clearly marking over-recording. (If this is an automatic control, then some means of manual override should also be incorporated.) A pause control is necessary, and volume and tone controls should affect only the level of signal being fed to the loudspeaker, not that appearing at any low level (line) input.

Other technical requirements are much the same as for radio receivers. Again, technical comparisons can be made on the basis of published specifications and field tests, covering matters as tape speed, wow and flutter (to be maintained within plus or minus 0.4 per cent peak). As regards output, 1 watt will cater for groups of about one dozen students, and for larger classes, 2 watts or more may be necessary. As with radio receivers, classroom tests should be conducted with comparative receivers to help assess performance.

For convenience, combined receivers/cassette recorders are useful and may produce overall financial savings. But such combinations will not always have the necessary output for classroom conditions, and tests should be made to see whether for a particular application separate receivers and cassettes are not required. If the majority of programmes are to be put on to cassette, either drawn directly from a tape bank or dubbed off air, monitored by a high quality receiver, then this method may also prove to be cheaper. For such a decision to be made, however, a good deal must be known about actual patterns of utilisation; once made, it will be difficult to change.

The TV receiver

The size of picture tube on a receiver is a matter for individual choice, but it should not be less than 21 in (53.3 cm) for anything other than small-group viewing; 23 in (58.4 cm) is the usual compromise, though some manufacturers offer larger educational models. (As these are not produced in bulk, the discount available may be less.) The larger the screen size, the more expensive the receiver (and the coarser the picture obtained), though the higher cost of larger models may be offset by the greater number of students accommodated.

There is more to the placing of the television receiver than considerations of visibility. It should also be located away from extreme moisture or dust, in a place where clean air circulates freely, out of reach of the casual passer-by and preferably in a room that can be made secure. Especially in countries where there are extremes of climate, the receiver must be turned on daily for at least an hour a day (in Samoa, for example, receivers were not turned off at all). It should be moved only when absolutely necessary.

Maintenance should, of course, be carried out by qualified technicians, and the inside of the receiver should never be touched: it has dangerous high voltage leads. Speed of repair is essential and it is advisable to write a clause into the contract by which the repairer (if he is an external supplier) guarantees to supply a replacement receiver if the repair cannot be carried out on the spot. It is also better for the service to keep a regular note of receiver performance; this means enlisting the help of the schools to supply information about breakdowns, but it will provide a guide to the quality of equipment purchases, and the efficiency of the repair service. Some questions on receiver performance should be written into the evaluation pro-forma in general use.

Security is essential. A television receiver is an expensive item of equipment and needs looking after properly. If it is pointed out to the viewing centres that they will be expected to pay for any loss or damage, this usually has the desired effect.

Maintenance is a skilled job, but every user needs to be familiar with normal receiver adjustment, and it should be a regular part of any utilisation training programme. Some reception faults will inevitably defy correction; this usually means that the aerial is wrongly positioned, or a more powerful aerial is required. However, it is worth pointing out that receivers should be given time to settle down after they are switched on, before tuning adjustments are made; often these will prove to be unnecessary.

Economy in receiver purchase is a poor principle for a media service. Front-speakers are essential, with a good sound system, and in tropical climates some protection against humidity is also required (some manufacturers produce special models for these conditions).

The mounting of television receivers presents special difficulties, as for maximum visibility they need to be raised high in the viewing room (see the section on seating arrangements below). Movable adjustable trolleys are available, which can offer variations in both the height and angle of receivers, but though these are flexible enough as far as positioning is concerned, they may become very unwieldy if more than 1 to 1½ metres in height. A satisfactory method of mounting, when possible, is from the ceiling, from the wall, or from a column running between ceiling and floor. Custom-built mounts are often locally available, at relatively low cost (a receiver manufacturer may be willing to provide them to the user's own specifications, in order to secure an order for his sets). Some characteristic mountings are illustrated in Fig. 17.3.

Video-recorders and cameras

No attempt will be made here to provide precise guidance on the selection of video-recorders; there are too many models available, and the technology is changing too rapidly. If purchase and servicing arrangements can be arranged locally, for most educational applications the videocassette is the best alternative, but much depends upon function. Specialist advice must be sought when making a decision, but the questions to be asked should include the following.

Function
What is the recorder needed for? If it is only for replay, a camera is not required; if micro-teaching or simple production are envisaged, the situation is different. Editing facilities will be needed in most production situations, but not for simple replay of hired or loaned materials.

Compatibility
There are several gauges of videotape (from ¼ to 1 inch for amateur applications) in use, and many models of recorder, of which the majority are incompatible with other makes (and often with recorders of the same make, if they come from different manufacturing batches). Standardisation is essential within any educational institution, and if tape exchange is contemplated this must extend to all other users in the proposed library

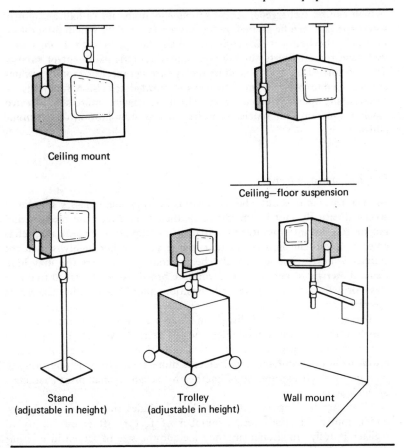

Fig. 17.3 Characteristic mountings for ETV sets.

system. Although dubbing between different models, and tape correction, are possible, they require expensive additional equipment.

Ease of operation
For most amateur uses, simple and automated equipment is desirable, with easy threading, automatic recording levels (for both vision and sound) and simple, well-marked controls.

Portability
For most users, a lightweight, portable machine will be required (and in the case of community media, which rely heavily on location work, port-a-pak camera and recording units are usually needed). The recorders have generally a 12 volt operation, have an integral omni-directional microphone as part of the camera, run for about an hour on an internal battery

(which can be recharged), accept spools containing up to half an hour of videotape, and can be carried by one person (since they weight about 9 kg, including the battery). Cameras are usually equipped with zoom lenses, and have remote starts for the tape, and automatic gain control circuits. Tapes recorded by portapak units replay through receiver/monitors which are switchable between monitoring and normal television functions, or through a.c.-operated video decks (which are heavier, more sophisticated machines, often with special facilities such as slow motion or electronic editing).

Seating arrangements

Seating for radio should be as informal as possible. Classes should be arranged casually, not in straight rows; they should face the receiver, and not be too distant from it. Semi-circular or group arrangements are preferable, to avoid the impression that this is yet another highly structured activity. The teacher will usually be in front of the class (he may have visual materials to demonstate during the broadcast, or be asked to direct class drills), but he should still position himself as unobstrusively as possible.

There is a good deal of disagreement on seating arrangements for ETV, mostly caused by the variable demands of users. If we wish to stipulate a 'maximum viewing distance' at which television can be 'seen' in a classroom, we must frame our requirements more precisely. It is one thing to take in a general picture, quite another to recognise small print characters on a TV screen.

If we are looking at a display which includes small print or figures, under controlled conditions, a number of factors affect our ability to register it fully. In particular, they include the size of screen in use, our distance from the screen, our angle of vision (both horizontal and vertical), the disposition of chairs or desks, the size of the smallest print used on the screen, the resolution of the picture (determined by the number of scan lines it contains), and the bandwidth employed. These are interdependent (for example, the maximum viewing distance for a particular class will correlate directly with the size of screen in use and the smallest print size employed to convey visual information), so that for analysis we shall have to take them in groups.

Fortunately, certain principles have been established empirically, which we can take as a starting point, always rembering to relate them (i) to the particular function of television in which we are interested (i.e. whether it is directly instructional, or only motivational), and (ii) to the realistic context in which we are operating (i.e. whether such sophisticated arrangements are actually possible at all). They are taken from studios made in the USA, by Educational Facilities Laboratories Inc.

We can assume, for example, that the student should be looking at the screen from as normal an eye line as possible: 30° is the *maximum vertical*

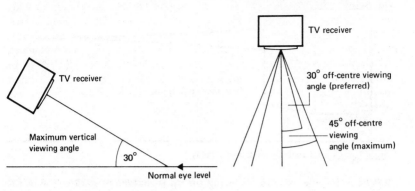

Fig. 17.4   Angle of vision for TV viewers.   **Fig. 17.5**   Off-centre viewing angles.

angle for comfort, and this may often necessitate tilting a set downwards (see Fig. 17.4).

We can also assume that the *horizontal, off-centre viewing angle*, (i.e. the angle between a line drawn perpendicular to the centre of the screen, and another line drawn from the centre of the screen to the viewer) should in no case exceed 45°, and preferably 30° (see Fig. 17.5).

Minimum viewing distance is another factor on which we can be fairly categorical. While the minimum viewing distance will grow greater as the screen size enlarges, in most cases it will average out at 1.2 to 1.5 m. Table 17.2 gives a general range.

Table 17.2   Minimum viewing distance

Screen size		Chairs close together		Chairs wider apart		Desks and chairs	
(cm)	(in)	(m)	(ft/in)	(m)	(ft/in)	(m)	(ft/in)
43.1	17	1.67	5 6	1.27	4 2	1.14	3 9
48.2	19	1.72	5 8	1.32	4 4	1.16	3 10
53.3	21	2.13	7 1	1.63	5 5	1.47	4 10
58.4	23	2.15	7 2	1.67	5 6	1.49	4 11
60.9	24	2.43	8 0	1.85	6 1	1.65	5 5

What other factors are involved? *Size of print* used on TV screens is an important consideration; ETV programmes, especially in the fields of science and mathematics, may include a volume of figured or printed information. A recent study indicated that, in a classroom television display, letters are needed large enough to produce at least 8 minutes of visual angle at the eye of the students in the last row (assuming that, with or without glasses, they have 20/20 vision (see Fig. 17.6).

This may mean that the ratio of character height to the total display

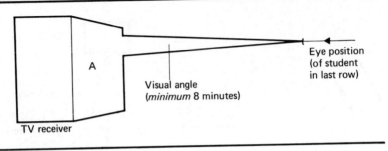

Fig. 17.6   Visual angle in classroom display.

height is as little as 1/33 (allowing for up to sixteen rows of characters to appear on the TV screen). So, in terms of picture resolution, on the US line standard of 525 lines (a practical 500 lines), an absolute minimum of fifteen lines is needed to accommodate each character in the display, or on the European, CCIR 625 line standard, a minimum of eighteen lines.

This ratio is calculated from a controlled viewing situation, with receivers perfectly adjusted and an excellent viewing environment. In practice, most producers will be best advised not to attempt to include character displays as small as 1/33 picture height; they should confine themselves to a 1/25 minimum, or better still 1/10 if possible.

We now have enough information to calculate another specific for ETV viewing — *maximum viewing distance*. Since this will depend upon the size of screen used and the smallest detail required on the screen, all these variables can be expressed in diagrammatic form. Figure 17.7 shows the maximum viewing distance, for a given range of minimum character heights, assuming 60.9 cm (24 in) screen and a 45° off-centre viewing angle.

Table 17.3   Maximum viewing distance

Screen size		Maximum viewing distance	
(cm)	(in)	(m)	(ft/in)
43.1	17	4.49	14 9
48.2	19	4.57	15 2
53.3	21	5.79	19 0
58.4	23	5.80	19 4
60.9	24	6.45	21 5

Table 17.3 provides a range of maximum viewing distances for a variety of screen sizes, assuming a minimum character height of 1/25 total picture height.

This leaves us with one major question to answer: how many students can be accommodated to view a programme? Again, there are variables; primarily the answer will depend upon the screen size used, the form of seating adopted and the spacing between chairs and desks.

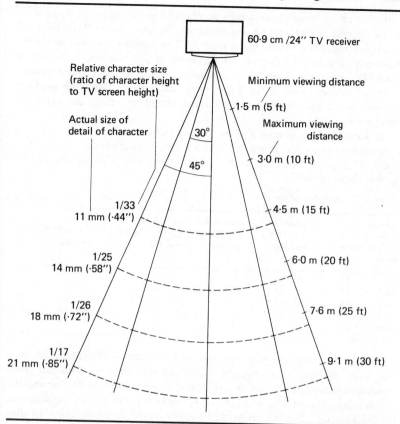

Fig. 17.7 Viewing distances with a 24-inch receiver.

We can begin by calculating the area available for viewing: this is done by extending the horizontal off-centre viewing angle (taken at its absolute maximum of 45°), and delimiting it according to the maximum and minimum viewing distances for any given screen size. The average viewing areas produced in square metres (and square feet) are given in Table 17.4.

Table 17.4 Average viewing area

Screen size		Approximate viewing area (30° angle)		Approximate viewing area (45° angle)	
(cm)	(in)	(sq. m)	(sq. ft)	(sq. m)	(sq. ft)
43.1	17	9.5	103	14.3	155
48.2	19	9.5	103	14.3	155
53.3	21	16.0	173	24.1	260
58.4	23	16.0	173	24.1	260
60.9	24	19.8	214	30.1	325

However, to translate area into numbers of potential viewers, we have to be specific about seating arrangements. We can assume three kinds of major seating: plain chairs; chairs with working arm-rests; desks and chairs. Naturally, the larger the piece of furniture in use, the less room will be available for seating. The choice is largely a matter of taste, but if a room is being used exclusively for TV viewing, and written follow-up work or normal schedules classes are conducted elsewhere, desks are certainly unnecessary.

If we therefore assume a 1 m spacing between chairs, a 1 to 1.3 m spacing between table armchairs, and a 1.5 m spacing between desks, then Table 17.5 gives a general range for the number of viewers who can be accommodated.

Table 17.5   Number of viewers

Screen size		Chairs 1 m (3 ft) spacing	Armchairs 1 m (3 ft) spacing	Armchairs 1.3 m (4 ft 4 in) spacing	Desk 1.5 m (5 ft 2 in) spacing
(cm)	(in)				
43.1	17	32−34	21	20−23	16−18
48.2	19	36−38	22	20−26	20−21
53.3	21	52−54	31	31−36	24−29
58.4	23	54−56	31	36−38	24−29
60.9	24	64−72	39	41−52	33−34

We are left, finally, with the question of vertical placement for the television receiver. As a rule, the closer the seat spacing, the higher the receiver will need to be positioned (and the more it will need to be angled for viewing comfort). In practice, this positioning will usually be affected by ceiling height; but in unrestricted conditions the optimum height of the television image is expressed in Table 17.6, showing the height from normal eye level, when seated, to the bottom of the TV image, for a range of screen sizes and student densities.

Table 17.6   TV receiver height*

Screen size		Row spacing 1 m (3 ft)		Row spacing 1.3 m (4 ft 4 in)		Row spacing 1.5 m (5 ft 2 in)	
(cm)	(in)	(cm)	(in)	(cm)	(in)	(cm)	(in)
43.1	17	66.0	26	43.1	17	35.5	14
48.2	19	68.5	27	45.7	18	38.1	15
53.3	21	86.3	34	57.1	22½	46.9	18½
58.4	23	88.9	35	58.4	23	48.2	19
60.9	24	97.7	38½	63.5	25	53.5	21

* Height of TV image above eye level only. Add average distance eye level to floor to obtain total height.

These figures do *not*, of course, allow for the distance between normal eye level and the ground, which will depend primarily on the age and physical characteristics of viewers. The range here will be from approximately 79 cm at an elementary level, to approximately 125 cm at a twelfth grade or sixth-form level; it should be calculated according to local circumstances and added to the figures derived from the previous table. But the fact that, for the average sixth-form student, watching a 58.4 cm (23 in) television screen from a row of chairs 1 m apart a total image height from the ground of 2 m is required, shows how important is the mounting of a television receiver. Flexible mounts are always needed which can be angled at will, and ceiling or wall mounting is clearly the most practical proposition. It is also worth stating the obvious: that students can be manoeuvred as well as television receivers, and in any television lesson the tallest students should be seated at the back of the room.

Power supplies

Radio reception poses few problems of power supply, even in rural areas, with a ready availability of batteries, many of which are now being manufactured locally. All batteries should be of the sealed variety, to prevent leakage. However, television is a different matter. One solution is to provide a portable 2-stroke generator, capable of developing up to 1,500 watts; small, inexpensive units are available, operating on petrol and these are powerful enough to handle a range of audio-visual equipment, apart from television. But there are obvious complications. First, petrol is not always available and is becoming increasingly expensive. Secondly, even with a simple generator, maintenance is essential, and rudimentary training must be provided for a local technician or custodian. If the fuel is impure, clogging will result, and on-the-spot repairs needed.

For the Ivory Coast, battery-operated receivers were especially designed, consuming 30 to 35 watts and employing industrial chemical batteries with a life of some 2,000 hours. A new receiver of this kind for colour television is about to be introduced (requiring less than 100 watts).

Currently, experiments with solar energy for television reception, conducted in Africa, are past the prototype stage. Such installations are now reducing considerably in price, and in combination with storage batteries should obviate the need for battery replacement at regular intervals, as well as minimising maintenance difficulties.

Maintenance

Maintenance is a function which is often overlooked; in one African survey of television utilisation, it was found that over 70 per cent of receivers were defective (though this fact had not been reported to the producing centre). It is not a matter which can be left to the receiving schools, even if repair facilities are available to them locally. Some regular system of inspection and repair for reception equipment has to be devised, which emphasises the principle of *preventive* maintenance.

One solution is to subcontract maintenance to a local supplier, on an annual fee basis. This has the advantage of economy, and in theory it allows specialists to perform specialist work. But it has substantial disadvantages as well. Unless maintenance arrangements are policed effectively, it is likely that the standard of service will decline, particularly once the manufacturer's warranty period has expired, and repairs will only be effected where they are specifically asked for.

It is preferable for a service to organise its own maintenance teams, operating on a regional basis if their catchment area is large, and adopting a routine schedule of visits. During this cycle, all equipment will be inspected in the schools and other educational institutions at stated intervals, basic repairs carried out on the spot and equipment which is seriously defective taken away for repair. (For this reason, it is important for each maintenance centre and team to carry spare receivers, or other items of audio-visual equipment, so that these can be left behind to replace whatever is being withdrawn for servicing.)

This kind of service need not involve enormous numbers of trained technicians, and their routine visits can be combined with other necessary functions; for example, the delivery of teachers' notes and pupils' pamphlets, or stocks of tapes, cassettes and other materials.

At the same time, it is useful to instruct teachers, especially technical and science teachers, in the essentials of equipment maintenance and repair, so that very minor defects can be corrected independently. Such basic instruction can be given at the time of a utilisation course, or short orientation courses can be mounted by the maintenance unit as it visits each school.

In this respect, a good deal depends upon the attitude of the teacher or monitor, and especially of supervisory staff. There are some countries where the very concept of maintenance is alien, and the notion of preventive maintenance is extremely difficult to communicate. Public relations statements by important persons who command the respect of the teaching force may help, if only to make sure that breakdowns are actually reported, or recorded on evaluation forms. It is important that, when such reports are made, the maintenance unit pays immediate attention to them, and reserves a proportion of its time for emergency visits. If a user has to wait more than a week for an answer to his call for help, he will be unlikely to cooperate on similar occasions in the future.

Improvisation – in context

Clearly, many of the prescriptions offered in the previous pages will be meaningless in some situations. A speaker at a recent international conference commented on the irrelevance of formulae specifying the numbers of children who should watch a television receiver, in a country like India when television is introduced for the first time into a remote village. In such situations, compromises have to be made; but they have to be made in context. A general interest or motivational programme may be viewed by up to 100 people (as was reported), but if specific skills are to be taught, then other arrangements have to be made. Either the numbers must be controlled, or the television programme must avoid introducing small-scale objects and figures as integral parts of its teaching, or the teacher must be encouraged (and trained) to follow up specifically those illustrations which many of his pupils will have missed. Or a combination of all three.

This is really a question of attitude: of perceiving constraints, seeing what can be done to minimise them, and trying to find ways around those which cannot be minimised.

SITE produced many examples of such creative improvisation. It developed a good deal of its own hardware, including some earth station antennae. But it has also paid attention to smaller, but equally fundamental problems. The problem of electrification is often quoted in discussions of educational television, and batteries, generators and solar-powered devices are all used to overcome this lack. But one of SITE's approaches proved much more radical: lobbying through the machinery of a State Government to secure an immediate, and permanent electricity supply. The problem of maintenance was approached in a particularly careful way, using a regional network of main and subcentres, with maintenance crews equipped with a specially designed test instrument (a signal simulator). By using this instrument, it was possible to make sequential tests on defective receivers, isolate the fault in the field in the majority of cases, and carry out repairs on the spot, without having to return the set back to base.

If this kind of creative attitude is adopted, then the principles cited above can be used as sets of indicators: not as absolute principles, but as guidelines, which need contextualisation. Providing a solution to a problem requires understanding of the problem, not following an arbitrary set of rules.

Chapter 18

Utilisation patterns and training

Utilisation needs

Physical environment and quality of equipment are important, but utilisation patterns — especially the interaction between teachers, materials and students — far more so. In this relationship, the following elements are critical.

1. *Flexibility* of materials — in timing, availability and content.
2. *Attitudes* of teachers and supervisors to the media, and *involvement* in the planning, production and evaluation process.
3. *Assistance and support* — in the form of facilities, adequate time for preparation, background and guidance materials.
4. *Confidence* in the potential of media, and *understanding* of their functions.
5. Concrete *results* for the educational system, which can be attributed unequivocally to media support.

What is involved in each of these? Many of the observations which follow are equally applicable to in-school and out-of-school uses of the media, but we will begin from the base of the school sector, and deal separately with any differences arising from the more fluid and informal arrangements which characterise adult and informal education.

Flexibility

Flexibility of programming — the provision of material which is both relevant and useful to the work of the teacher — is a matter of communication; it depends on the links which are set up between the media service and the educational system. At a distance from its subjects a service can only produce, in the first instance, what it thinks is required by its customers, but provided that communication lines are well enough drawn it can modify and streamline its products considerably at a later stage.

What are these links? We have already described the formal links — the policy-making machinery, and the machinery for programme planning. Another major link is through the evaluation system, which will be considered later in this section.

But other less formal contacts can also be established, which may be equally useful. Special surveys may be conducted, on an *ad hoc* basis, to find out user requirements, especially when new series or subject areas are planned; pilot programmes may be produced, and shown to groups of teachers and pupils before regular production is commenced. This will help resolve the more intangible specifics of pace, level and presentation format. A few classes or teachers can be invited to the media centre to view or hear programmes, or alternatively these can be replayed direct into the classroom from a portable recorder. In either case, as close a simulation of normal classroom conditions as possible should be insisted on. Some form of questionnaire may be distributed, but the real value of the exercise lies in the opportunity it gives for a personal interchange between users and production staff.

Seminars and workshops are also valuable, with representative groups of teachers coming together to analyse the success or failure of a series, or the validity of an approach. These groups should not be too general; a group of specialists, examining a particular series or subject area, is far more likely to produce concrete results than a complete cross-section of users, spread over a wide range of fields.

Flexibility of timing is a more mechanical, but nonetheless important process. In a small service, in a single school or college, timings can be arranged to suit a majority of users, even arranged to order. But the larger the audience, the more inflexible timings will become. Although such inflexibility is in the nature of the media some arrangements can be made to minimise its effects. In the first place, rather than choosing an arbitrary set of programme timings to suit the routine of the service, some attempt can be made to allocate times which suit whatever is known of school practice, based on enquiry and sometimes on specific research. This is simpler in a restricted or centralised educational system, where schools will, on the whole, be following a common programme. But even in a more decentralised system, it is possible to set up a survey of school timetables, either across the whole school population or from a statistical sample of schools (see Chapter 19), and to extrapolate from this a set of characteristic timings to suit a majority of users.

The procedure for such a survey is simple. Schools are asked to complete a pro-forma, stating when their periods commence and the subjects which are taught at a particular time of the school day. These results, after being returned to the service, are tabulated. There is an additional benefit in this procedure: not only will optimum timings be achieved, but the schools themselves should realise the care that has been taken to accommodate their requirements and be all the more ready to modify their own schedules where necessary.

The other arrangement is for repeat timings. Not only year by year, but within a single week, across the whole pattern of transmissions, each programme needs to be repeated as many times as possible. The reason for this is twofold. First, the greater the number of repeats available, the greater is the opportunity for each school to adjust to the media timetable; viewers are not limited to a single opportunity, which may well be inconvenient for them. Second, there is likely to be, at each academic level, a number of classes of roughly equivalent performance, many or all of whom may wish to hear or view the programmes. This is not possible without repeat transmissions (unless multiple exposure, with many classes combined, is adopted, and the disadvantages of such an arrangement have already been described). Consequently, there is no theoretical limit to the number of repeat transmissions which may be offered. In practice there are restrictions. Unless a number of separate channels have been reserved for education, only one or two repeats can be scheduled without reducing the number of original series, but with a carefully prepared schedule, as many as ten repeats may be arranged for large-audience programmes.

In the developed countries, at least, such issues are no longer a major problem for radio, and increasingly less significant for television, with improvements in recording technologies, and the evolution of cassette systems for both audio and video work. But in the developing world, the problem persists, and here it will be important for some years to come to do everything possible to anticipate, and plan for, timing difficulties.

It may also be useful at this stage to raise, and dispose of, a familiar argument, which is now heard much less frequently, since video-recording became more commonplace.

It is sometimes argued that, because of its limited flexibility, the television medium should be replaced in education by *film*, which can be distributed physically. Educational films have been a feature of classroom work for many years now and they can, of course, be used exactly as and when required.

There are a number of arguments against this position. Film is a more complex medium to handle than television; the projector has to be carried from place to place; there are large numbers of separate films to be stored, and repeated use wears out each copy. Moreover, film has to be seen in near-darkness, while television can be viewed in almost normal lighting conditions.

The main objection is, however, economic. A programme produced on film is far more costly than its television equivalent; it takes longer to produce (unless multiple camera techniques are employed), and the volume of programmes which can be expected from a television studio can never be matched by a film studio.

Furthermore, at the point of distribution the costs spiral enormously. A single print of a short educational film will cost upwards of $75 to strike, quite apart from the original production costs, and this figure does not reduce to rational proportions until a very high distribution figure is reached.

Attitudes and involvement

It would be mistaken to suppose that all users will adopt the mass media willingly. For some, it may imply a considerable amount of extra work (which may hardly be justified in the event); for others, it may represent a professional threat (like automation, television has been often promoted as a means of teacher-replacement). Since these objections are psychologically based, they can only be removed by a direct appeal. Apart from the evidence of results, which speak for themselves, a public relations programme is essential.

The public relations approach will be directed at two audiences: at teachers and educators, and at the general public, especially at parents. Press interest, and general publicity, is by no means to be scorned. Visits to the media centre are an important part of this programme; teachers, parents (and students) who have seen a little of the mechanics of media are much more likely to understand and sympathise with their workings than those who have made no contact. A member of the staff, possibly from the evaluation unit, or from the coordinator's staff, should be given responsibility for such visits. At intervals special displays and exhibitions can be mounted, and a house magazine containing general articles on media matters, both locally and in the world at large, may achieve a wide circulation. This need not appear frequently; quarterly intervals are about right. Occasional fuller reports, handout materials and résumés of seminars can also be published, for free distribution. (The more items that are free, the better.) Public relations should never degenerate into a routine; the objective of the service should be to create an image of flexibility, a willingness to experiment with new techniques and approaches.

At the same time, there is far more to involvement than public relations. It can extend to participation in production processes (especially true in the field of community media as will be seen later); in school services too, and at the local level, teachers can be encouraged to produce programmes and students to participate in them (in experiments, discussions, dramatisations).

One example of this type of production was a series of twenty broadcasts made for London schools on the topic 'Black Studies'. There was a great deal of concern in the schools over the fact that children from the West Indies, from parts of Asia and Africa, or the children of parents from these countries, had no information about their origins, and therefore lacked a sense of identity.

Teacher-advisers were consulted, and it was realised that this was the kind of project which called for closer liaison and cooperation than usual. The structure which emerged was based upon bringing together teachers working in the field, representatives from the Race Relations Board, community workers and other people who had some direct knowledge; it was proposed that this group decide the topics, the order of content, the material for the programmes and prepare the scripts. The producers saw themselves as coordinators, and as technical assistants, and were ready to help in any way the group wanted. They invited members of the team to present the programmes as well as to make recordings and choose music and effects. The larger group then broke down into smaller working teams of two or three people, who volunteered to prepare one or two of the programmes, and to collect and advise upon the pictorial and printed support material. Not every series lends itself to this kind of participation.

But as with most specialist areas, once teachers have a chance to experiment with production methods and techniques, they will evince much greater enthusiasm for the results.

Assistance and support

The proper utilisation of media is part of a regular teaching programme, which means that adequate time must be allowed for preparation and follow-up activity. Programmes viewed in isolation will be no more than semi-efficient; they are primarily sources, to be developed by the classroom teacher or lecturer. And for this to be done, not only is viewing time needed, but also an adequate period before and after for teachers to correlate their own objectives with those of the programme. To achieve this, the sympathies of those responsible for educational and school administration — inspectors, principals and headmasters — have to be enlisted. It is worth devising special appeals to these people, specific courses of training and explanation.

Facilities and support are another aspect of the same problem. For a close integration of media with normal teaching schedules, substantial advance information is required. At the time when the school curriculum is planned (i.e. when timetable and schemes of work are being drawn up, usually in the academic year preceding), full information must be circulated about projected series, stating their objectives and target audiences, and outlining their overall contents. This may be done in the form of a special bulletin, or published within the house magazine, preferably as a pull-out supplement. At a later stage, but still well in advance of actual transmission, teachers' notes are necessary, to allow individual teachers to plan their lesson approach and, where possible, study guides, workbooks and pupils' pamphlets for pupils to use, as well as any other supplementary material (e.g. specially conceived film strips, wall-charts, etc.).

The form of these materials will be tailored to suit each series, and it is a matter to which the planning cells must pay particular attention. However, any set of teachers' notes should contain the following:

(*a*) a clear statement of the objectives, target audience, level and ability range of the series;

(*b*) an explanatory introduction, describing in detail what the programmes hope to achieve and the form of presentation they will adopt;

(*c*) suggestions for preparation and follow-up activity for broadcasts, including possible correlations with the overall scheme of work;

(*d*) background information on individual programme topics which will not necessarily be found within the programme, but may be useful in follow-up work;

(*e*) as much detail as is available of individual programme formats and contents;

(*f*) suggestions for supplementary reading, appropriate visual aids, etc.

Pupils' materials should be added wherever possible (and relevant); they should contain specific projects and exercises associated with, and deriving directly from, the broadcasts, and as a general rule they should contain explanatory material difficult to obtain elsewhere, or not included in existing texts.

Confidence and understanding

Every producer experiences nervousness in the control room, or when his programme is being aired, but it may come as a surprise to him that the teachers who receive his materials may also be nervous. Unless a teacher understands how and why a mass medium is used, and is confident that he can handle it without looking foolish in front of students or colleagues, he will never warm to media in the classroom. His nervousness may take many forms, including aggressiveness and a strongly expressed disinterest in media, but it is often founded upon insecurity.

Utilisation training programmes

This lack of confidence can only be offset by carefully handled training programmes, at various levels of experience. They will cover primarily: (i) all users at the time of a media system's introduction; (ii) teachers in training; (iii) teachers involved in refresher or re-orientation courses (touching the media both directly and indirectly).

Orientation training

At the time of development, most users will be coming to the media as novices, and their willingness to make use of them, as well as the value of their efforts, depends on the completeness of their understanding. The basic training course provides an opportunity to explain a number of things to the classroom teacher or lecturer. First, the theoretical background needs clarification – why media are being used; what they offer; how they are used generally throughout the work programme; what specific contribution they will make locally. Second, the physical demands have to be explained – receiver placement, the use of simple controls, the selection of viewing and listening rooms, seating arrangements. And finally, there is the technique of classroom usage – the means whereby media can not only be taken as a motivating experience, prepared for and capitalised upon in follow-up periods, but can be written more significantly into a scheme of work as a method of introducing or reinforcing certain concepts, in the same way that text books and scientific demonstrations are automatically employed. This is the most important objective of all, especially in multi-media and systems approaches.

The length of the utilisation training course depends upon local conditions, but two aspects of its presentation are important. First, it must be fully illustrated, including varied examples of programming (if not yet

Table 18.1   One-day utilisation training course

Session	Subject	Illustration
1	What are media?	Examples of media programmes
2	Utilisation (1) – the physical environment	Demonstration of using receivers/recorders, etc.
3	Utilisation (2) – classroom work	Teaching demonstrations on tape, student practice
4	Evaluation and discussion session	–

available locally, then taken from other countries) and full demonstrations of follow-up approaches. Practical demonstration is worth far more, in the end, than theoretical lecturing. Second, it must try to reach every user, rather than confining itself to a select few.

Two possible formats for utilisation courses are reproduced in Tables 18.1 and 18.2. Table 18.1 provides an extremely short programme, merely a day or half a day (in many cases the maximum time available, if teachers have to be brought in from the schools, or recruited on an in-service basis). Table 18.2 is for a week's course. Other permutations can be derived easily enough from these examples to cover longer or intermediate periods of time.

In both courses, the practical element predominates. Film and tape examples of productions are available, showing the approach of a number of countries; most national services hire out or loan filmed examples, and there are several anthologies, produced in the United States and in Japan, which range over a variety of fields and modes of presentation. (A local embassy, High Commission, or broadcasting representative will supply the necessary addresses, and in many cases arrange the loan.)

Teaching demonstrations showing media in use in the classroom are

Table 18.2   One-week utilisation training course

Session	Monday	Tuesday	Wednesday	Thursday	Friday
1	What are media?	Mass media and the classroom situation	Planning for media programmes	Following up the broadcast	Evaluation and research
2	Examples of media programmes	Equipment practice	Programme literature and aids	Teaching demonstration (1)	New approaches to media
3	The production process	Specific types of programmes	Preparing for the broadcast	Teaching demonstration (2)	Final programme analysis
4	Discussion of different media programmes	Examples of subject approaches	Sample programme for analysis	Teaching demonstration (3)	Question and answer session

more difficult to secure. Some specific series have been mounted in the United States and in the United Kingdom on this topic and are worth viewing; but as utilisation will vary so much from place to place, a local example is far more valuable. As a last resort, it is possible to mount a teaching demonstration during the course, importing an experienced teacher and a small class of students. But television itself can be usefully employed for this purpose; the teaching demonstration, as well as the original programme, can be recorded in the studios and replayed as required, or mounted as an outside broadcast and recorded in an actual classroom if facilities are available for mobile recording. Indeed, to save time, the whole course can be largely pre-recorded, and producers brought in only at specific times for discussion periods. This may be necessary, if the numbers of teachers involved are considerable. A CCTV system is very useful for such exercises, as large numbers of users may be accommodated for a general session, and split up into smaller discussion groups only for practical question-and-answer periods.

If the environment is suitable, utilisation training need not be structured so tightly; or it can be structured at a local level, and suitable training materials provided, which are flexible enough to be used in a variety of different ways. In the United Kingdom, this has been one of the preoccupations of the Council for Educational Technology, which was set up in 1973 (as a successor to the earlier National Council for Educational Technology). The Council has produced a number of materials and case-studies, which can be used by trainers in whatever way they prefer, and where teachers are competent and motivated, it is not only an attractive approach, but far more in keeping with principles of self-development.

Full-time teacher training

Secondly, utilisation training should be written in as an ingredient of all full-time courses for teacher training: if the media are to become accepted, then they must be seen as a basic feature of pedagogical work. We are attempting in this way to achieve two objectives — to create an image of the media, an understanding of their functions and processes; and to make the image into a reality.

Such training should be properly integrated within the normal teacher education programme, not placed as an appendage. El Salvador's ITV system was in a particularly favourable position in this respect as, being a part of an overall Reform process, those teachers who were to operate within Reform schools were given specific training programmes over several months in methodology, principles of secondary education, the new curriculum, and television utilisation. Subsequently, ITV was included within complete 1-year retraining programmes (designed to recycle primary school teachers for secondary school teaching). This extended programme contributed, not only to effective utilisation within the classroom, but also to the favourable response among the teaching profession which ITV originally received in El Salvador.

Retraining

Finally, there is the retraining and renewal which must follow when a service is established, and its basic pattern of utilisation set. Techniques change, and refresher courses are needed to put them into a new context. Specialist courses, for presenters, scriptwriters and media specialists, will be required, and there is bound to be a nucleus of teachers who would welcome a more prolonged exposure to the principles and practice of media than their basic training afforded, simply out of interest. They should certainly be accommodated; their more detailed experience may well snowball throughout the system. At a later stage still it is also possible that advanced full-time and diploma courses will be asked for (within the senior teacher-training institutions, and possibly the universities), and while a service is not likely to be qualified to undertake these courses, it can — and should — make a substantial contribution.

Phasing

We have talked a good deal about utilisation patterns and training, because they are at the heart of the media process. Figure 18.1 attempts to put what has been said in perspective as far as the phasing of the programme is concerned; it is possible to suggest an appropriate timing for most of these training and promotional exercises. The completed blocks in this figure show the starting and finishing points of each activity in relation to the overall programme.

The blocks do not always represent actual *units* of time (these will often vary from one installation to another), but it is the way in which different activities interact, and overlap, that is most important.

The trainers

Who will carry out this training?

For full-time students, this poses no special problem; it is a matter of incorporating media studies into existing teacher-training courses, and making sure that qualified staff are available to teach them. If a college is already equipped with a CCTV system, so much the better, but if not, a modicum of reception and recording equipment will be needed (and programme materials for demonstration and analysis). It is assumed that in most cases the courses will be supervised by the college's audio-visual unit and its staff. There has been, in the past, a tendency to regard educational technology as an optional field. This is a mistake, if the media are to become an integral part of the educational system; while advanced options are certainly required for students who express a special interest, a basic knowledge is fundamental for all users. This knowledge cannot be purely theoretical — teachers must be asked to create simple audio-visual materials on their account, and to experiment with actual classes in using media as part of their teaching approach.

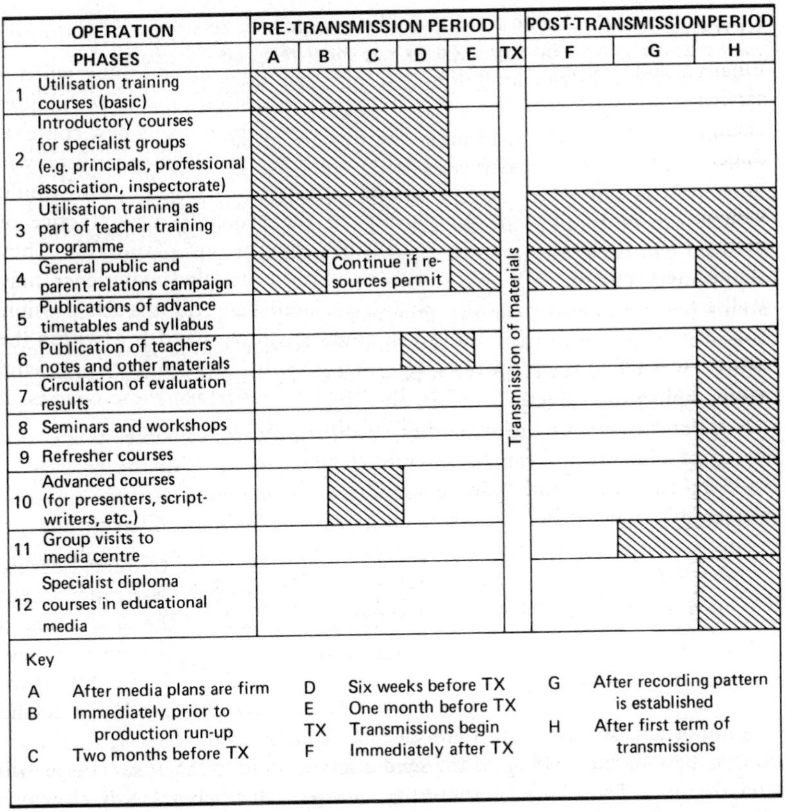

OPERATION	PRE-TRANSMISSION PERIOD						POST-TRANSMISSION PERIOD		
PHASES	A	B	C	D	E	TX	F	G	H
1 Utilisation training courses (basic)									
2 Introductory courses for specialist groups (e.g. principals, professional association, inspectorate)									
3 Utilisation training as part of teacher training programme									
4 General public and parent relations campaign		Continue if resources permit				Transmission of materials			
5 Publications of advance timetables and syllabus									
6 Publication of teachers' notes and other materials									
7 Circulation of evaluation results									
8 Seminars and workshops									
9 Refresher courses									
10 Advanced courses (for presenters, scriptwriters, etc.)									
11 Group visits to media centre									
12 Specialist diploma courses in educational media									

Key

A	After media plans are firm	D	Six weeks before TX	G	After recording pattern is established
B	Immediately prior to production run-up	E	One month before TX		
		TX	Transmissions begin	H	After first term of transmissions
C	Two months before TX	F	Immediately after TX		

Fig. 18.1   Utilisation patterns and relationships.

With refresher and reorientation courses, too, as the numbers involved can be regulated, no special difficulty should be experienced. Such courses can be run by teacher-training colleges and universities, in vacation periods or at weekends, or they can be mounted by the media centre itself. Whichever is preferred, media planners, evaluators and producers should be involved in the programme, invited to give guest demonstrations (and vice versa).

The main problem is encountered in the basic utilisation courses which occur at the time of a system's introduction. Here, if only because of the weight of numbers, some kind of snowball scheme must be devised. The media service will have a nucleus of utilisation staff, who will pay regular visits to training colleges, visit schools to listen to broadcasts and view television programmes, and make regular reports on what they see in the field. But at the time of development, they will be at their busiest (probably supplemented by short-term consultants and experts). They will have to begin a chain of training, in which they work, initially, with teacher trainers and audio-visual lecturers, and impart, not only the basics of media use, but also how these can be transmitted to others. In turn, the teacher trainers will be expected to run short-term courses for audio-visual supervisors at a district level — and so on until every user in the system is reached.

Some of this catalytic training can be carried out in the media centre itself. But utilisation supervisors will also have to tour in operational teams, setting up an intinerant programme in each region. Sometimes, teachers can be asked to attend a regional centre or college; at other times, the team can concentrate upon a particular town and assemble users for a brief course. The phasing of this programme is a complex undertaking. It cannot begin too early (or the momentum will be lost), but it must be devised in such a way that, by the time the service is in progress, all users have been reached. In large services, as much as 9 months may be needed to accomplish this target.

For touring training programmes, mobile units are valuable, as a basic library of illustrations can be assembled which can go on the road as a travelling exhibition and training support. It is also important for demonstration materials to be prepared well in advance (often a difficult undertaking, if no actual programmes are available). In such cases, utilisation training can usefully be associated with piloting, seeking a variety of reactions to prototype programmes as part of the basic training process.

Utilisation Supervisors

It is important that some staff are specially appointed to assist with utilisation, as part of the staffing of the media service (and in larger services, as a separate unit). These officers should be experienced teachers, with a knowledge of a wide variety of schools and levels, and with a declared interest in media. It will help a good deal if they can be given some training in production and evaluation techniques, so that they can better understand the work of their colleagues and act as a bridge between production departments and the educational system. Utilisation supervisors have many duties, but their principal activities are:

1. Visiting schools and educational centres, to hear and view programmes together with the pupils, and report on their findings (see Chapter 19 on reporting methods).
2. Conducting in-service training courses (especially for other trainers, so as to begin a snowball pattern of training, since they will not be able to handle the training job single-handed).
3. Contributing to courses in full-time teacher-training institutions.
4. Acting as resource members of course and programme planning teams.
5. Acting as a bridge between producers and educational personnel and agencies, and helping to set up arrangements for piloting programmes and for evaluation.
6. Monitoring the activities of regional centres, and such factors as maintenance arrangements.

7. Acting as public relations representatives, especially in talking to parental and community groups.

It is evident from this list that the utilisation officer has to be a mature, experienced, sympathetic and imaginative person, and in general older people, with a solid foundation of classroom experience, are preferable, provided that they can make the necessary adjustment to deal with innovative techniques. A familiarity with production goals and processes is extremely important, and quite apart from basic orientation training, they should be given the opportunity to produce occasional programmes for the media service, to keep their hands in.

Obviously, they will be expected to travel widely. In the schools they have a two-fold function, which needs delicate handling. They have to report on programmes and programme utilisation objectively, making sure that their presence in the classroom interferes as little as possible with normal routine and does not inhibit the teacher. It is as well for the utilisation officer not to make his visits too predictable, or to announce his arrival too far in advance, as he may find that special preparations are being made on his behalf (often with good intentions, but still impeding the task of objective reporting). Yet they also need, once this is done, to help teachers to use materials more effectively, and to carry out in their travels a continuous programme of updating and refresher training. They may also be asked to record good examples of classroom practice, for the information of producers and for use on training courses.

Above all, the utilisation supervisor must have good, informal relations with everyone in the media service, and especially producers and evaluators. He cannot afford to work purely through official channels if he is to be effective.

Media in the classroom

It may be felt that, in this general discussion, we have begged some of the basic questions. Most of our analysis has been centred on the *preconditions* for effective utilisation, but what of the process itself? What actually happens in a classroom, or lecture room, when educational mass media are in use? The traditional account of a mediated lesson runs roughly as follows.

1. Well before the broadcast

The main point of preparing for a broadcast (or for any audio-visual presentation) is to get students ready mentally for what is to follow, and receptive to its content. As with all teaching, the best kind of preparation makes demands on the students themselves and is not purely a passive exercise. So discussions can be held on what the class already knows about the topic, key concepts can be defined, questions can be posed (some of which are to be answered after the broadcast), responsibility for answering particular points can be divided up between pupils, supplementary media (e.g. film strips) can be used to explain some items in advance. If the teacher knows what is coming, and feels that certain concepts may produce difficulties in his class he can explain these in a preliminary fashion.

2. Immediately before the broadcast

Essential vocabulary or background information (marked out in the Teachers' Notes as being essential to a proper understanding of the programme) is presented, and explained. At the same time, the routine of switching on and adjusting the set is followed — ending in television with the 'schools' clock' or programme countdown.

3. During the broadcast

Correct conditions for learning are not purely a matter of seating and physical arrangement; the psychological environment is also important. Quiet conditions are needed, free from noise or sudden distraction. Note-taking during a programme should be avoided, unless it has been specifically requested by the production agency (for example, during a college overspill lecture it is a natural exercise, or during a televised 'quiz' of some kind).

The attitude of the class teacher or monitor is of paramount importance. If his attention lapses, or if he leaves the room during a transmission, the attitude of the viewing class will deteriorate rapidly. Especially with younger children, there is a tendency to accept a programme at the valuation of the teacher present. If cues are offered during a programme, requesting overt responses from students, there may be some initial embarrassment which the classroom teacher can overcome, by initiating the response; similarly, he can lead any oral drills which may be required; for example, in a language teaching programme.

As far as possible the routine of the programme should be adjusted to the routine of the school. This is not always possible, when programme timings cannot take local variations into account, but it is extremely distracting to view a programme while period changes and class movements are going on outside. Even more disconcerting is the split-second timetabling which brings a viewing class late into the television room, or takes it on to its next lesson immediately after the end of the transmission.

4. Immediately following the broadcast

A number of questions, incorporated in the programme itself or included in the teachers' notes, are discussed. From these the teacher can derive a fairly detailed knowledge of (a) how the broadcast was received; (b) what aspects appealed most to the students and held their interest most fully;

(*c*) what aspects were not properly understood; and (*d*) what is the best teaching strategy for further follow-up work. In this terminal period, he also assesses reactions, to be noted in the evaluation returns for the broadcast.

5. In periods following the broadcast

The stimulus of the programme is applied to classroom work. It may suggest avenues for project work, creative writing, oral practice or discussion, dramatisation and improvisation, individual or group research, or, in the case of science and mathematics programmes, specific experimentation and problem solving. Some of this work may be derived from the teachers' notes or pupils' pamphlets; if these materials were made available early enough, they should have been properly integrated with the teacher's own scheme of work. At times, special visits, related visual aids or invitation lectures may be included, assuming they are worth the time and energy involved. Some means of testing (probably objective) may also be arranged as a check on comprehension.

This is, as already stated, an account of traditional uses of media, arising from the hearing or viewing of a single broadcast. Is there any difference in multi-media presentations, or in systems approaches?

The decisive factor will be the level of integration of the media into the general curriculum. If this has been designed with mass media specifically in mind, there will be little wastage, and no room for the teacher's common complaint that working with media adds to rather than decreases or enriches his task because it works at a tangent to the main task. Associated with this principle is the availability of recorded, user-controlled materials. It will help enormously if the teacher can preview audio or video programmes in advance, can stop or start them at will, or repeat them after stated intervals and after group work with his class. It will also help if some programmes can be used for independent or small group study, either in remedial work or to serve as a refresher course. Once this kind of user control is assured, materials can be created, not as self-sufficient 'programmes' but as presentations (segmented if necessary) of particular themes or concepts.

Some of this is expressed diagrammically in Fig. 18.2. The media are seen, not as generalised teaching tools, but as aids to different kinds of learning behaviour stemming from different contexts. The figure (from Charles Klasek) illustrates one very important point: that in the end, the success of a multi-media or systems approach depends upon the understanding by the teacher of what the system is trying to do — the relationship of each piece of material to other materials, and to his own classroom models. The final objective of media is to serve as a resource and this means that the onus of responsibility falls back on teacher rather than producer. For this kind of understanding to be reached, long, practical experience is needed, beginning at the time of student professional career. The element can be communicated in training programmes, demonstration

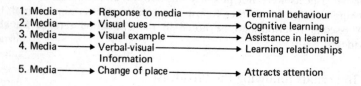

Fig. 18.2   Utilisation flow.

models and practice sessions can be offered, but in the end understanding comes from trial and error. Nevertheless, the learning process will be shorter if trial and error are not conducted in a vacuum, but also reflect communication between producers and users.

Utilisation out of school

What can be added to the foregoing of utilisation for adult audiences, in non-formal and informal education? Most of what has already been observed is still relevant, *as far as this is possible.*

Ideally, we would like to see the same degree of control applicable as can be hoped for (if not always secured) in the school sector. But here we are dealing with a situation where people are learning outside formal educational institutions, often without the benefit of trained teachers, sometimes as independent students, and very frequently without any real sense of continuity of purpose, or of motivation.

So each model must try, within the limits of its containing system, to set up the best pattern of utilisation that it can. The same elements are involved — a public relations campaign to inform and interest potential audiences; the involvement of adult education institutions, supervisors and teachers; cooperation with many extension agencies in agricultural and development fields; training programmes for teachers, field workers and administrative staff; the production of booklets, charts, posters and support materials, to intrigue and inform the target audience and to guide the work of animateurs, many of whom may be volunteers.

Utilisation supervisors

The duties of the utilisation officer in out-of-school education are consequently different from those of his counterpart in school education, though the same qualities of temperament and broad experience are needed. But for him, there will be less possibility of formal training programmes, of reporting on media use in structured situations, and a greater need for public relations and educational activities, and for guiding inexperienced monitors in handling an unfamiliar medium to advantage.

There will be a tendency for an out-of-school supervisor to concentrate too many of his energies on such elements as literacy classes, second chance education, etc., where the situation is more under monitor control and more akin to the school pattern, and while this is obviously important, he should not neglect the area of community media, or of gauging reactions to general programming. Much of this will have to be subjective, based on personal contacts, and for this reason a very broad base of enquiry will be needed. In the out-of-school area, in particular, the utilisation officer will be critical in setting up pilots for new series and media approaches. It follows that he must have a very good knowledge of the adult education network, and of the structures of community groups.

He will also have to contribute to the training of monitors or group leaders for community viewing or listening experiments, and often the task of setting up a network of groups will fall substantially on his shoulders. His relationship with the producers of such series has therefore to be especially close, and he will make a significant contribution to the task of programme development, since the producer may be working very much in the dark, with little knowledge of his target audience.

For some areas, such as distance education, a network of tutors and counsellors has to be created (such as is described later for the Open University). Here the problem is more complex, since special training programmes for these part-time workers have to be devised, and they have to be fed regularly with advance information, brought together for briefing sessions, and generally made to feel part of a coherent team. For such exercises, special units have to be created.

Utilisation models

The actual model for the utilisation system will therefore vary according to function. In an open-learning system, where there is no inbuilt contact between tutors and audiences, these are deliberately written into the system design, in the form of student programmes, summer schools, telephone tutorials and so on. In development campaigns, groups are specifically formed to hear or view programmes, and volunteers solicited to lead the groups and promote follow-up activities. In literacy classes, special study materials are provided for the groups to use, and seminars run for the tutors during vacation periods or in the evenings, mounted by a touring team of trainers.

Some examples are needed, to illustrate this variety. The first is of a development campaign run in Tanzania, which used radio and printed materials, together with a network of discussion groups. The following account, by Budd Hall, illustrates how the campaign was organised.

The 'Man is Health' development campaign fitted within the historical context of many development efforts and combined aspects of various antecedents in a national short-term (12-week), intensive campaign. It was an outgrowth of increased emphasis by the Ministry of Health on preventive or community medicine, an expansion of adult education experimentation with radio listening groups, part of the political party's concern with increased political consciousness and awareness of the politics of health, and fell within national policies for bringing about a socialist rural transformation.

The campaign had three objectives:

1. *To increase participants' awareness of and to encourage group actions on measures which groups and individuals can take to make their lives healthier.*
2. *To provide information about the symptoms and prevention of specific disease.*
3. *For those who had participated in the national literacy campaign, to encourage the maintenance of newly acquired reading skills by providing suitable follow-up materials.*

Two elements were fundamental to the fulfilment of these objectives. First, there were pre-existing structures available to implement the plans. Second, the planning was not rushed and it was thoroughly systematic.

Tanzania has built a widespread adult education network under the administration of the Ministry of National Education. It is composed of nearly 2,000 national, regional, district and divisional adult education coordinators and supervisors. These personnel are responsible to the thousands of adult education centres which operate using primary schools as bases. They are paralleled by a network of health education officers. Both sets of personnel were largely responsible for the day-to-day operation of the campaign, from the training of group leaders to encouragement during the broadcasting. They were supplemented by the networks of the political party and the Rural Development Division.

The planning for the campaign began 18 months before the first radio broadcast went on the air and was carried out under the guidance of a national coordinating committee which met as often as weekly during the more intense planning periods. The importance of this committee is that from the beginning as many agencies as were necessary to the success of the campaign were involved. A mass campaign at a rural level cannot be carried out by the activities of only one sector or one agency. It requires the coordinated efforts of all agencies working in the rural areas. At the village level in this campaign, the adult education personnel worked with the rural development extension officers, the local political officials and the health education personnel in organising groups before the campaign and in giving the groups support, once the radio programmes were under way.

Experience from the earlier radio study group campaigns indicated that a trained study group leader was essential to successful group activity. One of the most important reasons for training group leaders is to convey the message that group leaders are not teachers. A leader does not tell the group what to do or how to do it. The group leader is given training to guide group studies, to understand that he is only 'first among equals'. He must be trained in tact: to encourage the withdrawn, subdue the over-dominant and generally stimulate full participation. It is equally important to provide suggestions to leaders on how to move from discussion to action in the groups.

Logistically, the Tanzanian scheme required 75,000 study group leaders to be trained in 3½ months. This was done by means of a staged training system whereby regional team trained district teams who in turn trained the study group leaders at divisional level. There were 7 regional seminars for 200 participants (30 per seminar); 61 district level seminars for 1,400 participants (25 per seminar); and 2,000 divisional seminars for roughly 75,000 study group leaders (37 per seminar). All the seminars lasted from 2 to 3 days.

An important lesson from this experience of mass training is that it is possible to ensure that the central elements of the training message survive the diffusion process from the first through the last stages. That is, no vital element need be damaged by dilution. This is one of the most crucial aspects in the development of a mass campaign. In the Tanzanian case, the key elements of the training message were maintained by several devices: centrally prepared handouts (duplicated locally); the use of prepared flipover charts summarising the most important points of training; prerecorded cassettes of simulated radio programmes for role-playing experience; and copies of the actual materials to be used in the campaign.

The pattern which was most often followed by groups during the campaign was as follows:

1. *assemble during the gathering time — the radio plays music related to the campaign, political songs, poems and short announcements;*
2. *the group members listen to the 20-minute radio programme;*
3. *the group leader (or someone in the group who can) reads aloud the appropriate section of the text;*
4. *discussion begins first with the question of the relevance of the material presented to the actual circumstances of the group's members;*
5. *discussion takes place about various persons' experience with the disease, alternative causes of the disease and possible ways of preventing it;*
6. *resolutions are made and agreed upon by the group for specific actions which could be implemented in the village;*
7. *during the ensuing week — before the next programme — the resolutions are carried out by the group members and, most likely, others in the village.*

A major difference between this campaign and previous attempts was the importance placed on action following discussions. The type of activities which individual groups undertook varied according to the reality in various areas. In a survey of 213 groups, it was found that clearing vegetation from around the homes was carried out by 28 per cent of the groups; digging, repairing or rebuilding latrines by 20 per cent; destroying and cleaning the areas of stagnant water by 24 per cent; boiling water 12 per cent; and cleaning the area around water supplies 11 per cent. In one district, about 200,000 latrines were built during the campaign period. The result at the end of the campaign was that not a single house was without a latrine. This happened in an area where colonial officers had tried to enforce latrine construction nearly 50 years previously with dismal results and much rancour. In one other division the people decided that to have a latrine for each home was not enough. What, for example, could travellers use, while waiting on the side of the road for buses? The solution was obviously more latrines. It was agreed accordingly that one latrine would be built at each major bus stop in the area.

There are clear similarities of approach (though not of scale) between this project, mounted in a developing country, and an educational project in Quebec, designed to help disadvantaged adults — the TEVEC experiment, which is reported on below (by R. Lallez, for Unesco).

The Tevec project

TEVEC was a project, approved and financed by the Quebec Ministry of Education in 1967, which was directed towards adults living in the Gaspesie region of Quebec who had had only limited secondary education — a large number in an area where 73 per cent had not gone beyond 7th grade. The formal educational objective was to upgrade adult students to 9th grade level (reached by children of about 15 in the American school system) by means of a multi-media system which transmitted instruction in three 'regular' subjects — French, English and Mathematics — and in socio-economic issues relating to the region. After several months' preparation, enrolment began in December 1967 and courses were followed in two phases, from January to June 1968 and from October 1968 to May 1969, when examinations were held. Between September and December 1969 there was a short follow-up series and a second opportunity to take the examinations for those who had missed, or failed them the first time. The examinations were recognised and accredited by the Ministry of Education.

The courses

Tevec's communications system comprised daily television lessons and weekly 'tele-club' broadcasts, backed up by postal distribution of printed lessons, worksheets, questionnaires and IBM ('Sense-a-mark') cards for use by students in response to questionnaires.

Courses were administered by means of a regional structure of local, area and regional committees. Home visitors encouraged participation, concentrating on those with little previous education. Local committees

*organised tele-clubs (group discussions sparked off by tele-club broadcasts)
and set up revision centres which provided weekly lessons with a teacher
to discuss and resolve difficulties encountered during the week. These were
organised in the first stage by the regional educational commission, but in
the second stage revision centres were replaced by autonomous centres,
organised spontaneously on the basis of existing networks of family,
friendship or neighbourhood. These were visited from time to time by a
staff of educational development workers ('animateurs pédagogiques').*

*Two important points emerge from this. Firstly the Tevec team made a
distinction between the formal structure through which people could
make use of Tevec's resources, and the informal, casual arrangements
people made to help themselves and each other while working on Tevec
materials. Secondly, they felt that though both ways of working were
necessary, one of the key functions of the formal system was to provide
feedback to the organisers of Tevec so that it could be adapted as time
went on. And they stressed that feedback, and participation, is something
that needs to be built into a project the whole way through. In their case,
a whole series of changes were made to the second phase of the project, in
the light of reactions to the first. By having a structure of two-way communication between the project organisers and their 'students' (the Tevec
team, significantly, use the word 'clientèle') the participants themselves
could exercise some control over the whole project, and Tevec was able to
base its work very firmly on their real needs, interests and levels of knowledge or understanding. Their advice to others is to 'meet the people where
they are, socially, psychologically and culturally'.*

The staff

*In this light the work of the educational development workers and home
visitors is seen to be crucial. Only four field-workers (animateurs) could be
employed — clearly far too few for the 35,000 who followed the courses.
Their essential characteristic was that they were familiar with the area and
with its milieu, its cultural situation and its people. They regarded their
main function as being to stimulate the formation of groups — tele-clubs —
who would follow the course together. The educational function of the
tele-club was described by Tevec's director in this way: 'The chief thing
that interests us, in the tele-club formula, is students' regular participation
in the tele-club. What really matters is that it is a system of self-motivation
for the student which seems to us to be remarkably effective ... this is the
immediate and spontaneous use of knowledge recently acquired and, at
the same time, the student's perception of the breadth and value of what
he has learned.'*

*Apart from the animateurs, Tevec employed twenty part-time home
visitors who concentrated their visits on the students with the least
amount of previous formal education and appear to have succeeded in
raising the proportion of these who worked right through the course. Part-
time staff were employed too, at the beginning of the project, to help in*

the process of enrolling students. Tevec was publicised by television, radio and the press, by distributing pamphlets, and by the work of the animateurs. Part-time workers called from door to door to enrol students and were paid by results — a fee of $1.00 for each student they enrolled. As a result some undoubtedly pressed students into enrolling who would not otherwise have done so but, for all that, the enrolment figures are dramatic.

Achievements

Tevec, a project whose aims as well as methods were revolutionary in contrast with the formal education systems of North America, succeeded in enrolling around 35,000 people out of a total population of 275,000, or 12½ per cent. Roughly a quarter of this group worked right through the course. But the results are not to be measured in this way alone. The effects on individual students and individual communities are also significant, though more difficult to assess. But the Tevec staff talk of letters coming in with phrases like, 'I've never written a letter before' and of changes to communities like one where an unemployed Tevec student successfully ran for the office of mayor in place of the holder who had been in office for 25 years. Tevec groups gained the confidence necessary to summon before them the mayor, or the president of the school board or the curé: in one case a successful appeal to the bishop meant that the curé was drummed out of town. More generally the project seems to have resulted in a shift from traditional and religious local organisations to new patterns of organisation. (One of the Tevec workers talks too of the creation of a new elite in the working class of the area from the Tevec groups and of the consequent need for a 'revolution in the revolution' there to prevent a new stalemate situation.) Its concentration on the socio-economic conditions of the area clearly fitted with real local concerns — and produced results.

A third example at a very different level comes from the UK Open University. This experiment in part-time, home-based degree education has been referred to on a number of occasions in this handbook, as a careful model of multi-media teaching, with its mix of correspondence courses, broadcasting, specially written textual material, home study experiments, computer-marked assignments and so on. The design of the courses, from the very beginning, paid particular regard to trying to solve student problems in advance; the notes on correspondence courses try to anticipate difficulties (each text is piloted with a sample group of students, as well as reviewed by a complete course team), and attention is given in both supporting literature and in the media to the question of *how* (not just what) to study.

The following account (from a university study) describes its utilisation structure, and especially the arrangements which are made for student engagement, including a network of study centres.

The Open University

The University has established thirteen academic regions encompassing the entire United Kingdom. The staff at each Regional Office organise local student support services of which study centres are a part.

There are several components in the Open University teaching system. The basic component is the printed material. This consists of set texts, 'course units', and recommended texts, plus various supplementary printed materials (e.g. notes on the Open University radio and television broadcasts). Television, radio and other media are also integrated into this teaching system.

As the Open University is based on correspondence teaching, it is the function of the tutor to guide and evaluate the Open University student by assignments completed by the students and forwarded to the tutor by mail. These assignments completed by students at intervals during the course are designed to pace, instruct and assess the student. In some courses, especially in the Arts Faculty, assignments are marked by a part-time tutor, but in most courses, both computer-marked and tutor-marked assignments are used. The tutor-marked assignments are returned to the student with feedback on the level of the student's performance and comments on how to improve his work. Although tuition is carried out primarily by correspondence, the tutor also conducts face-to-face tutorials. These tutorials are held about once in every 3 weeks for foundation courses, but perhaps only two or three times in total for many post-foundation courses. Tutorials are designed to be chiefly remedial and not primarily for introducing new materials, and when students find that tutorial contact is too infrequent, they organise their own 'self-help' groups whereby the students help one another without an official organiser.

Every student is allocated to a personal academic adviser called a counsellor, who, like the tutor, is employed on a part-time basis. He acts as a permanent local representative of the Open University for the student. The counsellor advises students on academic matters at the foundation level. At post-foundation level, the counsellor concerns himself with the total academic progress of each of his students, irrespective of the courses followed, and probably for the duration of their Open University careers. The counsellor can help to humanise what might otherwise seem to students a remote and impersonal institution by advising on general academic, administrative, or (occasionally) personal, matters and, where necessary, acting as a student's advocate.

Some University courses, including the foundation courses with at least one of which all students must begin their studies, have a one week residential summer school component. Attendance at summer school is considered to be an essential part of these courses.

In order to offer additional human and technical resources to students, local study centres were established in each region. Study centre activities are optional and many students, already hard pressed for time, have to decide whether to attend the centre or work on the course material at home. It can by no means be assumed that students will automatically choose to participate in study centre activities.

The study centre

Study centres were created to fulfil various needs peculiar to the Open University's system of teaching. For instance, they provide a location where remedial face-to-face tuition is given, where counselling sessions are held and where student-led groups can form and meet to help one another. Study centres also help to increase the student's academic scope and enjoyment by eliminating isolation and developing a sense of corporate identity with the wider Open University student community and interdependence among study centres.

Counsellors pay particular attention to foundation course students, so there is usually high study centre attendance among this group. Tutorials at foundation level are also held at the study centre every third or fourth week and usually attract even more students than the counselling evenings. Among post-foundation students, study centre attendance is relatively infrequent. Such tutorials as there are may well be at a centre other than the local one, although locally based study groups may compensate for this to some extent. A majority of students will make an occasional visit to the study centre as shown by 50 to 70 per cent attendance at meetings arranged by regional staff to discuss, for example, conditional registration for courses in the following year.

As resource centres, the study centres are equipped with radio and television sets, and a super-8 mm film cassette machine with optical sound track. (However, Super-8 film cassettes of programmes are now being phased out because of technical problems with quality and reliability; in some centres experimental work with videocassettes is being tried and evaluated.) A library of audio cassettes is available and film cassettes can be borrowed from one of the thirteen Regional Offices, although neither type of cassette is available for courses offered in 1973 and 1974, following economic measures taken by the University at the end of 1972. These facilities are not heavily used, but there are usually a few students who regularly view their television programmes 'live' at the study centre.

Each study centre has a reference library of foundation course materials and students may also have access to any existing library facilities of the host institution. Selected study centres house a computer terminal as well which usually receives steady use from students whose courses contain a computing element. In physical terms study centres often consist of a few classrooms, two grey metal cupboards, a television set and perhaps a notice board. There are exceptions, but an empty study centre usually lacks any sense of atmosphere or warmth. In spite of such difficulties informal and social activities do thrive in some centres. These activities may vary from organised extra-curricular activities, both educational and purely social, to informal gatherings at a pub. Many study centres have a committee drawn from among students and counsellors which does its best to develop the sense of a 'local community' among all members of the centre.

Perhaps the most intriguing, and most fluid aspect, of utilisation is in the modern emphasis on access and participation. If a principal aim of utilisation strategies is to ensure that materials respond to the demands of audiences, and bridge the gulf between producers and users, then the active participation of the audience in programme planning, production and use goes a long way to bridging this gap totally.

The forms of community media extend from local to national levels, and include both radio and television. National systems have moved well beyond the simple 'phone-in' programme, to experiments such as that in Denmark, where the national radio organisation has set up a 'Radio Workshop' with its own production and editing facilities, designed for access to the public (both in using the technical facilities, and in air time on the second network). In Holland, a regular weekend programme features live discussions in which members of the broadcasting audience interview politicians, public figures and decision makers, in a studio which has been turned into a country restaurant, to create an atmosphere of informality. The BBC's 'Open Door' series offers air time on television to minority groups and the assistance of technical staff and producers who are there only to give technical assistance in realising the group's objectives, not as editors or censors. Another television series in Finland presents the opinion of minority groups in the form of a debate in the presence of the host community. Again the producer acts only as assistant; the tasks of research gathering, selecting questions, designing graphics, etc., are all undertaken by the group, and the programme includes items of local culture, music hall, satirical features.

The trend has gone furthest at the local community level, in the proliferation of video groups, usually expressing political or social convictions. Sometimes these groups replay their programmes through a local cable network; sometimes they use them as resource material in public meetings or community events, or as the nucleus of a local library.

In the account below, a Canadian author Linda Mitchell, examines community programming in a fictitious Canadian city, to see what kinds of solution are proposed for what problems. These accounts could be continued almost indefinitely, and in a handbook of this kind it is difficult to decide where to draw the line between 'educational' and 'community' media. Obviously community media affect all levels and styles of programming, and in many cases the educators are the least among the users. Indeed, in more than one city in Canada, because the tremendous potential of local media (and especially of cable television) was not finally realised, and many individual cable operators did not live up either to their own promises or to the general guidelines laid down by the Canadian Radio—Television Commission, resentment and frustration ensued, and the traditional adult education agencies all but abandoned the idea of using cable television for educational purposes, leaving the field to the community development-orientated groups. But hopefully, the pendulum will again swing the other way, and by this time the management and programming experience of the community groups, and their methods of coping with participatory formulae, will be of value. By this time too, another important issue may be clearer — to what extent community programming should be commercially sponsored (as in many cases it must, to survive). The problem is by no means confined to the industrialised world; a community newspaper started in Tobago experienced the same difficulty, and had to create its own advertising ring.

Community media in Canada

The easiest way to examine the various problems, solutions, alternatives, and decisions involved in community programming is simply to develop a fictitious group, environment and goal. We can use it to explore the real choices facing the people who become involved in this work.

Let's say our group exists in a middle-sized city, population about 100,000. The city has two major industries, a rolling mill and a potash plant just outside town; otherwise it exists as a service centre for the surrounding agricultural area. It has a university, an arts centre, a gallery, in fact all the usual amenities. It has a substantial Indian population concentrated in the poorer areas of town, as well as many second-generation people of Ukranian origin.

Our city possesses the following commercial media: one newspaper (morning and afternoon editions), three AM stations (one owned by the firm that owns the newspaper and one part of the national service), one FM station, two television stations (commercial and national), and two cable television systems, both with community programming channels, which geographically divide the city into two tidy halves.

There are also two weekly newspapers which are community-produced. One of these simply provides an information service about local events, the other offers a left-based interpretation and background of local political activities.

The two cable systems have a limited amount of portable VTR equipment and accessories, as well as studio facilities. There is also considerable audio and audio-visual equipment as well as a studio at the university and the technical high school, but this is not generally available for public use.

Our group (the North End Community Planning Association) has been engaged for 2 years with city hall in joint planning for their neighbourhood. The neighbourhood is older, heterogeneous, largely inhabited by workers, the elderly, some Indians, and a sprinkling of university students. Since they are close to the city centre, about a dozen high rises have been erected (at the expense of people's homes and park land), and this gave the neighbourhood of 16,000 the impetus to form the association and force the city to include it in the planning process.

The group has a broad membership but not a terribly broad base in the community; it has found keeping the neighbourhood informed of its progress its most difficult job. Although the members consistently place stories in the community newspapers, they realise they aren't reaching enough people. They sense a showdown coming with the city over the final stage of planning. This decides them. They must provide more information, more consistently, to their people if they can expect support when the crunch comes. But how?

Their first attempt is with the commercial media. The reaction is almost identical from them all. Broadcasters and newspapermen are more than willing to do a story, their only question is: what's the issue? The group executive hold a press conference and distribute a 'backgrounder'. As the stories come out they realise that the information they wanted to get across has been ruthlessly chopped, subtly altered and rearranged to suit the needs of 'the story' or 'the item' as seen by the reporter.

At this point the members realise that if the commercial media are to serve any useful purpose as far as they are concerned, they are going to have to control the information. But they can't and they know it. So, reserving commercial media for specific instances, they decide to look at alternatives which will enable them to control their material.

The first item is: what do they want to say? Just exactly what do they want to tell their neighbours? They agree they want to tell them three things: their plans for the neighbourhood; the city's plans; and their feeling that the city is about to disallow their plans and proceed with its own.

Their informal survey reveals that besides general meetings, posters and the community newspapers there are only two alternatives outside the commercial media available to them: producing a programme for one of the local cable television channels, and packaging freelance items for the national programme.

Our group lacks the skill to do radio items for the national network so the only alternative within the alternative media is cable television, about which the members also know next to nothing.

Upon investigation they learn that the two cable television owners in town have very different interpretations of community programming. One system believes in training community people in the techniques necessary to use the medium and letting them handle the equipment (even lending it to them to use outside the studio for location shots). This owner provides producers (animators or facilitators are other common terms) whose job is to help groups define their programming goals, prepare the programme, in short, any kind of assistance needed to produce the programme according to the group's specifications.

Also, this owner is well aware that once they've defined their needs groups may wish to produce one 1-hour programme, one ½-hour programme, or two 1-hour shows, etc. — in other words he realises that the frequency of their programming depends on their needs and will alter as their situation in the community alters. While this makes his scheduling a *fairly tricky process, he recognises rigidity is a disservice to the groups and the community he serves.*

The second cable system has elaborate studio facilities for the community channel, but because it programmes with expensive colour equipment it is reluctant to let groups do location work. It is also reluctant to let groups have hands-on equipment. From our group's point of view this system has two other major drawbacks: it is not fond of handling contentious political issues (and our group has sensed that its issue will definitely become contentious), and it prefers groups to agree to do a 13-week 'season' of ½-hour shows.

Our group knows that the members are all volunteers who work full time, ignorant of VTR work, and they just don't have that much to say right now. They can't commit the group to thirteen shows. At the same time four or five of their members are extremely interested in learning about the process and are willing to devote some time to training.

They approach the first cable television owner and discover that, since their neighbourhood is within the boundaries of the second system, they should be programming out of that studio. They manage to arrange to make the programme at the first system and have it bicycled to the second because the first owner decides that the general issue of citizens' participation in urban planning is important enough and has enough general interest to warrant its exposure to the total population.

Goals are clarified and the programme is planned with the aid of the producer. It is decided to use portapak footage of the neighbourhood as highlights and to display vulnerable areas. Interviews, also using portapaks, are conducted door-to-door soliciting various points of view. All of this work is done by the group. The city planners and politicians are interviewed for their views and graphics of the two alternative plans are prepared.

A format for this material is designed in conjunction with the producer, and the group selects three of its members who will appear as a panel in the last 10 minutes of the programme to put forward and clarify the group's point of view.

The cable television licencee schedules them editing time for their portapak footage and 2 hours of studio time to put the programme together. They decide it is too complex to do live and it is taped to be shown the following week.

The taping goes well. Those members functioning as technicians are obviously pleased with their newly acquired skills, and everyone agrees that the panel's presentation of the group's viewpoint was masterful. At the owner's suggestion they had advertised the programme in the TV listings and they also distributed a leaflet to every home in the neighbourhood. They settle back to wait, eager for next Monday.

During the making of the programme they noticed some changes in the group. Some people loved the work and had thrown themselves into it with more enthusiasm than they'd shown for anything to date. Others, disgruntled by the process, had gone around muttering darkly about video freaks and Marshall McLuhan.

Everybody had noticed those 3 weeks had eaten up enormous amounts of time and energy and they had neglected the group's regular business. They decided that whatever the result of the coming programme they couldn't undertake to programme regularly without some elaborate re-structuring and additional volunteers. There was also a general feeling that it had been a damn good learning experience for everyone, even the sceptics.

The programme was shown on Monday night and the members eagerly awaited feedback, expecting calls, letters, etc., from their constituents. They didn't get many so they checked out the cable television systems and found they hadn't received many either.

This led to serious discussion. Who had watched the show? How many? How were they to find out what the reaction had been? They decided to call a general meeting to try to answer these questions, although such meetings were difficult to organise and were usually reserved for very serious occasions. At the meeting they discovered a very small percentage had watched, but those who had were enthusiastic. In the discussion that followed the people who hadn't seen it on cable television wondered if they could see it. Could the group show it again in the community hall?

A call to the cable television company ascertained that the tape hadn't been erased yet and a screening was arranged. This time the group organised a telephone campaign to reach people and issued press releases to the local media. There was a good turn-out and, after the screening, a 2-hour discussion. There was unanimous agreement that this was the best meeting they'd ever had — people dealt with the issues raised in the programme and stuck to the point. The meeting arrived at a consensus about the presentation to be made to city hall in the next month.

After the general meeting the group sat down and assessed what had happened. Obviously, making the tape and showing it on cable television had been important. Equally obvious, having the general meeting view the tape had been important because the tape had provoked such a worthwhile discussion. Although the general meeting had been enthusiastic about making more tapes — maybe even making one to show city hall their needs — the group was cautious. All knew the enormous resources of time (and if they were to do it frequently, money) involved. They decided to appoint a sub-committee to find out if they should do more programming, and on what basis, and also to recommend a way the group could divide the work-load equitably if they continued to programme, even on a sporadic basis.

A fairy tale, obviously — no community group in Canada was ever so coherent and so together. But it is a convenient way to illustrate some of the alternatives and the hazards facing a group undertaking community programming.

Not surprisingly these trends are most advanced in the industrialised world; the equipment employed is relatively inexpensive, but still beyond the means of most developing countries, and the articulation of political or minority social viewpoints is something which would not recommend itself to many developing societies, where national integration is emphasised by government and political criticism discouraged. Nevertheless, there have been some experiments in the Third World, including Tanzania, Peru and Tobago. In Tanzania, the 'Year 16' experiment was a videotaping project which set out to produce a record of the Ujama movement (a cooperative approach to rural development, with national political backing). Videotaping and filming were intended to give to illiterate communities a means to express themselves and to establish communication between them and their outside leaders. In the end the project experienced a large number of practical difficulties, and took some members of the authorities by surprise in the forthrightness of its criticism. People who had passively supported an incompetent agricultural officer stood up against him and asked for his transfer. They began to say, 'We must not wait for the government to help us, but start work ourselves. If we wait for the government to help us, we can wait until paradise'.

Not surprisingly, in the Third World the video instrument may well be regarded as a double-edged tool, certainly by the authorities. A more cautious approach has been tried in Tobago, where a range of low-cost media facilities (radio, a community newspaper, video equipment) were made available to a small island community, as tools for whatever the islanders (especially women) considered important as development objectives. A completely different set of difficulties was experienced here, precisely because the project was left unfocused, and no attempt was made to impose a programme. The multiplicity of possible objectives created confusion, and without some structure, and especially without adequate community animation, the project remained inert for long periods. Eventually a community newspaper emerged as a regular product, but even this was largely the creation of the project's experts, rather than a community undertaking. It would seem that there is a fine line between access and chaos, and the interpretation of this line must be made by very skilful practitioners.

The Fogo Island experiments of the National Film Board of Canada and the Memorial University of Newfoundland remain the most important and detailed in this field. Originally conceived as a film project, they transferred to video as the technology improved and the possibility of instant replay gave the experiment a new orientation. Video was used, not to produce documentaries, but to show one community to another, and to open up debate within single communities. People saw themselves and their convictions replayed, juxtaposed with the sentiments of their neighbours. Whether or not the novelty of the video tool will remain constant is a doubtful question, but certainly when it was introduced into this small fishing community, it opened many eyes through its freshness and direct recording of reality. Most of all, it threw new light on the role of the animator. We have seen how different is the monitor (in a literacy class) from the school teacher, and how different in turn the group leader from the trained monitor. The animateur using small-format technology is different again. It is his role to provide instruments for social dialogue, without directly guiding or intervening; he has both a catalytic and a neutral role which is difficult to sustain. Some of the qualities of the animator can still be best described in terms of what he does not do, rather than what he actually does. He does not persuade people to make programmes; he does not invite them to put forward views on a specific topic; he does not try to edit material, or to pressurise audiences to respond in any way. He must learn by experience, not by training.

Such a role makes special demands and often poses ethical problems. Below is an account of how a woman, working in community media in Toronto, summed up her feelings about the job, and especially about the dilemma of working with tools which can be powerful instruments, without dictating the wielding of this power.

During this type of documentation — involving touchy areas like the use of police, the rights of working people to organise, management versus union, I had to deal with legal-type considerations — questions of legal rights, property rights, permission to tape and use material (i.e. police, company, government permission) and all the practical implications of deciding to handle this project. I decided in fact that I had to be prepared to take calculated risks — otherwise, I would really have to question whose interest I would be serving. In this kind of situation, I have to look at these risks in terms of who has power, and whose power I was trying to protect. In dealing with the issue of property (the police insist that picketers move off the company property in one sequence), I thought through a new interpretation of property — the property of civil and human rights. When you talk about property in that light, in this kind of situation, you run the inevitable risk of toe-stepping. If people have to move into conflict in winning these rights, then implied is another group (the police, government) giving up control over the rights of the demanding group. The property of rights must change hands — from being the property of establishment power to the rightful property of the people to whom those rights originally belong. You go from the arena of practical legality to that of ethical legality — who was I there for — whose rights was I trying to help protect. It seems to me that we always have to be prepared to look at these questions in an ethical, as well as a practical, light. To do this, we should develop an analysis of why we are involved in any particular project. This question is most graphic when we move within a group in conflict — the same question is more subtle when the conflict of interests is not as clear.

It is my experience that the issue and the political context of that issue has to be of common priority and concern to the media person and the community people. This, of course, is the logic for training some of the membership of that group in the use of that technology. It seems to me that our purpose in such a group is not to distract them with the power of the medium but to do whatever we can to support people to establish a very real sense of their own power.

Grierson said that film should be used as a hammer. I've heard too, that tape (or film) can be used as a mirror. There's a really important distinction between the two — one is a weapon and tool together and the other is simply a tool. If tape is used as a hammer, and the hammer is in the hands of the people to whom it belongs, you're really talking about political process. When tape is used politically — that is, to show how decisions get made, how and why people regard their sense of power — you're talking about using a hammer in the group's political education — or process. I think that tape — or any medium — is under-used when the material is simply descriptive, and shows no analysis. I really question the long term value of simply describing a situation — rather than analysing it. Simple descriptions can give all sorts of people lots of room to justify that they are doing something rather than looking at what they're doing and how they are prepared to plan for change.

I think too, that tape and film should pose important questions about an issue that will support people to go beyond the parameters of the visual material. The way I figure it, is that tape can act as a door-opener. In using this medium I am really knocking on the viewers' perceptual door — the best way to gain access to that person's process is through soliciting an emotional response. In the case of this strike, it may appear at first glance that the issue was diverted to one of police versus picketers. However, on second look, the issue becomes a very graphic one — the questions are who has power and who doesn't, and how does each side react in this kind of situation and what can and does each group do about it. The door-opener was that emotional response to a really graphic conflict. How can we, in using tape or film get beyond or behind the issue and use it educationally.

It is always super important to keep in mind that the media process is only a small corner of the organising process. It seems crucial for us to determine how we can guarantee community members access to their own media, without obstructing or obscuring their own political process. Perhaps the most effective way to do this is to share with them a common concern with their rights at large — their rights, and ours to gain access to a rightful sense of power and control of ourselves and our communities.

It is tempting to continue the discussion of community media, but in a handbook of restricted length, primarily concerned with instructional applications of media, limits have to be recognised. Community media push out the barriers of education; at a local, interpersonal level, they do not make arbitrary academic distinctions between what is educational and what is entertaining or informative, because individual experience is not categorised in such a fashion. The local environment is direct and personal enough for such distinctions to be both unprofitable and impossible. But the field is a major one for the future, introducing as it does new models of control, access and participation, and the reader is referred to Frances Berrigan's recent survey for Unesco (see Bibliography, p. 363) for an extended discussion of experiences in North America and Europe.

Can we, from all of this, construct a model of utilisation for media out

Table 18.3 Training for use of media out of school

	Open broadcasting	Development campaigns using group discussion	Literacy and non-formal classes	Open and distance learning systems	Community media
					All of these activities run together from the outset, since audience is involved at all stages, with or without technical support. Animator plays a continuing role, guiding but not dictating momentum.
Training for utilisation	Orientation training given to extension workers who may draw on programmes' stimulus	Training is given to discussion group leaders, using touring teams and snowball approach	Training is given to tutors or monitors, and guidance notes are provided	1. Guidance on independent study is given to students (in programmes, courses, texts) 2. Distance tutors are briefed on student difficulties (in programmes, courses, texts)	
Preparation for media use	Advance publicity for programmes, and sometimes published, print or AV materials	Posters and leaflets are distributed and advance programme details and venue	Monitor introduces key words, concepts, and theme, and supervises revision drills	Notes and support materials, including texts and home-study kits, are provided to students. In these function of media is clearly described	
Exposure to media	Individual views or listens at home, or in public meeting place	Groups meet with discussion leader to hear or view programmes in informal setting	Classes hear or view programmes together with tutors or monitors	Students hear or view either independently or in study centres. In the second case, they may view in company of resident tutor	
Follow-up	1. According to individual motivation, sometimes with assistance of materials published in association with programmes 2. Extension workers may follow-up broadcast's motivation	Discussion is followed by group decisions on practical follow-up actions	Discussion and practice follow the broadcast, with related reading, and associated exercises studies	Further assignments, correspondence study, objective and standard tests are given. In centres, discussions and group tutorial work may follow, before independent assignments	

of school? Almost certainly not; more than any other, the adult sector shows radical distinguishing features from place to place. But as a crude form of summary, we can present, in Table 18.3, the main ways in which five categories of adult media (*open broadcasting, development campaigns, using discussion groups, literacy and non-formal classes, open learning systems, and small-format community media*) cope with the essential components of *training* for leaders and monitors, *preparing audiences* for media, *using* materials and *following them up* with practical action.

The scale is one of adaptation to local conditions, and of increasing sophistication, ranging from the limited possibilities of engagement which occur in open broadcasting, to the controlled system of a distance learning system. Yet the impetus is the same in all cases — to create, by whatever means are available (albeit sometimes crude), a framework to support the media so as to make the best use of their potential.

Chapter 19

Evaluation and research

At one time evaluation was defined, and interpreted, in very narrow terms — a kind of *ad hoc* reporting on programmes, carried out by visiting school broadcasting officers, inspectors or utilisation personnel. This concept was later enlarged to include more scientifically based reporting procedures, based on sampling techniques, questionnaire forms and sometimes especially mounted surveys.

These procedures were, and still are, valuable, but they have two major drawbacks. They often isolate difficulties, or deficiencies, too late to incorporate changes into the system, and they do not show *why* things have gone wrong. Ideally, evaluation should be considered as a form of continuous monitoring, with evaluators included in the original course team which plans for a series, so that their comments can be built into the design from the outset.

Functions of evaluation

A major problem for managers and producers of educational media is that they have no direct knowledge of how their material is actually used in the school or home.

It is important to know, not simply whether the actual teaching objectives being supported by media are being achieved, and the extent to which the use of media is contributing to their achievement, but also whether the necessary conditions for an efficient media system (such as an adequate method of distribution) are being met. At the same time, because fields of knowledge and society in general are not static, the educational media system must be flexible enough to meet the demands of such changes. This means that there should be a continuous review not only of the effectiveness of the media design, but also of whether it is trying to do the right things.

Evaluation must consequently:

1. Ensure that there is as much knowledge as possible of what is happening.
2. Suggest possible changes that are likely to lead to improvements in the system.

3. Provide adequate information to assist and make possible rational policy making.

With this emphasis, at least initially, objectives for an evaluation system can be spelled out as follows:

(*a*) providing information, to assist with the selection of appropriate policies for an educational media system;
(*b*) providing information on the success or failure of educational media in meeting their educational objectives;
(*c*) providing information on the effectiveness of the various production and management elements involved;
(*d*) increasing knowledge of how to integrate media most effectively into an overall teaching context, in terms of both course design and production formats;
(*e*) increasing and spreading knowledge of the most appropriate production techniques in various education contexts;
(*f*) increasing and spreading knowledge of how to use media to their best advantage in actual teaching situations.

Organisation

In any but the smallest operations, a separate unit is needed to deal with evaluation problems. It may consist of only one or two people (though clerical support is essential). The number will depend on the size of the audience, the range of output and the complexity of the techniques employed, but there should be at least one person with a knowledge of statistical procedures.

The position of an evaluation unit within a media service is rather ambivalent. It is often said that research in media is best conducted by an external agency; this should lead to greater objectivity. But for continuous evaluation, different problems arise. In order to frame detailed questions about programmes an intimate understanding of producers' intentions is necessary, and some knowledge of the difficulties being faced. The intention is, after all, to initiate possible changes and improvements in programmes. This suggests that a regular contact with producers is essential. At the same time, detachment is also required, and this may be spoiled by too close an intimacy. A compromise is therefore in order. An evaluation unit is probably best housed within the centre; but it should either be a separate unit, responsible administratively to the main education authority, or at least work directly to the Head of the Service, with its independence from the rest of the service clearly understood.

Evaluation will require relatively little in the way of equipment, but in larger services access to data processing will be necessary, and this will in most cases be shared with other educational users (as with storage and computer facilities). Mostly, evaluation personnel work with other services (production, technical, curriculum, etc.), not on their own. It will usually be possible for the unit to acquire statistical and technical personnel, or to arrange for their training. But for senior media evaluation staff, special training programmes will have to be arranged, often overseas; the field is too new to have developed any volume of expertise.

Types of evaluation

Evaluation is therefore a complex subject, requiring very specialist disciplines. This is not the place at which to enter into techniques or statistical processes, but the planner should be aware of the various *types* of evaluation (in broad terms), and some of the *technical principles* which are employed by the evaluator.

Three authors from Stanford (John Mayo, Robert Hornik and Emil McAnany) outlined the main kinds of evaluation as follows:

Planning research entails the collection of essential data on a technology system before it is implemented and often before a decision is made to undertake it. Among the most common methods of data collection are feasibility studies which survey the key aspects of an educational environment, specifying the technical requirements for the transmission of radio or TV broadcasts and estimating how much effort will be needed to develop curricula, prepare learning materials, and train personnel. Planners often have much information of this kind already at their disposal. However, the scope of information needed to design and implement technology projects may warrant new studies. Planners of technology systems may want information on student ability and achievement levels in the past, as well as some notion of what teachers and students are expecting of radio or television in the classroom. Teacher attitudes toward instructional technology must also be well understood by planners of new classroom procedures and training opportunities are to be designed to equip teachers adequately for work in the new system.

The list of topics for planning research and the criteria for choosing among them could be extended considerably. In choosing areas for planning research, administrators and evaluators are able to focus their attention on the components of an educational system which are most fragile and therefore most likely to undermine project effectiveness.

Formative evaluation is a process of data collection during the development of a project so that revisions can be made to improve its functioning. Such evaluation touches decisions at every level of a project. Sometimes project administrators must decide whether to depend more on printed materials, classroom teachers, or television programs for a given course. Program producers need to know whether a given concept was learned satisfactorily and if students are ready for the next unit of material. Script writers need to know whether particular lessons were able to attract and hold the students' attention. When difficulties occur in these or other areas of an instructional technology system, formative evaluation is used to diagnose the problem and to provide some indication of what corrective steps are called for.

Summative evaluation *is a process of data collection designed to provide decision-makers with a more comprehensive understanding of how a project succeeds or fails in reaching its goals. It differs in time perspective from formative evaluation and is usually aimed at those decision-makers who control funds to continue or terminate the project. Nevertheless, the two approaches overlap in many ways. The variables or effects studied in both approaches may be quite similar. Formative evaluations of learning and attitudes often do contribute to summative evaluations of same phenomena. The most important differences between formative and summative evaluation pertain to the kinds of decisions which each is meant to influence. The need for immediate information to guide short range decisions (was last week's concept learned so that another one can be taught this week?) justifies a formative evaluation strategy with its inevitable compromises in methodology. However, when gathered in a systematic way, the data from formative evaluations often provide the basis for the longer range analyses and conclusions characteristic of summative evaluations.*

Techniques

Each of these three types of evaluation makes use of a battery of techniques, some of them objective and statistically based, some more subjective (and many of them still in the process of development). The main elements are summarised below.

1. Data collection

A considerable amount of information is needed for the evaluator to work effectively, on media as well as on educational topics. Most agencies now make routine statistical compilations of educational data, but there are obvious gaps as far as communications media are concerned. The evaluation unit should therefore make sure that it:

(a) has access to statistical data collected by other units;
(b) isolates the gaps in this data, and makes sure that these are rectified;
(c) adds to existing surveys (conducted on a regular basis by other agencies), specific questions in which it has a special interest.

One means of making the most of limited resources is to ensure that material is placed in a central data bank, and that methods of coding and retrieval are used in common with sister agencies (especially when computerised processes are employed). It will always be cheaper to place educational data together in this way, and it will often be possible, by pooling resources, to collect information which would be too expensive to acquire independently.

Some basic data will however have to be gathered by the evaluation unit, as it will not be available from any other source. This will include statistics on the following:

(a) Records of print-materials. One way in which accurate figures can be obtained of the number of adults seriously following broadcasts aimed at very small minority audiences will be by noting the number of requests received for supporting print materials. Standard ordering forms should be designed for such materials, so that the necessary information for both stock-control and evaluation can be collected and collated. The cost of providing supporting print materials should also be accurately accounted.

(b) Programme output figures. A basic statistic required is the yearly output of programmes in different programming areas, in some common unit of measurement (probably hours per year). The classification of different programming types will therefore need careful thought. Ideally, a system is required where output, audience size and direct programme costs can all be compared. The balance of programming also provides an indication of which of the educational objectives of the media system might be met.

(c) Utilisation of production facilities. Statistics need to be collected on the actual use made of production facilities, for two reasons. First of all, bookings have to be made and the future demand for facilities calculated. Secondly, as a rule-of-thumb it can be assumed that a wide use of the range of production facilities available indicates that imaginative and varied production techniques are being used: the use of portable recording equipment suggests there is a willingness to use local sources for programme material, and so on. It is therefore suggested that this information be collected in such a way that the utilisation of facilities can be analysed by various classifications of programme output.

(d) Remake and repeat figures. Statistics on the number of programmes remade each year are of obvious importance for evaluation. If the remake facility is not used, much of the formative evaluation effort will have been wasted. In fact, programmes can be categorised in four ways: new programmes in new series; remade programmes within a continuing series; programmes repeated within the year; programmes repeated from previous years. Statistics should indicate the proportion of programmes in each category, in each of the programme classifications.

(e) Delivery, maintenance and repairs. The maintenance service will need to keep its own records regarding costs and manpower usage. Regional centres and offices should, therefore, provide statistics on the number of particular items of equipment needing repair, the number of

repairs carried out on the spot by mobile repair vans, the types of repairs that have to be made at the local centres and the cost of spares as a proportion of the total value of the equipment available in the region.

(f) Budgetary analysis. This is perhaps the most difficult area of all for evaluation: obtaining figures for costs in such a way that expenditure is allocated in a realistic and meaningful way between different headings. However, if a reasonable classification of programmes can be produced, and if production costs between various media and programme areas can be meaningfully separated, then it should be possible to relate costs to output, and to measure with some degree of accuracy the amount being spent on each kind of programme and each kind of audience.

These are only examples of the kinds of data that are required; the list is not intended to be comprehensive. If special enquiries are foreseen (e.g. on the internal functioning of a particular aspect of the service, say convertibility between film and studio facilities) additional information will have to be collected. But as far as possible, a complete set of routine statistics should be gathered, decided at the time of the service's inauguration, and these can be supplemented for special needs as they arise.

2. Surveys and questionnaires

From time to time, and particularly before the inception of a media service, a general survey of viewing and listening habits should be carried out (which can be updated every few years). This is especially important in the area of adult and informal education, where regular contact with the audience is more difficult to obtain on a statistical basis.

A base-line survey will also be required of all schools and institutions in the system, giving numbers, classes, information about audio-visual equipment, etc. (this will be used as a coding base for surveys which follow).

Apart from these general surveys, special surveys will also have to be arranged; for example, when there are proposals to serve a new audience, or to introduce a new series. In the school sector (and as far as possible in the formal adult sector) regular weekly questionnaire surveys should ideally be undertaken, to provide an ongoing picture of media use and satisfaction. In a small environment this is easily achieved: the audience can be approached directly, either in person or through a form of questionnaire. In larger communities the problem is different, as the audience will be too large to deal with individually, and even questionnaires, if returned regularly each week, would bulk too large to be handled by other than a large and computerised staff. A sample is therefore required.

If possible, this sample should be statistically based, though even random returns are better than nothing. It is difficult, for example, for a national organisation such as the BBC to administer questionnaires to a controlled sample of schools; the form of the educational system militates against such an approach, being decentralised. In a single city, however, where there is only one education authority at work, or in a university, or even in a nation state (provided educational control is centralised), statistical organisation is quite possible. Each week, or month, if preferred, a representative sample of schools is asked to complete a questionnaire on programmes seen, and to return it to the evaluation unit. The sample can rotate, so that each school is involved only a few times each year, but there are two preconditions which must be met if the system is to yield valid results. The sample itself must be properly selected; and the returns must be as near 100 per cent as possible.

The first condition is a matter of technique, and a statistician is best employed. The principles involved in random sampling are straightforward enough. Say, for the sake of argument, that the total universe (i.e. the complete viewing audience) is made up of 160 schools. A one-in-four sample (of forty schools) would be sufficient to ensure valid results. If questionnaires were to be distributed weekly to such a sample (changing regularly), each school would be required to make returns only three times over a 12-week term. This serves two purposes: schools are not over-whelmed with demands from the service, and at the same time the volume of returns is not too great for the evaluation unit to handle.

To take a one-in-four sample from 160 schools, a list of *all* schools is arranged in random order (alphabetical order will do in this case, provided schools of a similar type are not grouped together). A starting point has to be chosen within the numerical range of one to four: any number lower than four will do. Say the starting point three is picked; the sample will then consist of the third school on the list and every fourth school there-after. This will yield a sample of forty schools, to which the first week's questionnaire can be administered. The following week, the sample will change. It will consist of the fourth school on the list, and every fourth school thereafter. The next week, it will be the first school (and every four following); the final week, the second school (and every four following). The cycle is now complete, and we return to the original sample. A principle of rotation has been established; and the results derived from these questionnaires, taken over a whole term or year, can be taken as reasonably representative of the entire school population. (The cycle of four is not invariable, of course: it is only used to achieve a one-in-four sample. For a one-in-six sample, a cycle of six is needed, and so on. The main reservation is that the sample should be large enough to be properly representative, and this will in turn depend upon the total number of schools in the 'universe'. The smaller the sample, the more important it becomes to achieve near-100 per cent returns.)

Regularity of returns is more difficult to achieve. Drop-outs can be written to or telephoned, to remind them that they have questionnaires outstanding, but in the end regularity will depend on the priority placed upon the system by the audience itself. Part of the remedy lies in utilisa-tion courses run by the service. The evaluation system must be explained, and its contribution emphasised. The attitude of the education authority is

Table 19.1 Evaluation questions and coded responses

1. Rate the level of attainment of the viewing class in regard to the subject Good Average Poor	6. What is your evaluation of the logical sequences of teaching points? Good Satisfactory Poor
2. Rate the level of attainment of the viewing class in relation to the Ministry's syllabus for this subject At the level of school syllabus Above the level of school syllabus Below the level of school syllabus	7. How were the individual teaching points handled? Completely adequately Fairly adequately Inadequately
3. Was the sound clear throughout the broadcast? Clear throughout Clear sometimes Not clear throughout	8. Were the illustrations effective? Yes No — they were too crowded No — they changed too fast No — some lacked precision No — too crowded and too fast No — too fast and lack of accuracy No — too crowded and lacked accuracy No — too crowded, too fast and lacked accuracy
4. Was the vision clear throughout the broadcast? Clear throughout Clear sometimes Not clear throughout	9. Were the visual materials well integrated into the lesson? Very well integrated Fairly well integrated Poorly integrated
5. Were there sufficient teaching points? Sufficient Too many Too few	10. Was the pace of the lesson correct? Yes No, too fast No, too slow

also crucial. A clear hint that the return of evaluation questionnaires is considered as important as, say, compiling school registers, is likely to improve reactions.

The *form* of the evaluation return is likewise a matter for an expert, especially when relatively complex questions are to be put. Questions have to be framed unambiguously, and in such a way that responses are easy to tabulate. Open-ended questions may be asked occasionally, but they cannot easily be assessed statistically, as 'Yes/No' or scaled responses can be. If, for example, the codes 'Very Good/Good/Average/Fair/Poor' have been allocated to a particular question, the total number of responses for each code can be tabulated, and a percentage result derived. The codes are generally comparable right across the responding schools. An open-ended question (with a blank left to fill, rather than a particular response to tick or ring) is of a different order. How is the evaluator to measure one subjective response against another?

Table 19.1 — *continued*

11. Was the level of the lesson
    suitable?
    Yes
    No, level too high
    No, level too low

12. Was the level of the language
    used correct?
    Yes
    No, too advanced
    No, too simple

13. How do you rate the presenter?
    Excellent
    Good
    Fair
    Poor

14. How would you evaluate the
    pupils' interest in this
    programme?
    Interest sustained throughout
    Interest on and off
    Not interested

15. What is your overall assessment
    of the programme?
    Very good
    Good
    Average
    Poor

16. In what ways can the Teachers'
    Notes be improved upon?
    Notes very good as presented
    Should be simplified
    Should be explained more clearly
    Should be amplified
    Should be simplified and
        explained more clearly
    Should be explained more
        clearly and amplified

17. How is this lesson related to the
    school syllabuses?
    Well related
    Fairly well related
    Remotely related
    Unrelated

18. What is the level of the lesson in
    relation to the school syllabuses?
    At the level
    Above the level
    Below the level

19. Were you able to integrate this
    lesson into your classwork?
    Yes – easily
    Yes – with difficulty
    No – programme cannot be fitted
        into my scheme of work
    Class level is such that it is not
        possible to integrate
    Material not in syllabus
    Too much material to be
        integrated effectively

When the number of questions asked is extended, and the audience sample is both large and regular, it is obviously preferable to use some form of mechanical sorting to tabulate responses, and the evaluation proforma reproduced (Table 19.1) is specifically designed for mechanical or electronic tabulation. A study of this document (evolved in Singapore) should illustrate some of the pitfalls involved in pre-coding questions of relative complexity (for example, in assessing the relationship of programmes to a general school syllabus or curriculum). There has been a consistent attempt to enumerate a whole range of possible responses, so that many shades of opinion can be registered by a simple tick. The approach is limited; it does not register minute variations, and the categories are not strictly comparable (the actual choice of response, after all, is still subjective), but it does provide the best available estimate of *total* audience reaction.

It is important to be quite sure of the limits of the questionnaire.

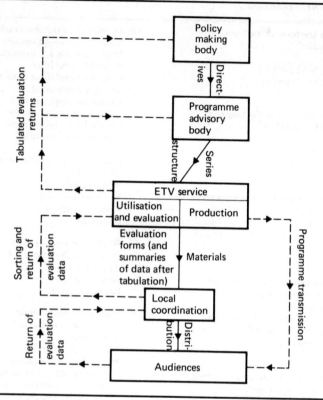

Fig. 19.1   The evaluation process

Specifically, the collective view of the whole audience on a number of subjects is being sought: subjective niceties are ignored in the interests of representativeness. Anyone devising an evaluation pro-forma must therefore ask himself: What are the main things I want to know? and also, What range of responses can there be to my question? All likely variants should be accounted for in the questionnaire — and for this reason the pro-forma must be vetted extensively before it is used, and piloted experimentally. In questions where more than a 'Yes/No' response is being sought, it is better to add a coding 'Any other reason' (with a blank space left below, where the reason can be explained), as well as all the other permutations. This, at least, will allow for the unexpected.

In principle, evaluation by questionnaire is a cyclic phenomenon, and the outlines of the cycle are shown in Fig. 19.1.

3. Performance testing

Performance and ability tests will obviously form a part of any research studies conducted in association with the media, if these are concerned with an analysis of learning gains, but apart from this there are both advantages and disadvantages in including performance testing in the regular schools' reporting system. The main advantage is that if there are tests on the broadcast material, teachers and pupils are likely to take the broadcasts more seriously. Tests are also useful because they allow the teacher to identify more easily the major points of the programmes, enabling him to plan follow-up activities if there are obvious weaknesses. Also, of course, if the students' answers to the tests are sent back to the programme designers, the data can be used for indicating areas in the programmes or materials, which need improvement in subsequent years.

There are also considerable disadvantages and difficulties. The tests must be designed well in advance of the actual transmissions, and they will add considerably to the workload of those responsible for the design of programmes, and to the teachers who will have to administer and mark the tests. Some programmes will not be appropriate for testing, particularly if multiple-response 'closed' tests are given. Furthermore, it will not always be clear whether score distributions will be due to the quality of the programme or the quality of the questions, since pre-testing of items, and tests of item reliability, will be difficult and extremely expensive for any meaningful coverage. Cost in fact is the main problem. It is recommended that a regular system of performance testing is first piloted on one or two programme series, to see if it can be extended to the rest of the system at a reasonable cost.

4. Direct observation

The statistical approach is acknowledgedly limited; it will list reactions, but it will not interpret them. For this purpose, other means must be found.

(a) Individual or group discussions. A useful technique for originating ideas about programmes is for an observer to hear (or view) a programme with a listener or group of listeners, in their own environment, and then discuss the programme immediately afterwards. These discussions may be carried out by school and adult education supervisors as well as by special media evaluators or producers. This method, which involves only a small number of discussions on any programme, should always be used in combination with other methods.

(b) Direct observation and personal interviews. Especially for teacher preparation and utilisation of broadcasts, direct observation will be necessary, accompanied by follow-up interviews. Since mainly quantitative information will be needed, it will be desirable to use large numbers of supervisors, and pre-designed forms, which can if possible be processed centrally by computer. The standard form could include the following types of questions:

- School and teacher details
- No of pupils in class
- Quality of reception
- Whether the radio or TV was ready and working
- Evidence of teacher's preparation
- Evidence of teacher's follow-up
- Evidence of pupils' participation during programme
- Evidence of pupils' participation after programme
- Whether teacher trained in utilisation
- Difficulties encountered during broadcast
- Attitudes of teachers and pupils to broadcast
- Whether teacher would use the programme next year
- How could the programme be improved

The last four questions which are open-ended need not be processed, but the answers can be given directly to the producers of the specific programme series. These 100 or so reports can provide them with invaluable information for remaking programmes.

Producers should also be encouraged (instructed if necessary; they are often reluctant) to visit the receiving end of their work. When they do so, they can report in the same manner.

5. Content analysis of programmes

Two criteria which are difficult to measure by surveys or official statistics are those concerned with the range of programme formats (used as a test of imaginative and appropriate programming), and those concerned with the teaching style used within programme materials. Thus special content analysis techniques have to be used for these purposes (classifications, according to predetermined criteria, of programme content). They concern:

(a) *Programme format.*   An examination is necessary of the relationship between programme format and levels of interest and learning. Two assumptions can be made, both of which will require testing for validity. The first is that a variety of programme formats within a series will lead to increased interest and learning; secondly that certain programme formats are more appropriate for some subject areas than for others. This kind of evaluation may be particularly important in a situation where new methods of teaching are needed, particularly in adult education, where it is important to find ways of interesting adults sufficiently strong to compete with alternative sources of entertainment.

(b) *Teaching style.*   It is often mooted that a major objective for a media system is to support curriculum innovation by encouraging rational and critical thinking, and that this may be carried out by incorporating into the programmes teaching styles which encourage individualised learning, small group learning, increased teacher:pupil and pupil:teacher interaction, and so on. One of the aims of content analysis is then to discover whether programmes actually do encourage such teaching styles.

For both these forms of analysis, there are certain requirements. Scripts for all programmes will be needed, or at least kept available, and preferably tapes of each radio and television programme.

Degrees of sophistication

Not all these forms of evaluation can be attempted at once; they need to be scaled according to the scope of the media operation, its resources, and above all its functional needs.

The reader who is interested in evaluation techniques would do well to refer to the report by Mayo, Hornik and McAnany on El Salvador, and to Gerald Lesser's survey of 'Sesame Street' (see Bibliography, p. 363). In these books he will find not only a highly readable account of process, but also examples of more sophisticated methodologies than are employed, say, in the questionnaire design of Fig. 19.1. But these refer to evaluation projects conducted by professional, external bodies, such as are unlikely to be available in the developing world (let alone the finance to employ them). El Salvador was fortunate in that its development was monitored for 5 years by members of Stanford University's Institute for Communication Research, who were interested in answers to questions far more wide-ranging than simple learning gain or programme appeal. The Children's Television Workshop had its own research department, but the summative evaluation of the series was carried out externally by the Educational Testing Service of Princeton University.

The emerging media service has to look first at what its needs really are, and correlate these with the resources which it thinks it can obtain. In such cases, the most likely need, and the most beneficial approach, is for formative research: research which is pragmatic, an integral part of the creative production process, highly compatible with the practice of defining instructional objectives precisely, and highly economic — because it aims to correct error *before* it is finally compounded into a production and distribution process.

Evaluation as a process

Although various techniques of evaluation have been described, we must remember that they are all part of a common process, which is in turn part of the overall media system. The tools, in other words, do not exist in their own right; they are means by which some of the fundamental questions posed by planners, producers and educators can be answered. The most important condition is, therefore, that the right questions should be asked — and this in turn comes back to the process by which media objectives and targets are derived through a corporate planning process. In this process, the user must never be forgotten. Not only should evaluation returns be published for the audience to see, but summaries of basic statistics should also be available, in a convenient pamphlet form, for all system users to consult as and when they are interested to do so.

Research

If we make a distinction between evaluation and research, this is mainly a distinction of convenience; both use the same methods and techniques, but from a different perspective. Evaluation seeks a continuous monitoring of the media system; research tries to answer specific queries, or concentrate upon a special subject, problem or audience.

Research is, in this case, particularly concerned with new developments, with areas of experimentation, or fields where insufficient is known upon which to base planning strategies. Some characteristic areas might be:

(a) *Studies of new utilisation approaches to media* — through distance learning systems, the use of media in non-formal education classes, the retraining of a teaching force with media assistance, etc. In such cases, the emphasis is upon deploying media in innovative ways, not so much upon their inherent characteristics.

(b) *Depth studies of media used within local communities*, as in the forms of community media. These are micro studies, in which interactions within a specific environment are being scrutinised, not generalised approaches across a whole system.

(c) *Studies of new applications of technology*, such as might occur with the introduction or videocassettes into a secondary school system. When such an innovation is contemplated, there will be many experimental snags — of technology, or organisation, of teacher attitude, of maintenance — all of which need to be smoothed out in pilot circumstances before large-scale expansion is contemplated.

(d) *Studies of media integration.* Particularly in mass media systems, where the broadcast media are often seen at a tangent to lower cost, local resource materials, a good deal of experimental work is needed to see how the two can interface. This equally requires work at a pilot level, using a limited number of schools, teachers and classes to evaluate alternate designs.

(e) *Studies of management and organisation.* A media service, or a communication system, needs to be evaluated to see whether it is really using appropriate organisational forms and structures. In particular, this includes course team planning methods.

(f) Studies of programme format and technique. As has been pointed out on several occasions in this handbook, there is still relatively little research data on what techniques are suitable for the presentation of what concepts, or appropriate to which learning tasks.

(g) Studies of learning behaviour. Although such studies are an accepted part of educational psychology, the involvement of media is by no means as accepted.

(h) Studies of socio-cultural effects. There are many studies of the impact of general communications media on society, fewer of the impact of educational media systems, especially when these are directed towards general adult populations.

(i) Studies of user and learner difficulty. Again, this is familiar territory for the educational psychologist, but not so much so in connection with mediated learning.

(j) Studies of user attitudes. If there is resistance to the use of media in education, from what circumstances do these difficulties derive? What means can be devised to overcome them?

Once again, this is not a comprehensive list, but if it is compared with the brief account of educational media research offered in Part 2 of this handbook, or with fuller research compilations, we can see how many gaps still exist in our knowledge.

The relative failure of evaluation

Why do so many gaps exist? And why has evaluation, in the past, made so little difference to media development? The Stanford authors, whose report to Unesco has already been quoted, see the answer to this question in these terms:

What studies there have been cluster into three basic groups. The largest group has been largely judgemental or subjective. An outside expert is asked to examine a project in a few days or weeks. He visits a few schools, catalogues facilities, speaks to some of the people involved, and sometimes obtains cost estimates. Such an approach may prove useful in many ways, depending on the ability and experience of the expert, but it rarely helps a project director to improve his system. A second and more sophisticated approach incorporates some attempt to measure effects. Its methods may include comparative before-and-after studies of short term learning or, more often, surveys of teachers' attitudes about a course or a television series. These results can be fed back to programme administrators or producers, but often they are of little use in suggesting pragmatic changes and may irritate rather than guide producers. The third and rarest type of approach consists of rigorous attempts to understand the functioning of an educational technology system. Here measures of effects are combined with analysis of the processes by which those effects were produced.

One of the reasons why there have been few evaluations of media systems in the past is perhaps that, in retrospect, there have been few users of the evaluations that have been done, and the information gathered in even the best formative or summative studies has rarely affected decisions in an important way.

One can point to several reasons why this is the case. First, the focus of study has more often than not been defined by the evaluator and not the decision-maker. Evaluations are often exercises planned by an academic with little empathy for the needs of a manager. Secondly, because administrators and programme producers are customarily under heavy day-to-day pressures to meet schedules, their receptivity to learning results from programmes broadcast weeks or months previously is likely to be quite low. Any information which does not respond to the priority concern of getting a programme prepared on time is apt to be ignored. The third reason is simply that evaluations are threatening. While the evaluator may claim that he is objectively evaluating a system and not individuals, those individuals justifiably assume that they will be accountable for any negative result.

Evaluators must respond to the concerns of decision-makers and report results in ways that bear directly on the latter's decision alternatives. Programme producers must be granted more time and encouraged to use evaluation results to improve the quality of their broadcasts. At the same time evaluators should recognise the real limits of time and action of producers and design their formative evaluations to fit within those constraints. Finally, project administrators must introduce a climate in which teaching effectiveness has first priority both as a general system goal and as a criterion for judging the success of the producing organisation and its personnel. Too often the responsibility of a production center ends when the programme is on tape and ready for broadcast. In broadening the concept of producer accountability to encompass what results in the classroom, the administrator must recognise that success and failure, while not divorced from the action of individuals, have multiple causes. Evaluation can best serve the principle of accountability only if it is used to improve programme effectiveness and not to lay blame at the feet of the easiest target.

Conclusion

This handbook has attempted, in a limited compass, to give an up-to-date commentary on the state of educational mass media, in terms which can be useful to planner, administrator, producer and user alike. Inevitably, in many cases it must fail, because it was bound to conduct the discussion at a number of different levels. It began with a scale of innovation, showing a wide variety in different parts of the world, and especially between industrialised and developed countries. It continued with a scale of function, attempting to argue positions which hold good for all media, whether used nationally, regionally or locally, but also to differentiate between them where there are significant differences of approach.

Partly, if there is disunity in the result, it is endemic to the mass media, which progress haphazardly, not in systematic order. Yet it is to be hoped that, from this discussion, one trend emerges — an attempt, in most places, to come to terms with media by recognising that they will be as good, not only as their productions, but as the use to which they are put. In this attempt, principles of rational planning, the synthesis of many disciplines and group activity are the most important factors. We would never wish to see identical uses of media common throughout the world, but a greater identity of purpose, and a greater reliance on systematic tools of analysis, would certainly not come amiss.

In many ways, the writing of this handbook has been easier than its predecessor (*Planning for ETV*) in spite of the much greater volume of experience and information available, because the character of media technology and its application is more coherent than 5 years ago. There has also been a marked increase in experimental work, and a greater willingness to evaluate, and report on, what is being done. Hopefully by the time that the book is updated, the task will be easier still.

Appendix:
Characteristic media installations

In the previous volume, *Planning for ETV*, the Appendix 'Characteristic ETV Installations' gave sample ranges of equipment, staffing lists, organisational structures and facilities layouts for a number of different environments, as a guide to the planner. This was probably useful; certainly the author has since had a good deal of opportunity to put the recommendations into practice, and to see how and where they are viable.

The present Appendix, however, is of a different character. Most of the discussion of ideal models has been conducted in the main body of this handbook, related to a variety of media beyond television. Here the intention is to give an account of real-life situations in a number of locations, where planners have had, of necessity, to come to grips with political and economic pressures.

Accordingly, in the next few pages, brief descriptions are offered of characteristic media services. The contexts chosen are at the *institutional* (college and university) level, that of the *community* or small city, the *city state*, and the *nation*. Also included in the national category is a distance learning system which employs media among its teaching tools.

Information is summarised in note form under the following headings:

(i) *Organisation*
(ii) *Staffing*
(iii) *Facilities and equipment*
(iv) *Output*
(v) *Audience*
(vi) *Recurrent expenditures*

The comparisons offered are therefore of a factual and logistical kind, and do not attempt to gauge quality or evaluate success. Examples are based upon data furnished by a number of services (from both the developed and the developing world), and although identities are not quoted, and in some cases figures have been rounded up, or situations simplified in the interests of intelligibility, realism is always maintained.

In the final part of the Appendix, some discussion is offered of the main drawbacks experienced by these services, or inherent in their structures and facilities, as well as of the reasons behind the limitations. The summary is then compared, briefly, with the planning model of educational mass media in Thailand already discussed.

It should be noted that the information given in this Appendix is drawn from sources consulted during the year *1974/5*. No attempt has been made to update examples since that time, particularly in relation to costs, in view of unpredictable trends in the world economy.

1. The institutional level

(A) A university media service in a developing country

(i) Organisation

The first example quoted is of an educational media centre, serving education and communication faculties in a developing country. This centre provides media services to the university as a whole, including advice on the purchase of equipment and materials, and also offers training facilities for educational technology and for communication students.

The Service is part, administratively, of a School of Education, but policy is formulated by a Media Advisory Committee, which is a Committee of the Vice Chancellor, representing all faculties.

(ii) Staffing

Head	1
Senior production and academic staff	4
Administrative coordinator	1
Engineer	1
Technical staff	11
Film/photographic technician	1
Library assistant	1
Designer and graphics artist	1
Clerks	2
Secretary/typists	2
General	2
Total	27

(iii) Facilities and equipment

The Centre is housed in a purpose-designed building, with one CCTV studio and control room, a radio studio and control room, associated technical areas, graphics and scenic service workshops, viewing theatre, library and review booths, classrooms and a lecture theatre, an audio visual laboratory and administrative areas.

There are three pedestal/tripod mounted plumbicon cameras (monochrome), telecine and slide projectors (with multiplexer) and a vision mixing unit with a special effects facility. Recording is carried out on 1 inch videotape machines (with electronic editing).

For audio work, the sound studio has a modular six-channel mixing unit, and a full range of microphones.

There is a selection of photographic and film equipment (for mute filming only), and a good supply of portable audio-visual equipment, including audio and video-recorders and videocassettes.

No distribution system is provided: transmissions can either be over an internal CCTV system within the Centre itself (with several fixed monitors), or materials can be taken by van to the desired location on the campus.

(iv) Output

TV programmes (courses)	3 per week
TV programmes (commissioned)	3 per week
Radio programmes (courses)	5 per week
Radio programmes (commissioned)	4 per week
Equipment loan to staff/students	50 items per week
Materials loan to teacher trainees	200 items per week
Photographic service	12 commissions per week
Audio tape duplication	200 items per week
Graphics and illustration service	8 commissions per week
Projection/viewing service	11 commissions per week
Teaching load (all staff)	37 hours per week

(v) Audience

Total audience	1,966 students
	275 academic staff
Specific courses	240 students follow a basic course in educational resources
	34 education students follow a special course
	46 communication students follow a special course

(vi) Recurrent expenditure

	(US $)
Staff	68,566
Materials	31,343
Maintenance	40,298
General	1,343
Total	$141,550

(B) A university television service in a developed country

(i) Organisation

The Centre is supervised by a Director, who is advised (on policy issues) by a committee which includes representatives of the University Senate and of the University's Governing Body. Day-to-day coordination is handled personally and informally, with the Director approaching university departments or faculty members directly, and not through formal committee channels.

(ii) Staffing

Director	1
Production Staff	3
Technical Supervisor	1
Technical Staff	11
Graphics	1
Photographic	1
Film	3
Administrative Supervisor	1
Clerical	3
General	3
Total	28

(iii) Facilities and equipment

The Centre has a three-camera facility (vidicon cameras, operating in monochrome), with the possibility of a fourth camera as and when required. Operation is from a specially converted studio; it is equipped with multiplexed 16 mm telecine, slide and scanner, and the vision mixing unit has a special effects bank. Recording is mainly on 1 inch machines, though one 2 inch transverse scan model is available. Experimental work with videocassettes is also taking place.

A distribution system connects the Centre to main lecture rooms and display areas, using a radio frequency system. A large stock of video monitors has been acquired, some of which are permanently installed (in high user locations), and others available on demand. A mobile unit is also available, with three vidicon cameras and control and recording facilities. This is a small mini-bus, designed to be as unobtrusive as possible.

Film facilities are available for colour working, including animation and dubbing; the only facility not offered is film processing.

The radio studio is small and self-operated, and is mainly used for commentary purposes, but more recently has also been used for interview and 'built' programming.

(iv) Output

Production of new TV recordings	93 annually
Production of new audio recordings (with other projected aids)	54 annually
Lecturing by television	208 hours annually
Transmission of recorded programmes via cable system	1,094 programmes annually

(v) Audience

Student numbers	9,000
Number of teaching departments	110
Departments regularly using TV	50

(vi) Recurrent expenditure	(US $)
Staff costs	124,200
Materials	12,650
Maintenance	9,200
Equipment	21,850
Fees and hire	1,150
Rental of cable system	11,500
Other	2,300
Total	$182,850

2. The community or small city level

(A) A local authority television service in a developed country

(i) Organisation

The Educational Television Service works as an independent unit, under its own Director, as one of the resource providers to the local education authority, by which it is financed. It shares facilities, and a good deal of equipment and expertise, with a polytechnic, which has a strong interest in electronic and electrical engineering.

There is a core staff of technical and support specialists, but producers are normally on secondment from the local teaching force. The main purpose of the service has been to complement national broadcasting services, providing an educational service to teachers, emphasising local subjects (and local elements and interpretations of other subjects) and coordinating wherever possible with other educational providers. There is a particular emphasis on innovation, with plans made (limited by finances at present) for the development of multi-media and community services touching a wider field than television, and a wider audience than the in-school segment.

(ii) Staffing

Director	1
Educational controller	1
Head of production	1
Head of graphics	1
Head of film	1
Chief engineer	1
Teacher/producers	3
Technical staff	4
Film technician	1
Graphics technician	1
Secretary	1
Total	16

(iii) Facilities and equipment

A single studio is equipped for both monochrome and colour operation, with both audio and video-recording facilities. As the studio is in an engineering centre, it is well placed for technical maintenance; it is also well equipped for film work, with shooting, editing and animation facilities. A good range of graphics is also available. The studio, although small, is professionally designed, with a flexible lighting system, and a three-camera operation.

Transmission is over a rented cable network serving the immediate environment; materials are also despatched physically.

(iv) Output

Sixty to seventy television programmes are produced each year, together with slide, tape/slide, audio tape, film and printed materials.

Transmissions provide eleven series per term (approximately seventy programmes), plus a record/replay service of network programmes for schools with timetabling difficulties.

A videocassette loan service is also operated for schools without a landline connection.

(v) Audience

Viewers	9,305
Viewing schools	62
Viewing groups	393

(vi) Recurrent costs

	(US $)
Staff costs	94,438
Building rental and services	3,128
Production costs	21,528
Network and receiver hire	52,497
General	1,955
Total	$173,546

(B) A community media resource centre in a developed country

(i) Organisation

The Centre is registered as a non-profit making association, with group and individual members and a Board of Directors (made up of community representatives), which formulates policy. The Board also appoints the professional Director, who in turn makes permanent staff appointments (subject to ratification by the Board).

The association offers:

(a) A *media resource centre*, with library facilities (for both hardware and software), and video and audio workspace.

(b) A *community development programme*, which conducts training programmes, and offers technical advice to community groups.

(c) An *experimental production centre*, for the preparation of low-cost materials (to order, and independently).

The Media Resource Centre is accommodated in rented premises; it has a deliberately small core staff, and depends heavily upon voluntary assistance from community groups and inviduals.

(ii) Staffing

Information and training officers	3
Producers	2
Community development workers	3
External relations director	1
Total	9

Secretarial and administrative staff recruited locally on contract basis.

(iii) Facilities and equipment

The Centre is housed in a converted building, with some specific technical areas (e.g. for VTR, audio and photographic work), but mostly arranged as workrooms.

The emphasis is upon easy-to-use, inexpensive equipment, including portable video equipment, audio equipment and a range of photographic and graphic production and display items.

There are six portapaks, three monochrome videotape recorders (with monitors, and electronic editing facilities), and a total of ten audio recorders (half cassette, half open-reel). Audio mixing is also possible and there is a small sound booth. The equipment is used by production staff to generate materials, especially of the experimental variety, but at any given time, half is on loan to community groups.

Two utility trucks are available, which are used for location work.

Some limited work on Super-8 is also carried out, but the main emphasis is on video activity. Distribution is by physical means: some materials are broadcast on local stations, others borrowed for display.

(iv) Output and (v) Audience

Output is not measured primarily in numerical terms, as the Centre's principal purpose is to stimulate community groups in production and utilisation in their own right. However, up to 500 'programme' items in various media are now generated annually, apart from a weekly schedule of workshops and seminars, ranging from equipment instruction to open-ended discussions of media use. The library already has a good stock of materials in all media, an information service, and over 150 groups and individuals are listed as members of the association.

A basic library is proposed as follows, for long-term build-up:

Books and periodicals	4,500
Videotapes	3,000
Audiotapes	800
Slide sets and other materials	6,000
Films	800

Of these, 65 per cent are to be locally produced.

(vi) Recurrent expenditure	(US $)
Regular staff costs	117,000
Other staff costs	20,000
Rent and utilities	19,300
Travel	13,000
Training	8,000
Maintenance	14,700
Insurance and depreciation	26,200
Materials	14,100
Administrative and communications	13,400
Total	$245,700

3. The city state level

(A) An island republic media service in a developing country

(i) Organisation

The Service is an independent section of the Ministry of Education, with policy and programme decisions guided by both an overall Advisory Committee and separate subject committees (all of which have teacher representation, as well as educational specialists, members of the Inspectorate and curriculum advisers). Originally a television service, though working within stringent financial limits, it has broadened its activity base to include the production of audio materials (for tape distribution, not for broadcasting), print and supporting audio visual materials, and a library service to schools, as well as a complementary development of learning resource centres, catering for teacher involvement in the production of low cost instructional aids. Emphasis is upon curriculum renewal and support.

The Service has also made preliminary forays into the area of adult and non-formal education, and is now linking its work with a regional agency for the production of adult television and film programmes. Plans have been prepared for a fully integrated media service, covering all media and levels of audience.

(ii) Staffing

Head	1
Deputy head	2
Senior engineer	1
Programme facilities organiser	1
Senior producers	2
Producers	4
Production and research assistants	12
Media specialists	4
Executive officer	1
Senior graphics artists	1
Graphic artist	3
Technical staff	6
Studio staff	6
Photographic staff	3
Administrative and clerical staff	7
General	8
Total	62

(iii) Facilities and equipment

The Centre operates from converted premises, and offers a two-camera (plumbicon) television studio, with telecine chain (16 mm film and slides). Recording is on two 2 inch transverse scan machines, with electronic editing; there are also 16 mm film facilities (shooting, editing and simple dubbing), a graphics workshop, photographic and support services. A comprehensive film and audio-visual library is maintained (both for production and for library use), and an audio dubbing room is available, which can be used as a small radio studio. All programmes are recorded for transmission by the main broadcasting organisation, to whom complete programme tapes are delivered.

(iv) Output

TV Production   17 Primary series (each of 15 minutes)
                  10 Secondary series (each of 20 minutes)
                    1 Pre-university series (of 45 minutes each)
Total about 300 programmes annually, with full support materials.

(v) Audience

Users of television	130,000 primary students
	70,000 secondary students
Users of all media	500,000 students

(vi) Recurrent expenditure

	(US $)
Staff costs	330,601
Programmes	36,000
Maintenance	18,000

Printing	22,500
Building rental	41,742
Utilities	6,480
Audio-visual aids	9,000
Travel	1,800
Office supplies	1,215
Other supplies and materials	765
Office furniture and equipment	2,286
Sundry	1,629
Total	$472,018

(B) A city state television system in a developing country

(i) *Organisation*

The Service is part of the Education Department, under its own Director; it is advised by Teachers' Committees on the planning of curricula, and by the Inspectorate on the suitability of programmes. The service is unusual in that it began at the primary level; it has since consolidated its experience, but has been unable to expand into the secondary sector, or to diversify its programming as it would wish. Although it produces print support materials, it has also not been able to move into multi-media work.

(ii) *Staffing*

Head	1
Assistant head	1
Senior engineer	1
Administrative supervisor	1
Producers	12
Station engineer	1
Technical staff	14
Production assistants	12
Graphics staff	6
Film and photographic staff	4
Administrative and secretarial	14
Carpenters	4
Electricians	3
General	12
Total	86

(iii) *Facilities and equipment*

The Centre is housed in a purpose-designed two-storey building. It has two studios, of which only one (the larger) is currently equipped, pending decisions on expansion. The studio is fitted with three image-orthicon cameras (monochrome), a grid lighting system and pedestal mountings. It has a multiplexed telecine facility, with two 16 mm film projectors, film strip projector, caption scanner and caption roller; the vision mixing unit has a thirteen-effect special effects generator. There is a range of film graphics and photographic equipment (including an animation bench). Recording is on three 2-inch videotape machines.

Programmes are broadcast by local commercial broadcasting companies, for which purpose special legislation was introduced: the Centre is connected by cable to each of these services.

(iv) Output

Annual production	120 new programmes of 15 minutes duration
	100 remade programmes of 15 minutes duration
Transmissions	Eight hours daily for 32 weeks in the year, from Monday to Friday

(v) Audience

Total number of children	400,000
Total number of teachers	10,000

(vi) Recurrent expenditure

	(US$)
Staff	459,701
Administration	32,388
Equipment and stores	66,155
Programmes	31,343
Transport and travel	3,239
General	14,104
Total	$606,930

4. The national level

(A) A national multi-media service in a developing country

(i) Organisation

The Service is an integral part of the Ministry of Education, and was originally formed by the amalgamation of existing school radio and audio-visual departments with a newly formed educational television section. The work of these three sections is integrated, with a common administrative and utilisation and evaluation unit.

Overall planning and policy-making is vested in an Advisory Committee chaired by the Director General of Education, with representatives of all divisions in the Ministry of Education, and nominees from other co-operating Ministries. Programme planning is through programme and subject committees, with specialist and teacher representation. A particular emphasis of the Service is on the introduction and support of new curricula.

(ii) Staffing

Director	1
Deputy director	1
Assistant director	4
TV production staff	22
Film and photographic	10
Design and graphics	10
Publications	2
Utilisation and evaluation	2
Research and training	2
Radio production staff	38
AV production staff	3
Technical staff	40
Administrative and secretarial	20
Subject specialists	7
General and manual	7
Total	169

(iii) Facilities and equipment

Pending the completion of a new purpose-built Centre, production is carried out in the radio and television studios of the parent organisation (a State-run broadcasting service). Additionally separate film shooting, some editing and animation facilities are available to the service, as well as graphic and photographic work.

The new Centre, now under construction, has two television and two radio studios (professionally equipped), and a very comprehensive range of technical, production support and audio-visual facilities.

(iv) Output

TV programmes	30 per week
Radio programmes	64 per week
Transmission hours — TV, 34 hours	
— Radio, 40 hours	

(v) Audience

Number of pupils viewing TV	490,135
Number of pupils listening to radio	304,068
Number of schools with TV sets	2,918
Number of schools with radio sets	1,573

(vi) Recurrent expenditure

	(US $)
Staff costs	360,000
Supplies and materials	110,598
Rental and hire	243,000
Printing	89,458
Travel and transport	23,946

Fees (artists), scriptwriters, etc.)	135,777
Furniture and equipment	10,460
General	3,507
Total	$976,746

(B) An open learning system in a developed country

(i) Organisation

The system is concerned with university level and post-experience courses, based on correspondence education and multi-media programmes. For this purpose, a new university has been created, but media production is entrusted to the national broadcasting organisation, which works in partnership with the University. Budgeting is centralised, coming from the country's Department of Education and Science, and channelled through the University administration.

The media component is produced by a special unit within the parent broadcasting organisation, with its own facilities. The educational broadcasting controller is a member of the University Council, and media representatives sit on all main advisory committees. Programme planning is a part of integrated course planning, achieved through course teams, based on university faculties.

(ii) Staffing

Management and administration	20
Production staff	62
Design and scenic servicing	32
Film (excluding outside hire)	14
Engineering (excluding crews on rota from parent service)	8
Administrative and secretarial	74
General and junior staff (cleaning, catering, house staff, etc.)	140
Total	350

(iii) Facilities and equipment

Facilities are contained in a renovated studio complex, with one TV studio (colour-equipped, three cameras), two radio studios (one of which is self-operated) and an outside broadcast mobile unit, with self-contained VTR (2-inch transverse scan). A video rostrum area is available for still and animated caption sequences; there are five film-cutting rooms, shooting, dubbing and review facilities. Full scenic, graphic and photographic facilities are available, and the Centre can also draw on its parent service for more complex requirements.

Recordings are made on the premises; transmission is via the parent organisation's country-wide transmission network, with some physical distribution of materials for isolated communities and study groups.

(iv) Output

Production output per annum	300 TV programmes of 25 minutes
	300 radio programmes of 20 minutes
Transmission output	TV — 2,500 transmissions
	Radio — 2,500 transmissions
Producer load	9 TV plus 9 radio programmes

(v) Audience

Registered students	50,000
Eavesdropping audience	100,000

(vi) Recurrent expenditure (US $)

Staff costs	2,300,000
Programme costs	1,380,000
Technical costs (including transmitter operations)	575,000
Rental and servicing of premises	460,000
General	92,000
Total	$4,807,000

Constraints

The data given in the previous pages cannot be a basis for rigorous economic analysis; it is too limited, and the figures are not comparable. Most economists working in the communications field are used to the frustrations arising from a shortage of data on which to base analyses; services are usually too busy with programme production to collect adequate background information or to present it in such a way that comparative studies can be made.

From these figures, nevertheless, a number of general conclusions can be drawn, which emphasise in practice what has already been argued, more theoretically, on several occasions in this handbook.

One of the major problems is that of *obsolescence*. Educational technology is a rapidly moving field, which tends to leave in its wake obsolete equipment, outmoded ideas, inadequate structures. In some cases, services overtaken in this way act like proverbial ostriches, and continue as they have always done; others, with an interest in new trends, re-order their thinking and try to improvise with what they have available.

This has affected media services in several ways. The first point to be noted is that many were created at a time when the emphasis was on educational television — when radio had been discarded as antique, and multi-media and systems approaches little known outside the text books. Some of the systems described are still confining their attention to television, with an increased amount of support and print material; others have diverted part of their attention to sound recording or audio-visual work. At times, they have placed an extreme burden on both resources and staff by doing so.

Linked is the problem of obsolescence in equipment. A few years ago, 1-inch technology and the videocassette were untried, and the earlier forms of helical scan machine often produced difficulties which did not recommend them to their pioneer users. The author himself remembers a slow-motion kit, offered as part of helical scan package, which not even the manufacturer's representatives could persuade to function. Supervisors are unfortunately not in a position to reject expensive videotape equipment, or to remove older image-orthicon cameras, unless expansion funds are available.

Similar issues affect CCTV distribution. In the universities, a considerable investment was often made in wired distribution systems (often on a radio frequency, with limited possibilities for expansion, or adaptation to feedback technologies). The newer installations have perhaps been fortunate in not committing themselves so readily to this expensive resource, leaving themselves flexible to cope with change as and when it arises.

But 10 years ago such trends were difficult to predict, and pioneers are necessary, even if they often seem to be left with more disadvantages than advantages through their willingness to experiment. Fortunately, in the case of open broadcasting, these problems are less likely to occur, since few services could ever afford their own transmission networks, and have necessarily worked from the backs of parent broadcasting organisations. This leaves them freer to cope with changing possibilities in physical distribution (or mixed transmission and recording systems).

It leaves open, however, the second major constraint, which is the difficulty of convincing authorities of the need for *expansion*. Without expansion, new audiences cannot be served (and all too often these audiences are at the primary level, larger than the original target audience addressed by the system). And in turn, it becomes impossible to reduce the unit costs of the system to a level at which expansion can be economically justified (quite apart from the fact that the system, being under-used, is simply not living up to its potential).

An inability to expand has many implications. It means that new technologies, such as colour working, cannot be introduced; it restricts professional opportunities; it inhibits experiment, discourages producers and support staff. And it means that new techniques (such as those described in our discussion of access and participation, including the various forms of community media) cannot be advanced. This affects national and local levels of operation alike. One community service described earlier, though fully conscious of new openings at the adult level, or in the more direct involvement of audiences, remains primarily a school-based system, producing a few programmes of its own and relaying network programming to its wired users. The second community service has perennial finding problems. Meanwhile, the various national or State services are forced to continue in the same mould as before, except for improvised experiments.

The final problem area shown up by the examples is in the critical areas of *utilisation, evaluation, research and training.* A cursory examination of staff lists and budgetary provisions shows in how few cases (and even then how nominally) these areas are catered for by full-time staff, or by significant resources. And again, as a result of political and economic refusals to contemplate these fields (for by now, most system producers and designers are aware of their necessity), adequate information is simply not available upon which to base the case for expansion and innovation.

Similarities

Constraints apart, there does seem to be some kind of pattern in the examples quoted. Although they have been drawn from different environments, and from different parts of the world, there is a similarity of scale and resources for comparable operations. If basic parameters of staffing, output, audience coverage and recurrent expenditure are averaged out, a picture emerges roughly like the following:

	Institution	State	Nation
Staffing	10–30	50–100	150 upwards
Output	100–300 programmes annually	200–300 programmes annually	600 programmes upwards annually
Audience	Up to 10,000	100,000–500,000	500,000 upwards
Recurrent expenditure in US $	150–200,000	500–600,000	1 million upwards

The one level which has been omitted from this table is that of the community system, which is the most difficult of all at the present time. Its scale and resources — ranging from local authority or school district systems, to media resource centres, community action groups, and so to local radio or local and cable television — are extremely varied. The difficulty of this area arises mainly, in fact, from its indefiniteness; it is the newest field, attempting to cater for a very wide range of demands, at all educational and social levels, and since it is often experimental, concerned as much with audience involvement as with materials production, and lacks the coherence of the formal instructional system with the latter's demonstrable cost effectiveness, it is a level at which not only a characteristic format, but also a guaranteed sponsorship, is hard to find. Community systems often emerge before their environment is ready to accept them, and their initial resources are often too few for them to provide the range of services necessary to make them a viable force in the community. It seems as if, whatever the economic or social arguments, a good deal of pragmatic experience will be needed before such systems can find consistent backing.

It is debatable whether the similarities (say between the college centre in a developed and a developing country) arise because each has found an optimal level of staffing in relation to output and budgetary possibilities, or because the developing country model has been drawn (as are most developing models) by experts recruited from the industrialised world. Yet it does seem that, for each level of operation, there is a ceiling beyond which it is difficult to pass, for political and economic reasons alike, without making radical changes in objectives and output. The unit costs per annum, for example, of the systems quoted above range from $1 to $50, but at all levels there appears to be a point, at about $50 annual unit cost, beyond which system financiers are naturally unwilling to proceed. At the same time, even in national systems, where very low unit costs may be achieved, there is also an *absolute* ceiling in recurrent expenditure (in the region of $1 million) beyond which sponsorship is difficult, because the expenditure required seems prohibitive, even if it can be justified theoretically. One cannot say that in educational media detailed economic arguments always or even often prevail, but at the same time, apparently there are subjectively based rules of thumb which have an economic foundation. This is especially true in the developing world, unless donors with ample resources the imagination can be found.

Comparison with a planned multi-media system

Finally, it may be useful to compare the preceding systems with a purpose-planned model: that already referred to on a number of occasions in this handbook, designed for the national development of educational mass media in Thailand. It must be emphasised that this was a preparatory, pre-investment study, and therefore did not suffer from the kinds of difficulty reported in the earlier, working models, though the study did attempt to take account of practical and political constraints, as well as meeting specific educational objectives. But in this design, essential elements of utilisation, evaluation, research and training were reasonably well retained, and the deployment of media within the system was based on educational need, with a strong emphasis on radio, as an ideal and cost-effective medium to reach rural and adult populations.

The comparison should therefore serve as an indicator of the effects of political and financial exigency. The same format of data presentation is retained as was used for the earlier examples, though it is described rather more fully.

For an account of the process by which objectives were determined, reference should be made to the main text of the handbook, though for convenience, a brief summary of the media justification is given below.

Summary of the justification for the project

Though Thailand is developing very rapidly in purely statistical terms, and her educational system is expanding at a fast rate, she is at the same time faced with increasingly severe social, economic, political and educational problems. Despite rapid growth the majority of the rural population (particularly in more remote areas) have not shared in the fruits of development and find it difficult to participate in democratic processes, as they are still steeped in traditional patterns of social relationships.

If rural development problems are to be solved, rural urban migration reduced to manageable proportions and the quality of life in rural areas significantly improved, it is essential to change the attitudes of rural people and to provide them with new and relevant skills and knowledge. Given the fact that there are 50,000 to 60,000 villages in Thailand, many of them only accessible on foot; that there are relatively small numbers of field extension workers; and that over 20 per cent of the rural population are illiterate, with a much larger proportion not functionally literate, only the mass media, and particularly radio (as over 60 per cent of rural households have radio sets), have the potential (combined and coordinated with other inputs) to act as the educational catalyst needed for development.

Similarly at the in-school level, the existing severe inequalities of educational opportunity can only be reduced if a means can be found to provide rural children with quality educational materials at a manageable cost (without further boosting urban schooling at the same time). Equally, means must be found to improve the quality of teaching, and to change teachers' and parents' assessments of the role of education. It is also essential, if the school is to play a positive role in the development process, for the fact-centered, often irrelevant curriculum to be transformed and radical innovation to take place. With a quarter of a million teachers (the majority of whom are not yet aware of the crisis facing the school system) spread through 30,000 schools, it is only the mass media which will be able, by their very nature, to provide an even spread of new educational materials and to multiply the initiative of the small number of innovative educators in existence.

The project therefore envisages:

(a) A considerable use of radio for all audiences, both in and out-of-school, including the establishment of an independent educational radio network.
(b) Television programming addressed initially to secondary schools and urban adult audiences, with an emphasis on curriculum support on the one hand, and on the other hand including experimentation with community programming. In addition there is a potential for expansion at a later date into the elementary and rural adult education fields.
(c) As wide a spread as possible of programming (apart from television) produced regionally, designed to help solve specific regional development problems.

(d) The experimental use of mobile audio-visual units in association with extension work.

(e) Experimental work in community video and audio techniques.

(f) As full a range of print support materials as is consistent with the resources available.

(g) A loan service for audio-visual equipment and materials, to allow for individual work by motivated teachers.

(i) Organisation and framework

The project includes facilities and personnel for producing or remaking 180 TV programmes for secondary school students and teachers per year and up to 200 programmes for general adult audiences, 69 series of radio programmes for schools, mainly at the elementary level, and of general educational programming per week with more during school holidays. In addition facilities are available for producing the necessary printed support materials and other audio-visual software needed for both in-school and out-of-school purposes.

Approximately 16 hours of TV programmes will be transmitted to schools each week through the expanded national TV network, and 16 hours a day of radio programmes through a specially created educational radio network. In addition films, slides and other AV software will be available on loan to schools and adult centres, and printed support materials will be distributed free to schools and adult groups where essential.

Receivers are to be provided to schools which will enable 8.5 million students and 300,000 teachers to use the TV programmes. In addition it is expected that the general radio and TV programmes will reach up to 7.3 million and 2.30 million adults respectively.

Centre for Educational Technology

The nucleus of the project is the location, in Bangkok, of a Centre for Educational Technology, to replace the existing limited facility. This Centre will provide studios, technical, projection and demonstration facilities, and accommodation for utilisation, training, evaluation and research functions.

The Centre for Educational Technology (ETC) will therefore act as a focal point for the planning, production, distribution and evaluation of the national media system, and will be the controlling point for other operations decentralised to the regional level. Its links with other sections of the Ministry of Education, with regional education offices, provincial administrations and out-of-school audiences are therefore crucial. Its function is to evolve a system which, through a process of planning, prototyping, training, evaluation and research, is flexible enough to keep its performance constantly attuned to educational priorities and user demands.

Policy planning for the Centre for Educational Technology will rest with an Educational Media Advisory Committee, with detailed operational planning in the hands of a number of Design and Strategy Committees for specific subject and topic areas.

Regional centres

Initially twelve regional centres have been planned (to be phased in, in groups of four, starting in the third year of the project); these will act as nuclei for local radio production, educational materials development and utilisation training. *No* television production facility is planned at the regional level.

The centres will also house a collection of audio-visual equipment and materials, for loan to schools and to supervisors for local offices once a month during term time; the van will be operated by a driver/technician who will collect equipment needing repair and deliver replacements, as well as carrying out simple repairs or adjustments on the spot.

Utilisation — Schools and teacher training

In the area of media utilisation three distinct priorities have been identified:

1. The introduction of a revised curriculum in Teacher Training Colleges, including media utilisation.
2. An in-service teaching programme designed to equip teachers in schools with the necessary skills to utilise the media service. This programme has been designed to provide courses for almost 200,000 teachers by the end of the project.
3. The appointment and management of a team of utilisation supervisors to plan, direct and evaluate the above courses.

Utilisation out of school

For out-of-school audiences, the media project has to adapt its approaches, not to a relatively uniform set of institutions (as with schools and colleges), but to the whole community of post-school adults, young and old. In some cases, it will be providing materials to support tutorially-based groups, but the majority of its audience will be found at random, in villages, in the fields and in private homes.

Utilisation procedures therefore have to cater for three distinct types of audience:

1. Those formed specially into groups to follow media programmes.
2. Those already meeting in groups, but for which the media are only of secondary or supportive interest.
3. For individual audiences.

The duties of the out-of-school utilisation supervisors parallel, in the adult field, those of their in-school counterparts. They will also be expected to travel widely within their region, visit classes and report on media use and liaison with local government offices and development workers.

Evaluation and research

A small evaluation and research section will be created, which will be responsible for the continuous monitoring of the media service.

The evaluation section does not have the capacity to initiate or conduct research, nor is this desirable for a functional unit of the Centre. However, it will act as the main coordinator of specific research projects, channelling information to researchers and acting as intermediary between research agencies and production staff.

(ii) Staffing

The full staff establishment proposed for the project in its final stage of development is summarised in the following table:

	Professional and adminis-tration	Technical	Clerical	General employees	Total
I. Bangkok centre					
Management and administration	17	3	67	22	109
Media production	77	5	–	–	82
Production facilities/technical services	15	86	3	3	107
Utilisation	5	–	–	–	5
Evaluation and research	12	–	–	–	12
II. Radio transmission network					
Transmission network	4	–	–	18	22
III. Community/mobile projects					
Community/mobile projects	15	13	–	–	28
IV. Regional centres					
Centres with radio	92	72	48	32	244
Other centres	20	24	20	16	80
Total	257	203	138	91	689

(iii) Facilities and equipment

The service is to be housed in a new Centre which is comprised of two buildings: a production block, and a smaller, adjacent services block (the latter for house services, workshops and storage areas and processing equipment). The Production Block is estimated at 49 m x 58 m, the Services Block at 20 m x 50 m.

In the Production Block, for radio one drama/music studio suite is provided, two talks studio suites, and two continuity suites, together with master control and all associated technical facilities. For television, two studios, each approximately 11 m x 15 m in area, are to be provided, with space for the addition of a third studio at a later date. Each studio is to be professionally equipped with three colour television cameras; the control rooms (for video) offer a vision mixing facility with a full range of special effects.

Complete technical services are available, including graphics and photographic workshops, film shooting, editing, dubbing, processing and animation, and scenic and carpentry workshops.

Library accommodation is for both print and non-print materials, and there is simple printing (offset) equipment, and facilities for audio and videotape dubbing and replication. Programmes for television are recorded and replayed on three transverse scan machines (with a 1-inch machine, and videocassette facilities available for experimental and community applications).

Observation, classroom and lecture theatre facilities are included for training and preview purposes, with a well-equipped audio-visual workshop (used both for training and for complex audio-visual materials production).

Transmission of radio programmes in intended to be over an independent educational radio network (operating on medium wave, with nine transmitters). Television programmes are to be relayed, by microwave or physically, to the national television network, as and when it is completed.

Regional centres are furnished with smaller radio studios, and can provide local programming to their own regions, and insert materials for the national radio network. They will also serve as bases for experimental work in community media, as well as administrative centres for equipment maintenance, loan and materials distribution.

(iv) Output

Programme preparation

Figures are given here for the production of radio and television programmes only. Other materials production follows the demands of mass media programming, as media support; the operations of mobile units and community media are determined by local needs.

Programme and materials production follow a cycle of planning (in interdisciplinary working committees), piloting, pre-testing and recording (with all television programmes, and the majority of radio programmes apart from general education, pre-recorded). The first new transmission cycle begins in Year 4, when the radio network is complete and studio facilities are equipped; thereafter output is gradually consolidated and expanded, with an allowance of up to 50 per cent of remade programmes in the early years. The pattern of programme development (by the end of the project) is shown in the following tables:

(a) *Number of programmes produced per year by end of project*
(OP = original productions, Rem = remakes)

	OP	Rem
(A) Radio		
Schools	504	224
Teacher Training	—	199
Ad. Ed. Central*	2,234	78
Ad. Ed. Regions†	750	78
Total radio	3,488	579
(B) TV		
Schools	112	40
Teacher Training	28	—
Ad. Ed. Rural	66	—
Ad. Gen.	52	—
Reserve	82	—
Total TV	340	40

* In addition there will be 28 hours 40 minutes of general programmes produced per week.
† In addition there will be 5 hours 20 minutes of general programmes produced per week.

(b) *Hours of transmission per week by end of project (during term time)*

	Hours Minutes
(A) Radio	
Primary 1—4	9.45
Primary 5—7	9.00
Middle School 1—5	5.20
Total schools	24.05
Specific adult	20.45
General adult	34.00
Total adult	54.45
Unallocated reserve	33.10
Total	122.00
(B) TV	
Secondary	14.20
Teachers	1.20
Ad. Ed. Gen.	0.20
Total	16.00

(c) *Average producer load*
(assuming assistance from support production staff)

Radio	— 70 original programmes and 30 remakes annually
Television	— 28 programmes annually

(v) Audience coverage (by end of project)

Radio	Primary	7,370,600	Teachers	62,554
	Secondary	1,099,503		
	Adult	7,327,000		
Television	Secondary	923,663	Teachers	11,669
	Adult	2,332,000		

(vi) Recurrent expenditure and financial analysis (US $)

Staff costs	880,650
Programme production	972,250
Training	128,400
Evaluation and research	17,500
Maintenance	54,150
Loan service	82,500
Radio transmission	684,650
Community media and mobile units	20,100
Other central costs	116,100
Regional centres	424,800
Contingencies	250,000
Total	$3,631,100

Within the system proposed the greatest emphasis is on adult education, followed by elementary education (which is the only schooling the majority of Thais receive). In order that these priorities can be met the project finally involves the following allocation of expenditures:

	Adult (%)	Elem. (%)	Sec. (%)	Total (%)	Radio (%)	TV (%)	Other media (%)	Total (%)
Capital	58.1	23.5	18.4	100.0	60.8	17.6	21.7	100.0
Recurrent	52.0	33.4	14.6	100.0	53.5	12.5	34.0	100.0

Though it is not possible to carry out any cost effectiveness analyses (as no other alternative educational approaches are likely to have comparable results), the unit costs of the educational media system are so low that it is obvious no alternative could have the same potential. This (in US $) can be seen in the following table (n.a. = not available):

	Radio		TV		Other media		Overall schools	
	Rec	Cap	Rec	Cap	Rec	Cap	Rec	Cap
Elementary	0.058	0.4665	–	–	0.0854	0.224	30	150
Secondary	0.1265	0.751	0.215	2.65	0.125	0.7045	62.5	530
Adult	0.165	1.27	0.0925	0.623	n.a.	n.a.	n.a.	n.a.

Finally, in order to give some further indication of the low unit cost of the media system, the following table (for illustrative purposes only, since it is not intended that media replace the formal school) compares (in US $) the total recurrent cost per viewer or listener per programme with the recurrent cost of an equivalent period (15 or 20 minutes) of formal schooling:

	Lowest in-school		Highest in-school		Highest out-school	
	Radio	TV	Radio	TV	Radio	TV
Cost per student per programme	0.000135	0.0135	0.00295	0.0385	0.02	0.1635
Formal school equiv.	0.008 (Elem.)	0.022 (Sec.)	0.022 (Secondary)		0.172 (Teacher training)	

Select bibliography

This selection of books on educational mass media in the English language has been designed to be practically useful; it is divided into three parts: *Books and Published Reports, Reference and Bibliographical Compilations* and *Periodicals.*

The books are selected to provide further reading and reference across most of the fields touched upon in this handbook: they therefore include a spread of titles on subjects ranging from research and utilisation to technical systems and media production. The majority of titles date only from the 'sixties, but some classic texts of an earlier date are also included.

I. Books and published reports

Academy For Educational Development. *Handbook on Use of Technology for Educational Change.* Academy for Educational Development, Washington, 1972.

Allen, D. and Ryan, K. *Microteaching.* Addison Wesley, Reading, Mass., 1970.

Armsey, J. W. and Dahl, N. C. *An Inquiry into the Uses of Instructional Technology.* Ford Foundation, New York, 1973, 113 pp.

Arnove, Robert. *Educational Television: a policy critique and guide for developing countries.* School of Education, Stanford University, 1973.

Aspinall, Richard. *Radio Programme Production: a manual for training.* Unesco, Paris, 1971, 151 pp.

Baddeley, H. *The Technique of Documentary Film Production.* Focal Press, London, 1970, 268 pp.

Bailey, K. *The Listening Schools: educational broadcasting by sound and television.* BBC, London, 1957, 184 pp.

Benton, C. W. *et al. Television in Urban Education: its application to major educational problems in sixteen cities.* Praeger, New York, 1969, 156 pp.

Berrigan, F. *Access: Some Western Models of Community Media.* Unesco, Paris, 1977.

Berrigan, F. *Mass Media, Family Planning and Development.* Unesco, Paris, 1975.

Bloodworth, M. *Highlights of Schools using Educational Media.* National Education Association, Washington, 1967, 306 pp.

Bloom, B. S. *et al. Handbook on Evaluation of Student Learning.* McGraw-Hill, New York, 1971, 920 pp.

Bosley, Howard E. and Wigren, Harold E. *Television and Related Media in Teacher Education: some exemplary practices.* Multi-State Teacher Education Project, Baltimore, Maryland, 1967, 53 pp.

Bretz, R. *Techniques of Television Production.* McGraw-Hill, 1962, 517 pp.

Bretz, R. *The Selection of Appropriate Communication Media for Instruction.* Rand, Santa Monica, California, 1971.

Briggs, L. J., Campeau, R. L., Gagne, R. and May, M. A. *Instructional media: a procedure for the design of multimedia instruction, a critical review of research, and suggestions for future research.* American Institute for Research, Pittsburg, Pa., 1967, 176 pp.

Brown, J. W. and Norberg, K. D. *Administering Educational Media.* McGraw-Hill, 1965, 363 pp.

Brown, J. W. and Thornton, J. W. (eds.). *New Media in Higher Education.* National Education Association, Washington, 1963, 182 pp.

Burder, J. *The Techniques of Editing 16 mm Film.* Focal Press, London, 1968.

Bushell, J. (ed.). *The Use of Audio-visual Aids in Education for International Understanding.* Unesco Institute for Education, Hamburg, 1966, 106 pp.

Canadian Broadcasting Corporation. *Challenge for Change.* CBC, Toronto, 1972.

Canadian Broadcasting Corporation: Research Department. *Educational Television for Farmers: a study in audience reactions.* CBC, Ottawa, 1964, 101 pp.

Canadian Radio-Television Commission. *A Resource for the Active Community,* Ottawa, 1974, 125 pp.

Carlisle, R. B. *College Credit through TV: Old Idea, New Dimensions,* Great Plains National Instructional Television Library, Lincoln, Nebraska, 1974, 194 pp.

Carnegie Commission On Educational Television. *Public Television: a program for action.* Bantam Books, New York, 1967, 254 pp.

Carpenter, C. R. and Greenhill, L. P. *Instructional Television Research.* Report no. 2, Pennsylvania State University, 1958, 110 pp.

Cassirer, H. *Television Teaching Today.* Unesco, Paris, 1960, 268 pp.

Castaldi, B. *Creative Planning of Educational Facilities.* Rand McNally, Chicago, 1969, 360 pp.

Calvert, C. E. *An Approach to The Design of Mediated Instruction.* Association for Educational Communication and Technology, Washington, 1974, 271 pp.

Cherry, C. *World Communication: threat or promise.* John Wiley and Sons Ltd, London, 1971, 229 pp.

Children's Television Workshop. *The Electric Company: an introduction.* New York, 1971, 120 pp.

Chu, G. C. and Schramm, W. *Learning from Television: what the research says.* National Association of Educational Broadcasting, Washington, 1969, 116 pp.

Coffelt, K. *Basic Design and Utilisation of Instructional Television.* University of Texas, Austin, 66 pp.

Committee On Education And Labor, House of Representatives. *To Improve Learning – A Report to the President and Congress of the United States by the Commission on Instructional Technology.* US Govt. Printing Office, Washington, 1970, 124 pp.

Commonwealth Secretariat. *New Media in Education in the Commonwealth.* Commonwealth Secretariat, London, 1974.

Connochie, T. D. *TV For Education and Industry.* Mitchell Press, Vancouver, 1969, 195 pp.

Coombs, D. H. *One Week of Educational Television:* no. 5, May 6–12, 1968: UHF–VHF, closed circuit and ITFS (2500 MH) activity. Sponsored by National Educational Television and the National Instructional Television Centre. NITC, Bloomington, 1968, 75 pp.

Coppen, H. *Aids to Teaching and Learning.* Pergamon Press, 1969, 230 pp.

Corder, S. *English Language Teaching and Television.* Longman, 1960, 107 pp.

Corder, S. Pit., *The Visual Element in Language Teaching.* Longman, 1966, 96 pp.

Costello, L. and Gordon, G. N. *Teach with Television: a guide to instructional TV.* 2nd edn., Hastings House, New York, 1965, 192 pp.

Council Of Europe: Council for Cultural Co-operation. *Direct Teaching by Television.* Report of the European seminar, Rome, 1966. The Council, Strasbourg, 1967, 94 pp.

Council Of Europe: Council for Cultural Co-operation. *The Use of Closed Circuit Television in Technical Education.* The Council, Strasbourg.

Council Of Europe. *Direct Teaching by Television.* Report of the European seminar, Rome, 1966. The Council, Strasbourg, 1967, 94 pp.

Council Of Europe. *European Research in Audio-Visual Aids.* Parts 1 and 2. The Council, Strasbourg, 1966.

Council Of Europe. *The Use of Radio and Television in Institutions of Higher Education in CCC Member States.* The Council, Strasbourg, 1967, 65 pp.

Cowlan, B. and Foote, D. *A Case Study of the ATS—6 Health, Education and Telecommunications Project, A.I.D. Studies in Educational Technology,* A.I.D. Washington, 1975.

Cowlan, B., Jamison, D., Porcyn, K., Singh, J., Smith, D., Wolff, L. *Broadcast Satellites for Educational Development: the experiments in Brazil, India and the United States.* Academy for Educational Development, Washington, 1973.

Crawford, R.H. and Ward, W. B. *Communication Strategies for Rural Development.* New York State College of Agriculture, Cornell University, Ithaca, 1975.

D.A.V.I. *Planning Schools for use of A—V materials: classrooms, auditoriums, audiovisual instructional materials centre, audiovisual centres for colleges and universities.* Dept. of A-V Instruction, Washington DC.

Davies I. K. *The Management of Learning.* McGraw-Hill, New York, 1971, 256 pp.

Davies, I. K. and Hartley, J. *Contribution to an Educational Technology.* Butterworth, London, 1972, 394 pp.

De Korte, D. A. *Television in Education and Training.* Philips, Eindhoven, 1967, 175 pp.

Diamond, R. A. (ed.). *A Guide to Instructional Television.* McGraw-Hill, New York, 1964, 304 pp.

Dieuzeide, H. *Teaching Through Television.* OEEC, Paris, 1960, 71 pp.

Dodds, T. *Multi-Media Approaches to Rural Education.* International Extension College, Cambridge, 1972, 48 pp.

Dodds, T. and Hall, B. *Voices for Development: the Tanzanian National Radio Study Campaigns.* International Extension College, Cambridge, 1974, 51 pp.

Dumazedier, J. *et al. Television and Adult Education: the teleclubs in France.* Unesco, Paris, 1956, 276 pp.

Edstrom, L. O. *et al.* (ed.). *Mass Education: Studies in adult education and teaching by correspondence in some developing countries.* Almquist and Wiksell, Stockholm, 1970, 380 pp.

Educational Media Council. *New Relationships in ITV.* EMC, New York, 1968, 157 pp.

Erickson, C. and Curl. *Fundamentals of Teaching with AV technology.* Collier Macmillan, London, 1972, 381 pp.

European Broadcasting Union. *Third EBU International Conference on Educational Radio and Television,* Paris, March 8—22, 1967. ORTF, Paris, 1968, 682 pp.

European Broadcasting Union. *Fourth EBU Seminar on Teaching by Television: adult education.* Basle, 30 November—7 December 1966. EBU, Geneva, 1967, 64 pp.

European Broadcasting Union. *Fifth EBU Seminar on Teaching by Television: schools, summary.* Basle, 13—20 December 1967. EBU, Geneva, 1968, 61 pp.

Farmer, M. and Weinstock, R. *Schools without Walls.* Educational Facilities Laboratories Inc. New York, 1965, 56 pp.

Firth, B. *Mass Media in the Classroom.* Macmillan, London, 1968, 127 pp.

Foote, D., Parker, E. and Hudson, H. *Telemedicine in Alaska: The ATS—6 Satellite Biomedical Demonstration,* Institute for Communication Research, Stanford, Calif., 1976.

Fuglesang, A. *Applied Communication in Developing Countries.* Dag Hammarskjöld Foundation, Upsala, 1973, 124 pp.

Fuglesang, A. *The Story of a Seminar in Applied Communication.* Dag Hammarskjöld Foundation, Upsala, 1973, 142 pp.

Fund For Media Research. *School Television: Great Cities 1967: a study of the status* *and needs of the schools, as served by television in sixteen great cities.* Fund for Media Research, Chicago, 1967, 140 pp.

Gattegno, C. *Towards a Visible Culture: Educating Through Television.* Outerbridge and Dienstfrey, New York, 1969, 117 pp.

Gerbner, G., Gross, L. P. and Melody, W. H. (eds.). *Communications Technology and Social Policy: understanding the new 'Cultural Revolution'.* Wiley, New York, 1973, 573 pp.

Gerlach, V. S. and Ely, D. P. *Teaching and Media: Systematic Approach.* Prentice-Hall, Englewood Cliffs, New Jersey, 1971, 392 pp.

Gibson, T. *Closed-Circuit Television Single-Handed.* Pitman, London. 1972, 143 pp.

Gibson, T. *The Practice of ETV.* Hutchinson Educational, London, 1970, 189 pp.

Gibson, T. *The Use of ETV: A Handbook for Students and Teachers.* Hutchinson Educational, London, 1970, 127 pp.

Goodwin, L. G. and Koehring, T. *Closed-Circuit Television Production Techniques.* Foulsham, 1971, 191 pp.

Gordon, G. N. *Classroom Television: New Frontiers in ITV.* Hastings House, New York, 1970, 248 pp.

Gordon, G. N. *Educational Television.* Centre for Applied Research in Education, New York, 1965, 113 pp.

Green, Alan C. (ed.). *Educational Facilities with New Media.* (3rd edn). Department of Audio-Visual Instruction, National Education Association, 1972.

Greenhill, J. P. *Closed-Circuit Television for Teaching in Colleges and Universities.* Pennsylvania State University, 1961 and 1963.

Groombridge, B., (ed.). *Adult Education and Television.* National Institute of Adult Education and Unesco, London, 1966, 143 pp.

Groombridge, B. *Television and the People.* Penguin Books, 1972, 254 pp.

Guimary, D. L. *Citizens' Groups and Broadcasting,* Praeger, New York, 1975, 170 pp.

Guttenberg, M. (ed.). *Handbook of Evaluation Research.* Sage Publications Inc., Beverley Hills, Calif., 1974.

Halloran, J. D. *Attitude Formation and Change.* Working paper no. 2 of the Television Research Committee. Leicester University Press, 1966, 167 pp.

Halloran, J. D. *Mass Communication Research and Adult Education.* University of Leicester, Department of Adult Education, 1968, 75 pp.

Hancock, A., (ed.). *Producing for Educational Mass Media.* Longman and Unesco, 1976.

Hanf, H., Koppes, W., Green, A., Gassman, M. and Haviland, D. *New Spaces for Learning designing college facilities to utilise instructional aids and media.* Center for Architectural Research. Rensselaer Polytechnic Institute, New York, 1966, 137 pp.

Head, S. W. (ed.). *Broadcasting in Africa,* Temple University Press, Philadelphia, 1974, 453 pp.

Head, S. W. *Broadcasting in America,* Houghton Mifflin Company, Boston, 1972, (2nd edn), 563 pp.

Heinich, R. *Technology and the Management of Instruction.* Association for Educational Communications and Technology, Washington, 1970, 198 pp.

Hickel, R. *Modern Language Teaching by Television.* Council of Europe, Strasbourg, 1965, 185 pp.

Himmelweit, H. T. *et al. Television and the Child.* Oxford University Press, for the Nuffield Foundation, 1958, 522 pp.

Hooper, R. (ed.). *The Curriculum: Context, Design, and Development.* Oliver and Boyd, Edinburgh, 1971, 505 pp.

Hopkins, J. *et al. Video in Community Development.* Ovum Ltd, London, 1972, 146 pp.

Hornik, R. C., Ingle, H. T., Mayo, J. K., McAwany, E. G. and Schramm, W. *Television and Educational Reform in El Salvador: Final Report.* AID Studies in Educational

Technology, ICIT (Information Center on Instructional Technology), Academy for Educational Development. Washington, 1973, 322 pp.

Industrial Council For Education And Training Technology. *A Guide to the Specification and Purchase of Wired Distribution Systems for Educational Television.* ICETT, London, 1971, 26 pp.

Ingle, H. T. *Communication Media and Technology: A Look at Their Rôle in Non-Formal Education Programs.* ICIT, Academy for Educational Development, Washington, 1974, 62 pp.

International Council For Educational Development. *Instructional Broadcasting: A Design for the Future.* ICED, Washington, 1971, 37 pp.

ITV Humanities Project. *The ITV Humanities Project: a history of five experimental programs for instructional television.* WGBH Educational Foundation, Boston, 1967, 144 pp.

Jamison, D., Klees, S. and Wells, S. *Cost Analysis for Educational Planning and Evaluation: Methodology and Application to Instructional Technology* Educational Testing Service, Princeton, New Jersey, 1976.

Jamison, D., Suppes, P. and Wells, S. *The Effectiveness of Alternative Instructional Media: a survey.* AID Studies in Educational Technology, ICIT, Academy for Educational Development. Washington, 1973, 72 pp.

Jamison, D. and Wells, S. *The Cost of Instructional Radio and Television for Developing Countries.* AID Studies in Educational Technology, ICIT, Academy for Educational Development, Washington, 1973, 57 pp.

Johnson, T. *et al. Guide to VTR: A News Report on Equipment, Suppliers and Applications.* Ovum Ltd, London, 1971, 108 pp.

Kinross, F. *Television for the Teacher.* Hamish Hamilton, London, 1968, 140 pp.

Klasek, C. B. *Instructional Media in the Modern School.* Professional Educators Publications Inc., Lincoln, Nebraska, 1972, 102 pp.

Klein, G. and Hockley, J. *Television Teaching Techniques.* Angus and Robertson, Sydney, 1972, 143 pp.

Knezevitch, S. T. *Instructional Technology and the School Administration.* American Association of School Administration, Washington, 1970, 146 pp.

Koenig, A. E. and Hill, R. B. (ed.). *The Farther Vision: educational television today.* University of Madison Press, 1967, 371 pp.

Lallez, R. *The Tevec Case: an experiment in adult education using the multi-media system.* Unesco, Paris, 1972, 64 pp.

Lesser, G. S. *Children and Television: Lessons from 'Sesame Street'.* Random House, New York, 1974, 290 pp.

Levin, H. L. and Gillespie, R. W. *The Use of Radio in Family Planning.* World Neighbours, Oklahoma, 1972, 160 pp.

Lewis, P. *Educational Television Guidebook.* McGraw-Hill, 1961, 238 pp.

McAnany, E. *Radio's Role in Development: five strategies of use.* ICIT, Academy for Educational Development, Washington, 1973, 28 pp.

Maddison, J. *New Trends in Educational Technology and Industrial Pedagogy.* International A.V. Techniques Centre Foundation, Antwerp, 1971.

McIntosh, N. E. and Calder, J. *A Degree of Difference: A Report to the Social Science Research Council,* July, 1975.

MacKenzie, N. *et al. Teaching and Learning: Introduction of New Methods, and Resources in Higher Education.* Paris, 1971.

MacKenzie, N., Postgate, R. and Scupham, J. *Open Learning: Systems Problems in Post-Secondary Education.* The Unesco Press, Paris, 1975, 498 pp.

Mackenzie, O. and Christensen, E. L. *The Changing World of Correspondence Study: International Readings.* Pennsylvania State University, 1971, 376 pp.

McLaughlin, G. H. *Educational Television on Demand: an evaluation of the Ottona IRTV Experiment.* Ontario Institute for Studies in Education, Toronto. 1972, 167 pp.

McLean, R. *Television in Education.* Methuen, 1968, 151 pp.

Mayo, J. K., Hornik, R. C., McAnany, E. G. *Educational Reform with Television:*

The El Salvador Experience. Stanford University Press, Stanford, 1976, 216 pp.

Millerson, G. *The Technique of Television Production.* Focal Press, London, 1972, 440 pp.

Millerson, G. *The Technique of Lighting for Television and Motion Pictures.* Focal Press, London, 1972, 366 pp.

Moir, G. *Into Television.* Pergamon Press, 1969, 94 pp.

Moir, G. (ed.). *Teaching and Television: ETV explained.* Pergamon Press, 1967, 170 pp.

Moriarty, J. B. *The Third Eye: A Portapak Handbook for Teachers.* Toronto, OECA, 1972.

Morphet, E. and Jassen, D. *Planning for Effective Utilisation of Technology in Education.* Citation Press, New York, 1969, 372 pp.

Murphy, J. and Gross, R. *Learning by Television.* The Fund for Advancement of Education, New York, 1966, 95 pp.

National Association Of Educational Broadcasters. *Television in instruction: what is possible?* NAEB, Washington, 1970, 24 pp.

National Association Of Educational Broadcasters. *Toward a Significant Difference.* Final report of the National Project for the improvement of televised instruction, 1965–1968. NAEB, Washington, 1969, 43 pp.

National Association Of Educational Broadcasters Research Committee. *Educational Broadcasting Research.* Report of a survey of personnel, projects and publications. NAEB, Washington, 1964, 59 pp.

National Cable Television Association. *Cablecasting Guidebook.* Washington DC, 1973.

National Committee For Audio Visual Aids In Education. *Survey of British Research in audio visual aids.* NCAVAE, London, 1965, 75 pp. Supplement no. 1 (H. Coppen, comp.), 1966, 23 pp.

National Council For Educational Technology. *A Survey of Video Distribution Systems for Educational Purposes.* NCET, London, 1973, 87 pp.

National Council For Educational Technology. *Staffing and Training for Educational Closed-circuit Television.* NCET, London, 1971, 32 pp.

National Extension College. *A Survey of Audio-visual Activities in Universities and Colleges of Advanced Technology.* NEC, Cambridge, 1966, 51 pp.

National Extension College. *University Intercommunication.* Pergamon, 1966, 92 pp.

Nippon Hoso Kyokai. *Proceedings of the Second International Conference of Broadcasting Organisations on Sound and Television School Broadcasting.* HNK, Tokyo, 1963, 881 pp.

Nisbett, A. *The Technique of the Sound Studio.* Focal Press, London, 1970, 559 pp.

Ohliger, J. *Listening Groups: Mass Media in Adult Education.* Center for the Study of Liberal Education for Adults, Boston, 1967, 78 pp.

Oswald, I. and Wilson, S. *The Bag is not a Toy.* Council on Social Work Education, New York, 1971, 134 pp.

Owings, M. *Basic Planning for Television Distribution Systems: a guide for administrators.* Maryland Center for Public Broadcasting, 1969, 12 pp.

Perraton, H. *Broadcasting and Correspondence* (NEC Reports series 2 no. 2). National Extension College, Cambridge, 1973, 42 pp.

Perraton, H. D. *Correspondence Teaching and Television.* National Extension College, Cambridge, 1966, 19 pp.

Perry, W. *Open University,* Open University Press, Milton Keynes, 1976, 298 pp.

Polcyn, K. A. *An Educator's Guide to Communication Satellite Technology.* ICIT, Academy for Educational Development, Washington, 1973, 99 pp.

Polsky, R. M. *Getting to Sesame Street: Origins of the Children's Television Workshop.* Praeger, New York, 1974.

Pool, Ithiel de Sola and Schramm, W. (eds) *Handbook of Communication.* Rand McNally, Chicago, 1973, 1,011 pp.

Putting Research Into Educational Practice. *Instructional Television Facilities: a guide for school administrators and board members.* US Department of Health, Education and Welfare, Washington, 1969.

Quick, J. and Wolff, H. *Small Studio Videotape Production.* Addison-Wesley, London, 1972, 229 pp.

Radiotelevisione Italiana. *Proceedings of the International Conference of Broadcasting Organisations on Sound and Television School Broadcasting.* RAI, Rome, 1962, 721 pp.

Razik, T. *Systems Approach to Teaching, Training and Curriculum Development.* Unesco/IIEP, Paris, 1972, 156 pp.

Rigg, R. P. *Audio-visual Aids and Techniques in Managerial and Supervisory Training.* Hamish Hamilton, London, 1969, 198 pp.

Robinson, J. (ed.). *Educational Television and Radio in Great Britain.* BBC, London, 1966, 292 pp.

Robinson, J. and Barnes, N. (eds.). *New Media and Methods in Industrial Training.* BBC, London, 1967, 221 pp.

Romiszowski, A. *A Systems Approach to Training.* Kegan Page, London, 1970, 95 pp.

Roper, B. W. *Emerging Profiles of Television and Other Mass Media: public attitudes 1959—67.* New York Television Information Office, 1967, 26 pp.

Rossi, P. H. and Biddle, J. (eds.). *The New Media and Education.* Aldine, 1966, Chicago, 417 pp.

Rossi, P. H. and Biddle, J. (eds.). *The New Media and Education.* Doubleday, 1967, 460 pp.

Saettler, P. *A History of Instructional Technology.* McGraw-Hill, New York, 1968, 399 pp.

Schamberg, M. *Guerilla Television.* Holt Paperback, New York, 1971.

School Broadcasting Council. *Using Radio and Television: a guide to classroom practice.* BBC, London, 1969, 15 pp.

Schorb, A. O. and Bakker, F. J. *The Attitude of Teachers to the Use of Television: methods and materials.* Council of Europe, Strasbourg, 1968, 59 pp.

Schramm, W. *Big Media—Little Media.* AID Studies in Educational Technology, ICIT, Academy for Educational Development. Washington, 1973, 333 pp.

Schramm, W. *Instructional Television in the Educational Reform of El Salvador.* ICIT, Academy for Educational Development, Washington, 1973, 89 pp.

Schramm, W. *Instructional Television: promise and opportunity.* NAEB, Washington, 1967, 23 pp.

Schramm, W. *Mass Media and National Development.* Stanford University Press and Unesco, Paris, 1964, 333 pp.

Schramm, W. *ITV in American Samoa — after nine years.* ICIT, Academy for Educational Development, Washington, 1973, 55 pp.

Schramm, W. *Notes on Case Studies of Instructional Media Projects.* ICIT, Academy for Educational Development, 1973, Washington.

Schramm, W. *Notes on Instructional Cross-Media Comparisons.* AID Studies in Educational Technology, ICIT, Academy for Educational Development. Washington, 1971, 53 pp.

Schramm, W. (ed.). *Quality in Instructional Television.* University Press of Hawaii, 1972, 226 pp.

Schramm, W. *et al. Television in the Lives of Our Children.* Stanford University Press, 1961, 324 pp.

Schramm, W. *The Audiences of Educational Television: a report to NET.* Institute for Communication Research, Stanford, 1967, 90 pp.

Schramm, W. (ed.). *The Impact of Educational Television.* University of Illinois Press, 1960, 247 pp.

Schramm, W. *et al. The People Look at Educational Television.* Stanford University Press, 1963, 209 pp.

Sloane Commission On Cable Communications. *On the Cable; the Television of Abundance.* McGraw-Hill, New York, 1971, 256 pp.

Schueler, H. and Lesser, G. S. *Teacher Education and the New Media.* The American Association of Colleges for Teacher Education, National Education Association, Washington DC, 1967, 122 pp.

Scupham, J. *The Open University.* International Broadcast Institute, 1972, 32 pp.

Smith, M. H. (ed.). *Using Television in the Classroom: Midwest program on airborne television instruction.* McGraw-Hill, 1961, 118 pp.

Speagle, R. E. *Educational Reform and Instructional Television in El Salvador: Costs, Benefits.* AID Studies in Educational Technology, ICIT, Academy for Educational Development. Washington, 1973, 333 pp.

Stanford University, Institute Of Communication Research. *Educational Television: the next ten years.* Stanford University Press, 1962, 375 pp.

Stasheff, E. and Bretz, R. *The Television Program, its Direction and Production.* McGraw-Hill, 1962, 335 pp.

Stufflebeam, A. *Educational Evaluation and Decision Making.* Peacock, Ithaca, Illinois, 1971, 386 pp.

Takeo Furu *et al. Television and Children's Life.* Japanese Broadcasting Corporation, 1962, 34 pp.

Tate, C. *Cable Television and the Cities.* The Urban Institute, Washington DC, 1972.

Taylor, S. W. *Radio Programming in Action: realities and opportunities.* Hastings House, New York, 1967, 183 pp.

Television Research Committee. *Problems of Television Research: a progress report.* Leicester University Press, 1966, 38 pp.

Tickton, S. G. (ed.). *To Improve Learning: an evaluation of instructional technology.* R. R. Bowker, New York and London, 1970, 2 vols.

Trenaman, J. *Communication and Comprehension.* Longman, 1967, 212 pp.

Tunstall, J. (ed.). *The Open University Opens.* Routledge and Kegan Paul, London, 1974, 191 pp.

Unesco, Reports and Papers on Mass Communication. Unesco, Paris.

  An African Experiment in Radio Forums for Rural Development, Ghana, 1964/1965. 1968.

  Broadcasting from space, 1970.

  Cinematographic Institutions, 1973.

  Communication Satellites for Education, Science and Culture, 1967.

  8 mm Film for Adult Audiences, 1968.

  A Guide to Satellite Communication, 1972.

  Mass Media in an African Context, 1973.

  Mass Media in Society. The Need of Research, 1970.

  National Communication Systems. Some policy issues and options, 1975.

  Planning for Satellite Broadcasting: The Indian Instructional Television Experiment

  Radio Broadcasting serves Rural Development, 1965.

  Radio and Television in Literacy, 1971.

  Radio and Television in the Service of Education and Development in Asia, 1967.

  Script Writing for Short Films, 1969.

  Technology and Access to Communications Media, 1975.

  Television and the Social Education of Women, 1967.

  Television for Higher Technical Education of the Employed. A first Report on a Pilot Project in Poland, 1969.

  Television for Higher Technical Education of Workers. Final Report on a Pilot Project in Poland, 1973.

  Television Traffic — a one-way street? 1974.

  The Mass Media in a Violent World, 1971.

  The Practice of Mass Communication: some lessons from research, 1972.

  The Role of Film in Development, 1971.

  Training for Mass Communication, 1975.

Unesco/IEEP *New Educational Media in Action: Case Studies.* Unesco, Paris, 1967, 3 vols.

Unesco/IEEP, *The New Media: Memo to Educational Planners.* Unesco, Paris, 1967, 175 pp.

United Nations, *Manufacture of Telecommunications Equipment and Low-cost Receivers.* United Nations, New York, 1972, 96 pp.

University Grants Committee *et al. Audio-visual aids in Higher Scientific Education.* HMSO, 1965, 153 pp. (Brynmor Jones Reports.)

Unwin, D. *Media and Methods: Instructional Technology in Higher Education.* McGraw-Hill, New York, 1969, 219 pp.

Unwin, D. *Educational Technology.* OECD/CERI, Paris, 1971, 86 pp.

Unwin, D. *Educational Programme in 1980,* OECD/CERI, Paris, 1972.

Unwin, D. *The Fourth Revolution: Instructional Technology in Higher Education.* (Carnegie one million.) McGraw-Hill, New York, 1972.

Waniewicz, I. *Broadcasting for Adult Education.* Unesco, Paris, 1972, 132 pp.

Wedell, E. G. and Perraton, H. D. *Teaching at a Distance: an appraisal of the co-ordinated teaching of 'O' level physics using television, correspondence and special aids.* National Institute of Adult Education. London, 1968, 64 pp.

Weiner, P. *Making the Media Revolution.* Collier Macmillan, Toronto, 1973.

Wilson, A. J. *Education by Television.* Report of the mission for the evaluation of educational television in Niger, El Salvador and American Samoa; Ivory Coast, Unesco, Paris, 1969.

Wilson, A. J. *ETV Guidelines: writing, directing and presenting.* Hutchinson Educational, 1973, 144 pp.

Wilson, A. J. *Multi-media Systems in Adult Education.* Descriptions of 12 projects in 9 countries. Internationales Zentralinstitut für das Jugend- und Bildungsfernsehen, Munich, 1972.

Wiltshire, H. and Bayliss, F. *Teaching Through Television.* National Institute of Adult Education, London, 1965, 34 pp.

Wittich, W. A. and Schuller, C. F. *Instructional Technology: its nature and users.* Harper and Row, New York, 1973 (5th edn.), 737 pp.

Wortman, L. A. *Closed-circuit Television Handbook.* Foulsham-Sams, Slough, 1964, 286 pp.

Zettl, H. *Television Production Handbook.* Wadsworth Publishing Company, Belmont, 1968, 541 pp.

Zelmer, A. C. Lynn *Community Media Handbook.* The Scarecrow Press, Inc. Metuchen, New Jersey, 1973, 241 pp.

II. Reference and bibliographical compilations

Aspen Institute. *Aspen Handbook on the Media.* Aspen Institute Program on Communications and Society, Palo Alto, California, 1975, 182 pp.

Dale, E. and Belland, J. *A Guide to the Literature on Audiovisual Instruction.* Stanford Educational Resources Information Center, Clearinghouse on Media and Technology, 1971, 17 pp.

Educational Resources Information Center, Clearinghouse on Media and Technology. *Instructional Technology Subject Matter Descriptors: A Subset of the ERIC Thesaurus.* Stanford, 1971, 21 leaves.

Eraut, M. and Squires, G. *An Annotated Select Bibliography of Educational Technology.* National Council for Educational Technology, London, 1971, 90 pp.

European Broadcasting Union. *Selected Bibliography: Part 1 Broadcasting in Education.* EBU, Geneva, 1967, 25 pp.

European Broadcasting Union. *Selected Bibliography: Part 2 Broadcasting in Society.* EBU, Geneva, 1968, 25 pp.

Focal Press Limited. *The Focal Encyclopedia of Film and Television Techniques.* London and New York, 1969, 1,100 pp.

International Audio-Visual Technical Center. *Closed Circuit Television and*

Educational Television: Bibliographical References Parts 2–8. Antwerp (n.d.), 7 vols.

Internationales Zentralinstitut für das Jugend- und Bildungsfernsehen. *Bibliographie. B.I. Deutschpachige literatur zum Bildüngsfernsehen.* The Institute, Munich, 1966.

Internationles Zentralinstitut für das Jugend- und Bildungsfernsehen. *Bibliographie E.1. Television and Adult Education.* The Institute, Munich, 1966, 61 pp.

Internationles Zentralinstitut für das Jugend- und Bildungsfernsehen. *Bibliographie S.1. School Television.* The Institute, Munich, 1966, 76 pp.

Internationles Zentralinstitut für das Jugend- und Bildungsfernsehen. *Bibliographie S.2. Instructional Television.* The Institute, Munich, 1968, 185 pp.

Internationles Zentralinstitut für das Jugend- und Bildungsfernsehen. *Bibliographie J.1. Television and Youth.* The Institute, Munich, 1967, 128 pp.

Internationles Zentralinstitut für das Jugend- und Bildungsfernsehen. *Bibliographie J.2. Television and Youth.* The Institute, Munich, 1969, 60 pp.

Kato, J. *Japanese Research on Mass Communication: Selected Abstracts.* East–West Communication Institute, University Press of Hawaii, Honolulu, 1974, 128 pp.

Lomisse, J. and Brichet, N. *La television et l'enseignement, Bibliographie Internationale Commentée.* Librairie Universitaire, Louvciun, 1968, 476 pp.

Morgan, R. P. and Singh, J. P. *A Guide to the Literature on Application of Communication Satellites to Educational Development.* Stanford Educational Resources Information Center, Clearinghouse on Media and Technology, 1972, 19 pp.

National Council for Educational Technology. *Copyright and Education: A Guide to the Use of Copyright Material in Educational Institutions.* NCET, London, 1972, vii, 91 pp.

Niemi, J. A. and Anderson, D. V. *Television: A Viable Channel for Educating Adults in Culturally Different Poverty Groups? ... A Literature Review.* Syracuse University, Educational Resources Information Center, Clearinghouse on Adult Education, New York, 1971, 16 leaves.

Ohliger, J. *The Mass Media in Adult Education: A Review of Recent Literature.* Educational Resources Information Center, Clearinghouse on Adult Education, Syracuse, 1968, 123 pp.

Razik, Taher A. and Ramroth, Delgra M. *Bibliography of Research in Instructional Media.* Educational Technology Publications, New Jersey, 1974, Volume 2, 441 pp.

Reid, J. Christopher and Maclennan, Donald W. *Research in Instructional Television and Film.* Office of Education, U.S. Department of Health, Education and Welfare, Washington, 1967, 216 pp.

School Broadcasting Council. *Selective Bibliography of Titles: 1. Radio and Television Broadcasts to Schools. 2. General Broadcasting.* SBC, London, 1967, 48 pp. with Supplement, 1967.

Sparks, K. R., comp. *A Bibliography of Doctoral Dissertations in Television and Radio.* Syracuse University, 1965, 68 pp.

Sparks, K. R. *A Bibliography of Doctoral Dissertations in Television and Radio.* Syracuse University, Newhouse Communications Center, School of Journalism, New York, 1971, iv, 119 pp.

Stroud, W. *Selected Bibliography on Telecommunications (Cable Systems),* Madison, Wise, Wisconsin Library Association, 1972.

Twelker, P. A. et al. *The Systematic Development of Instruction: An Overview and Basic Guide to the Literature.* Stanford Educational Resources Information Center, Clearinghouse on Media and Technology, 1972, 24 pp.

Unesco. *An Annotated Bibliography of Unesco Publications and Documents Dealing with Space Communication 1953–1970.* Paris, 1971, 44 pp.

Unesco. *World Communications.* Paris, 1975, 533 pp.

Van Bol, J. M. and Abdelfattah, F. *The Use of Mass Media in the Developing Countries.* International Centre for African Social and Economic Documentation, Brussels, 1971, 751 pp.

III. Periodicals

Access, three or four times per year. National Film Board, P.O. Box 6100, Montreal, Quebec.

Audio-Visual, monthly, MacLaren Publishers Ltd., P.O. Box 109, Croydon, Surrey CR9 1HQ, England.

Audio-Visual Instruction, monthly. Association for Educational Communications and Technology, 1201 16 St., N.W., Washington D.C. 20036, USA.

AV Communication Review, quarterly. Association for Educational Communications and Technology, 1201 16 St., N.W., Washington D.C. 20036, USA.

British Journal of Educational Technology, three per year. Councils and Education Press Ltd., 10 Queen Anne Street, London W1M 9LD, England.

Broadcasting, weekly. Broadcasting Publications Inc., 1735 De Salas St., N.W., Washington D.C. 20036, USA.

Challenge for Change newsletter. National Film Board, P.O. Box 6100, Montreal, Quebec.

Educational Broadcasting International, quarterly. Peter Peregrinus Ltd., Station House, Nightingale Road, Hitchin, Herts SG5 1RJ, England.

Educational Broadcasting Review, bi-monthly. (National Association of Educational Broadcasters), Ohio State University, 2400 Olentangy River Road, Colombus, Ohio 43210, USA.

Educational and Industrial Television, monthly. C. S. Tepfer Publishing Co., Inc., 607 Main St., Rigdefield, Conn. 06877, USA.

Educational Media, Educational Media Publishing Co., 1015 Florence St., Fort Worth, Texas 76102, USA.

Educational Media International, quarterly. Modino Press Ltd., 6 Conduit St., London W1R 9TS, England.

Educational Technology, monthly. Educational Technology Publications Inc., 140 Sylvan Ave., Englewood Cliffs, N.J. 07632, USA.

Eric at Stanford – the Newsletter. Institute for Communication Research, Clearinghouse on Educational Media and Technology, Stanford, California 94305, USA.

ICB – International Communications Bulletin, quarterly. ICB, College of Journalism, University of Maryland, College Park, Md. 20742 USA.

IFTC Newsletter, every 2 or 3 months. International Council for Film and Television, Unesco, Rue Miollis, Paris.

Instructional Technology Report, bi-monthly. Information Center on Instructional Technology, Academy for Educational Development, 1414 22nd St., N.W., Washington D.C. 20037, USA.

Journal of Communication, quarterly. Annenberg School of Communications, P.O. Box 13358, Philadelphia, Pennsylvania 19101, USA.

Mass Media/Adult Education. Georgia Center for Continuing Education, Athens, Georgia, 30602, USA.

Media and Methods, nine per year. North American Publishing Co., 134 N. 13th St., Philadelphia, Pa. 19107, USA.

Open Line, quarterly. The Open University, Information Services, Walton Hall, Milton Keynes MK7 6AA, England.

Programmed Learning and Educational Technology, bi-monthly. Sweet and Maxwell Ltd., 11 Fetter Lane, London EC4 P4EE, England.

Public Telecommunications Review, bi-monthly. PTR/National Association of Educational Broadcasters, 1346 Connecticut Avenue, N.W., Washington D.C. 20036, USA.

Radical Software. Suite 1304, 440 Park Avenue South, New York, NY 10016.

Screen, quarterly. The Journal of the Society for Education in Film and Television, SEFT Publications, 63 Old Compton Street, London W1V 5PN.

Visual Education, monthly. National Committee for Audio-Visual Aids in Education 33 Queen Anne Street, London, England.

Index